Annals of Astoria

ANNALS
of
ASTORIA

The Headquarters Log
of the Pacific Fur Company
on the Columbia River, 1811–1813

Edited by

ROBERT F. JONES

Fordham University Press
New York
1999

Copyright © 1999 by The Rosenbach Museum and Library.
All rights reserved.
LC 99-20823
ISBN 0-8232-1763-9 (clothbound)

Library of Congress Cataloging-in-Publication Data

Annals of Astoria : the headquarters log of the Pacific Fur Company on
the Columbia River, 1811-1813 / edited by Robert F. Jones.
   p. cm.
   Includes bibliographical references and index.
   ISBN 0-8232-1763-9
   1. Pacific Fur Company--History. 2. Fur trade--Columbia River
Valley--History--19th Century. 3. McDougall, Duncan, d. 1818
Diaries. 4. Astoria (Or.)--History. I. Jones, Robert Francis,
1935- .
HD9944U48P333 1999
380.1'456753'09797--dc21   99-20823
                                                   CIP

Printed in the United States of America

For Elizabeth and Caroline
First of the new generation
Godspeed

CONTENTS

LIST OF ILLUSTRATIONS

INTRODUCTION

Fur trapping, the fur trade, "Mountain Men"—expressions such as these bring up images of men working in unexplored wilderness, tending extended trap lines, usually alone, meeting once or twice a year to sell their furs in a grand rendezvous, drinking most of the proceeds away with fellow trappers, and, then, having restocked with the provisions they could not kill and the tools they could not make, going back into the wilderness. There is a good bit of truth in this picture, but it ignores the merchants and trading companies also essential to the process of taking the fur from where it was trapped to its eventual use, as a hat in London or a garment in Canton. The document presented here is part of the story of one of the earliest of those companies and of some of the individuals who, after the furs were gathered, started them on their way.

Like much of the economic history of the United States during the early republic, this document is closely associated with John Jacob Astor. Astor, born in Waldorf, Germany, in 1763, came to the United States in 1784 after a stay in London. He brought with him a selection of musical instruments to sell, as well as a grand ambition to become rich. On the ship that brought him over were a number of fur merchants and, listening to them and probably questioning them, the young emigrant decided to see what he could do for himself in that area.[1]

More than ambition and information gained in shipboard conversations would be needed to succeed there, however. Like most areas of the American economy, the fur business was greatly affected by the newly independent status of the United States. Many of the pelts marketed through New York were actually trapped in Canada and were bound for Great Britain, usually

---

[1] Kenneth W. Porter, *John Jacob Astor: Business Man*, 2 vols. (Cambridge, Mass.: Harvard University Press, 1931), I, 6–24; hereafter, Porter, *Astoria*. See also John Denis Haeger, *John Jacob Astor: Business and Finance in the Early Republic* (Detroit: Wayne State University Press, 1991), especially his discussion in chap. 1 of the various studies of Astor done over the years; the Pacific Fur Company and Astoria are covered in chaps. 4–6; hereafter, Haeger, *Astor*. The most recent study of the enterprise and one that will be frequently used is James P. Ronda, *Astoria and Empire* (Lincoln: University of Nebraska Press, 1990); hereafter, Ronda, *Astoria*.

London. Moreover, the richest areas for trapping then being exploited were divided by the still partially undefined boundary between the United States and Britain's colony, Canada. Some of these uncertainties were resolved by Jay's Treaty of 1794, but the boundary remained to be fixed. Astor worked hard in this shifting commercial world and prospered, both in the general mercantile line and in the fur business. But, in the new century, his interests became increasingly international, and he grew to be especially interested in the burgeoning trade with China. However profitable this trade might be, Europeans in general and Americans in particular had a marked difficulty: they had little that interested the Chinese. Initially, American merchants exported coin and ginseng, a root gathered in the eastern states and much prized in Asia generally and China in particular for its presumed aphrodisiacal potency. These commodities purchased tea and luxury goods such as dishes ("china"), furniture, and textiles. During the 1780s, American merchants had begun sending ships with trading goods to the northwest coast of North America to trade furs with the natives there, then taking the furs to Canton, the only Chinese port where Westerners were permitted to trade. Later, they added sandalwood from the Sandwich Islands (now known as the Hawaiian Islands). Astor involved himself in this already well developed trade in 1800 when he bought an interest in the ship *Severn* and its cargo. He did well enough to order the ship *Beaver* in 1805, a vessel built for the special demands of the northwest coast–China trade.[2]

Coincidental with this new interest was the substantial addition to the United States of the Louisiana Purchase (1803), by which France sold most of the trans-Mississippi west to the young republic. Astor, who had previously shown patriotic ire by claiming to be very much annoyed at having to buy furs in Montreal that had been trapped in American territory in the upper midwest, realized that the Purchase had extended the still-undefined boundary between the United States and British Canada. One of the factors that would help to define the boundary would be the activity of fur trappers and traders working out of St. Louis under American auspices. Mixing in with this was a concern of the American government: that the United States

---

[2] Foster Rhea Dulles, *The Old China Trade* (Boston: Houghton Mifflin, 1930), especially chaps. 3, 4, 5; Philip Chadwick Foster Smith, *The Empress of China* (Philadelphia: Philadelphia Maritime Museum, 1984), passim; Porter, *Astor*, I, 164–65. Throughout this work, the term "European" is used to indicate persons not native to the region in question. The Pacific Fur company and the North West Fur Company employed Britons of English as well as Scottish extraction, French Canadians, and American citizens of various ethnic backgrounds. In an effort to avoid lengthy and perhaps inaccurate designations, "European" is used to describe groups comprising all or several of the categories mentioned.

secure a portion of the Pacific coast of North America. In 1792, Robert Gray, a Boston ship captain, had been the first explorer known to have sailed into Columbia's River (named for his vessel), thus, according to Western notions, becoming the discoverer of the river. American captains had been trading on the coast before this, and they were followed by others in increasing numbers. To bolster the American claim to the area, President Thomas Jeffferson sent the Lewis and Clark Expedition overland from St. Louis; it reached the Pacific coast at the mouth of the Columbia in November 1805. However, also claiming a share of the coast were the British in Canada, the Spanish from the south, and the Russians from the north.[3]

Sometime, someone is supposed to have said that God created Spain and the Ottoman Empire to hold large expanses of territory without prejudice to the interests of the great powers. In the late eighteenth/early nineteenth century, Spain was playing that role on the Pacific coast. Having moved up the west coast of Vancouver Island, she was turned back by Britain during the Nootka Sound controversy in 1789–90. She retreated to San Francisco, but did not renounce her claim to the entire coast. Tsarist Russia was not that passive. The Russian American Company, under the direction of Count Alexander Baranov, from its post at New Archangel (Sitka), had opened another at Fort Ross, about seventy miles north of San Francisco. This aggressive move concealed a basically weak position. The vast distance across the Eurasian continent which separated European Russia from its colony posed very difficult supply problems. It lacked the shipping to bring the furs to St. Petersburg and to supply the Alaskan colony as well as carry them to the alternative market at Canton. Further, its position at Sitka itself was challenged. Its brutal policies had antagonized the Tlingit Indians of the mainland and Kodiak Island, an antagonism made effective by muskets, shot, and powder traded by American and British captains. The Russian government had already attempted, unsuccessfully, to have the United States forbid this trade.[4]

John Jacob Astor moved into this mix of international tensions, national concerns, and private ventures. One of Astor's employees once remarked on his "comprehensive mind," that he could see connections in apparently disparate circumstances and relationships. So it was with the tangle of the

---

[3] Ronda, *Astoria*, pp. 29–38; F. W. Howay, "A List of Trading Vessels in the Maritime Fur Trade, 1785–1825," Royal Society of Canada, *Transactions*, Ser. 3, Sec. 2, 24 (1930), 111–34 [1785–94], 25 (1931), 117–49 [1795–1804], 26 (1932), 43–86 [1805–14].

[4] Hector Chevigny, *Russian America: The Great Alaskan Adventure, 1791–1867* (New York: Viking, 1965), pp. 32, 55, 86–88, 93, 96–97, 100–101, 116.

American–British rivalry for furs, the tension between the United States and Great Britain over the undefined northwestern boundary, the desire of both countries for a share of the Pacific coast of North America, as well as Spain's pretensions in the area, and Russia's difficulties in Alaska. When Astor first proposed what became the Pacific Fur Company, all these factors (except the Spanish whom he, along with others, ignored) were brought together to the advantage of the United States and, to be sure, John Jacob Astor. He envisioned a chain of trading posts on the upper Missouri, along the Lewis and Clark route, a fleet of trading vessels that would supply posts on the Columbia River, trade along the coast, and supply the Russians in Alaska. These ships would carry the furs of the American and Russian companies to Canton and to the northeastern United States, along with the prized merchandise of China. As an added advantage, these traders would, because of their superior economic position, drive the gun-trading captains away from Alaska and improve the Russian situation there. All this would also strengthen the position of the United States along the upper Missouri and on the northwest coast.[5]

This grand plan was first revealed to DeWitt Clinton, mayor of New York City, in 1808. Astor wrote to Clinton as a preliminary to seeking the assistance of the federal government in, first, doing away with a federal monopoly on trading with the Indians, and, second, securing a monopoly for Astor of the same activity. Clinton's uncle, George Clinton, the former governor of New York, was then serving as vice president under Thomas Jefferson. DeWitt could also be helpful in getting a charter of incorporation for the enterprise through the New York legislature.[6]

This was easily obtained. In April 1808, the American Fur Company was incorporated under the laws of the State of New York; it had an initial capitalization of $1,000,000, and a life of twenty-five years. Mentioned in the charter were the necessity of competing with the foreign monopoly which controlled the fur trade in the United States and the desirability of securing the "good will and affections" of the western Indians toward the United States. Not so easily obtained was the assistance of the federal government. Several letters to President Jefferson elicited only the vague promise of "every reasonable patronage and facility in the power of the executive." Astor

---

[5] Alexander Ross, *Adventures of the First Settlers on the Oregon or Columbia River* (London: Smith, Elder and Co., 1849 [University Microfilm ed., 1966]), p. 4; hereafter, Ross, *Adventures*; Ronda, *Astoria*, pp. 37–38.

[6] J. J. Astor to DeWitt Clinton, January 25, 1808, DeWitt Clinton Papers, 4:5–6, Butler Library, Columbia University, New York City.

had hoped for a good bit more than this. A visit to Washington and an interview with the President and Secretary of State James Madison in April 1808 followed. As Astor later recalled, when the possibility of interference by the British was mentioned, the President promised government protection "in the most Desided & explicit manner." A promise of this sort by Jefferson is most unlikely. Vague words of support, yes, but an explicit promise, no.[7]

To the American President, Astor said nothing whatever of Canadian interests, other than to portray them as the agents of British colonialism. But his mercantile contacts and business with various Montreal fur houses were extensive and various. At that time, the North West Company and a subsidiary, the Michilimackinac Company, were operating in Canada outside the area monopolized by the Hudson's Bay Company and in the upper midwest of the United States. In the fall of 1808, Astor made an offer to buy the subsidiary, whose operations were concentrated in the Great Lakes, an offer that was refused by the North Westers. But he continued to be interested, for when Astor thought of a monopoly of fur trading in the west, he meant from the Great Lakes to the Pacific, and to do this, he would have to eliminate British/Canadian competition in the upper midwest. The shifting trade legislation of the American Congress as it tried vainly to devise a non-violent, economic way of coercing Great Britain and France, then in the midst of the Napoleonic wars, to abandon their onerous and harassing regulation of American neutral commerce exasperated fur merchants in Canada. They realized that their over-the-border operations were hostage to whatever temporary majority might govern American policy. Some of them decided that the best way to deal with this dilemma was to cooperate with an American citizen, thereby avoiding the strictures on alien commercial operations which were an intermittent feature of American trade policy. In the fall of 1809, Astor repeated his offer of the previous year. He offered to buy a half-interest in the Michilimackinac Company in return for the North Westers' purchasing a third of his Pacific venture. The character of the North West

---

[7] Ronda, *Astoria*, pp. 37–47; "An Act to incorporate the American fur company, Passed April 6th, 1808," in Porter, *Astor*, I, 413–20; see J. J. Astor to James Madison, July 27, 1813, in Dorothy Wildes Bridgwater, ed., "John Jacob Aster [*sic*] Relative to His Settlement on the Columbia River," *Yale University Library Gazette*, 24, No. 2 (October 1949), 62, for Astor's record (the only one) of the 1808 meeting. In 1813, Jefferson praised Astoria as " 'the germ of a great, free, and independent empire,' " which would help to establish liberty and self-government over the entire continent; Thomas Jefferson to J. J. Astor, November 9, 1813, in Richard W. Van Alstyne, *The Rising American Empire* (Chicago: Quadrangle, 1960; repr., 1965), p. 93. Thus, there is no reason to doubt Jefferson's basic sympathy with the proposal, but Astor had hoped for far more than that.

Company, which was a number of "interlocking short-term agreements between wintering partners, Montreal merchants, and London supply houses"
ruled out a quick and decisive answer to Astor. But in February 1810,
several Montreal merchants, representing the North West Company, visited
Astor in New York and began serious conversations about taking a partial
share in the new company. Emboldened by this development, Astor organized the Pacific Fur Company on March 10, 1810, as a simple partnership,
having recruited three former North Westers, Alexander McKay, Donald
McKenzie, and Duncan McDougall. The concern had 100 shares (to be
increased to 200 if the North Westers signed on), of which Astor held one-
half; each partner held five. American partners, Wilson Price Hunt, Ramsay
Crooks, Robert McClellan, and Joseph Miller, were also added (the remaining shares were held back for any additional partners), and clerks, *voyageurs*,
trappers, hunters—all the various skills needed to get the enterprise going—
were hired.[8]

Here, the informal character of the North West Company complicated
things considerably. The "wintering partners" referred to above were those
who supervised what might be called field operations, often also going out
into the country. They did this from Fort William, at the northwestern
corner of Lake Superior (near present-day Thunder Bay, Ontario). Believing
the Montreal merchants had given their assent to a bargain with Astor, the
wintering partners agreed, after having made several qualifications. In July

---

[8] Porter, *Astor*, I, 182; Ronda, *Astoria*, pp. 55–61; the description of the North West Company is from Ronda. See Ann Carlos, "The Causes and Origins of the North American Fur
Trade Rivalry: 1804–1810," *Journal of Economic History*, 41, No. 4 (December 1981),
774–94; Dr. Carlos treats only the rivalry between the North West Company and the Hudson's Bay Company. North Westers and any Astorians associated with that company are
treated in "A Biographical Directory of the North Westers," Appendix A in W. Stewart
Wallace, ed., *Documents Relating to the North West Company* (Toronto: The Champlain Society,
1934); hereafter, Wallace, *NW Documents*. Donald McKenzie's name is sometimes spelled
Mackenzie in the log. Wilson Price Hunt was a New Jersey native who was a merchant and
fur trader in St. Louis in the early years of the nineteenth century. He had some familiarity
with the west through conversations with Meriwether Lewis and William Clark and an asso-
ciation with Manuel Lisa, one of the most important fur merchants working out of St. Louis.
Astor probably selected Hunt to head the company because of his American citizenship, as
he was not experienced in field operations. Most of those who were experienced and were
willing to work with Astor were British subjects from Canada. Ramsay Crooks, Robert Mc-
Clellan, and Joseph Miller were Americans who had worked with Hunt previously; after
going overland with him, all three resigned their partnerships on reaching Astoria and left
with Robert Stuart on June 29, 1812, when he carried dispatches to Astor in New York City.
Crooks continued to work with Astor, acting as president of the American Fur Company in
the 1830s. Ronda, *Astoria*, pp. 50–51; T. C. Elliott, "Wilson Price Hunt, 1783–1842,"
Oregon Historical Quarterly, 32, No. 2 (June 1931), 130–34.

1810, they ordered David Thompson west to meet Astor's party on the Columbia and offer them his cooperation along the lines of whatever agreement was finally worked out in Montreal or New York. However, a serious division had developed among the Montreal merchants, and a majority had decided to go it alone and tough it out against the American competition. This decision was reached too late to affect Thompson's mission, and there would be, for a while, a substantial misunderstanding on the western side of the Rocky Mountains regarding the relationship between the two companies.[9]

As Thompson's errand indicates, Astor had not waited for a final agreement with the Canadians before acting. He went ahead with a three-pronged movement to the northwest coast. Wilson Price Hunt was to lead a company overland from St. Louis, roughly along the route of Lewis and Clark. He was to be the supervising partner at a post to be established near the mouth of the Columbia River. Along the way, he was to select sites for trading posts. A second group was to go by sea, around Cape Horn, on the newly purchased ship *Tonquin*, commanded by Captain Jonathan Thorn, on leave from the United States Navy. It carried provisions, heavier trade goods, tools, etc., for the post, and the frame of a shallop, to be completed at the Columbia. The smaller vessel was to trade along the Pacific coast, while the *Tonquin* proceeded up to Vancouver Island. The third unit was to be brought to the Columbia by a second ship, *Beaver*, loaded with trading goods and supplies; it left New York in the fall of 1811 and arrived at Astoria in May 1812. Astor's plan also included trade with the Russian American Company's post at Sitka; after preliminary agreement was reached with Andrei Dashkov, the Russian *chargé d'affaires* in Washington, Astor sent his son-in-law, Adrian Bentson, to St. Petersburg. There, the best he could do was obtain a tentative agreement, notable more for its vagueness than anything else.[10]

Leaving New York in September 1810, the *Tonquin* made a tense and unhappy voyage around the Horn. Captain Thorn brought notions of discipline and order to his position that would have been extreme on a naval ship in time of war. Even before they left New York, there was a quarrel over the quarters assigned to the partners (McKay, McDougall, David and Robert Stuart, all Canadians of Scottish origin) and the clerks. During a layover to water at the Falkland Islands, David Stuart, McDougall, and several clerks

---

[9] Ronda, *Astoria,*. pp. 62–64.
[10] Ronda, *Astoria*, chaps. 3–6.

did not hear the signal to return to ship. Enraged at what he was certain was their deliberate defiance of his authority, Thorn ordered the ship to set sail. What ensued was well described by one of the marooned clerks, Gabriel Franchère: ". . . nothing could excuse his cruelty in abandoning us on the bare rocks of Falkland, where we must surely have perished except for the intervention of Mr. R. Stuart, whose uncle was with us in the boat, determined to blow the Captain's brain out—which he would have done, if the latter had not turned the ship about to let us come aboard."[11]

Franchère's description of the captain as a "precise and rigid man, naturally hot-tempered, expecting instant obedience" seems fair. After a short layover in the Hawaiian Islands to purchase fresh provisions and livestock, and to hire native laborers for both the ship and the post, the *Tonquin* reached the mouth of the Columbia in March 1811 where it took three days and the lives of eight of the crew before Thorn took the vessel through the perils of the shoals and currents of the river. It is at this point that a detailed and daily account of events on the river and at the post starts in the manuscript presented here. However, the *Tonquin* does appear again in the log. As soon as he could, Thorn took his vessel, on orders from Astor, to Sitka, trading along the way on the west coast of Vancouver Island. Alexander McKay, a partner, and James Lewis, a clerk, went along to assist with the trading. While in Clayoquot Sound, Thorn, true to form, insulted one of the local chieftains by throwing a pelt in his face. This chief, who was in the habit of taking umbrage, later returned with others, ostensibly to trade. By a stratagem, the natives obtained knives from Thorn and then turned on the captain and crew. Since no precautions had been taken, they were virtually defenseless. During the fighting, several of the men, perhaps badly wounded, hid themselves below decks. When they realized how the fight had gone, they scattered gunpowder along the deck and lit it. This started a fire which in time caused the powder magazine to blow, destroying the ship and everyone on it, including possibly two hundred natives. The only survivor was an interpreter, Joseachal, a Quinault Indian who had been taken on board along the Washington coast. He was thrown into the water by the explosion and later survived only because his sister had married into the tribe some years

---

[11] The most recent description of the voyage of the *Tonquin* is in Ronda, *Astoria*, chap. 4; Gabriel Franchère's record of events there and at Astoria is in *Journal of a Voyage on the North West Coast . . . 1811, 1812, 1813, and 1814*, ed. W. Kaye Lamb, trans. Wessie Tipping Lamb (Toronto: The Champlain Society, 1969); the passages quoted in this and the next paragraph are on pp. 55, 56; hereafter, Franchère, *Journal*. The first four chapters of Alexander Ross's *Adventures* describe his experiences on board the *Tonquin*.

previously. The loss of the *Tonquin* was a serious setback for the Astorians as well as a shocking event. Within months, it was known throughout the northwest coast and even as far as Hawaii. All direct knowledge of it comes down through the native interpreter. In the spring of 1813, working through Comcomly, the local Chinook chief, McDougall had him brought to Astoria, where he was closely questioned and his answers transcribed into the log. The result is the most reliable record known of the loss of the *Tonquin*.[12]

As uncomfortable and unpleasant as the trip from New York on the *Tonquin* was, it was a pleasure trip when contrasted with the experience of the overland party, headed by Wilson Price Hunt. The party moved from Montreal through the river-and-lakes route to Fort Mackinac, thence down the Mississippi to St. Louis in the summer of 1810. It wintered about 350 miles up the Missouri, near present-day Oregon, Missouri. Leaving there in March 1811, Hunt decided to abandon the Lewis and Clark route and headed instead on a more southerly route along the Yellowstone River in pursuit of a hoped-for southern pass. It did not materialize, and the trip was a long and grueling exercise in how not to cross from the Mississippi to the Pacific. Eventually, the overlanders divided into several parties, the largest of which reached Astoria in January and February 1812, with some stragglers taking until the summer to arrive. Hunt had been designated as the supervising partner at Astoria, but his long-delayed arrival meant that Duncan McDougall, next in line, exercised the authority that was supposed to be his for almost a year.[13] This loss of control was then compounded by Hunt's

---

[12] See below, entries of June 15, 18, 1812; see E. W. Giesecke, "Search for the *Tonquin*," *Cumtux*, 10, No. 3 (Summer 1990), 3–8, No. 4 (Fall 1990), 3–14, and 11, No. 1 (Winter 1990), 23–40 for a description of the various efforts to find the wreckage of the *Tonquin*. The site of the encounter remains unknown. This was the first voyage the *Tonquin* made as an Astor ship; it had been built for Captain Edmund Fanning in 1807. Fanning included a rather fanciful version of the vessel's end in his memoirs; it had been gotten at second hand from a mixed-race Indian, Ramsay ("Lamazee" and other spellings), who claimed to be the interpreter. Edmund Fanning, *Voyages to the South Seas, Indian and Pacific Oceans, China Sea, Northwest Coast, Feejee Islands, South Shetlands, &c, &c.* (New York: William H. Vermilye, 1838; repr. Fairfield, Washington: Ye Galleon Press, 1970). See Robert F. Jones, "The Identity of the *Tonquin*'s Interpreter," *Oregon Historical Quarterly*, 98, No. 3 (Fall 1997), 296–314, for a discussion of the question of the native interpreter's identity. The name of the *Tonquin* is a variant of "tonka," the black, almond-shaped seed of a large leguminous tree, *Dipterix odorata*, used to scent and flavor various products (*Oxford English Dictionary*). The tree is found throughout Asia and may have been selected in consideration of where Captain Fanning expected the vessel to sail.

[13] Ronda, *Astoria*, chaps. 5 and 6, describes the overland passage; for a more picturesque and reasonably reliable version, Washington Irving's *Astoria, or, Anecdotes of an Enterprise Beyond the Rocky Mountains*, ed. Richard Dilworth Rust (Boston: Twayne, 1976), chaps. 12–38, may be read; hereafter, Irving, *Astoria* (Rust, ed.).

decision to accompany the *Beaver* on a trading mission to the Russians at New Archangel, thus getting a vital part of Astor's plan under way. He left early in August 1812, intending to return later that fall. Instead, a combination of events and poor judgment kept him away until August 1813, at which point most of the major decisions that ended Astoria's existence had been made. Hunt left again soon after his return to charter or buy a ship in Hawaii, returning to evacuate Astoria. By the time he returned with the brig *Pedler*, in March 1814, Astoria had been sold to the North West Company and was now Fort George. Thus, the man whom Astor had intended to be the supervising partner was absent from the post for all but seven months of its two and one-half years of existence.[14]

Since contacts with the North West Company marked several significant points in the history of the Pacific Fur Company's operations on the Columbia, it is appropriate to describe these contacts briefly here. The first was the visit of David Thompson to the new post, named Astoria, in July 1811. As noted above, he brought with him notice of an apparent agreement between the two companies which, at the least, meant cooperation and not competition west of the Rocky Mountains. After a stay of a week, Thompson left on his return east, in the company of David Stuart, who was leading a party up to the Okanogan River and beyond. Thus reassured, the Astorians concerned themselves with possible problems with the Indians rather than North West competition.[15]

The next contact came in January 1813 when Donald McKenzie returned unexpectedly from the interior, bringing news given to him by a party of North Westers who had come to John Clarke's post at Spokane. Clarke was a Pacific Company partner who had come out on the *Beaver*. The news was

---

[14] Hunt arrived at Astoria on February 15, 1812. The decision to go to New Archangel with the *Beaver* was made on June 29, and the ship managed to get over the bar on August 3, having been kept by contrary winds and heavy seas. He returned on the *Albatross* on August 20, 1813, and left on the 26th. The *Albatross* had already been chartered to carry sandalwood to China and could not serve the Astorians' needs. Hunt returned early in March 1814, after McDougall had stopped keeping the log; after a brief visit, he departed on the *Pedler* for New Archangel with merchandise for the Russians and three of the Pacific Fur Company's clerks who had not signed on with the North Westers. See entries for the dates given above, and Ronda, *Astoria*, pp. 194, 242, 283, 297–98

[15] Thompson's visit lasted from July 15 to the 22nd; he carried back with him an answer by Duncan McDougall who was, at that time, senior partner at the post. This was apparently in answer to a letter to him from the wintering partners informing him of the probable agreement. See the exchange of correspondence between Thompson and McDougall in the introduction to Franchère's *Journal*, p. 11. Ronda, *Astoria*, pp. 63–64. David Thompson and David Stuart are in Appendix A to Wallace, ed., *NW Documents*.

of the declaration of war on Great Britain by the United States the previous June. This immediately cast doubt on Astor's sending of the yearly supply of provisions and trade goods necessary for continuing operations. McDougall and McKenzie, the only partners then at Astoria, decided on a policy of retrenchment with an eye to the likely evacuation of the post in the spring. Also instrumental in this decision was the boast by the North Westers that an armed vessel was on its way to take the post by force.[16]

Finally, the North Westers brought about the end of Astoria as an American enterprise. In April 1813, the post was surprised by the visit of three North Westers, John George McTavish, Joseph Larocque, and Michel Bourdon, with fifteen men supporting them. They brought news of the imminent arrival of the *Isaac Todd*, an armed vessel earlier spoken of only vaguely. Despite the non-arrival of the vessel, May and June only magnified the fears of the Astorians. By the end of June, the partners present, McDougall, McKenzie, David Stuart, and Clarke had confirmed the decision to abandon the post, but decided that it was too late in the year to start parties overland to St. Louis. They would have to stay another year on the Columbia. In the meantime, the fur business in the area was divided between the two companies. By July 5, McTavish was on his way back to Fort Spokane, a post the North Westers would maintain, while Clarke gave up his nearby establishment.[17]

In October, McTavish returned for what would prove to be Astoria's last act. This time he brought more definite news of the long-awaited arrival of the *Isaac Todd*, in the form of an excerpt of a letter from Montreal to the wintering partners at Fort William. The British ship was escorted by a Royal Navy vessel, and their purpose was to "take and destroy everything that is American on the North West Coast." McTavish also brought a surprising offer, to buy the post and all it contained, pelts, provisions, tools, buildings, everything. On October 16, McDougall signed the final agreement with McTavish, and the Pacific Fur Company post on the Columbia River was dissolved.[18]

---

[16] Ronda, *Astoria*, pp. 264–65. John Clarke and Donald McKenzie are in Appendix A, Wallace, ed., *NW Documents*.

[17] Ronda, *Astoria*, pp. 277–83; see pp. 282–83 for the partners' explanation of their decision. Documents relevant to this are in T. C. Elliott, ed., "Sale of Astoria, 1813," *Oregon Historical Quarterly*, 33, No. 1 (March 1932), 43–50, especially 44–46. McTavish and LaRoque are in Appendix A, Wallace, ed., *NW Documents*. Michel Bourdon (No. 15) is listed as a freeman and interpreter in the roster of Pacific and North West employees for the winter of 1813–14 given as the Appendix to this work.

[18] Ronda, *Astoria*, pp. 287–90; see Elliott, "Sale of Astoria, 1813," cited in n. 17 for the

The manuscript presented here has been known as the "Duncan McDougall Journal"; however, for reasons presented below, I believe it is more accurately described as the "Headquarters Log of the Pacific Fur Company Post at Astoria on the Columbia River, 1811–1813." Whatever the most accurate title might be, McDougall was the supervising partner at the post during most of the time covered by the log and was probably responsible for what was recorded (or not recorded) in it. Further, he may have been the most significant person in making the important decisions that marked the history of the post on the Columbia. Thus, it seems proper to give him a brief biographical notice here.

As the name indicates, McDougall was of Scottish stock, possibly born in Scotland, the son of Duncan McDougall, a lieutenant in the 84th Regiment of Foot. Both parents died when he was still a boy, and it is thought that his uncles, Angus Shaw and Alexander McDougall, saw to his employment with the North West Company, probably around 1801. He worked for the company at various posts in present-day Quebec and Ontario provinces until 1806 when he dropped from the record. He was next seen as one of the former North Westers recruited by Astor in 1810. His activities from then until the sale of the post in 1813 are chronicled in the log. Following the sale, McDougall joined the North West Company as a partner, something that was suspected at Astoria in February 1814. Thus, he was believed to be a North Wester while he was liquidating the Pacific Fur Company's inventory, etc., at Astoria, nominally as Astor's agent. This may have been responsible for his disagreement with Hunt when the latter returned to Astoria in March 1814, having purchased a ship in Hawaii. Before any treachery was suspected, however, Alfred Seton, one of the American clerks, characterized him as "a compound of all the mean & petty passions that generally disgrace the lowest of animals" and accused him of employing one of the Hawaiian boys to spy on the men and of slandering Hunt in his absence. As if that were not enough, McDougall also hoarded various delicacies for himself, while claiming a full portion from the common stock.[19] Alexander Ross,

---

letter quoted above and the bill of sale signed on October 16, 1813; see also "Letter from Astor to J. B. Prevost . . . , November 11, 1817, Giving An Account of the Loss of Astoria," in Porter, *Astor*, II, 1154–57 for Astor's view of the bargain.

[19] Robert F. Jones, ed., *Astorian Adventure: The Journal of Alfred Seton, 1811–1815* (New York: Fordham University Press, 1993), pp. 148, 132–33; unless otherwise indicated, the information in this notice is taken from Jennifer H. S. Brown, "Duncan McDougall," *Dictionary of Canadian Biography*, V, 525–27; according to Ms. Brown, McDougall did not become a partner until 1816; John Haeger (*Astor*, p. 167) has him becoming a partner in July 1814. Thus, no matter whether Brown or Haeger is correct, McDougall was not playing a double role while he was dealing with the North Westers.

another of the clerks, was no kinder: "He was a man of but ordinary capacity, with an irritable, peevish temper; the most unfit man in the world to head an expedition or command men." Ross also accused McDougall of hoarding delicacies while the men lacked necessities. Further, during the arduous work of clearing a plot for the post, Ross recorded three deaths and three serious injuries, none of which were entered in the log.[20] Another clerk, Gabriel Franchère, noted several instances when McDougall was confined to his bedroom by illness and characterized his health during the entire period on the Columbia as "precarious"; most of this was not entered in the log.[21]

The most controversial event of McDougall's stewardship was the sale of the post to the North West Company; this has been surrounded with clouds of acrimony since the transaction occurred. The affair is much too complicated, with too many factors to be considered, to be treated here. Washington Irving, probably reflecting Astor's judgment at the time he wrote *Astoria* (some twenty years after the event), is severely critical of McDougall's conduct. Modern writers are more lenient in their verdicts, pointing to the isolated position in which the post had been placed by the war, the uncertainty of any help arriving from Astor, and the generally bad luck the enterprise experienced. Focusing on these factors avoids the quagmire of judging personal motives and justifications. John Haeger sums up the matter well: "it seems more important to observe that Astor's conception of Astoria was sound, but timing and luck were not his allies. Astor gambled and he lost."[22] One more point should be made: in his will, drawn in March 1817, McDougall insists "that I did every thing in my power to do the utmost justice to the trust and confidence reposed in me by John Jacob Astor . . . agreeable to, and in conformity with, the Resolves of the Company passed and signed by my late Associates and myself [these resolves would demonstrate] how much and how unjustly my character and reputation has suffered and been injured by the malicious and ungenerous conduct of some of my late Associates in the late Pacific Fur Company."

It seems only right to let him have the last word.

As to the title for the manuscript presented here: while a journal can be the official record of some organized body—the journal of a legislative assembly,

[20] Ross, *Adventures*, pp. 70, 74–76.

[21] Franchère, *Journal*, pp. 116–17.

[22] Irving, *Astoria* (Rust, ed.), chap. 59, pp. 342–45; Haeger, *Astor*, pp. 161–69 (quotation on p. 167). See Porter, *Astor*, I, 227–29, Ronda, *Astoria*, pp. 288–91, 298–301 for other modern treatments.

for example—when it is connected to a person, it is usually a record of the impressions, judgments, thoughts, and activities of that person. As the reader will soon discover, there is little of Duncan McDougall in the document presented here. Rather, it is a record of the allocation of resources, especially manpower, economic activity, that is, the buying and selling of provisions, pelts, and trade goods, and the status of the post, for example, the daily sick list—in short, the record of post as a business enterprise. Any personal references must be gleaned by inference rather than from any direct statements: for example, his protest on July 20, 1813, that his marriage to Comcomly's daughter was a "means of securing to us [Comcomly's] friendship . . . and for which purpose only it was proposed" (p. 203). This is almost certainly due to the snickers and asides on the part of the clerks and perhaps the lower ranks at the union, as reflected in Irving's treatment in Chapter 56 of *Astoria*. Thus, although it might be incomplete either as a personal or a business record, it is closer to a headquarters log than to a journal of Duncan McDougall's.

The manuscript is physically unprepossessing. Volumes I and II are notebooks, 8 x 13 inches, soft bound with marbled paper covers. Volume III is the same size, but bound in cardboard covered with marbled paper. On alternate pages there is a a watermark of Britannia seated within an oval frame, surmounted by a crown; the facing pages bear a "Lydig & Mesier" watermark. There is no watermark visible on Volumes I and II, which are completely filled with entries. Only about one-third of Volume III was used. This edition was transcribed from these three volumes, not the "Fair Copy" referred to below. The volumes are held by the Philip H. and A. S. W. Rosenbach Foundation at its library in Philadelphia. It was probably sent east with other company papers to Astor in New York City and was available to Washington Irving when he wrote his study of the enterprise in the 1830s. The description of the volumes in the Rosenbach Library catalogue states that it was used by Irving in writing *Astoria*. When Irving started work on his history, he hired his nephew, Pierre Irving, as a research assistant; in describing the task, he mentioned Astor's offer of an "abundance of materials in letters, journals." There are pencil marks on the left margin of many pages of the manuscript. Checking a number of the passages marked against the same events as described in *Astoria* showed them to correspond with each other. To mention just a few: Captain Thorn's refusal on April 22, 1811, to allow trading on the *Tonquin*, forcing McDougall to move ashore (Rust ed., 62); the report by natives of Europeans active in the interior on April 30, 1811, interpreted by McDougall as North Westers (64); the January 25,

1813, council of partners and clerks called in consequence of news of the declaration of war by the United States (316–18). Irving also mentions "the 'journal of Astoria' . . . which was kept under [McDougall's] own eye" (328). Thus, there is ample evidence to support the conclusion that John Jacob Astor made the log available to Washington Irving who used it, along with a number of other sources, in the writing of *Astoria*. In 1968, it was discovered among the holdings of a distant, indirect Astor descendant in Britain during the liquidation of an estate. The Rosenbach Foundation purchased the volumes in 1970.[23]

The McDougall manuscript is the only significant document of the Astoria venture that remains to be made generally available to students. Paradoxically, it can claim to be the most authentic, as it was written at the time of the events under the direction of someone who was at the center of the Pacific Fur Company's activities on the Columbia. All the other Astorians' memoirs, with the exception of the journal of Alfred Seton, were composed later, sometimes much later, and often apparently without written reminders of events then years in the past. Whatever the defects of this document, and they have been discussed above, it is the most complete contemporary record of events on the Columbia extant.

Also at the Rosenbach Museum and Library is a second copy of "Duncan McDougall's Journal." This is complete in one volume, ending on October 28, 1813, and has been labeled the "Fair Copy" by the Library. The volume is $7^3/4$ x $12^1/4$ inches, bound with a leather spine and cardboard covers. It is labeled "Journal at Astoria" and bears the penciled marginal note: "This is kept by one of the party set out by Jn Jacob Astor from New York—viz. Duncan McDougall." A pencil note glued to the title page lists this volume, a ring, and a traveling trunk as having been willed to Duncan McDougall Campbell, son of McDougall's cousin, Isabella Shaw McDougall Campbell. A typewritten statement, notarized at Detroit, Michigan, August 9, 1894, claims it as the property of W. A. Campbell, son of Duncan McD. Campbell. It also describes the document as McDougall's "original diary written in his own handwriting." I did not have any reliable copies of McDougall's handwriting, against which this statement could be tested. Unlike the three-

---

[23] Washington Irving to Pierre Munro Irving, September 15, 1834, October 28, 1834, in Pierre Irving, ed., *The Life and Letters of Washington Irving*, 4 vols. (New York: G. P. Putnam, 1864; repr., 1967), III, 60–64. Clive E. Driver, compiler, *A Selection from Our Shelves: Books, Manuscripts, and Drawings from the Philip H. and A. S. W. Rosenbach Foundation Museum* (Philadelphia: Rosenbach Foundation, 1973), No. 179.

volume journal, which is written in a number of hands and has erasures, interlinear and marginal notes, and words lined over, this volume is written in the same neat hand throughout and has no apparent revisions. A review of the text revealed no significant alterations, additions, or subtractions. Thus, it is probably just what the library title states, a "fair copy," made from the original after that had been completed. If this is the case, it could have been copied from the original by McDougall between the end of the original record and the departure on April 4, 1814, of the remaining Astorians.

Work began on the publication of this manuscript in the early 1980s with the preparation of a transcript of the three volumes by Professor Werner L. Gundersheimer, then at the University of Pennsylvania. The work of editing the log was started, but then, for various reasons, laid aside. Professor Gundersheimer moved on to the Folger Library, Washington, D.C., and the project remained in a state of suspended animation. At the time of the initial work, plans had been made for a joint edition of the Seton and McDougall journals. After I picked up the task of editing the former journal and completed it in 1993, Saverio Procario, Director of the Fordham University Press, proposed following up on Seton with the McDougall journal. The Rosenbach Museum and Library generously agreed to allow me to take up the work suspended when Professor Gundersheimer moved on. Assisted by his transcript and notes, I began my editing in January 1995. Ms. Elizabeth Fuller, Librarian of the Rosenbach Museum, generously and graciously assisted me during a visit there. In addition to agreeing to publish the log, Fordham University also gave me a leave from my teaching during the spring semester of 1996. Several of my Fordham colleagues helped with answers to such problems as the nutritional value of wapatoes and other anti-scorbutics. They include Robert D. Cloney, S.J., Monica Kevin, R.U., Martin Hegyi, S.J., and Henry Schwalbenberg. Ms. Maureen Dolyniuk, Archivist of the Hudson's Bay Company Archives in Manitoba, graciously extended the Archives' permission to publish the roster of North West and Pacific Company employees presented as an Appendix to this work and helped me determine the likely size of point blankets in 1811–13. Rita C. Jones carefully transcribed the roster from a copy of the original. Robert Sweeny of the Memorial University, Newfoundland, helped with various of the job titles current in the fur industry in the early nineteenth century. E. W. Giesecke, Olympia, Washington, drew my attention to material pertaining to the *Tonquin*. As always, the staffs of the New York Public Library as well as the New-York Historical Society and, especially, the Fordham University Library gave essential assistance. Where would we be without libraries and librarians? Mr. Procario of the Fordham University Press kept "urging" me on, pleasantly but insistently. Dr. Mary Beatrice Schulte, executive editor of the press, worked her customary magic on my sometimes wandering prose. I decided on the editing procedures used in preparing the text, and any mistakes in it or in the accompanying notes are my responsibility.

Fordham University Robert F. Jones

EDITORIAL PROCEDURES & GUIDELINES

I have intended to present the log as a readable document with the assistance and within the constraints of sound scholarship. The expanded method of historical editing, which aims at presenting a readable text with the fewest possible changes, has been used, with the following rules and adaptations. (The expanded method is described in Oscar Handlin, et al., *Harvard Guide to American History* [Cambridge, Mass.: Harvard University Press, 1955.])

1. Spelling, capitalization, and punctuation appear as in the original document, with the exception of capitals being supplied at the beginning of sentences and periods at the end, where they are lacking.

2. Author's dashes at the end of sentences are replaced by periods.

3. Daily entries are generally printed as one paragraph.

4. Abbreviations and contractions are generally spelled out, except for those still in common use (months, proper names, titles) and those readily understandable from the context.

5. Accidental repetitions are silently corrected.

6. Superior letters are brought down to the line of text, i.e., Feby appears as Feby. No punctuation is added.

7. The ampersand—&—remains.

8. Except at the top of a page and at the beginning of a month, the writer did not repeat the month, rather employing the ditto sign—". The ditto has been omitted and the month and year placed at the top of each page. Months appear in the text only where they are in the original.

9. Interlineations are brought down to the line of text where indicated by the writer.

10. Marginal annotations are inserted into the text where indicated by the writer.

11. Erased or lined-out passages are explained in footnotes.

12. Where necessary information is lacking in the manuscript—a first

name or part of a date, for example—the omission is made good in a foot-note. Any words in brackets are part of the original document.

13. The manuscript is in excellent condition and in all but a very few instances completely legible; any disputable readings are indicated in a foot-note.

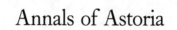

Annals of Astoria

Journal
Commencing Septr. 6th, 1810
Ending 18th April 1812

1810

Septr 6th. At 7 A.M. we set sail from New York, on board of the Ship Tonquin, Jonathan Thorn Commander, having a complement of 21 men, <u>viz</u>. E. D. Fox, Chief-Mate, William P. Mumford, 2d ditto, Peter Anderson Boatswain & 18 seamen.[1] Our party consisted of 32 persons, <u>viz</u>.

Alexander Mackay	
Duncan MacDougall	Proprietors
David Stuart	
Robert Stuart	
Alexander Ross	
Russel Farnham	
Donald MacGillis	
Gabriel Franchere	Clerks
Benjamin Pillet	
James Lewis	
Thomas Mackay	
Job Aiken	Master of Shallop[2]
Donald MacLenon	Clerk
Wm. Wallace Mathews	Ditto
William Wallace	Ditto
Paul Jeremie	Ditto & Labourer
Ovid Montigny	Ditto
Augustin Roussel	Black-Smith
Giles Leclerc	Silver-Smith
George Bill	Cooper

---

[1] A list of the *Tonquin*'s crew is reproduced as an enclosure in Edmund Fanning, *Voyages to the South Seas, Indian and Pacific Oceans, China Sea, Northwest Coast, Feejee Islands, South Shetlands, &c, &c.* (New York: William H. Vermilye, 1838; repr. Fairfield, Washington: Ye Galleon Press, 1970), hereafter, Fanning, *Voyages to the South Seas.*

[2] In a penciled note, "drowned 25 Mar 1811."

Johann Kaster	Ship-Carpenter[3]
Michel Laframboise	Labourer/Carpenter by Trade/
Benjamin Roussel	Ditto/Shoe-Maker by Trade/
Ignace Roy Lapansé	Labourer[4]
Basil Roy Lapansé	Ditto
Olivier Roy Lapansé	Ditto
Jacques Lafantasie	Ditto
Joseph Lapierre	Ditto
Louis Bruslé	Ditto[5]
Joseph Nadeau	Ditto[6]
Jean Belleau	Ditto
Antoine Belleau	Ditto
William Perreault	An Apprentice Boy for [blank] Years and 10 Years of Age.[7]

Octr 6th. Passed the Cape Verd Islands, all hands enjoying a good state of health, excepting a few affected with the Venereal.

25th. Crossed the Equator, when the customary ceremony of ducking and shaving was performed in high stile.[8]

Decr. 4th. Arrived at the Falkland Islands, entered Port-Egmont the 7th for the purpose of watering, etc., had excellent diversion shooting Sea-Lions, Seals, Foxes, Geese, Ducks, & Penguins; all of which are very numerous in those parts, having completed all our operations on shore we weighed and stood to sea the 11th, all in perfect health and high spirits.[9]

---

[3] In a penciled note, "lost in the Tonquin."

[4] In a penciled note, "drowned 22 Mar"—Immediately below this, ditto marks are penciled in along Basil Roy Lapansé.

[5] In a penciled note, "lost in the Tonquin."

[6] In a penciled note, "drowned 22 Mar."

[7] McDougall, or the person transcribing the log, apparently omitted Perreault in arriving at a total of thirty-two company partners and employees. Duncan McDougall has been identified in the Introduction. The proprietors and clerks of the Pacific Fur Company are identified in the Appendix. Other significant individuals will be identified as they appear in the log. Since many persons are repeatedly listed, they will be identified only at the first mention. Note that there is no mention of the tension and bad feeling which had already started to build up, mostly because of Captain Thorn's unreasonably dictatorial command.

[8] Ironically, or paradoxically, Captain Thorn permitted this customary ritual, which usually included a good bit of drinking and fraternity-initiation–style high jinks directed at those crossing the Equator for the first time, while the much more relaxed commander of the *Beaver*, the supply vessel that followed the *Tonquin* some months later, Cornelius Sowle, refused to allow it on his vessel. See Robert F. Jones, ed., *Astorian Adventure: The Journal of Alfred Seton, 1811–1815* (New York: Fordham University Press, 1993), pp. 32–33; hereafter, Jones, ed., *Astorian Adventure*.

[9] Incredibly, McDougall omits any mention of a quarrel between the captain and several

25th. Passed Cape Horn with a fine favorable gale, tolerable moderate but cold weather.

Feby 11th. Arrived off Owyhee (one of the Sandwich Islands) entered Karka bay the 12th, here our Boatswain & a Sailor deserted, the latter however was soon after brought back, but the Capt. would not receive the former, altho the Natives offered to bring him on board: Our not being able to procure all the necessary supplies either there or at Tochigh without losing much time determined us to proceed to Woahou where we arrived on 21st and engaged 12 natives for the establishment, exclusive of 5 the Capt. engaged for the Ship, of which she will soon stand in need, he having discharged one of his best sailors at this place, which with the loss of the Boatswain (who was an excellent sailor) will be most seriously felt as the greater part of his Crew are green hands, having got our Men & necessaries on board we took our departure on the afternoon of 28th, lost sight of the Islands on the 2d of March.[10]

March 22d. Arrived off the Columbia River, but as it blew a very fresh Gale from the Northward & Westward the Capt. did think[11] it prudent to approach within less than about 3 Leagues of the entrance untill the bar should be sounded across on which service he ordered Mr. Fox his chief mate, John Martin seaman & 3 of our Canadians viz. Ignace Lapansé, Bazil Lapansé & Joseph Nadeau; they accordingly set off in our Whale Boat

---

of the partners and clerks who had gone ashore to hunt and stretch their legs. Those on shore, misunderstanding the signal for returning to the ship, lingered, and Thorn ordered the crew to set sail without them. Realizing that the captain did not intend to come about when the shore party appeared in a small boat, Robert Stuart (whose uncle, David, was in the boat) threatened Thorn with a pistol. He then ordered the crew to lower sails and allow the boat to catch up with the ship. Gabriel Franchère (*Journal of a Voyage on the North West Coast . . . 1811, 1812, 1813, and 1814*, ed. W. Kaye Lamb, trans. Wessie Tipping Lamb [Toronto: The Champlain Society, 1969], pp. 55–56; hereafter, Franchère, *Journal*) is one of the boat's passengers who described the incident. After this, the atmosphere on the *Tonquin* was, if possible, even more strained.

[10] Owyhee is now usually spelled Hawaii; the bay is Kealakekua, where the British explorer James Cook was killed in 1779. Alexander Ross (*Adventures of the First Settlers on the Oregon or Columbia River . . .* [London: Smith, Eden and Co., 1849; repr. Readex Microprint, 1966], chap. 3; hereafter, Ross, *Adventures*) describes the stay in the islands as something less than idyllic. Several sailors attempted to desert, with one, who returned voluntarily after having been caught ashore overnight, being refused entry by Thorn. The boatswain who deserted, Peter Anderson, had quarreled several times with the captain. Tochigh may have been Kailua Bay, where the governor, a Briton, John Young, who had come off the American ship *Eleanora* in 1790, lived. He advised Thorn that provisions, etc., could be obtained only through King Kamehameha in Honolulu on the island of Oahu, where the restocking was completed and twenty-four Hawaiian natives (then most frequently called Sandwich Islanders) were hired. Franchère also describes the stay in the islands. *Journal*, pp. 58–70.

[11] Clearly, the captain did NOT think it prudent to approach the bar at the mouth of the river.

about 1 P.M. blowing very fresh, & squally which incited us to express our disapprobation of sending them off to the Capt. but without effect; as they did not return in the evening we were under great apprehension for their safety, being well aware that it is hardly possible for such a boat to live in the breakers on the bar even in moderate weather.[12]

23d. Being equally squally we stood off & on with anxious solicitude having seen nothing of either Boat or Men.

March 24th. Ushered in very pleasant weather, but being for the greater part calm we found it impossible to near the River untill the morning of 25th when a light breeze sprung up of which we took advantage and succeeded in getting to Anchor about 4 Miles N. N. W. of Cape Disappointment; from thence Messrs. McKay & D. Stuart went off with a party in the Pinnace in order to get some information if possible of the Whale Boat & Crew, but the surf broke with such Violence all along the shore that they found it impractible to land and therefore returned on board.[13] About Meridian a fine breeze sprung up from the Northward & Westward which induced us to get under weigh and stand in for the Channel about 1 P. M. but before we got within a League of the bar the Captain became so alarmed at the appearance of the breakers that he hove to and sent Mr. Mumford his 2nd mate & 4 hands in the Pinnace with orders to sound across the channel untill he should find 4 fathoms water, but by the time he found himself in 5 fathoms the Surf began to break all around them, they therefore thought it high time to retreat & made the best of their way back to the Ship; the Captn. not satisfied with Mr. Mumford's exertions & supposing that he kept too far to the southward; sent Mr. Aikin, the Armorer, the Sail-Maker with two Sandwich Islanders, Harry & Peter, in the Jolly Boat (which was at the time without a Rudder & only an old broken oar to steer her) to sound ahead, but the Ship drifting fast to the Southward he judged it necessary to make sail shortly after the boat went off, and either forgot or neglected to make a signal for their return; by the time the Ship got abreast of them the ebb tide was making so strong ahead that we could not take them on board

---

[12] Franchère, whose description is somewhat less circumstantial than McDougall's, adds that the boat did not have a proper sail and a bed sheet had to serve that function. *Journal*, pp. 71–75. Ross has a very detailed description of the events at the bar, including the statement by Fox that his uncle had been drowned there not many years before "and now I am going to lay my bones with his." *Adventures*, pp. 54–56. He was correct.

[13] In place of McDougall's somewhat laconic recounting of this effort, Ross notes that those in the pinnace felt themselves in danger most of the time they were away from the ship. *Adventures*, pp. 57–59. Cape Disappointment is the northern promontory marking the mouth of the Columbia River.

without heaving to or standing out to sea again rather than which he (not withstanding our remonstrating against it) left them to their fate; a few minutes afterwards we entered the breakers steering by the directions of 2 Men in the fore top, and Messrs. McDougall & D. Stuart went up the Mizzen top to look for the Boat which they saw making toward us, & shortly after broaching broadside too, this increased our apprehensions, as from the ebb tide making strong, the surf had now become so violent that the Ship struck repeatedly but without receiving any apparent injury, by the time we had almost got over the Bar, the Boat was once more seen broad side to; next morning parties were sent in all directions to look for them, and about 11 A. M. the Armorer made his appearance on the beach opposite to where the ship lay at anchor in Bakers bay, this for the moment gave hopes of their having been all saved, but how sadly were we disappointed when he informed us that they had not passed more than 3 or 4 of the breakers before a huge one came rolling after them and broke right over the stern of the Boat which ingulphed them all in an instant, and he could see nothing more of either Mr. Aiken or the Sail-Maker, however he and the 2 sandwich Islanders succeeded in getting to the Boat which was floating by them bottom uppermost, they made a Shift to right her & throw out the water, whilst they were thus employed the ebb tide fortunately drifted them out to sea, where they remained all night in a most miserable state: about midnight Peter, one of the Sandwich Islanders, died in the Boat. The Armorer however, with what assistance the other could afford him got a shore in the morning, about 4 or 5 Miles to the Northward & Westward of Cape Disappointment, where he was obliged to leave his fellow sufferer (by the Boat,) who by the time had become so feeble & benumed that he could not proceed: a party went off immediately to his assistance, but before they had arrived at the place the Armorer pointed out; the poor fellow had recovered & made the best of his way to the beach, where he was found next Morning (27th) laying almost lifeless on the sand, however they got him on board and before next morning he was considerably recovered, but his feet were much swollen & torn, by the Cold & walking through the bushes.[14]

---

[14] The armorer was Stephen Weeks. He and the Hawaiian native were the only survivors of the ten men sent out in the pinnace and the jolly boat. The sail maker was Aaron Slaight. Ross comments that, with regard to the time of sounding the water and the time chosen to enter the breakers, "In respect to both, there was an unwarrantable precipitation—a manifest want of sound judgment." *Adventures*, pp. 59–65. Franchère comments that the loss of eight men, especially considering the circumstances under which they died, was "a bad augury, and we felt it very keenly." *Journal*, p. 76. Caution is still needed when entering the Columbia; see Hobe Kytr, "The Lady Is Changeable. Catch Her When She Is Angry," *Sea History*,

28th. Fresh gales & cloudy, about 11 A. M. Messrs. Franchere & Pillet were sent with six sandwich Islanders to inter the remains of their Country Man Peter, which having performed they returned in the evening. Landed our live stock, consisting of 1 Ewe & 1 Ram, 4 Goats, viz. 3 males & 1 female, 14 Hogs, to wit 4 males & 10 females, two of which a male & a female made their escape into the woods before they could be got into the Pen, left 3 hands to attend them.[15]

29th. Pleasant weather, preparations making for the departure of the Launch to sound up the River, and in hopes of seeing or hearing something of the Whaleboat's Crew. Harry the sandwich Islander, convalescent.

30th. Clear & agreeable weather, about 9 A. M. Capt Thorn, Messrs. McKay & D. Stuart set off in the launch to sound the River etc. with a party of 10 Men & an Indian Chief (Dhaitshowan) exclusive of Messrs. Alexr. Ross & Benjn. Pillet, and Benjn. Roussel whom they were to land on the Southern Shore in hopes that they might gain some intelligence of the fate of those who unfortunately left us on 22nd Inst.[16]

31st. Mild & pleasant weather, In the forenoon Mr. Robert Stuart with a party of 7 Men went to endeavor to get off the Jolly Boat, that the Armorer left on 26th Inst. on N. W. side of the Cape, which by 6 P. M. they effected with considerable difficulty the only practicable way being through a marsh which Mr. McDougall had been examining the day previous.[17]

April 1st. Monday weather much the same as yesterday: Landed the two Blacksmiths & forge to work for the Ship, & Mr. Robt. Stuart with a party to make Balls, Cut Fire-Wood etc; Mr. McDougall attending the trade on

---

No. 61 (Spring 1992), 46. Baker's Bay, where the *Tonquin* was anchored, is on the north shore of the Columbia, immediately within Cape Disappointment. McDougall often indicated individuals by their function, occasionally leaving the name of the person in doubt. The armorer and the sail maker have been identified from the *Tonquin* crew list enclosed in Fanning, *Voyages to the South Seas*, 1970 reprint.

[15] Benjamin Pillét, one of the French Canadian clerks, is better known in the history of the Northwest as B. C. Payette; he is memorialized in southwestern Idaho with a town, county, and river named after him.

[16] Although this is the first mention of contact with the natives, the Chinooks and other tribes in the area had become accustomed to the occasional visits of Europeans since Robert Gray's discovery of the Columbia in 1792. Dhaitshowan was the chief of the Clatsops, a tribe within the Lower Chinook division of that river people. They lived south and west of Astoria, in the area where Lewis and Clark wintered in 1805–06. Robert H. Ruby and John A. Brown, *A Guide to the Indian Tribes of the Pacific Northwest* (Norman: University of Oklahoma Press, 1986), pp. 30–31; hereafter cited as Ruby, Brown, *Guide*.

[17] Apparently, they dragged the jolly boat across the Cape rather than risk running the dangers of the mouth of the river, an eloquent testimony to how the company men felt about the events of the past few days.

board & looking over some hands employed in breaking up the hold for Articles of Trade. In the afternoon Messrs. Ross & Pillet, with B. Roussel returned in a Canoe but brought no tidings whatever of those whom they had been looking for, which no longer leaves any doubt of their unfortunate fate; thus have we lost 8 fine fellows either through the obstinacy, ignorance or imprudence of Capt. Thorn.[18]

2d. Tuesday Clear & agreeable weather: Mr. R. Stuart went on shore with a party to make Balls, Cut Fire-Wood, wash clothes, etc. Mr. McDougall traded a few skins.

3d. Wednesday, Continues pleasant. As no Indians were about the Ship Messrs. McDougall & R. Stuart went ashore with a few Men to fill water, cut Firewood, make Balls, etc: Black Smiths employed making Axes, as those on board cannot be got at.

4th. Thursday cloudy with frequent showers of rain: Blacksmiths ashore making Axes, and Mr. R. Stuart with a party cutting Firewood & filling water, etc: In the evening Capt. Thorn & Mr. D. Stuart with 8 Men & the Indian chief, returned in the Launch; Mr. McKay & 2 Men having parted with them near the Cowlitsk River on 1st Inst. for the purpose of exploring farther up the River, & in order to look for a convenient spot to build upon, they having not seen any eligible place this side of the chelwit's village, a little above which the Launch returned, Capt. Thorn alleging that he could not think of carrying the ship so far up.[19]

---

[18] Despite the clear reference to two blacksmiths, McDougall notes only one blacksmith on the *Tonquin*, Augustin Roussel; the second blacksmith may be Giles Leclerc, listed as a silversmith in the log. Carl Russell mentions William Cannon, who came to Astoria with the overlanders in 1812, as a blacksmith. Carl Russell, *Firearms, Traps, and Tools of the Mountain Men* (New York: Alfred A. Knopf, 1967), pp. 381–82; hereafter, Russell, *Firearms*. See below, II, n. 29 for more men working as blacksmiths at Astoria. See also the Appendix for a reasonably complete listing of those at Astoria in 1813–14 and their listed skills. The balls mentioned are doubtless musket balls. Also, note that McDougall has begun to trade, probably with either the Clatsops from the south shore or the local Chinooks (frequently spelled Tshinook) on the north shore, or with both. For an idea of the variety of goods traded, as well as the items needed to carry on the work of the post, see the inventory of merchandise, etc., shipped on the *Beaver*, the supply ship sent out to Astoria in 1811. Kenneth W. Porter, *John Jacob Astor: Business Man*, 2 vols. (Cambridge, Massachusetts: Harvard University Press, 1931), I, 484–507; hereafter, Porter, *Astor*.

[19] The Cowlitz River (spelled variously throughout the log) flows into the Columbia from the north about fifty-five miles from its mouth, at the present site of Longview, Washington. The Chelwits (also spelled variously), a Lower Chinookan group, lived near Oak Point, a name then used for a point on the south shore of the Columbia, about forty miles from its mouth. See Robert H. Ruby and John A. Brown, *The Chinook Indians: Traders of the Lower Columbia River* (Norman: University of Oklahoma Press, 1976), pp. 120–21 and n. 173; hereafter cited as Ruby, Brown, *Chinook*.

5th. Friday cloudy with heavy showers of sleet: Messrs. McDougall and
D. Stuart, with 4 Men & an Indian chief went off in the Pinnace about 1
P. M. for the purpose of looking out for some convenient spot to build
upon, as all hopes of getting the Vessel much farther up are now given over;
Several parties employed on shore cutting & piling Fire-Wood, filling water
etc. See * opposite page.[20]

April 5th. * This morning Captain Thorn without consulting any of us
on board went ashore & pitched upon a place to build a shed to receive the
rigging, etc. belonging to the shallops and gave orders to land some of them
which was the first intimation we had of it, and it was in consequence of the
conversation that passed then, that Messrs. McDougall & Stuart determined
on going in search of some more eligible place than Bakers Bay to build our
shallops and trading establishment.[21]

6th. Saturday. Cloudy & disagreeable weather, with frequent showers of
snow: Capt. Thorn with 15 Men went ashore in the forenoon to build a shed.
Mr. Stuart with another party making Balls, cutting & piling Firewood, etc.
Blacksmiths principally employed for the ship.[22]

7th. Sunday. Squally with showers of sleet, several parties ashore, working
at the shed, cutting & piling Firewood, making Balls, etc. Blacksmiths employed for the ship.

8th. Monday. Cloudy & rainy weather which prevented the people from
going ashore to work.

9th. Tuesday. Continues boisterous with incessant rain which has prevented any work going either on board or ashore.

10th. Wednesday. Squally with frequent showers of hail & rain. Messrs.
McKay, McDougall & D. Stuart returned in the forenoon partly by land &
partly in a canoe; the two latter having been upset on their return 7th Instant

---

[20] This refers to a second entry for April 5th; in the manuscript, the second entry appears
after that of April 11th. It has been placed here as corresponding to the intention of the
writer. The Indian chief referred to may have been Comcomly (sometimes Comcomley), the
chief of the Chinook village opposite where the post will be placed.

[21] The content of this note may give a clue as to its out-of-order location in the journal.
Up to now, McDougall had been discreet in criticizing Thorn's conduct throughout the
voyage and even going over the bar at the Columbia's mouth. Now, he had perhaps lost
patience and decided to record clearly and unmistakably just what Thorn was doing and the
Astorians' response. The "shallops" referred to were small sailing vessels, intended to carry
on a coastal trade with the natives in the area around the mouth of the Columbia. Despite the
plural used, only one was apparently built. It is frequently mentioned in the log.

[22] This is another example of Thorn's precipitate and arbitrary conduct. The shed was for
the protection of trade goods unloaded from the *Tonquin*, but McDougall and the other
partners had not yet fixed on a permanent site for their establishment.

on the N. E. shore of Bakers bay, where they were obliged to leave the Boat, having lost several articles and narrowly escaped with their lives, from thence they made the best of their way to the Tshinook's Village, where they were detained for 3 days in consequence of bad weather, but Comcomley the Chief entertained them in a most hospitable manner, & accompanied them on board.[23]

11th. Thursday. Weather much the same as yesterday, preparations making for proceeding up to point George, near which Messrs. McDougall & Stuart have pitched upon, as the fittest place for the establishment that they had any knowledge of.[24]

12th. Friday. Clear & pleasant weather. In the forenoon Capt. Thorn with 4 hands went off to sound the channel, in order to ascertain whether the ship could be taken to Pt. George. Messrs. McKay & D. Stuart set off at same time in the Launch, to begin clearing a spot to build upon (in case the channel should be found Navigable) having a party of Men, viz.

Alexr. Ross	
Russel Farnham	
Donald MacGillis	
Gabriel Franchere	Clerks
Benjn. Pillet	
Thos. McKay	
Donald McLenon	Clerk
Wm. Wallace Mathews	Ditto
William Wallace	Ditto
Ovid Montigny	Labourer
Augustin Roussel	Blacksmith
Giles Leclerc	Silversmith
Michel Laframboise	Labourer/Carpenter by trade
Benjn. Roussel	Ditto/Shoe Maker by ditto
Olivier Roy Lapansé	Ditto
Jacques Lafantaisie[25]	

---

[23] The canoe had possibly been borrowed or purchased from the Chinooks. This is the first explicit mention of Comcomly, whose position as chief of the Chinook village opposite Astoria made him very important to them. He also acted as intermediary and, until the Astorians realized it, middleman between the traders and the other tribes, especially those further up the Columbia.

[24] Point George is on the south (Oregon) bank of the Columbia, about twelve miles south, southeast of Baker's Bay.

[25] Lafantasie's name was written diagonally in the left margin, with a cross marking its place in the list.

Joseph Lapierre	Ditto
Louis Bruslé	Ditto
Jean Belleau	Ditto
Antoine Bellow	Ditto
William Perreault	apprentice Boy

George Naaco ⎫
Toby Too
Peter Pahia
Paul Pooar
Jack Powrowrie ⎬ Sandwich Islanders
Bob Pookarakara
Dick Paow
William Karimou ⎭

Remained on board the Ship, <u>viz</u>.

Mr. Duncan McDougall
–"– Robert Stuart
–"–James Lewis   Clerk[26]
George Bell   Cooper
Johann Kaster   Ship Carpenter[27]
Harry (a cripple since the Boat wreck) ⎫
Thos. Tuana (affected with the venereal) ⎬ Sandwich Islanders

Remained on Shore in charge of Live stock, etc.

Paul Jeremie ⎫
Edward Cox ⎬ Sandwich Islanders
James Keemoo[28] ⎭

A party employed bringing off several articles which had been left ashore. Mr. McDougall traded a few Skins.

13th. Saturday, fine clear weather, a considerable number of Indians about the Ship. Mr. McDougall traded a few skins & some Fish. In the evening Capt. Thorn with 4 hands returned in the Launch, bringing a pretty favor-

---

[26] Penciled note, "lost in the Tonquin."

[27] Penciled note, "lost in the Tonquin."

[28] This list differs from the first chiefly in the addition of the Hawaiians (Sandwich Islanders), the mention of members of the ship's crew, and notes as to the medical condition of two of the Hawaiians. Thomas Tuana never recovered sufficiently to work and was sent home in 1813.

able account of the channel; having in the forenoon left Messrs. McKay & Stuart with their party at work, clearing a place for the buildings.

14th. Sunday. The morning tolerably fair, the Capt. made some dispositions to proceed up the River, but about 10 A. M., the weather became so hazy & rainy that he thought it imprudent to ventur out untill more favorable weather, as the channel is somewhat intricate.

15th. Monday. The morning cloudy with frequent showers of rain, towards noon it cleared away, began to prepar for getting under weigh, got 2 of the Goats & 7 of the Hogs on board, leaving the remainder, to wit, 2 Sheep, 2 Goats & 3 Pigs in charge of Jeremie & the 2 Sandwich Islanders, as the Capt. pretended he had not time to bring them off. At 2 P. M. got under weigh and came to anchor about ½ a league to the North & Eastward of Pt. George at a quarter after 4, when we were saluted with 3 Vollies of Musketry & 3 Cheers by the party ashore, which we returned with thre Guns, etc., etc.

April 16th. Tuesday. Mild & pleasant weather. All hands on board employed mooring the Ship. Our party on shore busy clearing a place to build upon in which they have been engaged since they left the Ship, but owing to our not having got at the Axes, they are able to make but little progress. Mr. McDougall remains on board to attend the trade, etc.[29]

17th. Wednesday. Agreeable Weather. Our party on shore employed as yesterday. The people on board variously engaged in breaking up & sending some articles belonging to the Shallops etc. ashore. In the forenoon Mr. R. Stuart went off with Comcomley in his canoe, to bring up Jeremie, the two Sandwich Islanders and what part of our live stock remained with them; the latter he left at the Tshinook Village in charge of Comcomley the chief, and with the former returned about 5 P. M. Two days ago Mr. McKay had a very bad fall, in consequence of which he was considerably indisposed all yesterday, but this morning he grew much worse & is since confined to bed. The rest of our party enjoy a tolerable state of health, excepting Harry and Thos. Tuana who are both very much indisposed. Mr. R. Stuart left the ship to remain on shore.

---

[29] James P. Ronda, *Astoria and Empire* (Lincoln: University of Nebraska Press, 1990), pp. 200–202, gives some of the details of this very arduous task; hereafter, Ronda, *Astoria*. As McDougall notes, it was made more difficult by the unavailability of the felling axes. Thorn will depart on a trading voyage without all the cargo meant for the post having been unloaded, thus leaving them, until the arrival of the *Beaver*, deprived of some essential tools. This may have been owing as much to the limited storage space thus far constructed at the post as to Captain Thorn's typical impatience.

18th. Thursday. Clear & pleasant weather. All hands both on board &
ashore employed much the same as Yesterday. Mr. McKay considerably
recovered.

19th Friday. Weather continues fair. In the afternoon the carpenter & 4
Men began to cut down & square timber for the store. All the rest still
employed in clearing away, which we find a much more difficult & tideous
job than was at first imagined. The Ship's Company busy disembarking the
several articles belonging to the Shallops, & building a shed for their reception, etc.[30]

20th. Saturday. Cloudy with light Showers of rain. All hand, both on
board & ashore, employed as Yesterday.

21st. Sunday. Cloudy with a few partial showers of rain. A little before
daylight the Ship (not being properly moored) tailed on a sand bank &
struck several times with some violence but received no perceptible injury.
About 10 A. M. she was got off and anchored farther from shore. All hands
have a holiday to scrub & wash themselves & clothes. Ever since we landed
here we have been daily visited by a number of Tshinooks, Clatsops, Cathlamets, and Wakicoms.[31]

April 22nd. Monday. Cloudy with frequent showers of hail & rain. People employed at diferent work, the Carpenter & his gang working constantly
at squaring & hewing the frame of the Store, which is to be sixty feet by
twenty five, inside. We make but little progress in clearing, the place being
so full of half decayed trunks, large fallen timber & thick brush. In the
forenoon Mr. McDougall, with his baggage, came ashore, Capt. Thorn
having refused to allow his trading any longer on board.[32]

---

[30] Note that McKay's fall was not connected, directly or indirectly, to the work of clearing
the land. According to Alexander Ross, that task cost several injuries, some serious, most of
which McDougall did not mention; see Ross, *Adventures*, pp. 73–74.

[31] Note that McDougall is not cutting Thorn any more slack. It was the captain's responsibility to see that his vessel was moored properly, and noting the failure to do so in the log was
an implicit criticism of Thorn's command. Later, however, McDougall will note that there is
no good holding ground in front of the post; see below, November 22, 1811. The Tshinooks
(an alternative spelling of Chinook) and Clatsops have already been identified; the Cathlamets
and Wakicums were part of the Chinook family. The former had recently moved from the
south bank of the Columbia, from Tongue Point, about six miles east of Astoria, and incorporated themselves into the Wakicums, on the north bank, near present-day Cathlamet, Washington. Both groups were Upper Chinookan linguistically, Lower Chinookan culturally.
Ruby, Brown, *Guide*, pp. 11–12, 257–58. See also Ruby, Brown, *Guide*, p. 24.

[32] The "store" referred to here is the building which will be used to store or safeguard the
trade goods as well as those items needed by the Astorians themselves. Eventually, several
buildings will be constructed and surrounded with a wooden palisade, surmounted by two
blockhouses.

23rd. Tuesday. Clear & pleasant weather. People at work as usual.

24th. Wednesday. Cloudy with frequent showers of rain. Our People employed as heretofore, excepting 4 of the Sandwich Islanders who began this morning to prepare a piece of ground in which we intend to sow some Indian corn, a few garden seeds, & about 30 or 40 Potatoes we have brought safe from New York out of near half a bushel we put up very carefully in Paper, etc., to secure them from the sea air. This afternoon the carpenters were sent a shore to lay the keel of one of the shallops. Traded a few shines & some Venison.[33]

25th. Thursday. Mild & pleasant with a few light showers of rain. Our people employed as usual; the Natives informed us of their having seen a Brig out side of the Breakers, but after firing a few guns she sheered off.[34]

26th. Friday. Pleasant weather. People variously employed. Saw the Vessel the Indians reported Yesterday, passing and repassing the entrance of the River, which inclines us to think that she intends to come in.

27th. Saturday. Cloudy with a few showers of rain. This morning Messrs. McKay & D. Stuart set off for the Tshinook and Clatsop Villages, to endeavour to secure any furs they may be possessed of (as well as a party of the Clemax nation who are at the latter place on a visit) in case the sail we saw Yesterday should enter the the River, as hitherto our ship has been so lumbered that few of the trading articles could be got at, which compelled us to put off the greater number of those who came to offer skins, etc., for sale. People employed as usual.[35]

April 28th. Sunday. Rainy & disagreeable weather. Messrs. McDougall & R. Stuart with 4 of the young Gentlemen Dined on board; Messrs. McKay & D. Stuart have not returned according to expectation; we suppose that their detention is occasioned by the stormy weather.

---

[33] In spite of the work done on this garden, there will be little mention of its produce. Just what the "shines" were is not clear. Later, the Astorians buy large quantities of "uthlecan," actually a variety of smelt (*Eulachon*), with a very high oil content. These were sometime called "candlefish," because if hung from a string, they would burn like a candle. Any connection of them with "shines" is entirely the fancy of the editor, as "shines" could also be a miswriting of "skins." See Ruby, Brown, *Chinook*, p. 12, for a description of uthlecans.

[34] This is the first mention by the natives of a European ship outside the mouth of the Columbia. There was an active trade up and down the coast with the natives of the area, and such vessels may actually have existed, but almost invariably the Astorians were not able to catch any sight of them and they did not enter the river. This time they did see the vessel and moved, see below, April 27th, to buy up all the available skins before competition occurred.

[35] Clemax was a local name for the Tillamooks, a Salish-speaking tribe living further south, along the Pacific coast. See Ronda, *Astoria*, pp. 223–24, and "Early Indian Tribes, Culture Areas, and Linguistic Stocks," *National Atlas of the United States* (U.S. Geological Survey).

29th. Monday. Weather as yesterday. All hands however turned out to work as usual. Messrs. McKay & D. Stuart returned in the evening, after making a very satisfactory trip. We have two or 3 Men every day unwell and unable to work.

30th. Tuesday. Wet & disagreeable weather. People employed as usual. An Indian from the Rapids informed us of his having seen a party of about 30 Men building Houses, etc., near the second Rapid, and from the description he gave of them we conclude that they must belong to the <u>N. W. Company in Canada</u>, to ascertain which and in order to take the fittest measures in case of an opposition, a party will set off as soon as a few articles of trade can be got ready <u>from on board</u>. Traded a few skins & Geese.[36]

May 1st. Wednesday. Dirty rainy weather, wind S. W. Men variously employed, a party hauling out timber. In the afternoon got a few articles ready for Messrs. McKay & R. Stuart to proceed up the River.

2nd. Thursday. Showery, wind S. W. Messrs. McKay, R. Stuart & Franchere with 5 Men departed in a large Canoe about 9 A. M. People employed as yesterday. <u>Two unwell</u>.

3rd. Friday. Wind variable with rain. Four persons unwell. Mr. Pillet cut his foot with an Axe. Some of the Men hewing timber, others rolling logs. Sandwich Islanders making a Garden & clearing the point.[37]

4th. Saturday. People employed as usual. The Ship's carpenter & our own employed at the Shallop, but make little progress having so many jobs from the Ship.

5th. Sunday. Heavy rain all day.

6th. Monday. Wind S. W., dry & pleasant. Began hauling out the timber for the Store. Preparing a shed to receive goods, &c for trade.

7th. Tuesday. Pleasant weather. Received sundry articles into the Shed & traded a number of Beaver. People at their usual labour.

8th. Wednesday. Pleasant weather. Part of the People hauling out timber, clearing a foundation for the store, digging & clearing a cellar, etc. Mr. Mumford, the Tonquin's Chief Mate, came ashore & acquainted us that he was sent out of the Ship, consequently wished to make some arrangement

---

[36] This is the first mention of the possibility of competition from the aggressive North West Company. As noted in the Introduction, Astor had proposed an amalgamation of the two companies, but this had been turned down by the Montreal group within the North Westers. Notice also the implicit criticism of Thorn's unloading of the *Tonquin*, in that the goods needed for trade with the natives were not yet available.

[37] Pillet's accident is the first mention of a casualty because of the clearing and construction work going on. The number of sick is always given, but the cause or nature of their ailments is not usually mentioned.

with us, to remain as Master of one of the Shallops, but we gave him no decisive answer untill we should see Capt. Thorn.[38]

9th. Thursday. Mathews, Laframboise & Jos. Lapierre framing the store since the 6th instant, and still busy at it. The rest employed as usual.

10th. Friday. Some rain. People employed as yesterday. Told Capt. Thorn the purport of the conversation that passed between Mr. Mumford & us, & that we would not interfere in any manner between him & his officers.

11th. Saturday. Agreeable weather. Mr. Mumford goes on board in consequence of Capt. Thorn having sent for him. People at their usual labour.

12th. Saturday. Dry & pleasant. All last week we had on an average four Men unfit for duty. Those with the six that are with Messrs. McKay & Stuart, the Carpenter & Cooper who are constantly employed at the Shallop & Ship made the number we had here but <u>small indeed</u> out of the number of labouring Men embarked at New York.[39]

13th. Monday Rainy weather. All hands employed as usual. Received a long Letter from Capt. Thorn addressed to Messrs. McKay & McDougall.[40]

14th. Tuesday. Gloomy weather. The frame of the Store ready to raise. Wrote an answer to Capt. Thorns Letter. Mr. D. Stuart very much indisposed, having strained himself hauling out the timber for the Store.

May 15th. Wednesday. Cloudy with some showers of rain. Wind S. W. Messrs. McKay & Stuart arrived about 7 A. M., being as high as the grand rapid, where they met some Indians from near the Rocky Mountains, who as well as the Natives there, assured them that no white People were seen in any part of the River, but said that they had paroles with some Tobacco from

[38] This interview resulted in Mumford's staying at Astoria, where he was put in charge of the shallop then being constructed. However, he was no more satisfactory to McDougall than he had been to Captain Thorn. It seems that even Thorn could, on occasion, be correct in his judgment.

[39] Exclusive of the clerks and skilled craftsmen, thirteen laborers and the ten-year-old apprentice, Perreault, had embarked at New York. However, three of the Canadians had been lost in crossing the bar. McDougall was apparently including the clerks, ten of whom had come on board in New York, among the number of laboring men. The contract signed by the clerks who came out on the *Beaver* in 1811–12 made no specific mention of the duties the clerks were expected to perform; see Porter, *Astor*, I, 475–78. McDougall almost invariably refers to clerks as "Mister" while not so honoring the Canadian *voyageurs* and laborers, or the Hawaiians. Presumably, he considered the former gentlemen, but, it seems, gentlemen who might be expected to work for a living from time to time. More important, his comment underlines the real labor shortage that did occur from time to time at Astoria.

[40] This letter begins an exchange of correspondence which will finally end on May 23rd when McDougall and McKay go on board the *Tonquin* "to put an end to such unnecessary & trifling communications."

the other side of the Rocky Mountains, by which they understood that a party somewhat similar to Capts. Lewis & Clarke's were on their way hither, who we suppose can be no other than our own people. Being fully satisfied that no strangers were establishing on any part of the River, and having got what information they could regarding the adjacent Country, they thought it unnecessary to proceed farther. They gave a favorable account of the appearance of the Country, & the Natives appeared all very friendly, but they understand little or nothing of hunting Beaver (altho' very numerous on their lands) a convincing proof of which is our people bring down no more than 16 skins, notwithstanding they visited every Village this side the Rapids. Making preparations to raise the frame of the Store. Busy making out a general requisition of sundries to be landed from on board. Mr. D. Stuart & 2 of the men very much indisposed, the latter having strained themselves also carrying out the Timber: & 3 more are laid up with a kind of flux.[41]

16th. Thursday. Clear & pleasant weather. All hands employed raising the store. Nine persons unfit for duty. Messrs. McKay & McDougall wrote a Note to Capt. Thorn, enclosing a Memo of the whole Pieces & articles that would be most in the way of restowing the ship. In the afternoon they received a long Letter from him respecting the detention of the ship & Mr. Astors Instructions, say regarding his own conduct & ours on board & at Bakers Bay, etc. In the forenoon, Mr. McDougall set off with Dhaichowan, a clatsop chief, to his Village on Pt. Adams, to visit a party of 80 or 90 Men

---

[41] The rapids referred to are probably those encountered on the eastern slope of the Cascade Mountains, about 145 miles from the mouth of the Columbia. Some forty-five miles further on, the Astorians would encounter the Dalles, where the Columbia was funneled down a narrow rock chute for ten miles below Celilo Falls. The Dalles was the long portage where the Astorians and other European travelers encountered difficulties time and again from the natives. Another set of rapids, "Priest Rapids," is 200 miles farther up the river. It will not always be clear from the log just which one of these natural obstacles (and there were others farther on) was the location of one or another incident. "Paroles" is probably an antique usage, meaning a semi-formal conference of some kind; notice that tobacco was smoked, usually a sign of friendship between those present. Whoever the approaching party was, and it may have been the overland Astorians who did not begin to arrive there until January 1812, McDougall took false comfort in assuming there was no competition elsewhere on the river. His assumption will be disproved with the arrival of David Thompson of the North West Company on July 15th. Notice the complaint about the shortage of beaver skins among the natives, especially of the upper Columbia. Since beaver was not a good source of food and they clothed themselves with other material, the natives did not commonly hunt or trap them. This was sometimes taken by the whites as proof of their inveterate laziness or stupidity, possibly both. McDougall's mentions of injuries, possibly hernias, from the clearing and construction show that such were constituting a serious problem, in the light of the labor shortage mentioned above. The "flux" was possibly a diarrhea or dysentery from the very oily salmon of the summer run; see Ronda, *Astoria*, p. 204.

of the Clemax nation, whose Lands adjoin the former's & live along the sea shore; they came there two days ago in consequence of some serious difference which has lately taken place between them and the Tshinooks. Both parties are making preparations for War. Mr. McD pointed out to them the impropriety of such conduct & that we could not countenance it, etc. They approved of our sentiments, saying that there was nothing farther from their wishes than to be at variance with any of their neighbours, but said that the Tshinook's conduct forced them into those disagreeable broils, etc., etc.[42]

17th. Friday. Mild but gloomy weather. The people variously employed about the store, etc. In the afternoon, Mr. McKay went over to the Tshinook Village in hopes of prevailing on them to come to some accomodation with the Clemax. Sick list much the same as yesterday.

18th. Saturday. Clear & pleasant, wind S. W. Part of the People busy about the store, & the rest hauling out timber. Mr. McKay returned in the afternoon being employed all the morning sowing Timothy, clover & a variety of garden seeds, &c. on Comcomly's point. From what he could learn there is reason to suppose that all differences between them and their southern Neighbours will be amicably settled, as both parties from knowing our sentiments seem averse to commence hostilities. Sent a general requisition on board for the Capt.'s perusal, & Mr. Lewis to make out a fair copy. Traded a good many skins.[43]

19th. Sunday. Mild & pleasant. Our Invalids are in a fair way. Traded between 25 & 30 skins from about the same number of Indians, who are constantly visiting us either from one tribe or another.

20th. Monday. Agreeable weather, wind S. W. Signed & sent the general Requisitions on board. All those who have been unwell resumed their work this morning, excepting Mr. D. Stuart who is still very weak but in a state of recovery, and Mr. Pillet & Tom Tuana who are both cripples from the nature of their complaints. Visited by 50 or 60 Indians, who traded 100 or 120 Skins.[44]

21st. Tuesday. Fine weather, wind. S. W. Mr. Robert Stuart went off in search of cedar bark to cover the store, with five men & provisions for one

---

[42] Point Adams was the southern cape of the mouth of the Columbia River.

[43] Recall that some of the Astorians' livestock was left on the north bank of the river in Comcomley's care when Captain Thorn would not transport it across to Point George; see April 17. The planting of timothy, etc., may have been an attempt to provide pasturage for the animals.

[44] Since McDougall has already noted that Tuana's ailment was venereal disease, possibly Pillet was laid up with the same disease.

week. People employed squaring and hauling out timber, & filling in the store, digging another cellar and making a wharf. Received a Long Letter from Capt. Thorn stating his interpretation of Mr. Astor's instructions to him, etc. Mr. Lewis came to remain a shore, having been left on board untill now to bring up the Captain's & our own accounts.[45]

22nd. Wednesday. Fine weather. People employed as yesterday. Messrs. McKay & McDougall sent an answer to Capt. Thorn's Letters of 16th & Yesterday. The Shallops finished to the binns. Jeremie received a bad blow & is laid up. Four more are sickly & unfit for duty. Mr. D. Stuart went over to the Tshinook Village to secure what furs they might have, in consequence of the Indians having reported that a Vessel was seen off the entrance of the River.[46]

23rd. Thursday. Clear & pleasant weather. People employed as usual. Messrs. McKay & McDougall received an answer to their letter of yesterday from Capt. Thorn, wrote an answer to his, and in order to put an end to such unnecessary & trifling communications, they went on board in order to bring the business to a final termination. Mr. D. Stuart returned in the afternoon, with about 20 Beaver, which were all he could find amongst them.

24th. Friday. Agreeable weather. People employed as yesterday. Mr. R. Stuart, 1 Man, & 2 Indians arrived with 20 boards and about 100 pieces of Cedar Bark. He returned again with the flood Tide & took provisions with him for the People. Visited by 4 or 5 Canoes of Tshinooks & Clatsops; traded a few skins.

25th. Saturday. Disagreeable rainy weather. Wind S. W. People variously employed.

26th. Sunday. Weather much the same as yesterday. Mr. R. Stuart, 1 Man, & 3 Indians arrived with two canoes' load of Bark. The effects of the late Mr. Fox, Mr. Aiken, & Jn. Coles were disposed of on board the Ship.[47]

---

[45] The cedar bark was to be used as both a siding and a roofing material. "Mr. Astor's instructions" presumably refer specifically to Astor's wish that Thorn move north along the Pacific coast, securing as many pelts, especially sea otter, as possible, before leaving Astoria to carry the furs to Canton, their intended destination. Thorn was probably arguing that McDougall and the other partners were detaining him unnecessarily.

[46] "Binns" has not been traced; its obvious resemblance to bin, or a storage area, leads to the surmise that it may refer to storage areas in the hold or along the side of the vessel. Wilfred Granville notes that the word's original meaning was a receptacle for stores; see *A Dictionary of Sailors' Slang* ([London] André Deutsch, 1962). Notice the Indians' sighting of another vessel and the traders' response. It may have been a stratagem on the part of the former to secure better prices, perhaps for inferior skins. There is no further news of this vessel.

[47] Just where the Astorians were securing the boards and cedar bark is not apparent. Cedar

27th. Monday. Clear, dry weather. People variously employed. Erected a sawpit.

28th. Tuesday. Rainy weather. People employed as usual.

29th. Wednesday. Dry & pleasant weather. People variously employed. Mr. R. Stuart arrived with Cedar Bark.

May 30th. Thursday. Clear & pleasant weather. People employed as usual. Mr. Mumford brought his things ashore in consequence of our arrangement with himself and Capt. Thorn, who discharged him entirely from the Ship, & we give him the birth of Master of the Shallop that is now building. We however sent a Man on board to perform the Voyage to the Northward in his place.[48]

31st. Friday. Agreeable weather, Wind S. W. People variously occupied.

June 1st. Saturday. Gloomy Rainy Weather. Messrs. McKay & McDougall signed the receipts for the goods landed here. Mr. McKay sent his things on board this morning, in order to be ready to repair thither himself at a moment's warning. He performs the Voyage to the Northward as Joint Supercargo with Capt. Thorn. Louis Bruslé also goes round in Mr. Mumford's place. Our Carpenter, Jn. Castles, went on board in place of Henry Wicks, who remains to build the Shallops, the former not being fit for the task. The Cooper came ashore in the forenoon, having been employed on board ever since our arrival. The wind springing up from the Northward & Eastward induced Capt. Thorn to get under weigh about 3 P. M. & anchored in bakers bay between 8 & 9. Messrs. McDougall & D. Stuart being on board and their Canoe having returned to the shore for some things that were forgotten, those in it could not overtake them & the channel was so narrow that the ship could not be hove to, they were consequently obliged to remain on board all night.

2d. Sunday. Fine clear weather, with light airs from the Northward during the forenoon, & we think fair for the Ship to cross the Bar. Mr. McKay feeling lonsome and wishing much to have some one from here along with him; since the Capt. was so determined to allow none of our other young Gentlemen on board, but Mr. Lewis; it was agreed the latter should accompany him as Ships Clerk, on condition of his making out duplicates of the Ships transactions during the Voyage, which was acceded to by Capt. Thorn.

---

trees grew in many areas along the river; thus, it was probably not far away. An auction was the common means of disposing of the personal effects of those lost at sea.

[48] Unfortunately, as events would prove, the agreement between Mumford and McDougall (and perhaps also with Thorn) was entirely oral, and would produce a good bit of contention. The exchange of men took place on June 1st.

Messrs. McDougall & Stuart, having hired an Indian Canoe to convey them hither, took their leave of the Ship about 2 P. M. & arrived in the evening. Three Men unwell. Visited by 4 or 5 Canoes of Indians who brought some fish to Trade.[49]

3d. Monday. Wet & unpleasant weather. People employed at different work; Mr. Mumford & the Cooper work with the Carpenter at the Shallop. Sent Mr. Pillet & 2 Men to Baker's Bay with Letters & clothes to Messrs. McKay & Lewis. Visited by Comcomly & a number of other Indians. Four Men sick.

4th. Tuesday. Agreeable weather. Three Men began felling & squaring timber for a House 60 feet by 20 inside. The rest of the people at different work. Mr. R. Stuart set off with 3 Men for Cedar Bark.[50] One of the Sandwich Islanders being merry & rather forward, was struck & cut very ill with a bone by Mr. Mumford, who was also Gay & glorious.

At sun set Mr. Pillet returned from Baker's Bay, where he left all hands on board well but fatigued, having tried to get out, but without success.

5th. Wednesday. Pleasant weather. People variously engaged. Moved the Goods, our Baggage, etc., out of the trading Shed into the Store, & about ²⁄₃ of the people are to sleep in it with us in case of any alarm from the natives. Mr. McDougall handling one of the Blunderbusses, it went off unexpectedly & hurt him considerably [in the genitals] the shot passed through the side of the Tent & Mr. D. Stuart, who was standing near by, very narrowly escaped. Mr. R. Stuart arrived with near 200 pieces of Bark & brought down Benjn. Roussel. The Sawyers make but little progress owing to the bad quality of the saws (there also being no proper files to set them), and the quantity of sap in the Timber.[51]

---

[49] In the light of the later loss of the *Tonquin* and all those who left the Columbia on it, the exchanges, especially that of James Lewis, were especially unfortunate for those who would otherwise have stayed at Astoria. It should also be noted that a significant quantity of trade goods was still on board the ship, probably owing as much to the lack of suitable storage space at the post as to the understandable desire of McDougall to be rid of Captain Thorn for a while.

[50] At this point in the manuscript, four lines are heavily crossed out. The matter begins "In the afternoon, all" but cannot be read further. A fifth line is erased, except for the phrase beginning "one of the Sandwich Islanders. . . ." What follows is one of McDougall's rare mentions of a drunken brawl. Either the Astorians were extraordinarily temperate and easygoing, or he did not record other such "discussions." Notice that the Hawaiian is implicitly reproved for being "forward" or moving beyond his station, while Mumford was simply "Gay & glorious."

[51] For whatever obscure reasons of delicacy, the material in brackets has been lightly crossed out in the manuscript. A blunderbuss is a short musket, with a large bore and flaring muzzle, suitable for short-range use where aim is not important. More than seventy files were

For the last five weeks we have had on an average three Men unwell, & rather more. Bought four large salmon. At 7 A. M. the Tonquin Sailed out with a fine breeze.

6th. Thursday. Agreeable weather. People employed as usual. A number of Indians visit us daily but seldom bring more than 2 or 3 Skins each. They have salmon in great plenty, but from a superstitious idea they entertain that boiling & cutting it across will prevent them from coming into the River untill the next new Moon, they have brought us Very few & those they insisted on dressing & roasting themselves. We at first suspected it was from some plan they had formed to starve us, but are now agreeably disappointed.[52]

Being anxious to acquire a knowledge of the country & the prospects of trade, in any place where the Natives are assembled in any numbers, that is within our reach; we got a Tshinook Indian named Calpo to take Mr. R. Stuart to Queenhalt, in order to ascertain the situation of the Place & prospects of Trade, with a small assortment of trading articles, to find out their prices for furs, etc. The Blacksmith made a broad Axe.[53]

7th. Friday. Fine warm weather. Our Cathlamet hunter came to inform us that he had killed an Elk near Capts. Lewis & Clarks house in Youngs

---

recorded in the inventory presented by Astor to the President in 1823 (Russell, *Firearms*, p. 405), but they could have been part of the more than one hundred files of various descriptions shipped as part of the *Beaver's* cargo in 1811; Porter, "Inventory of Merchandise Shipped on the *Beaver*," *Astor*, I, 496, 502, 505. Presumably, the files McDougall missed were still on board the *Tonquin*.

[52] A description of the Chinook beliefs regarding, and the ceremonies followed with, the first salmon of the summer run is given in Ruby, Brown, *Chinook*, pp. 12–13. Note the lack of regard for native religion and practice typical of European traders and others. There were at least four species of salmon (*Oncorhynchus*) that spawned in the Columbia, the largest being the chinook or king (*O. tshawytscha*) salmon, which came in three successive runs, from spring through fall. Sockeye (*O. nerka*) salmon came in the late summer or early fall, while the coho (*O. kisutch*) came only in the fall. The toughest or driest species, the chum or dog (*O. keta*), also comes only in the fall; it was probably this species that the French Canadians called *poisson à sept écorces*, literally, "the fish of seven layers," as one supposedly went through seven layers and still had nothing good to eat; see Franchère, *Journal*, p. 97. A. J. McClane, ed., *McClane's Standard Fishing Encyclopedia* (New York: Holt, Rinehart & Winston, 1965) and Richard White, *The Organic Machine: The Remaking of the Columbia River* (New York: Hill & Wang, 1995), pp. 16–20.

[53] The Quinaults, a tribe of the Salish linguistic stock, lived along the Pacific Ocean and in the interior along the river of the same name, above Gray's Harbor, about eighty miles above the mouth of the Columbia. Ruby, Brown, *Guide*, pp. 174–77. A description of how a broad ax (and other types) was made is in Russell, *Firearms*, pp. 257–59. Calpo, presumably from Comcomly's village, across the Columbia, will perform a number of tasks for the Astorians in the future.

River. Mr. McDougall & 3 Men went off with him in a canoe and brought it home about 3 P. M. Settled with our hunter, to give him one Blanket, 2½ pts for every large male elk he brought us. The Indians about us as usual & notwithstanding all our precautions, they pilfer every thing they can lay their hands upon, particularly Tools. Today they stole an axe and tho' it was missed a few minutes afterwards, we could not discover the Thief. Blacksmith made a square for the house Carpenter. Sowed some Indian corn.[54]

June 8th. Saturday. Wea: as yesterday. Our hunter brought an elk, for which we paid him 1 Blanket, 2½ points & made him a present of one small Axe & 2 feet Iron hoop. Several Clatsops visited us & traded a few skins. Gave leave to the people to wash their clothes, etc., after 3 P. M.

9th. Sunday. Blowing fresh from the Northward, light showers & cold for the season. This climate we find not near so warm as that of Montreal, altho' in the same Latitude. From one cause or another we have continually two or three on the sick list. It must be owing to the change of diet, and the fatigues they undergo in hauling out the Timber, which is uncommonly heavy & large.[55]

---

[54] The Cathlamet hunter is Watatcum (various spellings), whose agreement, presented above, will have to be renegotiated at least once; see below, September 18, 1812, May 26, 1813. Lewis and Clark's house refers to "Fort Clatsop," where the explorers wintered, 1805–06; it is about six miles south and west of Astoria on what is now called the Lewis and Clark River. Young's River is about three miles east of the Lewis and Clark River. The blankets the Cathlamet hunter agreed to receive for his work were probably similar to what are today referred to as "Hudson's Bay blankets," and were a kind of standard currency with the fur traders. At one time, the "point'" referred to the number of beaver skins needed to secure the blanket—the larger the blanket, the more points. Since the sizes of Hudson's Bay blankets were not standardized until 1860, there is no way to be certain just what the size of these blankets were. However, shortly before this, in 1808, the U.S. Office of Indian Trade ordered blankets shipped to the post at Mackinac in the strait between Lake Huron and Lake Michigan. The stipulated sizes for 2½- and 3-point blankets were, respectively: 5'4" x 4'3" and 6' x 5'2". It seems reasonable that McDougall's blankets were of similar, if not identical, sizes. See Charles Hanson, Jr., "The Point Blanket," *The Museum of the Fur Trade Quarterly*, 12, No. 1 (Spring 1976), 5–10. The present Hudson's Bay Company, a general retail chain in Canada, does not sell 2½-point blankets; their smallest blanket generally available is 3½-point, suitable for a single bed, approximately 60" x 85" in size. I have not been able to determine why the meat (or the skin) of the male elk was preferred; see below, June 13, 1811. Notice McDougall's complaint about the natives' pilfering of tools, etc., from the post and its vicinity.

[55] McDougall would seem to have been wrong in his climatic observations, although he was correct in his locations. Astoria is about 46°, 15' north latitude, while Montreal is 45°, 30', but their average July temperatures are just about the same. Taking the average for Portland as an equivalent for Astoria, the high is 80°, the low, 57°, while in Montreal during the same month, the high is 78°, the low, 61°. *The World Almanac: 1995* (Mahwah, New Jersey: Funk & Wagnalls, 1994), pp. 181, 184, 550–51. His observation about the number

10th. Monday. Rainy & disagreeable weather. The Sawyers making a shed for the Saw pit. Mathews, Jeremie & Farnham preparing rafters, etc., for the roof of the Store. McGillis, Ross, Pillet, Wallace & Benjn. Roussel felling & squaring timber for the Mens house; Franchere & the Sandwich Islanders clearing around the buildings, and particularly between the store & the bay. Mr. D. Stuart & 4 Men went up the River for Bark. A Tshinook being caught in the act of stealing, Mr. McDougall had him put in Irons, & a sentry over him for the Night.[56]

11th. Tuesday. Cloudy weather. People variously employed. Mr. D. Stuart arrived with 170 pieces cedar bark. It seems the Indians have stolen about 100 pieces from our people up the River. The Tshinook Mr. McDougall had confined made his escape about dawn & carried off both Manacles & Shackles, & to punish the sentry he was put in his place untill 11 A. M. In the afternoon, Comcomly's Son & Brother came on a visit & volunteered to bring back the Irons, returned with them about dark. Gave them 1 Butcher's Knife, ½ Measure shot, 7 Balls, & 2 heads of Tobacco for their trouble.[57]

12th. Wednesday. Clear & pleasant weather. Mathews & 2 Men employed at the store as usual. Got the 3rd pit saw prepared for sawing, & both saws are now at work, one sawing timber for the Shallop, the other Boards for Doors & Window sashes. Five Men squaring & hauling the frame for the Mens house. The Sandwich Islanders hewing & rolling logs off the point. Messrs. D. Stuart & Franchere sowing garden seeds, etc. Kamaquiah arrived in the forenoon & brought us 3 Axes that were stolen & traded by the Tshinooks to the Indians up the River. Rewarded him for his trouble. Saw several flocks of Pigeons.[58]

13th. Thursday. Weather much the same as yesterday. Mathews & his party setting up the rafters & Laths on one end of the store, all the rest

---

of men on the sick list is pertinent, and was possibly owing not only to the causes he ascribed, diet and hard and dangerous work, but also to the general level of morale which had not seemed to improve since the dispiriting events experienced crossing the bar at the Columbia's mouth in April. The departure of the *Tonquin* may also have induced a feeling of isolation among the men.

[56] This was certainly a sign of McDougall's exasperation over the constant thievery by the Indians, although in this case, as seen in the June 11th entry, his punishment backfired.

[57] A "head" of tobacco possibly refers to a bunch, hank, or handful of cured tobacco leaves, before they were cut for smoking. Comcomly's brother may have been Kamaquiah, as noted below; Comcomly had three sons, Gassagass, Chalowane, and Shalakal. See J. F. Santee, "Comcomly and the Chinooks," *Oregon Historical Quarterly*, 33, No. 3 (September 1932), 271–78.

[58] Kamaquiah was a Chinook headman whose village was one of several upriver from Comcomly's on the north bank of the Columbia. Ronda, *Astoria*, p. 231.

hauling out timber untill noon, & employed at different work the remainder of the day. Five Indians living up Young's River brought (as they said) a male elk, for which they got 12 strings of Beads, & 2 Clasp Knives. But on spreading out the skin, we found it was a female. On every occasion they try to overreach us, & on this they succeeded. Two Sandwich Islanders sick.[59]

14th. Friday. Fine warm weather. Mr. D. Stuart with 5 Men went up the River for Cedar bark. McLenon & Laframboise sawing for the Shallop, the other two Sawyers made so little progress that we made them give it up, employed them with Farnham and Franchere putting up the bark. Mathews & Jeremie preparing window sashes, etc., the rest hewing and squaring timber. Comcomly & Kamaquiah paid us a visit, the former brought 15 small Salmon for a feast, but the whole to be eaten before sun set, & had it prepared by his own people. The Sandwich Islanders still sick. Kamaquiah informed us of two strangers (Indians) from a great way inland being at the Cathlamet Village, & a long story about their mission hither, of which we could understand very little.[60]

June 15th. Saturday. Pleasant weather. People employed as usual. The two strangers, a Man & woman, arrived about noon with seven Indians (in a middle sized canoe) mostly Clatsops. The rest were from the Rapids. Soon after their arrival the man handed us a Letter directed to Mr. Stuart, Estekakadme Fort, which Mr. McDougall opened & perused. It had been written at Flat head Fort 5th April last by Finnan McDonald. We cannot make out the motive of his journey hither either from his conversation or the tenor of the Letter he brought. Mr. D. Stuart arrived with 180 pieces of Bark. Sent off both Canoes for another load.[61]

---

[59] Again, I have not been able to determine the preference for the male elk, either for meat, as would seem to have been the case with the Cathlamet hunter, or, as in this case, for the skin.

[60] The injunction to consume all the salmon before sundown was part of the natives' rituals with the first salmon of the summer run; see above, n. 52. The strange Indians make their appearance on June 15th.

[61] The two Indians, apparently a man and a woman, puzzled McDougall no end. But when David Thompson of the North West Company arrived in July, he immediately recognized the "man" as a woman who had, some years back, been the wife of a French Canadian servant of his. When Thompson had ordered her away from his post, the local Indians would not accept her. She wandered from tribe to tribe "to the Sea. She became a prophetess, declared her sex changed, that she was now a Man, dressed, and armed herself as such, and also took a young woman to Wife, of whom she pretended to be very jealous" (pp. 366–67). She either predicted or threatened outbreaks of disease and engendered a good bit of enmity among the Columbia River tribes. Richard Glover, ed., *David Thompson's Narrative, 1784–1812* (Toronto: The Champlain Society, 1962), pp. 366–69. Thompson, along with the Astorian Robert Stuart, escorted the couple through the hostile natives when they left for the interior late

16th. Sunday. Fine agreeable weather. People variously employed. Kamaquiah visited us previous to his setting off for the Cowlitsk River. Judging it to be a good opportunity to gain information respecting the Natives & productions of that River, we gave him an assortment of goods to the amount of 112 Beavers, to trade, on condition of his taking Mr. Pillet with him. He set off with the goods about 5 P. M. Mr. Pillet is to join him tomorrow when he sends back our largest Canoe & borrows another in its place. Both canoes arrived with 180 pieces of Bark & the four Men who were raising it. Bought a few Salmon for Gurrahs & Tobacco. Our inland stranger begins by degrees to speak the Sauteaux or Knistineuax tongue. We strongly suspect him to be a half Breed from the N. W. & a spy from that Company.

17th. Monday. Mild & pleasant weather. Blacksmith working for the Shallops. The Sandwich Islanders hoeing the Garden, & the rest employed as last week, etc. About noon Mr. Pillet went off with Kamaquiah's people. Sent Montigny with them to see if any Bark could be got in the Small River near their Village. Finished covering one half of the Store.[62]

June 18th. Tuesday. Rainy wea: The hewers & squarers employed making a Magazine of half of the Cellar. The others employed at intervals, setting up the Rafters, fixing the laths, etc. Broke the canoe of one of the Tshinooks who was seen stealing, but could not lay hold of him.[63]

19th. Wednesday. Wet disagreeable wea: Men employed as yesterday. Our hunter brought us a black Bear he shot this morning. A number of Indians about us, traded a few skins. Montigny arrived having found tolerable bark, but was scurvily treated by the Indians after Kamaquiah set off.

20th. Thursday. Dirty Rainy wea: People variously occupied. The Natives

---

in July. They separated from the Astorians on the Okanogan, after causing more difficulties with the tribes there. Ross, *Adventures*, pp. 142–44. There appears to be no ready explanation for the vague message from Finnan McDonald carried by the Indian; it may have been simply a subterfuge on his part to get rid of them. Fort Estekakadme is unknown. The significance of the episode, if it has any, is that by its revealing the presence of North Westers at Spokane House (Flat Head Fort), McDougall had become aware of the presence of possible competitors relatively close. Ronda, *Astoria*, pp. 230–32.

[62] Even with François Pillet going along, this was an extraordinary action by McDougall, trusting the relatively unknown Indian with a substantial quantity of trade goods. See the *Beaver*'s inventory, Porter, *Astor*, I, 484–507; and Hiram M. Chittenden, *The American Fur Trade of the Far West*, 3 vols. (New York: Francis P. Harper, 1902), I, 3–6, for the kind of merchandise used in trade. Gurrahs were a muslin, usually made in India and traded in fathom-long lengths (i.e, a man's armspread, about five- to five and one-half feet). I have not been able to identify the "Sauteaux or Knistineuax" language.

[63] Stoving in the canoe of the Chinook who was seen stealing was certainly done only by McDougall's orders and is a sign of his exasperation at the constant pilfering by the natives.

brought about 20 Salmon. Two of the Men very unwell, say McLennon & Mathews.

21st. Friday. Rainy forenoon, clear & pleasant the remainder of the day. Purchased 60 fine salmon, the largest weighing about 45 lbs. Our hunter Shot a small buck elk last night near Capts. Lewis & Clark's House. Sent 3 Men in a Canoe, who returned with it about noon. Comcomly came upon a visit & acquainted us that some of his family had arrived from Quinhalt & left Mr. Stuart well there; also that two of his tribe saw the Corpse of a white man not quite 15 days ago, at the foot of a large tree near Cape Disappointment. We suppose it to be some one who met his fate in the same manner as the late Mr. Fox & his crew. The Tshinooks threaten to kill our inland stranger & he is anxious to be off. 4 persons unwell, only 1 saw going. This evening they finished covering the Store.

June 22d. Saturday. Cloudy wea: Mathews & McLenon still indisposed, which puts a stop to one saw & the Carpenters work, 4 others much indisposed, the late wet weather we suppose to be the cause of so many being unwell, particularly as they mostly complain of cholics & stitches. 4 men hewing & squaring timber, the rest laying skids (& clearing the shore) to haul the canoes upon, during the forenoon, & in the afternoon took 2 Casks Bread, the Sandwich Islands cordage & other rigging belonging to the Shallops, from the shed & lodged them in the Store. Blacksmith mending tools & making bolts, etc. for the Shallop those 4 days back. The Carpenter & Cooper have made but little progress this week in forwarding the Shallop, & the sawyers as little owing to their Saws being so very bad. Mr. Pillet arrived at 5 P. M. with Kamaquiah & 3 other Indians. They found the waters so high by the time they reached the Chelwits village (at least their present place of residence as they remove from place to place as they find it convenient for the fishery) that Kamaquiah found it impracticable to proceed farther. He traded 15 Beaver & 1 Otter at this village, & returned on the morning of the 21st. We have reason to suspect that he had predetermined to proceed no farther when he set off, & his objection respecting the height of the waters is evidently an excuse. Paid him however for his trouble. It seems the Natives all along the River are determined to kill our strange visitor. A Tshinook sold us an elk for 16 strings of Beads & 2 heads of Tobacco. Purchased 40 salmon.[64]

---

[64] The reference to "colics & stitches" would usually indicate some kind of abdominal distress, probably owing to the diet at Astoria; hence McDougall's connecting them to the wet weather is confusing. The Chelwits lived near Oak Point on the south shore of the Columbia; see above, n. 19. See also Ruby, Brown, *Guide*, p. 208. Kamaquiah's quick turn-

23rd. Sunday. Fine wea: Mr. Stuart embarked with 4 Canadians & 4 Sandwich Islanders, first to visit Comcomley & from thence to Cape Disappointment to examine the Corpse the Indians discovered. Traded 20 fine Salmon.

24th. Monday. Agreeble wea: People variously employed. At 3 P. M. Mr. D. Stuart arrived in company with Mr. R. Stuart & Calpo, the former saw instead of a Corpse an old elk head with moss growing through it. He saw the tracks of our 2 Pigs, but could not trace them out. The latter has been as far as Quinhalt or Point Grenville Lat. 47°20'N. & Long. 124° W. in Calpos Canoe, & brings a very favorable account of the country, which abounds in Beaver, Otter, Sea Otter, Elk, Deer, Bears, Wolves, Fish, etc. and is thickly inhabited. But the natives are remarkably indolent, & understand very little about hunting. However it is his opinion that an establishment in that quarter (with a few good Kodiak Indians) would turn out well, as they would not only make a good hunt themselves, particularly in sea otter, but secure the most of the furs this side of Neweetie or the Straits of Juan De Fuca, which according to what he could learn, would be no small object. For besides 2 or 3 small tribes, there is a very numerous (& reported wicked) nation called the Culewits about 3/4 of a days paddling to the N. W. of Quinhalt, or near Destruction Isle Lat. 47°34' N. Long. 124°10' W. They are said to kill a great many Beaver & dispose of them (as well as the Quinhalt people, of their sea otter, of which they kill a considerable number) to the Neweetians for Hyquoyas, etc. Should an establishment be formed on that side the Columbia he thinks that Grays Harbour is the most eligible situation for an establishment, etc., but would give the preference to Quinhalt, being a much more centrich place, were it not for the want of a harbour, and the difficulty of finding a convenient spot to build upon. His returns amounted to 20 Beaver & would have had a great many more, but his guides were unwilling he should shew his articles of Trade. They however bought but 10 Beaver and 4 Sea Otter after all their trouble. Gave Calpo & his Wife 4 fathoms long cloth for Mr. Stuarts passage, etc. Henry Wicks, Ship Carpenter, unwell.[65]

---

around may have been an effort to keep Comcomly's Chinooks as middlemen between the natives of the upper Columbia and the Astorians; Pillet would have had little recourse but to assent to turning back.

[65] According to the longitude and latitude given, Point Grenville would be four miles east of Highland Heights on the central coast of Washington. Point Grenville today is two and a half miles south of the mouth of the Quinault River. It is likely that the latitude and longitude calculations were in error. The reference to the natives' indolence probably means nothing more than that they could feed themselves and secure whatever they needed by trade without

25th. Tuesday. Pleasant weather. Mathews much worse than yesterday & bled by Mr. Stuart. McGillis unwell of a strain. McGillis, Ross, Pillet, McLenon & Jos. Lapierre felling, squaring & hewing timber. Messrs. Franchere & Farnham laying the upper floor of the Store. Jeremie & Laframboise making window sashes & putting up boards to the North end of the Store. LeClair & Dick Cooking, Black Smith making Hinges for the Cellar Door, Jean & Aontine Belleau Sawing, Ship Carpenter & Cooper unwell, 1 Sandwich Islander do. Sent Montigny, Olivier Roy Lapansé, Jacques Lafantasie & Cox over to Grays Bay to raise cedar bark, with about 4 days provisions.

26th. Wednesday. Agreeable weather. Mr. D. Stuart Sowing Garden Seeds. People employed as usual. Mathews rather better. Wicks worse, 1 Sandwich Islander sick.

27th. Thursday. Wea: as yesterday. Mathews has a relapse & is very weak. Bled the Ship Carpenter. Jeremie & Jean Belleau sick; Sandwich Islander still unwell. Montigny & the other 3 Men returned, not being able to find good Bark. Began to cut poles for enclosing the garden. Mr. Mumford & Jeremie unwell.

28th. Friday. Cold raw wea: People variously employed. Mathews & Wicks appear to have the fever & Ague & are very weak. Jeremie complains of a pain in his breast & head. Whatever arrangements may be entered into by the Co. for the future, with any of their servants, etc., it should be an established rule to have it regularly made out in writing: Having had several

---

much trapping or hunting. Kodiak Indians were used by the Russians at their Alaskan posts to take the especially valuable sea otter. Neweetie was a village located on Templar Channel of Clayoquot Sound, on the west coast of Vancouver Island; see Ross Cox, *The Columbia River*, ed. Edgar I. and Jane R. Stewart (Norman: University of Oklahoma Press, 1957), p. 63, n. 2; hereafter, Cox, *Columbia*. Thus, "Neweetians" means the Nootka Indians who lived there; these were the Indians who attacked the *Tonquin*, in an incident that ended in the explosion of the ship's powder store, with the consequent loss of the crew and many natives. See August 11, 1811, for the first reception at Astoria of the news of the tragedy. The fullest account of the incident was given by a native interpreter, Joseachal, on June 15 and 18, 1813. See July 27 and September 4, 1812, for other instances of hostile behavior by this band of Nootkas. Vancouver Island is separated from the Olympic Peninsula of the present state of Washington by the Strait of Juan de Fuca. The Culewits (Quileute, of the Chimakuan linguistic stock) lived about the mouth of the Quillayute River and up its banks. They were noted deep-sea whale and seal hunters and frequently fought with other tribes. Ruby, Brown, *Guide*, pp. 171–74. "Hyquoas" refers to a kind of shell (*ioqua*) found along the shores of Nootka Sound and to the northward on Vancouver Island. They were tubular, with a slight curve, and a quarter of an inch to three inches in size. The natives used them as ornaments and a form of money. See Frederick Merk, ed., *Fur Trade and Empire: George Simpson's Journal*, rev. ed. (Cambridge, Massachusetts: Harvard University Press, 1968), p. 31. See June 6th for the purpose and beginning of Stuart's mission.

conversations with Mr. Mumford previous to his being discharged from the Ship, respecting his coming on shore to take charge of the Shallop that was building, we did not take the precaution of making him sign articles immediately while on board or on landing, relying on the promises he made to continue with us for one or more Seasons, for the same wages he had on board the Tonquin. We, however, proposed making out his engagement, but being busy at the moment, the Tonquin on the point of Sailing, & he himself saying it would do at any convenient time hereafter, we deferred it. We have had every reason to be satisfied with his conduct untill those few days past, when to our great surprise he proposed following Captains Lewis & Clarks route across the Continent, after previously trying to debauch some of our People to accompany him, & had the assurance to ask our assistance, which we refused, acquainting him at the same time of the verbal arrangement he had entered into with us; to which he replied that he considered it in no wise binding & merely as a mercantile transaction which, not being put to paper, might be retracted at pleasure. We pointed out to him the ingratitude and impropriety of his conduct, & requested him to give us his final determination as soon as convenient. Paul Jeremie, who pretended Sickness for some time back, requested permission to accompany him, for which he received a severe reprimand.[66]

29th. Saturday. Pleasant Wea: People employed as usual. Mr. Mumford acquainted us that he had made up his mind to remain for one season, but would ultimately cross the Continent. Paul Jeremie wrote us a Letter repenting of his past conduct and promising better for the future. McGillis, Mathews, Jeremie, Mumford, Wicks & 3 Sandwich Islanders sick.

30th. Sunday. Agreeable Wea:, but cold for the Season. Sick list the same as yesterday.

July 1st. Monday. Wea: as yesterday. People hauling out timber for the dwelling House, making a fence round the Garden. Two Men sawing timber, two preparing boards for Doors, etc. Black Smith made an Iron Laddle to make Balls, & making anew the half & small Axes, made at New York, being made too thin & of bad Steel. Visited by two canoes of the Cathlanami-

---

[66] This refers to an oral agreement among McDougall, Captain Thorn, and Mumford, arrived at shortly before the *Tonquin* left the Columbia; the details were entered into the log on May 30th. Mumford would continue to be uncooperative. Jeremie's request is the first sign of what would be an especially vexed relationship between him and McDougall. It may also be noted that McDougall would record, on June 18, 1813, that it was about this time, late June 1811, that rumors of the loss of the *Tonquin* first came to Astoria. The first mention in the log of the loss of the ship and its crew is on August 11, 1811.

nimin Nation, from the entrance of the Multonomat or Wallamat River. They traded two indifferent Sea-otter & 3 Beaver. They went on to the Clatsops with the rest of their cargo, which consisted of sweet potatoes & dried fish. Served out 26 lbs. Navy Bread to the Carpenter, being his monthly allowance of that article. Mathews, Jeremie & Wicks recovering but not fit for duty. Mr. Mumford and Sandwich Islander still sick. Our inland Visetor extremely anxious to return among his friends, as he finds the Natives here waiting only for an opportunity to destroy him. We took pains to convince him to the contrary, altho' we knew his fears to be too well founded, and if we had not taken him under our protection from the moment he arrived, he would have fallen a sacrifice to the dread they entertain of his power to introduce the Small Pox, which he very imprudently boasted of on his way down. The Chiefs of the Tshinooks & Clatsops have frequently requested us to deliver him & his wife up to them, as their slaves or to retain them as such ourselves. The latter we feigned to agree to, knowing if once in their power, their destruction was inevitable.

His fears however rendered him more communicative, regarding the Natives & productions of the interior, & particularly the distance & situation of the N. W. establishments from the grand falls of this River, which to our surprise we found not to be more than 14 days march (at most) on horseback. From the different sketches he made of the upper parts of the River, his favorable account of the numerous tribes on its banks, added to our apprehensions of his making his escape, & losing so favorable an opportunity of gaining more certain knowledge of the Country, particularly as Messrs. McDougall, D. Stuart and Pillet understood his language. After mature deliberation it was resolved that Mr. D. Stuart with * 8 Men and a small assortment of Goods, should accompany him if possible to the banks of the Wahnaaihee, or as he calls it Iaaggama Nibi, & there form an establishment, should the manners of the Natives & appearance of the Country be sufficiently flattering to induce him to remain among them with so few men; if not, to return as the knowledge he will acquire of the Country must be of essential service another season.[67]

---

[67] Three lines are erased, beginning at the asterisk. "8 Men" was written in at the start of the erasure, with the rest, at the bottom of a page, left vacant. The Cathlanaminimin were probably part of one of several Chinook tribes which clustered about the mouth of the Willamette (also referred to as the Wolamat or McKay's River) River, the present site of Portland, Oregon. In the light of Stuart's eventual establishment on the Okanogan, near the present U.S.–Canadian border, the Wahnaaihee may have been that river. The "Navy Bread" was probably a form of hardtack. The carpenter was Henry Wicks (or Weeks), who had switched places on the *Tonquin* with the unfortunate Johann Kaster.

2nd. Tuesday. Pleasant. Wind S. W. Blacksmith & Sawyers employed as yesterday. Farnham & Jeremie finished the Garden fence. The Sandwich Islanders carrying out small timber. The rest of the People occupied about the buildings, etc. Sicklist as yesterday, excepting Jeremie who is at work. Mathews was able to go & point out to Laframboise how to frame the dwelling house.

3rd. Wednesday. Agreeable weather. Blacksmith and Sawyers occupied as usual. Sandwich Islanders clearing the ground between the Fort & the River. H. Wicks & Mathews recovering but slowly. Mumford resumed his work; two Sandwich Islanders still unwell. The Chief of the Chilwits left us after trading a few skins & some Cedar Bark. He promises to provide a quantity of dried venison & salmon to trade when the Shallop goes up the River.[68]

4th. Thursday. Wet weather. People employed about the buildings, excepting the Sandwich Islanders who are bur[nin]g up what they gathered the day before. Of late there have been but few of the Tshinooks about us. This being the anniversary of the independence of the U. S., fired three rounds of Musketry, & treated all hands with grog. Kamaquia arrived & presented us with 4 large and 7 small salmon.[69]

July 5th. Friday. Agreeable wea: People employed as yesterday. Visited by a few Tshinooks, who brought a few Skins & fresh Salmon to trade.

6th. Saturday. Rainy in the forenoon, clear the rest of the day. People occupied about the buildings, etc. H. Wicks is still weak & complains of a sore throat, has not done any thing since he fell ill. Mathews recovering, but not fit for duty. Received a formal Note from him complaining of want of food for these three days past. If he has the least shadow of complaint he could blame but himself, having been repeatedly told to acquaint us with anything he thought could be of service to him, & that he should have it provided it was in our power. It being late in the evening & raining, instead of sending for him, an answer was handed him to the above purport. The Cooper has been making Kegs these 3 days back, & Blacksmith making sundries for Mr. Stuart's adventure. The Sandwich Islanders still ill of the Venereal. Mr. R. Stuart with 4 Men & 2 Canoes went off for Cedar Bark.

7th. Sunday. Fine weather. Comcomly & two Clatsop Chiefs visited us, with their followers in 3 Canoes; traded a few Skins & Salmon from the

---

[68] The chief of the Chilwits (also Chelwits) was "Ka-las-kan"; see below, April 29, 1813.

[69] Considering that a majority of those at Astoria were Canadians, the celebration of American independence was restrained. The issuing of grog, when liquor was part of the daily ration, could not have been too big a treat, and the men were not relieved of work for the day.

former. Sold at auction the effects of the late Ignace & Basil Lapansé who were lost in the Whale Boat, on 22d March last. Gassagass brought us back a Jacket & Axe stolen by the Clatsops from the People, & promises to bring our canoe in a day or two, (that was some time ago). Mr. R. Stuart arrived with 130 pieces Bark.

8th. Monday. Dirty rainy wea: People employed at the buildings between the showers. Mathews still weak but able to go about. H. Wicks & 1 Sandwich Islander still indisposed. Laid out the goods for Mr. Stuart's adventure up the River. Blacksmith making a marking Iron for do., Taylor making a Canoe Sail.

July 9th. Wednesday.[70] Wea: as yesterday. People occupied at different work by intervals. The invalids nothing better.

10th. Wednesday. Cold & raw with frequent showers. People employed as usual. The wet & disagreeable weather that prevailed this some time back, & Mathew's indisposition, have retarded the buildings considerably. The sick list as usual.

11th. Thursday. Clear & agreeable wea: People variously employed about the buildings, falling & cutting up timber that is too near us, in case of high winds or fire. Mathews has continued in a very weak state, altho' the violence of his complaint had abated some days ago. Yesterday he felt some symptoms of a relapse, and to day had a fit of the ague. H. Wicks recovering, & expects to be able to resume his work tomorrow. Mr. R. Stuart & 4 Men went for Cedar Bark.

12th. Friday. Wea: as yesterday. People employed as usual. Our hunter brought us word of his having Killed two Elk, up a small river called the Sosoné, on the North side of Youngs Bay. Sent off a Canoe & five Men for them. Mr. Stuart arrived at 9 A. M. with 130 pieces Bark. Gassagass, Comcomly's son, dangerously wounded a Tshichilish Chief, while playing Ball. The Tshinooks are much alarmed that the wound should prove mortal, as in all probability it would be the cause of war between the two Nations. It will probably be of some service to us, as they had several conferences to cut us off as soon as the Ship left us in the fall for Canton. Settled with several natives to bring us 100 pieces Timber 15 feet long for Picketing * in the buildings, for 1 Blanket, 2½ pts., 1 Knife, 1 fm Gurrahs & 2 heads Tobacco, with a treat of Molasses & rice for every 100 they render on the Spot.[71]

---

[70] Note that this is actually a Tuesday. The next day is correctly given as Wednesday.

[71] Young's Bay was between Astoria and the peninsula ending in Point Adams. The Sosoné could be the river now known as the Walooskee. The Tshichilish are the Chehalis, a tribe who lived north of the Chinook, along the Washington State coast, around Gray's Harbor

July 13th. Saturday. Clear wea: with high wind from S. W. People variously employed, one party filling up the frame of the dwelling house. Those sent off yesterday with our hunter returned early this morning with the two Elk, but a considerable part of one of them was ate up by the wolves, before they reached the place. The Carpenter has resumed his work, but Mathews is rather worse, & this morning took an emetick. Kamaquia arrived & brought us four salmon. A party of the Chilwits arrived with 100 Pickets (but smaller than the standard) for which they received 6 fms of gurrahs & some Tobacco.

14th. Sunday. Mild & agreeable Weather, Wind West'ly. Sick List the same as yesterday. Visited by a number of Tshinooks & Clatsops, who brought us a few furs, and salmon.

15th. Monday. Wind & wea: as yesterday. People variously employed. Mr. R. Stuart with 3 Sandwich Islanders in two Canoes went off for Cedar Bark. Mr. Thomson of the N. W. Co. in <u>Canada</u>, arrived about 1 P. M. in a Cedar Canoe (made after the manner of a bark Canoe) manned by eight Men. All hands enjoy tolerable health excepting Mathews & Tuanna, who are still in a very weak & debilitated state.[72]

16th. Tuesday. Clear wea: with high wind from west'd. People occupied

---

and Point Chehalis; the first name is probably derived from "tsels," a Chehalis word meaning "sand." They frequently went to the beach for whatever they could obtain there. Ruby, Brown, *Guide*, pp. 105–106. See also Jones, ed., *Astorian Adventure*, p. 91, for a description of their habits which supports the identification. McDougall's fears of native hostility and a possible combination of tribes against the Astorians were not foolish, considering the small number usually at the post and, now, the rumors of the loss of the *Tonquin* and the non-arrival of the overland party sent out from St. Louis the previous spring. The Astorians were isolated. The trade goods include 2½-point blankets and a fathom of gurrah cloth. At the asterisk, the words "for the fort" have been lined out and "in the buildings" written above. This will be repeated on several occasions, as if McDougall was afraid of giving offense to the local Chinooks by making clear his fear of them.

[72] McDougall's lack of comment on the arrival of David Thompson, the first European to come down the Columbia from its source, is surprising, if only for his failure to note that feat. Thompson brought with him news of the approval by the wintering partners (those headquartered at Fort William, at the northwest corner of Lake Superior) of the cooperative arrangement of the North West Company and the Pacific Fur Company. Neither man knew then that the North Westers in Montreal had convinced a majority of the partners not to go through with the agreement. Also, as its terms were vague, it seems evident that the wintering partners did not believe everything west of the Rockies would be the province of the new company, but that some kind of a division of the area would be effected. See Ronda, *Astoria*, pp. 59–64. Thus, McDougall's hospitality to Thompson and his apparent readiness to cooperate with his former North West colleague were not signs of disloyalty to Astor; nor did Thompson consider himself as running a race with the American company for an establishment at the mouth of the Columbia, as Irving wrote. See Irving, *Astoria* (Rust ed.), pp. 65–66.

as usually. Mr. R. Stuart arrived with 130 pieces Bark, & brought down the Men who were raising it, as we expect having a sufficient quantity of that article for this season. Visited by Comcomly & Dhaichovan with a number of their tribes who brought a few skins. The Cooper indisposed & unfit for duty. Mathews & Tuanna much the same as yesterday.[73]

July 17th. Wednesday. Pleasant, wind N. W. People variously employed. Messrs. R. Stuart, Farnham & McGillis went out a hunting, accompanied by two of Mr. Thomson's best hunters. Preparations making for Mr. D. Stuart's departure. Sicklist as yesterday.

18th. Thursday. Clear & agreeable wea:, wind from west'd. People employed as yesterday. Our hunters ret'd without success. Comcomly & a few of his followers paid us a visit, & traded a few Beaver and Salmon.

19th. Friday. Calm & excessively hot wea: People occupied about various jobs. In the morning, Messrs. Thomson & D. Stuart went over to visit the Tshinook village, and in order that the former might have a view of the sea, they returned in the afternoon but were not fortunate enough to see either of the Chiefs. Visited by a few of the Natives who brought some fresh salmon to trade. The Cooper resumed his work. Mathews & Touanna are still very weak. The former, however, is on the recovery.

20th. Saturday. Wea: as yesterday, Wind N. W. People occupied as usually. In the afternoon, Messrs. Farnham & McGillis went out a hunting. Visited by two or three canoes of the Natives, who traded a few Beaver & a good many salmon. Sick list as yesterday.

21st. Sunday. Cloudy but mild wea:, wind west'y. Preparations making for Messrs. Thompson & D. Stuart's departure. Messrs. Farnham & McGillis returned about noon, but had killed nothing. Visited by Comcomly & Calpo, who brought 3 or 4 Sea Otters & as many Beavers. Mathews rather better.

July 22nd. Monday. Wind & wea: as yesterday. People occupied as follows, viz., The Carpenter, Cooper and Mr. Mumford working at the Shallop, Farnham & Jeremie raising a chimney in the dwelling House, the Sandwich Islanders carrying stones for ditto. Laframboise making Doors, etc. for the Store, and the rest employed about different jobs.

Messrs. Thompson & Stuart took their departure about 1 P. M. The former (who came across the Rocky Mountains in the months of Decr & Jany last) is to proceed direct for Montreal. He told us that no doubt remained with him, but ere now a coalition of the two companies had taken

---

[73] Dhaichovan is an alternative spelling for Dhaitshowan, the Clatsop chief identified above, n. 16.

place, regarding which he wrote us on his arrival, and also handed us an extract from a Letter (on the same subject) addressed to Mr. McGillivray of Montreal, by the wintering Partners, the following day (say 10th instant). We returned him an answer.

The latter had three Canoes loaded with Goods & necessaries for forming an establishment, and manned by 8 Men, viz., Messers. Ross, Pillet, McLenan & Montigny, Benj: Roussel, Jacques Lafantaisie, & two Sandwich Islanders (Cox & Bob).

Visited by a few of the Natives who brought several Beaver, etc. Mr. McGillis & Antoine Belleau sick.[74]

23rd. Tuesday. Forenoon pleasant with a light breeze from the East'd, afternoon cold & high wind from West'd. The People employed as yesterday, excepting two Parties, who are cutting & carrying out Pickets, & cutting wood to make char-coal. Visited by a small party of the Natives who brought a number of Salmon to trade; but we could not accept of many at a time, not having salt to cure but very few. Mr. McGillis at work. Mathews, Belleau & Tuanna much the same as yesterday. Three Sandwich Islanders laid up with sore Backs, Bellies, & limbs.

July 24th. Wednesday. Pleasant wea: Wind S. W. People occupied much the same as yesterday. Blacksmith working for the Shallop those few days past. Visited by a number of the Clatsop Nation, who brought a few Salmon. Sick-List as yesterday.

25th. Thursday. Cold raw weather, Wind from S. W. People employed much the same as yesterday. The Cooper building a chimney in the dwelling house, he being the only one we have who understands anything of Masonry. Black-smith, & Joe Lapierre sick, the other invalids no better. Visited by a few of the Natives, who brought some Fish, etc.[75]

26th. Friday. Mild but cloudy weather: Wind Westwardly. People occupied as yesterday. In the morning we were informed that Jeremy had packed up his clothes, etc., and hid them in the wood some days ago, with the intention of deserting tomorrow evening, having made an engagement with four of the Natives to conduct him some distance up the River. We immedi-

---

[74] This effort of the Astorians is the largest and deepest penetration of the Columbia to date; it will result in the establishment of a post on the Okanogan from which David Stuart will move into present-day British Columbia, establishing a post near Kamloops. It may also be noted that the two strange Indians who had arrived at Astoria on June 15th accompanied the party at least as far as the Okanogan. Ross, *Adventures*, pp. 142–44; see also William C. Brown, "Old Fort Okanogan and the Okanogan Trail," *Oregon Historical Quarterly*, 15, No. 1 (March 1914), 1–38.

[75] The cooper who can also do masonry work is George Bell (or Bill).

ately called him, with a few of the People, & proceeded to the place where he had secreted them. When the whole were exposed to view, to identify them, and among them we were not a little astonished to find: 1 Bottle of Wine, 1 Do. Rum, 6 Biscuits, 6 oz. Butter, 2 heads of Tobacco, 1 Powder Horn, 23 oz. Gun Powder, 31 oz. Ball & Buck Shot, 1 fine cocoa nut shell belonging to Mr. McKay, 1 Butcher's Knife, 1 Cross cut Saw file, 1 Small Ball of Twine, & 5 Gun Flints, belonging to the Company. We made him carry the whole home again, and after reprimanding him for his conduct, as well as the rest of our people, who were well aware of his proceedings (excepting McGillis) he was ordered to give us in writing the Manner in which he intended to conduct himself for the future, that we might know in what manner to treat him, etc. He shortly after handed us the following lines, viz.

Fort Astoria, 26th July 1811

This may sertify that I hame Gouing a Way on account of Not a free with this contray and Ill Youse. I Hame Makin my was home as soon as possibel, and will Not Yous No bade Story. Nor ill languuge agints the Company of the Collumbeá, I shall say Nothing of wat as Happen.

Plis to let me Gou Free, You will OBlige me the Mos, on Commenly,

Your Most Obediant Servent

(signed) Paul Jeremy

Mr. McDougle & Stuart

By which it appeared that so far from repenting of his folly, he was determined to persist in getting off the first opportunity. He was consequently put in Irons and ordered to be fed on the Biscuit & Butter he stole. An Inventory was now taken of all his things and put under Lock & Key. Ever since we landed, all hands were indulged with Liquor three times a day. But for the future they shall have it but twice a day, for their late passive conduct. Sick list as yesterday, excepting Mathews who feels himself considerably better, & in the afternoon resumed his work, for the first time since 20th Ultimo.[76]

---

[76] As Jeremie had shown signs of discontent previously, this should not have surprised McDougall. What was probably most disquieting about the incident was the apparent complicity of the rest of the men, albeit a passive complicity. They probably considered McDougall's punishment unduly severe. Several of the Astorians' memoirs, most especially Alexander

27th. Saturday. Pleasant Wea: Wind N. W. People employed as usual. Mathews has a relapse. Antoine Belleau recovered & at work. Roussel & LaPierre on the recovery, but still unfit for duty.

28th. Sunday. Cold, raw wea: Wind West'y. Our Hunter came to inform us that he had killed a Deer, & wanted assistance to bring it home. Sent two Men in a Canoe along with him, who brought it in towards night. All our Invalids in a state of recovery. Turned all hands out to drill, & see whether their arms were in good order.

July 29th. Monday. Pleasant Wea: Wind West'y. People variously occupied about the Buildings, cutting and rafting Pickets, etc. etc. For some time back a few of our friends among the Tshinoooks have been hinting that they were suspicious the Tshichilish (who are all assembled in Bakers Bay for the purpose of catching Sturgeon) had some intention of attacking us, of which we generally made light (at least pretended so), altho' pretty well informed of those fellows treachery. However, one or two of our particular friends came this morning in great perturbation, & informed us that they had been with the Tshichilish yesterday, who imparted their intention of attacking us in three nights hence. This with some other news we heard of: 40 or 50 Canoes being expected soon from the North'd and a number from the South'd, to wage war (as was pretended) against one another, etc., inclining us to think that a general combination has taken place, & something serious to be expected. We therefore concluded that the only chance of our being able to contend with such numbers, rests in immediately throwing up a temporary Fort & Bastions. In the evening the party who have been after Pickets arrived with two rafts (say 50 or 60), so that we are now ready to begin the fort in the Morning. Calpo, one of the Tshinooks, brought us a small Deer. All hands in tolerable health, but Mathews & three of the Sandwich Islanders are still too weak to attend regularly to work.[77]

30th. Tuesday. Wind and wea: as yesterday. Early in the morning all hands commenced raising the[78] Pickets and making other necessary preparations for our defence. Jeremy wrote us a very penitential Letter, expressing his regret for his late conduct, and promising to behave well for the future;

Ross's, speak of the low morale at the post. Aside from the rather high proportion of men on the sick list from time to time, especially given the character of many of their complaints, there is little definite sign of this, until now. Ross, *Adventures*, pp. 74–76. Nor was this the last of Jeremie's escapades.

[77] See Jones, ed., *Astorian Adventure*, p. 91, for a description of the Chehalis (Tshichilish) as dangerous, already having cut off several trading vessels in the Columbia.

[78] "Fort" is heavily crossed out at this point, with "Pickets" written above.

in consequence of which he was allowed to return to his duty. Visited by none of the surrounding Tribes, which is rather unusual.

31st. Wednesday. Wea: still pleasant, Wind S. W. All hands employed raising the * Pickets, putting the great Guns, Swivels, etc., in order. Visited by a few of the Natives, who did not appear to half relish our War like appearance. Brought the Carpenter's & Coopers baggage & Tools, as well as the greater part of the Blacksmiths from the Shallops so that we are now all lodged together in the Store. We are informed that Kamaquiah has one of the Cathlaputle Chiefs in irons (he having stole one of his women) which they say will bring on an immediate war between the two Nations. In the afternoon finished & hung the Doors of the store.[79]

Augt. 1st. Thursday. Mild but gloomy Wea: Wind S. W. People employed much the same as yesterday. Brought up the Black Smith's forge, etc., from the Shallop. After Dark, cleared (& laid part of the flooring for) the Store. Four or five of our People very unwell, but make a shift to assist at the work. None of the natives about us for some time past have brought any furs, or in fact, but few visit us at all.[80]

2nd. Friday. Pleasant Wea: Wind N. W. Part of the People cutting & carrying out Pickets, the rest began in the forenoon to make a Bastion, having finished the upper side of the Picketing.[81] In the evening we were favored with a visit from Comcomly & his son who remained with us all night.

3rd. Saturday. Wind and wea: as yesterday. People employed cutting & carrying out Pickets for what remains to be enclosed.[82] Kamaquia arrived with a few pickets, the greater part of his raft having gone adrift. Comcomley & his son set off in the afternoon promising to return in two days with

---

[79] At the *, "Fort" has been lined out and "Pickets" written above. The Cathlaputle (Calthlapootle) were an Upper Chinookan tribe who spoke the Clackamas dialect; they lived on the north bank of the Columbia River, opposite the mouth of the Willamette and along the Lewis River. Ruby, Brown, *Guide*, p. 13. The war was something less than immediate; it did not come about until August 1813; see below, pp. 206–209. When completed, the fort covered an area 75′ x 80′, with pickets 17′ high. The storehouse was 60′ x 30′ high, and the dwelling, 60′ x 25′. A second dwelling, 60′ x 30′, two stories high, was built after this, as well as two bastions. Philip Ashton Rollins, ed., *The Discovery of the Oregon Trail: Robert Stuart's Narrative . . . , 1812–1813* (New York: Edward Eberstadt, 1935), pp. 4, 28; hereafter, Rollins, ed., *Stuart's Narrative*. See following page 142 for an illustration of what Astoria may have looked like.

[80] Perhaps nothing demonstrates the air of tension and anxiety in the post as much as the willingness of those on the sick list to do what they could to prepare the post's defenses.

[81] "Fort" lined out, "Picketing" written above.

[82] The original phrase, "the remainder of the fort" has been lined out, and "what remains to be enclosed" written above.

50 large Pickets, but we were obliged to make him believe that they were intended for building a house to the Black Smith as he seemed quite averse to bring them for the purpose of enclosures.[83] The Black Smith, Laframboise, Lapierre, Antne. Belleau & 2 Sandwich Islanders sick.

4th. Sunday. Forenoon wet raw wea: Wind South East; in the afternoon it cleared up & the wind veered around to the West'd. All hands turned out to drill, and had their arms examined, which were all in pretty good order. The Blacksmith much better, but the others (almost) in same State as yesterday. All hands turned out to drill again in the evening.[84]

5th. Monday. Agreeable Wea: wind Westwardly. All hands Cutting & Carrying out Pickets, excepting Mathews & three hands, who are finishing the lower story of the Bastion, & placing the swivels, etc.[85]

The carpenter is constantly employed at the Shallop, but comes on very slowly. However, we are in hopes that she will be launched by the latter end of this month. Laframboise, Lapierre & Antne. Belleau still unfit for duty, as well as the two S. Islanders.

6th. Tuesday. Mild but cloudy wea: Wind S. W. People employed as yesterday, all hands at work excepting the two Sandwich Islanders.

7th. Wednesday. The morning cloudy with a few Showers, wind S. E. Towards Noon it cleared away & the Wind veered to the Westward. People variously employed about the Fort, etc. One party cutting & drawing out Pickets, another cutting & hewing posts for the Fort-Gate, etc., a third digging a trench to receive the pickets, and a fourth laying out & mortising the Posts. In the Morning Mr. Franchere & two Men went out a seining but returned without success. Visited by a number of the Chinooks & Clatsops, the former brought us a few fresh Fish & the latter, some furs, etc. Jeremy laid up with the venereal. Three Sandwich Islanders unwell. Lapierre working at the Shallop along with the Carpenter.

8th. Thursday. Pleasant wea: Wind S. W. People employed as yesterday. Our hunter arrived overnight and informed us of his having killed a deer. Three Men in a canoe went off with him about 2 A. M. to fetch it, in which they did not succeed untill 3 P. M. It had a good deal of tallow, & is the first fat one we have yet seen. In the afternoon, a party began to set up the

---

[83] Here, "raising a fort" is lined out and "enclosures" written above.

[84] The drilling on a Sunday, generally observed as a day of rest for the men, as well as the readiness of weapons, were more indications of the genuine fear of attack throughout the post.

[85] Swivels were generally small cannon (although they could be blunderbuss-style muskets), usually one or two pounders, which, as the name indicates, could be easily turned on a pin or swivel mounting; see Russell, *Firearms*, pp. 45–48, for a description and illustration.

Pickets. Mathews finished the lower story of the Bastion. Planked the swivels, etc. Sicklist as yesterday.

9th. Friday. Wind and Wea: as yesterday. People variously occupied, viz., one party raising the Pickets, another employed (in the forenoon) hauling out Posts, etc., for the Fort Gate; in the afternoon they went to cut timber for the Bastion. Visited by a few of the Natives who brought us some fresh Fish. Sicklist as yesterday.[86]

10th. Saturday. Cloudy but mild Wea: Wind West'y. People employed much the same as yesterday. Visited by a number of the Chinooks, Clatsops & three or four of the Quinhaltians, who traded some fresh Salmon and a few Furs. Jeremy and one Sandwich Islander resumed their work; the other two are still very unwell.

11th. Sunday. Mild & pleasant Wea: Wind Westwardly. Visited by a few of the Natives, & among them was a Chinook who arrived from the Southward a few days ago. He informed us that about twelvemonths since, he went to the Northward in a Boston Ship, but on their return the weather was so boisterous that the capt. would not venture into the River, consequently was obliged to carry him to Canton, where the Cargo was disposed of, and after receiving a few supplies on board, they repaired to the Spanish Main, where Captain Ebbets, and two or three other american Vessels met them about four Months ago, and the Captain of one of them decoyed him & ten Neweetians who were with him from the Ship they were then in, and on getting them on board, set sail for this River; but soon after he had passed the Spanish settlements, a violent snow storm overtook them, and in the night they ran the vessel among some Islets or Rocks, where she soon went to pieces and all hands perished, excepting him and his companions, who took to the whale Boat and by that means got safe a shore. From thence they proceeded along shore & for seven days could procure neither Fire or Aliment. At length, however, they arrived at a few huts. [The inhabitants offered them some food but they declined it, (being afraid of getting poisoned) & preferred living upon Snakes and Frogs.] But the inhabitants had no other food to offer them than a few snakes & frogs. Here they reposed themselves for two days, & then resumed their march. A few days after, the country began to assume a more favorable appearance, and became pretty populous, but the Natives seem to be very ferocious, & ill affected

---

[86] The combination of conventional tasks, the fishing and hunting, for example, as well as the occasional visits of natives, along with the continuing work of fortifying the post seem to have put the Astorians in a state of semi-preparedness, several steps down from the anxiety of the past week.

towards strangers, having attacked those poor fellows, en passant and massa-
cred seven of them, the remaining four they retained as slaves, untill Dhaichouan, a Clemax Chief, went down (to Trade) a fortnight ago & ransomed
them.[87]

In the afternoon we received a visit from one of our Chinook friends, who
informed us that some Indians have lately arrived from Neweetie with a
report that the Tonquin was cut off at Nootka in consequence of some misunderstanding with the [blank], viz. "On her arrival there, the Natives went
on board to trade, but Capt. Thorn giving them only two Blankets for a Sea
Otter displeased them so much that one of their chiefs gave him some inso-
lent language, which he resented by rubbing the Otter across his face, this
so enraged him that he ordered all his tribe immediately ashore. Next day
the ship proceeded to Nootka, and they accompanied by a considerable number of the Neweetians (say 50 or 60 canoes in all) followed her. On their
arrival they requested the Nootka Chief to join them, to which he at length
assented, and next day they all repaired on board with their furs, which they
traded at the rate of two Blankets & two knives for each Sea Otter, appeared
very well pleased and carried on a pretty brisk trade, untill they had a sufficient number (on board) with knives to answer their diabolical purpose:
when a signal was given, and four of them laid hold on Capt. Thorn whilst
a fifth stabbed him in the Neck. A number got round Mr. McKay, but he
made his way to the forecastle, where he killed three of them with his Dirk.
However, they at length got hold of him and one gave him a mortal blow
over the eyebrow with an Iron Bludgeon. Whilst this was going on, two had
sprung on each of the ship's crew, and after a short conflict killed every man
on board excepting four, who got into the Magazine and there heroically
terminated their fate by blowing up the Ship, with about 100 of the Indians
who were on board." We heard a vague account of this about a month ago,
but gave it no credit. However we now find that the Chinooks have been
circumstantially acquainted with the whole affair for some time past. But
Comcomly, their chief, gave strict orders that no one should mention a word
of it, on pretence that it would too much afflict us. However, we have pretty

---

[87] McDougall's reason for including this improbable, but not impossible story is not at all
clear. The bracketed words were a marginal addition. Captain John Ebbets commanded
Astor's ship *Enterprise* in the first voyage the entrepreneur sponsored to the Northwest. He
visited Sitka in 1809. See Ruby, Brown, *Chinooks*, p. 119, and Ronda, *Astoria*, pp. 72–74. It
should be noted that previously (see above, May 16, 1811), Dhaichouan was mentioned as a
Clatsop chief who accompanied McDougall on a visit to the Clemax (Tillamooks) to settle a
controversy between them and the Chinooks.

good reasons to believe, particularly from his late conduct and several suspicious circumstances that have taken place, his pretended friendship all along has been a mere train of deceit, and his sole object in not informing us of this circumstance was to put us off our guard untill they should find it convenient to cut us off, which we are convinced they have had in contemplation ever since the Ships departure. Turned all hands out to drill, & examined their Arms.[88]

12th. Monday. Clear agreeable Wea: Wind N. W. Part of the People employed, digging a trench for the Bastion; another party preparing pickets for the Fort, and setting up the King Posts. Mathews & Laframboise making the Fort gate; Jean & Antne Belleau began to saw planks, a party of the Sandwich Islanders bringing Pitch, Tar, Rosin, Turpentine & Varnish up from the shallop, & another party rolling logs & clearing about the Fort, etc. All hands enjoy pretty good health, excepting the two Sandwich Islanders, who have no symptoms of recovery.

13th. Tuesday. Cloudy, with a few light showers, Wind Southerly. People employed much the same as yesterday. Sick-list the same.

14th. Wednesday. Wea: as yesterday. Wind South East. People employed as yesterday. In the afternoon, Mr. Mumford & 4 of the Sandwich Islanders hauling out Bowsprit, etc., for the Shallop. The Carpenter & Lapierre finished laying the Deck. The * outside or large pickets all set up.[89]

15th. Thursday. Clear pleasant Wea: Wind North'y. People variously occupied, viz., one party setting up the small or inside pickets, Mathews &

---

[88] This is the first recorded description of the destruction of the *Tonquin*; it resembles in most details what would later become known about the event. The only important error is the place, which was probably Clayoquot Sound, some distance north of Nootka Sound on the west coast of Vancouver Island. See E. W. Giesecke, "Search for the *Tonquin*," *Cumtux*, 10, No. 3 (Summer 1990), 3–8; No. 4 (Fall 1990), 3–14; and 11, No. 1 (Winter 1990), 23–40 for a description of the effort to find the wreckage, so far fruitless. The leader of the Indians was one Wikinanish, a Nootka chief, whose power and influence in the area made him the paramount native leader. Both he and his father (of the same name) were quite aggressive in dealing with the Europeans since the trading vessels first came to the area; see Jones, ed., *Astorian Adventure*, p. 72, n. 26, for other instances of bad feeling between Wikinanish and traders. See *Dictionary of Canadian Biography*, IV, 767–68 for a biographical note of the elder Wikinanish; his name is spelled variously, the spelling used here is taken from the *Dictionary*. The only survivor of the *Tonquin* explosion was an Indian interpreter, Joseachal, a Quinault, who was taken on board near Destruction Island. He survived because his sister had married into Wikaninish's tribe. In June 1813, McDougall had him brought to Astoria where he was closely questioned about the event and his replies transcribed; see below, pp. 191–95. McDougall's suspicions of the reasons for Comcomly's reticence seem unduly harsh and he, in time, will think better of the old chief; see below, p. 148.

[89] "Fort" is lined out at the asterisk.

Laframboise still working at the Gate. Black smith making irons for Do. Another party cutting & hewing timber for the N. E. Bastion. Jean & Antne Belleau sawing plank, the Sandwich Islanders clearing about the Fort, Piling & burning Logs, Brush, etc. Visited by a few of the Natives who traded several Beaver, salmon, etc. Jeremy & 3 Sandwich Islanders still laid up.

Augt. 16th. Friday. Cloudy but mild Wea: Wind North'y. People occupied much the same as yesterday. A party bringing clay (from a little this side of Tongue Point) to build the chimneys. Mr. McGillis, Jeremy, Olivier Roy, & 3 Sandwich Islanders sick.[90]

17th. Saturday. Cloudy with frequent, light showers; Wind N. W. Finished the Fort & hung the Gate. Blacksmith making irons for the Shallop. Visited by (Comcomly &) a number of the Natives, who brought several Beaver, etc. Sick list as yesterday.[91]

18th. Sunday. Clear & pleasant Wea: Wind N. W. In the forenoon turned the people out to drill, & examined their arms, which were all in excellent order. Visited by a few of the Clatsops, who traded several Beaver & 40 or 50 Salmon, which are now getting very scarce. Mr. McGillis rather better, the remainder of our invalids much the same as yesterday.

19th. Monday. Wind and Wea: as yesterday. People variously employed; one party raising the Bastion, another levelling, etc., about the Fort; the Cooper (with two hands attending him) building the chimney; a party bringing clay down the River, & another cleaning & arranging Fish; Mr. Franchere working at the Shallop, along with the Carpenter & Lapierre. The two Belleaus sawing plank. Visited by several canoes of the Natives, who brought us a considerable quantity of small Salmon & sturgeon. Sick list as yesterday.

20th. Tuesday. Wea: clear and remarkably hot. People employed much as yesterday. In the afternoon, a party began to set the rafters on the dwelling house. Mr. Mumford working at the shallop. Visited by a few of the Chinooks, who brought several salmon and sturgeon.

Augt. 21st. Wednesday. Wea: as yesterday, Wind N. E. People employed as yesterday. Visited by a few of the Natives, who brought some fresh Salmon. McGillis, Jeremy, Laframboise, & two S. Islanders sick. In the afternoon Olivier Roy cut his foot very ill with an axe, which will render him unfit for duty for some time.

22d. Thursday. Clear & pleasant wea: Wind N. W. People differently employed; raising the Bastion, Building the chimney, covering the dwelling

---

[90] The clay was for mortar for the chimney; see below, August 22nd.

[91] Three lines were erased at this point in the manuscript.

House, cutting grass, bringing home clay (for Mortar), & curing salmon, etc. Sick list as yesterday.

23d. Friday. Agreeable wea: high Wind West'y. People occupied as yesterday. In the afternoon, a party went off for small pickets to line the Bastion. Visited by a few Clatsops & Tshichilish, who brought several Beaver & sturgeon. We asked the Tshichilish party why their tribe did not come to trade their furs, etc. (which they generally sent by the Chinooks) like the other People around us. They told us that being cautioned by the Chinooks, against coming, as we were very inveterate against their Nation, for their conduct to former Visetors they did not wish to put themselves in our power. This we made them sensible to be an egregious falsehood imposed upon them by the Chinooks, merely to monopolize the Trade, and added should they behave well, that so far from bearing them any antipathy, we would always be their particular friends, etc. etc. Laframboise resumed his work, the rest of our invalids much the same as yesterday.[92]

24th. Saturday. Fine clear Wea: Wind South West. People employed much the same as yesterday. Visited by several of the natives, who brought a few Beaver & Sturgeon to trade. 7 Men sick (3 of whom are S. Islanders).

25th. Sunday. Wind & Wea: as yesterday. Visited by a number of the surrounding Tribes, who brought several skins & a few salmon. Sick list as yesterday.

26th. Monday. Mild Wea: with a few showers of rain. Wind south'y. People employed as follows, to wit; Mathews & Jeremy finishing the lower story of the Bastion, Farnham & the Cooper building the Chimney with Roussel & 4 Sandwich Islanders attending them (bringing stones, Morter, etc.); Franchere & Wallace & Olivier Roy putting the Bark on the dwelling House; the two Belleaus sawing Rafters and curing fish; 3 Sandwich Islanders bringing home clay; Mr. Mumford, the Carpenter & Lapierre working at the shallop. Visited by a few Indians who brought some fish & 2 or 3 skins. McGillis, Laframboise & 3 Sandwich Islanders sick.[93]

27th. Tuesday. Pleasant Wea: Wind S. W. People employed as yesterday,

---

[92] Tshichilish is more commonly spelled Chehalis; see above, n. 71. This incident illustrates the extent to which Comcomly was monopolizing the trade of the area and the means he used. His potential for profit in doing so is obvious. For this, he has frequently been characterized as a crafty old pirate, etc. J. F. Santee in "Comcomly and the Chinooks" (*Oregon Historical Quarterly*, 33, No. 3 [September 1932], 271–78), has made the pertinent observation that such tactics on the part of a white businessman would have been characterized as shrewd, or by a political leader, as statesmanlike.

[93] The bark referred to above was the cedar bark which the men had gathered from various locations. It was used as both siding and roofing material.

excepting Mathews, who with Laframboise is fixing the upper part of the kitchen chimney. In the morning, Farnham & the Cooper began the other. Towards evening the weather became cold & it blew very hard; some showers of rain.[94]

28th. Wednesday. Clear & pleasant Wea: Wind West'y. People occupied much the same as yesterday. McGillis, Jeremy, & the 3 S. Islanders still unfit for duty.

29th. Thursday. Cold & raw Wea:, with frequent showers of rain. High Wind from the South'd & East'd. People employed as yesterday, excepting Mathews, who is making Doors for the dwelling House, & the Blk-smith working for the Shallop. Visited by a number of the Natives, who brought several Beaver. Sick-list as yesterday, with the addition of Lapierre.

30th. Friday. Fine Wea: with a few showers in the mor'g. Wind S. W. People employed, & sick-list as Yesterday. Visited by several of the Natives, who brought a few Beaver & some fresh Salmon.

Augt. 31st. Saturday. Disagreeable rainy Wea: Wind S. by W. People employed much as yesterday; in the afternoon, two men went out a hunting. Sicklist as yesterday.

September 1st. Sunday. Wea: as yesterday. Wind S.E. In the afternoon our hunters came home, but without killing any thing. Lapierre much better, the rest of our invalids rather in a weak state.

2d. Monday. Clear & pleasant Wea: Wind Southerly. People variously employed: building chimnies, carrying stone, Making Morter, covering the Dwelling House, making Doors & windows for ditto, curing salmon, etc. The Carpenter, Mumford, & Lapierre working at the shallop. 5 Men sick. Visited by several of the natives, who brought a few sturgeon to trade.

3d. Tuesday. Wind & Wea: as yesterday. People occupied much the same also. A few of the Natives about us, who brought some sturgeon, & 12 or 13 Beaver. Sick-list as yesterday.

4th. Wednesday. Fine warm wea: Wind N.E. People occupied as usual. Our hunter arrived in the morning, with a Deers head, & requested assistance to fetch the rest. A canoe was consequently dispatched with 4 Men who returned with it, late in the evening. Sick-list as yesterday.[95]

5th. Thursday. Wind & Wea: as yesterday. The Black-smith working for

---

[94] By the "other," McDougall is referring to a second chimney, apparently on the dwelling house; the kitchen may have been an attached shed or a separate building, in either case requiring a separate chimney.

[95] When McDougall refers to "our hunter" with no further description, he is probably referring to the Cathlamet Indian who had been hired previously; see above, n. 54.

the Shallop. The rest of the People at various jobs about the dwelling House, etc. Visited by a number of the natives, who traded a few Beaver & Clemels. 4 Men sick.[96]

6th. Friday. Cloudy with a few showers of rain; Wind Southerly. People employed as yesterday. Sick-list the same.

7th. Saturday. Pleasant Wea: Wind Eastwardly. People occupied pretty much the same as the rest of the week. Visited by a few of the Natives who are now retiring into winter quarters. 5 Men sick. The Cooper working at the Shallop.

8th. Sunday. Mild agreeable Wea: Wind South'y. All hands turned out to drill & get their Arms inspected, which were in pretty good order, but had remained rather too long loaded. A Target was therefore set up, at which they all fired, very much to our satisfaction. Visited by a few of the Natives, who brought two or three sturgeons. Sick-list as yesterday.[97]

September 9th. Monday. Clear & pleasant Wea: Wind N. W. The Carpenter, Cooper, Black-Smith, Mr. Mumford & Lapierre working at the Shallop; the two Belleaus sawing plank for ditto; the House Carpenter fixing Doors & windows in the dwelling House; the rest of the People Laying the floors, building the chimnies, hearths, plastering, etc., etc. Visited by a few of the Clatsops, who brought several Beaver and some fresh Sturgeon. 4 Men sick.[98]

10th. Tuesday. Very mild & pleasant Wea: Wind North'y. People occupied as yesterday. Sick-list much the same also. Visited by several of the natives, who are daily bringing in what few skins they have to dispose of, as they are on the eve of * departure for their Winter Quarters.[99]

11th. Wednesday. Clear & agreeable Wea: Wind N. W. People employed as yesterday. Three Men sick. Visited by two or three of the Clatsop Tribe, who traded a few Beaver.

12th. Thursday. Wind & Wea: as yesterday. In the Morning a party

---

[96] The "clemels" (sometimes referred to as clamons or clemons) were either elk skins or upper body armor made of elk hide, resembling a European cuirasse; here, the context suggests that they were the latter. See below, August 10, 1813, for a specific identification of them as war garments; Ruby, Brown, *Chinook*, p. 15, describes them; several examples of highly decorated "clemmons" are pictured in Thomas Vaughn and Bill Holm, *Soft Gold: The Fur Trade and Ethnographic Exchange* (Portland: Oregon Historical Society, 1990), pp. 84–85.

[97] The satisfactory state of the weapons is another indication that not only McDougall but also the men took the danger of an attack by the natives seriously.

[98] The house carpenter was probably Michel Laframboise.

[99] * - A single word was erased from the journal at this point and the resulting gap filled in heavily with XXXs.

arrived from our hunter, with information that he had killed a Deer, & requesting some assistance to bring it home. Four Men were accordingly dispatched in a large Canoe; and shortly after, we sent two more men out a hunting. The rest of the People occupied much as usually. Late in the evening the men returned with the Deer. Sick-list as yesterday.

13th. Friday. Pleasant Wea: Wind N. E. People occupied as usual about the Buildings, Shallop, etc. In the forenoon our two hunters arrived, but had killed nothing. Visited by a few of the Tshinooks, who brought several Beaver, & some Sturgeon to trade.

14th. Saturday. Wea: as yesterday. Wind S. W. People employed about various necessary jobs. 4 Men sick.

Sept. 15th. Sunday. Mild & pleasant Wea: Wind S. E. In the morning Tucan (a Clatsop) arrived with information of his having killed a Deer, & wanted some assistance to bring it along. Six Men were consequently sent off in a Canoe, who arrived with it about Midnight; but it must have been killed a considerable time longer than the fellow pretended, as it was in a very forward state of putrefaction. Visited by a few of the Cathlamats, who brought us some fresh Sturgeon.

16th. Monday. The morng. fair, but the afternoon cloudy with considerable deal of rain. Wind S. E. In the morning, the Hunter's wife arrived & told us that her husband had killed a Deer & wanted a few men to bring it home. Five were instantly dispatched, who returned in the evening with two Deer, he having killed another before they reached the place appointed. The rest of the People variously employed about the buildings, & bringing Timber for the Black-Smith's Shop. The Carpenter, Cooper, Black-Smith, Mumford and Lapierre still working at the Shallop. Six Men sick, i.e., unfit for duty.

17th. Tuesday. Clear & pleasant Wea: Wind N. W. People employed Cutting & hauling out Timber for the Black Smith's shop, excepting Mathews & Laframboise, who are fixing partitions & Windows in the Dwelling House, & the Belleaus, who are sawing plank. Sick-list as yesterday.

18th. Wednesday. Mild but cloudy Wea: Wind South'y. People employed as yesterday. 5 Men unwell.

19th. Thursday. Morning pleasant, the afternoon cloudy with a few showers of rain. A party began raising the Black Smith's Shop. Mathews, McGillis & Laframboise laying the floor & fixing windows in the Dwelling House; Mr. Franchere cutting Hay & the rest of the people employed as usual. Sick-list as yesterday. Visited by a few of the Cathlamets, who brought some fresh Sturgeon, to trade.

20th. Friday. Mild with partial showers of rain. Wind S. W. People occupied at several necessary jobs about the buildings. The Hunter brought us 1 young fawn and 2 Bear Cubs.

21st. Saturday. Wind & Wea: as yesterday. People employed much the same, principally at the Black Smith's Shop. Visited by Kamaquiah & a few of his tribe, who brought several Beaver & some smoked salmon. Sick list as on Thursday. In the afternoon sent out 2 hunters.

Sept. 22d. Sunday. Clear & pleasant Wea: Wind S. W. In the forenoon all hands turned out to Drill, had their arms inspected, which were all in tolerable order. Visited by several of the Cathlamets, who brought a few Beaver, etc. 4 men sick, of a kind of Dysentery, which is a general complaint ever since our arrival here.[100]

23d. Monday. Pleasant, with a strong gale from S. W. In the morning our two hunters returned, having killed but 2 or 3 Ducks, altho' they saw a great number of Geese, etc. etc. People employed laying floors & fixing Doors in the Dwelling house, covering the Black Smith's Shop; Sawing plank, making Hay, & bringing home clay to plaster the Black Smith's Shop. The Carpenter, Cooper, Lapierre, & Messrs. Mumford and McGillis working at the Shallop. In the afternoon, sent Mr. Franchere out a hunting.

24th. Tuesday. Clear & agreeable Wea: Wind S. E. People employed much the same as yesterday. In the forenoon, Mr. Franchere returned, having lent his fowling piece to our Cathlamet Hunter, his own being out of order. 4 Men sick.

25th. Wednesday. Pleasant, Wind S. W. People occupied as yesterday. In forenoon, we were honored by a visit from Kamaquiah's Wife, who brought us half an Elk. In the afternoon, visited by Gassagass & a few of his followers, who brought a few Beaver & Smoked Salmon. Sick-list as yesterday.

26th. Thursday. Clear mild Wea: Wind S. W. People employed as yesterday. In the evening, all hands moved into the dwelling house (it now being in a tolerable state for our reception) & were treated with Grog on that occasion. 3 Men sick.

27th. Friday. Wind & Wea: as yesterday. In the morning, all hands were

---

[100] McDougall may mean a simple diarrhea rather than the more serious dysentery; either could be owing to the diet at Astoria, which tended heavily to fish, both dried and fresh, and game, with few vegetables. They may also have been short of food on more occasions than are recorded in the log. Franchère records that the men ate varieties of berries, etc., obtained from the natives for their antiscorbutic qualities. *Journal*, pp. 97–98. See below, n. 106, for a description of one of the most plentiful of these native vegetables.

employed hauling out Ways for the Shallop. In the afternoon, occupied much as usual, but mostly about the Blacksmith's Shop. Olivier Roy has been working at the Shallop for 3 days past. Visited by Kamaquiah, who brought us the 4 Qrs of an Elk. Towards evening we heard two Guns fired in the offing, by which we concluded that some vessel was at Anchor there, waiting a fair wind to come in. One of our breeding sows piged & had 8, one of which died.[101]

28th. Saturday. Pleasant Wea: Wind S. E. People occupied as yesterday. Visited by a few Chinooks, who brought us a Sea-Otter & some Beaver. 4 Men sick. [At sunrise fired two Guns in <u>response</u> to those fired outside last evening, this being the signal agreed upon with the Tonquin; besides, we thought that should it be any strange Vessel, she would not come in, after this warning of our preoccupation.][102]

29th Sunday. Cloud Wea: Wind S. W. In the morning, Mr. R. Stuart went off with a party of 7 Men, to look for the two Hogs that made their escape at Cape Disappointment, an Indian having brought us word that they had six young ones, which were laterly seen by himself & some others. In the afternoon, our Cathlamat Hunter brought us a small Bear. Sick-list as yesterday.

30th. Monday. Boisterous Wea: with frequent showers of Hail and rain. Wind S. S. W. The Carpenter & his party laying the Shallop's Ways. Mathews making a slide for the [gap]. The Black-Smith also working for Ditto. The two Belleaus sawing plank. Mr. Franchere & the rest of the people raising the furnace, & at other necessary jobs about the Black-Smith's shop. About 11 A.M., Mr. Stuart & his party arrived, but saw nothing of the Hogs, or Ship that we supposed to be laying outside. 3 Men sick.[103]

October 1st. Tuesday. Cloudy, with some Thunder & partial showers of rain. People employed as yesterday. In the forenoon sent out a person to hunt. A great number of Seals & porpoises have been seen in the River for 3 or 4 days past, as well as Pelicans, Geese, and Ducks, all of which, the

---

[101] "[W]ays for the shallop" refers to preparations for its launching; see below, October 2, 1811. The cannon were heard from the direction of the mouth of the Columbia. This occurs on several other occasions, when no vessel makes its appearance; see below, p. 124.

[102] The bracketed words are a marginal notation. McDougall can hardly doubt that the *Tonquin* has been lost, so he is probably referring to the agreed-upon signal in the expectation that the supply ship which Astor was to send would respond to the same signal. See below, p. 88, for the arrival of that vessel, *Beaver*, in May 1812.

[103] The gap noted here is about one word long. Possibly, "hull" or "launching" was intended.

Indians inform us, are here in great plenty the whole winter. Sick-list as yesterday.[104]

2d. Wednesday. Through the Night, heavy peals of Thunder, with a great deal of rain. Towards morning it cleared somewhat away, but continued showery. Wind S. E. People variously employed. About 11 A. M. the Shallop was launched, which went off exceedingly well; and will (we calculate) be ready to sail towards the latter end of next week; three Swivels were fired on the occasion, & all hands treated with Grog. Visited by Kamaquiah, who brought us the greatest part of an Elk. The hunter we sent off yesterday returned with Calpo, who had accompanied him. They killed 5 Brant Geese and 9 Ducks. All hands in a tolerable state of health excepting Tuanna, who has no symptom of convalescence.[105]

October 3d. Thursday. Cloudy with frequent showers. Wind N. E. The Carpenter, Mr. Mathews, the Cooper, Blacksmith, Lapierre, & Mr. Mumford, fixing Masts, Spars, etc., etc. in the Shallop; the rest of the people employed between the Black-Smith's Shop, Sawing Plank & making Hay. Visited by a number of the Natives, who brought a few Beaver, & Wapatoes, or small potatoes.[106]

4th. Friday. Clear & pleasant Wea: Wind South'y. People employed as yesterday. Sent off Thomas McKay & Calpo to hunt. 2 Men sick.

5th. Saturday. Wea: yesterday. Wind + S.E. and ± S.W.[107] People employed between Roussel's Shop, building a Hog Pen, Sawing Plank, making Hay, & transplanting Turnips, at which Jeremy has been employed for some days back. Towards evening, we were agreeably suprized by the arrival of a canoe from * Mr. D. Stuart's establishment on the Okannaakken

---

[104] The Indians were wrong. For whatever reason, they misinformed McDougall about the prevalence of waterfowl on the Columbia during the winter, something they should certainly have known. This would be no trivial matter, as the coming winter would be a difficult one for the Astorians. They also misinformed the trappers about vessels lying about the mouth of the river or exaggerated the severity of attacks on parties moving into the interior.

[105] The hunter who accompanied Calpo seems to have been either one of the clerks or, more likely, one of the French-Canadian laborers.

[106] Wapatoes are a form of Arrowhead (*Sagitarria latifola*), sometimes known as the swamp potato. They are a water plant, common throughout North America, whose bulbous roots could be eaten either raw or cooked. Like potatoes, they could be kept through the winter. See Raymond Stark, *Guide to Indian Herbs* (Blaine, Washington: Hancock House, 1981), p. 8; or Charlotte B. Clarke, *Edible and Useful Plants of California*, California Natural History Guides 41 (Berkeley: University of California Press, 1987), pp. 140–42; hereafter, Clarke, *Edible Plants*. These were one of the roots, berries, etc. referred to above, n. 100. See below, II, n. 1, for the antiscorbutic effect of these plants.

[107] In the margin, McDougall noted "+ A.M. ± P.M.," as symbols used to make his description of wind direction more specific on this date. They were not used again.

River, manned by Messrs. McLennon & Pillet, Benjamin Roussel, Bob (the Sandwich Islander), Ignace Shoriowane (our Iroquoi hunter, with his wife and two children) & Mr. Bruguiere, a freeman, who Mr. Stuart prevailed on to descend & try his luck in this quarter. They gave a very gratifying account of the hospitality, docility and honesty of the Natives above the falls, as well as of the appearance and productions of that part of the country, etc., etc. Visited by several Chinooks who brought some fresh salmon to trade. Sick-list as yesterday.[108]

6th. Sunday. Clear & pleasant Wea: Wind S. S. W. In the morning, sent out four Men to hunt. Towards evening, two of them returned having only killed a couple Ducks. 3 men sick.

7th. Monday. Clear, mild Wea: Wind East'y. In the forenoon, Messrs. McGillis & Mathews (who had not returned from hunting last night) arrived with intelligence of their having killed two Elk (the first that have been killed by any of our people); a canoe was immediately dispatched in which they returned, accompanied by Jeremy, our Iroquoi hunter & 4 S. Islanders. The rest of the people variously employed. Visited by Calpo & his Wife who brought us three Geese, 5 Ducks. 2 Sturgeon, and 4 Sea Otters. Sick-list as yesterday.

8th. Tuesday. Wea: as yesterday. Wind S. W. In the morning our Cathlamet hunter came for some assistance to bring home an Elk, which he killed yesternight. A canoe was consequently sent off with 6 Men, who returned about Midnight. Mr. Mathews & his party arrived in the evening, but one of the Deer was entirely destroyed, they not having taken out the intestines. Mr. McGillis & our Iroquoi hunter have not returned. The few People we had about the fort variously employed. Visited by Kamaquiah, who brought us two sturgeon.

Octr. 9th. Wednesday. Cloudy, with frequent showers of rain. Wind S. S. W. People variously employed between Shallop, Packing up Goods, etc., piling timber for char-coal, etc., etc. Visited by a few of the Clatsops, who

---

[108] At the *, "Fort George" is lined out. Ironically, this was the name the North Westers gave Astoria after their purchase in November 1813. Stuart's first post was located on the Okanogan River, near its confluence with the Columbia; see above, n. 74. Bruguier is identified as a free trapper, working for "Spokane House," the North West Company post near the present city of that name. By one means or another, he had come to the post on the Okanogan where he was convinced to cast in his lot, also as a free trapper, with the Pacific Company. Irving in *Astoria* (Rust ed., pp. 81–83), writes of both him and the Iroquois hunter, Ignace, who had apparently made his own way west through Canadian territory. See the Appendix, below, where no. 3, Pierre Brugier, "Gouvernail," and no. 161, Ignace Salioheni, "Guide," are listed.

brought several Beaver & two Clemels. In the forenoon sent off Messrs. Pillet & Bruguiere, with two Sandwich Islanders, to look for the best Beaver Country in our vicinity. 2 Men sick.

10th. Thursday. Clear & pleasant. Wind S. W. People occupied as yesterday. Visited by a few of the Chinooks, who brought us some fresh Sturgeon, etc. Sick-list as yesterday.

11th. Friday. Cloudy with incessant rain. Wind S. S. W. People variously employed, laying the upper floor in the dwelling House, cutting Saw logs, & removing several articles out of the lower cellar, which were put in the upper, in consequence of the Water having made its way thither, as well as into the Powder Magazine. Yesterday evening Messrs. Pillet and Bruguier returned & give a favorable account of Baker's Bay & its environs as Beaver country. Visited by a few Indians who brought us some fresh Salmon. Sicklist as yesterday.

12th. Saturday. Cloudy with frequent showers. Wind S. S. W. People variously employed. In the forenoon the Dolly departed for the first time on a voyage up the River, having the following persons on board; viz.: William P. Mumford, Master; Robert Stuart, R. Farnham, Donald McLennan; George Bell; Joseph Lapierre; Paul Poar; & William Karimoo (two Sandwich Islanders). In the afternoon got the upper cellar bailed out, and the Powder taken out, in order to elevate the lower floor. The Blacksmith fixing Beaver Traps for Mr. Bruguier. Sick list as yesterday.[109]

13th. Sunday. Clear & pleasant Wea: Wind S. W. Mr. Bruguier set out for our Hunter's House to purchase a Canoe, but was informed on his way, by some of the natives, that the hunter had removed to Captain Lewis' old House, adding that there were great plenty of Salmon. Accordingly a Canoe was immediately dispatched to that place, & returned about 7 P.M. with intelligence that there were but very few Salmon. Two of the Natives brought our she Cat & four kittens. Sick-list as yesterday.[110]

Oct. 14th. Monday. Clear & agreeable Wea: Wind S. S. W. People employed as follows: Mr. McGillis & Olivier Roy hewing timber for two gutters; Laframboise & Jeremy squaring saw logs; Mr. Pillet & the Sandwich Islanders making a drain from the upper cellar. In the evening got out two saw logs. Three Men sick.

---

[109] For the first time, the shallop was given a name. *Dolly* was named after Astor's daughter, Dorothea. Some writers have suggested it was christened in honor of Mrs. Astor, but her name was Sarah. Dolly is a much more likely diminutive for Dorothea than for Sarah.

[110] The hunter is probably the Cathlamet Indian previously hired by Hunt to supply the post; see above, n. 54.

15th. Tuesday. Cloudy with partial showers of Rain. People employed as yesterday. In the morning got out the two gutters. Our Iroquoi hunter went out in the morng but returned about dusk without success. Visited by a few Indians, who brought some Beaver, Wapatoes, fresh & Smoked. Gassagass (Comcomleys son) was permitted to stay in the fort overnight, in order to go & shew our people a fishing place in Bakers Bay. Sick list as yesterday.[111]

16th. Wednesday. Boisterous Wea: with frequent showers of sleet & Rain. People at different jobs: draining the cellar, digging the Gutters, Laframboise & Jeremy sawing Plank. 2 Men sick. Took a fine large Cocumber out of the Garden, the only one that came to perfection, altho they were sown in May last.

17th. Thursday. Wea: as yesterday, with strong wind S. W. People employed much the same as yesterday. Being short of provisions & hearing from the Indians that there are abundance of Salmon up Young's River, a Canoe was sent off with five Men to set the Nets, but were compelled to return, owing to the high Wind, etc. In the forenoon, Mr. Mumford arrived at the Fort, he having shamefully thrown up his charge, on board the Schooner <u>Dolly</u> on Monday the 14th, Instant. Three men sick.[112]

18th. Friday. Clear wea: Strong Wind West'y. People employed as yesterday. Weeks, the Carpenter, fixing a Bench for the Black Smith's shop. In the morning a canoe was sent off to set the Nets, but was as yesterday compelled to come back. Our Iroquoi hunter went off in the morning, & returned in the afternoon with the pleasant intelligence of having killed an Elk not far from the fort. Visited by a few Indians (one a Chinook), brought us three quarters of an Elk; & some of the Chilwits brought 25 bags of Wapatoes and a few fresh Salmon. 3 Men sick.

Oct. 19th. Saturday. Cloudy Wea: Wind N. E. Early in the morning, Messrs. Pillet & Bruguier left the Fort to hunt at the Chilwits Village, having been informed by one of the Natives of that village that there are plenty of Beaver and Salmon. Mr. McGillis with three Men accompanied them in order to procure Fish, etc. Sent five Men with our hunter to fetch the Elk that was killed yesterday. They arrived after dark, but were obliged

---

[111] Wapatoes were frequently dried and strung on cords by the natives; the Astorians may have assumed that they were smoked from their appearance. See Clarke, *Edible Plants*, p. 140.

[112] Young's River flows into the bay of the same name immediately to the west of the peninsula on which Astoria is located. There is no immediate reaction to Mumford's refusal to captain the *Dolly* other than McDougall's accusation of shameful conduct on his part. The vessel was apparently not well suited for use on the river and that may have been part of the difficulty with Mumford, who easily found reasons for not staying with a job.

to leave ½ of the meat behind on account of the darkness of the Night. Last night it froze about ⅛ of an Inch thick. Three Men sick.

20th. Sunday. Cloudy with rain. Wind East'y. Six Men were sent off early for the rest of the Meat, who returned about 10 A.M. Sick list as yesterday.

21st. Monday. Cloudy wea: with rain by intervals. Wind East'y. Part of the people fixing the cellars; the pit-saws (two) going. 4 Men sick.

22nd. Tuesday. Cloudy, with thick haze. Messrs. Pillet, Bruguier & Mc-Gillis with their party returned without success. Mr. McGillis & party were dispatched immediately to the Chinook side, where we hope they will be more fortunate. Our hunter went out in the morning, but killed nothing. People employed as usual Sawing, clearing behind the Fort, filling the Cellars with gravel. The Carpenter making a Gate for the back part of the Fort.[113]

23rd. Wednesday. Thick hazy wea: Wind S. W. People employed as yesterday. Our hunter went out in the morning accompanied by a Sandwich Islander. Passed the Powder into the Magazine. Visited by Kamaquiah, who brought us a few salmon. Sick list as yesterday.

24th. Thursday. Calm, with thick mist. People employed as yesterday. Towards noon Messrs. Bruguier, Pillet & McGillis returned, having gone no farther than Comcomley's point, on account of the sea breaking with much violence in the Bay. About dusk our hunter arrived, having killed two Bears, i.e., a large female & a cub.

25th. Friday. Cloudy wea: Wind S.W. Early in the morning, Mr. McGillis with a Sandwich Islander left the Fort on a Jaunt as far as the Chilwits, to procure some oak. Thomas McKay, Laframboise & two S. Islanders were sent across the River to try the Nets. The rest of the People employed as usual. Finished the cellars. 3 Men sick.[114]

26th. Saturday. Clear by intervals, with intervals of rain. People employed as usual. Mr. Bruguier clap boarding the chimneys, to prevent the Clay falling off. In the afternoon, the Belleaus & Olivier started on a hunting excursion, as we are very scarce of provisions. Sick list as yesterday.[115]

---

[113] With no further identification, "hunter" here probably refers to Ignace, the newly arrived Iroquois Indian. Presently, on October 28, he and his family will move to Young's Bay, just west of the post.

[114] As noted above (n. 64), the Chilwits lived on the north bank of the Columbia, near Oak Point, about forty miles from the ocean.

[115] Olivier is Olivier Roy Lapansé, usually referred to as Olivier Roy. Given the seasonal character of the salmon runs, and the poor quality of the fish taken at that time, a shortage was especially troubling. Notice that the next day, possibly in desperation, as no other stratagem seems to work, McDougall sends everyone out to hunt, "without success."

27th. Sunday. Cloudy with some rain. In the morning, all hands turned out a hunting, but returned without success. Our hunter returned likewise without having killed anything, Thomas McKay also arrived with two S. Islanders, bringing news that Walaly, a Cathlamet Chief where he had been, was catching a great many salmon, but would send none to the Fort untill a certain time of the Moon, on account of some superstitious idea. He likewise kills a great many sturgeons, of which he would send us none except roasted; but said that he would feed our people, were they sent to his house. Sick list as yesterday.[116]

28th. Monday. Fine wea:. Wind N. E. Early in the morning Mr. Franchere, Mumford, T. McKay & 4 S. Islanders were sent off to Wallaly's to procure provisions, Fish and hunt, etc. The Belleaus, Jeremy & Olivier sawing; Benjamin, etc., clearing behind the Fort; Weeks mending canoes; Mathews making sashes for Store Windows. Our Iroquoi hunter and family left the fort to live in Youngs Bay, it being as he thinks good hunting ground. Bob, a Sandwich Islander, was sent with him. Sick-list as yesterday.

29th. Tuesday. Clear with flying clouds. Wind N. E. People employed as yesterday. In the afternoon Mr. Franchere, Mumford with 3 S. Islanders returned unsuccessfully. They left T. McKay, Laframboise & a Canaka to attend the fishing and hunting. Mr. McGillis arrived from our Cathlamet hunter's, & brought two quarters of an Elk. Visited by several of the Natives, who brought us 25 fresh Salmon.[117]

30th. Wednesday. Cloudy with a few showers of rain. Wind East'y. People employed as yesterday. About noon, Messrs. Pillet & Bruguier arrived, having killed only five Ducks. Visited by a few of the Chilwits & Wakikums, who traded about five Bushels of Wapatoes & a few Beaver. 3 Men sick.

31st. Thursday. Cloudy, rainy Wea: Wind S. W. In the morning sent off a canoe with 3 Canakas, with orders for Laframboise & his party to return with what provisions they had procured. They all returned in the evening, but had killed nothing. In the evening set a Sturgeon Line. 3 Men sick.[118]

Nov. 1st. Friday. Cloudy. Wind S.S.W. This being all saints' day all

---

[116] Walaly's (various spellings) reluctance to sell the salmon may have been connected with the various rituals that accompanied the consumption of the first salmon in the spring; see above, n. 52, and Ruby, Brown, *Chinook*, p. 13. Note that when he does hand over some salmon on November 2, he does so personally and gives the Astorians fish already roasted.

[117] A "Canaka" (also spelled Kanaka and, on at least one occasion, Kanaker) was another term for the Sandwich (often abbreviated to S.) Islanders, all contemporary references to Hawaiian natives.

[118] A sturgeon line was probably a long line with multiple baited hooks held out into the river from the shore.

hands got a holyday, & as good a feast as the season could afford. Two men sick.[119]

2nd. Saturday. Cloudy, with a strong breeze from S. W. People employed as usual. Towards evening, Thos McKay came down with the three S. Islanders accompanied by Wallaly, who brought us 10 roasted salmon. Sick-list as yesterday.

3rd. Sunday. Clear, with a fine sun shine. After breakfast, Laframboise, T. McKay & 3 Canaks were sent off with Wallaly. They took a scoop Net to fish salmon after the Indian fashion. Our Iroquoi hunter arrived with an Elk. Sent two Canakas along with him. A Chinook Indian brought us six Geese, & told that there were plenty of salmon up the small Creeks about his house. Mr. Franchere was therefore sent along with him to view the place, as we could no longer put any confidence in their reports. Sick-list as yesterday.[120]

4th. Monday. Clear, pleasant wea. Wind N.W. All hands employed as usually. Visited by Gasagass, who brought us upwards of 50 Salmon and several Beaver skins. Visited by a few Wakicums, who brought us two sturgeon.

5th. Tuesday. Cloudy with Scotch Mist. Wind S.S.W. People variously employed. Mr. Franchere returned with the Indian having killed eleven Geese and five Ducks. He gives a favorable account of the place both for fishing & hunting (one of the Natives speared 120 salmon in one morning.) Messrs. McGillis & Pillet were immediately sent off with one of the S. Islanders. Our Cathlamet hunter arrived with part of an Elk which he had purchased. Two men sick.[121]

6th. Wednesday. Clear wea. with flying clouds. Wind. N. E. Mr. Bruguier making a canoe 31 feet long, out of a large Spruce tree which lies behind the Fort. Visited by Wallaly, who brought some pounded Fish, our people having ate the little Salmon they were able to catch. Sick list as yesterday.[122]

---

[119] McDougall, in spite of his presumed status as a Protestant, probably a Presbyterian, was ecumenical enough to allow his French Canadians (and everyone else), a day off in recognition of the Roman Catholic feast of All Saints' Day.

[120] Wallaly's willingness to allow the Astorians to fish now may be owing to the completion of certain rituals. Also, observe the explicit copying of native fishing methods. Note McDougall's new caution in accepting the word of the natives as to the availability of fish, etc. Ironically, this time the report will be correct; see November 5, 1811.

[121] "Scotch Mist" is a dense mist, mixed with drizzle.

[122] The wording of the entry indicates that Bruguier was making a dugout canoe. Indian canoes on the Columbia were constructed in this fashion, generally from the cedar logs commonly found throughout the valley. Lewis and Clark described them, noting especially the skill of the natives in handling them and the speed and craftsmanship of their construction.

7th. Thursday. Cloudy with intervals of rain. Wind N.E. People differently occupied. Purchased a considerable number of salmon, which were immediately salted. Sick-list as yesterday.

8th. Friday. Cloudy wea. Wind S.W. People employed as yesterday. Mr. Mumford & the Canakas who were at the Cathlamets arrived & informed us that they had caught little or nothing since they went up, & that Wallaly refused them victuals when they requested them, which with the loss of their line & Hooks (which were stolen) occasioned a refusal of such presents as Mr. McDougall had promised Wallaly.[123]

9th. Saturday. Pleasant wea. Wind N. E. People employed as yesterday. Visited by a few of the Natives, who brought 80 fresh salmon. Toward evening the two Belleaus & Jeremy went out a hunting.

10th. Sunday. Cloudy wea. Wind Easterly. Visited by Cassacas who brought 73 smoked salmon & 20 fresh ones that his father sent as a present. About noon, we were informed that the Belleaus & Jeremy had deserted, which was found out by some of the Men having missed their clothes. Messrs. Franchere & Mathews, with two Men & 5 Indians were immediately dispatched to try & overtake them or prevent their passing the rapid by means of the Natives, to whom a handsome reward was offered for bringing them back. Sick-list as yesterday.[124]

11th. Monday. Cloudy with frequent showers. Wind Easterly. Sent off Mumford, T. McKay & 3 Canakas, to recall Mr. Pillet. Sick list as yesterday.[125]

12th. Tuesday. Wet, disagreable wea. Wind S. W. People variously employed. 3 Men sick.

13th. Wednesday. Cloudy, with partial showers. Wind N. E. People em-

---

Meriwether Lewis, *The Lewis and Clark Expedition*, ed. Archibald Hanna, 3 vols. (Philadelphia: J. B. Lippincott Co., 1961), January 20, 1806, II, 523–25; see also, Ruby, Brown, *Chinook*, pp. 17–19. There are frequent references throughout the log to various kinds of river craft. In addition to the shallop, *Dolly*, the Astorians built one or more whaleboats, some row barges, and canoes, as well as purchasing canoes from the natives. The pounded fish were probably dried, flaked salmon.

[123] There is no further reference to or explanation for Wallaly's hostile behavior.

[124] Cassacas's (Gassagass) father is Comcomly. Offering a reward for the deserters is an interesting indication of either McDougall's confidence in the natives or his willingness to do anything to prevent any further desertions. See below, November 17, for another effort to hire natives to find and return the deserters.

[125] Pillet had gone to the fishing and hunting site first mentioned on November 3rd and assessed favorably by Franchère on November 5th; it is not clear just where it was. "Chinook" was usually reserved for Comcomly's band which lived opposite Astoria, on the north bank of the river.

ployed as yesterday. Mr. Pillet & his party returned toward evening. Sick-list as yesterday.

14th. Thursday. Clear & pleasant wea. We were informed by some of the natives that the Belleaus & Jeremy had arrived at the Clatsop Village with the intention of proceeding towards the Spanish Settlements. Mr. Wallace was immediately sent after them, accompanied by one of the Natives as guide. Traded several fresh salmon & Wapatoes. Sick-list as yesterday.

15th. Friday. Cloudy with strong Wind from N.E. People employed as usually. Killed a Deer which happened to be sweeming across the Bay in front of the Fort. Plucked a Turnip in the Garden weighing 8 lbs; Circumference 28 Inches.[126]

16th. Saturday. Rainy weather. Visited by a Chief from the Rapid who brought us intelligence of the Shallop's being at the Chilwitz, cutting Timber. He also reports that Mr. D. Stuart is on his way down with a great number of white people. Mr. Wallace returned in the evening, being obliged to give up the pursuit, as his guide refused to proceed. Traded some fresh salmon. Our Iroquoi hunter brought us the meat of 2 Elk.[127]

17th. Sunday. Disagreable wet Wea: Word was sent to Mr. McGillis & his party to return, in consequence of some suspicions we entertained of the Rapid Chief's intention in sending for the Chinook & Clatsop Chiefs, etc. Mr. Wallace went off early in the Morning with the intention of engaging some of the Natives to pursue the Diserters, but could not prevail upon any of them to accompany him; consequently was necessitated to return. Traded several Salmon.

18th. Monday. Wea: as yesterday. Wind N. E. People employed as usual. In the afternoon, Mr. McGillis and his party arrived, having caught 18 Salmon. In the morning sent off a canoe, to recall our Iroquoi hunter having so few hands in the Fort (in case of an attack). Sick-list as yesterday.[128]

---

[126] McDougall is not including everything in the log, or is being purposely vague. On this date, Franchère noted the acute need for fresh food, as several of the men were suffering from scurvy. Since Franchère wrote his journal in his old age, the date should be taken only as an approximate one. Nevertheless, he is accurate where references can be cross-checked. He also observed on several occasions, this being one of them, McDougall's poor health. *Journal*, pp. 116–17.

[127] David Stuart would arrive on January 27, 1812, from a season of trading near present-day Kamloops, British Columbia; see Ken Favrholdt, " 'Cumcloups' and the River of Time," *The Beaver*, Outfit 67, No. 4 (August–September 1987), 19–22.

[128] McDougall may be reacting not only to the small number of men at the post or, as he puts it, "in the Fort." He may also be fearful that the desertion of several men had given the natives an indication of the Astorians' weakness and disunity; notice his fear of an Indian alliance expressed on the 17th, when he summoned McGillis back to the post.

19th. Tuesday. Flying clouds. Strong Wind S. W. Part of the people employed in cutting wood for char-coal, others clearing away brush, etc., behind the Fort. Mr. Bellair and Benjamin making a Canoe. The Carpenter still mending Canoes.[129]

20th. Wednesday. Fine mild wea: People variously employed. Thomas McKay, a Canaka & Lamasey (a Chinook) arrived with 26 fresh salmon which they had caught in some small creeks about Comcomley's point. Sicklist as yesterday. Transplanted six Turnips as an experiment, to ascertain whether they would survive the Winter. Towards evening, Mr. Mathews, Olivier Roy, Laframboise and the Natives who accompanied them in pursuit of the Deserters arrived, without gaining any intelligence of them untill their return to the Chilwit Village, near which they had been seen by the Natives; & Mr. R. Stuart, who was there with the Shallop, sent 4 Canoes manned by his own people & the natives in search of them. But at the end of two days, they returned unsuccessfully, altho' the Natives maintained that they must still be in the environs. This determined Mr. S. to leave Messrs. Franchere & Farnham at said Village, in hopes of their making their appearance after his departure with the Shallop, which Mr. Mathews & his party left above Kamaquiah's, the wind having come a head.[130]

21st. Thursday. Rainy with strong East'y Wind. People variously employed. Laframboise & Olivier sawing. The Powder being found damp, it was put up stairs in the store & covered with Oil cloths, Blankets, etc. Visited by a few Indians who traded some fresh salmon. 3 Men sick.

---

[129] "Mr. Bellair" is probably Registe Bellaire (Appendix, No. 16), listed on the 1813–14 roster as a "Freeman & H[unter]." Freemen were those under no contractual obligation to a company.

[130] "Lamasey" is better known as Jack Ramsay, the son of a shipwrecked Briton and a Chehalis woman; apparently his last name was pronounced as spelled because the natives had difficulty pronouncing the letter "R." Alexander Henry describes him as having "extraordinary dark red hair and is much freckled," with an appearance more white than Indian; Elliot Coues, ed., *New Light on the Early History of the Greater Northwest: The Manuscript Journals of Alexander Henry and of David Thompson, 1799–1814*, 3 vols. (New York: Francis P. Harper, 1897), II, 768; hereafter, Coues, ed., *New Light*. Franchère, *Journal*, p. 124, n. 1, and others have identified him as the Indian interpreter recruited by either Captain Thorn or Alexander McKay after the *Tonquin* left Astoria on its last voyage. See below, June 15–18, 1813, for the visit to Astoria of Joseachal, described as a "Queenhilt" (Quinault) Indian from the central Washington coast. He was identified explicitly as the sole survivor of the *Tonquin* by McDougall and sent for, through Comcomly, with the promise of a generous compensation. McDougall and others questioned him closely as to the circumstances accompanying the loss of the *Tonquin* and recorded his answers under the dates of June 15th and June 18th, 1813. As noted, the Chilwits lived near Oak Point, about forty miles up the Columbia from its mouth. "Mr. S." was Robert Stuart, as given above. "Kamaquiah's" would be on the north bank of the Columbia, somewhat above Astoria.

22nd. Friday. Flying clouds with frequent showers. In the course of the Night stormy, with Thunder & lightning. Wind easterly. Sent off our Iroquoi hunter with two Sandwich Isldrs. The <u>Dolly</u> arrived about 9 A. M., having been in a very perilous situation off Grays bay for the two last boisterous Nights. However she got off clear with the exception of her Anchorstock, which gave way last night, in consequence of which she dragged upwards of a Mile before daylight & was within very little of being cast away upon a sand bank. In short, coming to anchor about this place ought always to be avoided, if possible, as it is bad holding ground & is exposed to every Wind, etc. Traded 80 fresh Salmon. One Man sick.[131]

23rd. Saturday. Cloudy with frequent showers. Wind East'y. People variously employed, unloading the Shallop, making & mending Canoes, clearing away brush, etc. about the Fort, sawing Plank, salting salmon, etc. Sick-list as yesterday.

24th. Sunday. Clear & pleasant Wea: Wind South'y. In the morning a canoe was sent off for Mr. McGillis & his party, all of whom arrived in the afternoon, having caught about 20 Salmon. About 2 P. M., Messrs. Franchere & Farnham arrived with the three Deserters, who they found prisoners at the Cathlanaminimins. Dodilcham, the Chief, having taken them up some days previous, but would part with them upon no account without a considerable reward. On their arrival here, they were put in Irons, & on half allowance. [What articles they left at the Fort were forfeited to the Company.] Traded a few fresh salmon. Two Men sick.[132]

25th. Monday. Calm cloudy wea: People variously employed, viz., making a coal pit; making and mending canoes; sawing Boards; Mr. Mathews making Window frames, etc., for the shop. Visited by Comcomley, his

---

[131] See above, April 21, 1811, when the *Tonquin* dragged its anchor and struck aground; McDougall recorded it as owing to the vessel's not being properly moored by Captain Thorn. Apparently, there was no way of securely mooring in front of the post without a dock or similar structure.

[132] McDougall had not recorded just where McGillis had gone to fish. Previously, November 17, he had been recorded at "the Rapids," probably at the Cascades, but it is doubtful McDougall sent him back there, as he was fearful of a native attack. Dodilcham and the Cathlanaminimins lived near the mouth of the Willamette River, at the present site of Portland; see above, June 1, 1811. The bracketed words are a marginal addition. This was the last real trouble from Jeremie, at least as far as McDougall was concerned. In December 1813, following the sale of the post to the North West Company, the H.M.S. *Raccoon* visited Astoria. Jeremie took advantage of its presence to sign on as an assistant clerk. In November 1818, he was in Lima, Peru, where he presented himself to J. B. Prevost, U.S. Special Agent, on his way to reclaim Astoria for the United States. Jeremie then claimed to have been the only true American at the post, the only one to try and stop its sale to the North Westers! For this he had been kidnapped and sent to England. See Ronda, *Astoria*, pp. 216–17.

sons, & a number of his people. His son brought several smoked salmon & a few Beaver. The days being now very short & provisions not over plenty, we begin taking two Meals a day only. Sick-list as yesterday.[133]

26th. Tuesday. Cloudy. Wind N. E. People employed as yesterday. Dug the remainder of our potatoes, say 60. 60 turnips were also put in the Cellar as also nine carrots which are intended for seed, in case the others should fail. Sick-list as yesterday.[134]

27th. Wednesday. Cloudy wea: Wind N. E. People variously employed, a party finishing the coal-pit, another getting saw logs. Packing up sundries for the Dolly and Mr. Stuart's expedition up the Cowlitsk. Sick-list as yesterday.

28th. Thursday. Cloudy wea: with rain. Wind N. W. The wind being favorable, the Dolly got under weigh for the Chilwits, to get timber for the Shallop, staves, timber for Whale Boat, Barges, etc. In her embarked Messrs. McLennan & Pillet, George Bell & Dick (a S. I.). Toward evening, Mr. Farnham & his party arrived with the meat of two Elk. Sick-list as yesterday.[135]

29th. Friday. Rainy wea: wind S. E. People employed about the Coal-pit, getting saw-logs, etc. Visited by some Indians, who brought us about 30 fresh salmon and a few smoked ones. Towards evening our Iroquois Hunter sent us part of a young Elk. Sick-list as yesterday.

30th. Saturday. Rainy wea: Wind South'y. People occupied as yesterday. Commenced burning the Coal-pit. Sick-list as yesterday.

Decr. 1st. Sunday. Flying clouds with a strong S.E. wind, during the day some hail fell. Mr. Franchere was sent over to the Chinooks in order to

---

[133] The coal pit was in preparation for making charcoal, the principal fuel for the blacksmith's forge; see Russell, *Firearms*, pp. 379–80, for a description of the process. He makes the point that constant attention was needed for it to succeed. McDougall's rationalization that the short days were a partial justification for only two meals a day does not hide his fear that the Astorians will not be able to secure sufficient food during the coming winter.

[134] One of the few mentions by McDougall of the relative success of the garden plots, for the quantity of potatoes left at that late date indicated a large yield. Further, if the harvest had been small, why would any pains be taken to preserve seed for the next year? See below, December 20th, for further evidence of the garden's productivity; see also Franchère, *Journal*, p. 96.

[135] The whale boat mentioned here may have been one of the vessels begun earlier when McDougall mentioned building more than one shallop. The utility of the barges is not entirely clear. If, indeed, they were barges, they would be cumbersome and possibly dangerous in the fast-flowing Columbia. They were meant to be propelled by oars; see April 16, 1812, below for a reference to oars being made for a barge which was being painted by Mumford, the erstwhile skipper of the *Dolly*. George Bell was the cooper for the post, so possibly some of the wood was needed for barrels.

procure a Native to go with Mr. Stuart as Interpreter. Sick-list as yesterday.[136]

2nd. Monday. Clear wea: with a strong S. E. wind. The most of the people getting out Saw-logs. The Black-Smith & Harry attending the Coalpit. Visited by Comcomly & 10 natives of Queenhalt. The former brought us 150 dried Salmon; the latter came in consequence of a report that Mr. Stuart & Calpo, with some of our people, had been made prisoners by the Cathlanaminimins. Sick-list as yesterday.

3rd. Tuesday. Showers of rain & hail, with a strong S. E. wind. People employed as yesterday. 2 Men sawing plank. About noon Mr. Franchere returned, accompanied by the Native he went in search of. In the evening, sold part of Mr. Lewis's things. 2 men sick.[137]

4th. Wednesday. Cloudy wea: with a heavy gale from the S. E. It blew so fresh during the Night that several trees were thrown down very near the Fort. The wind continued all day with the same impetuosity. Hauled out three saw logs. Sold the remainder of Mr. Lewis' things. Sick-list as yesterday.

5th. Thursday. Clear wea: with a moderate breeze from S. W. About Noon Mr. Robert Stuart left the Fort, accompanied by Messrs. McGillis, Farnham & Bruguier, the Carpenter, Joseph Lapierre, George & Peter (two Sandwich Islanders). Messrs. McGillis, Pillet & Bruguier, Lapierre & the two Sandwich Islanders were to proceed up the Cowlitsk, with Mr. Stuart & the others to remain on board the Shallop. The Belleaus, having got Roussil, the Black Smith, & Olivier Roy to become security for the payment of what expences, etc., were incurred in pursuit of them, as well as for their future good conduct, were let out of Irons. 4 men sawing, Mathews joining the floors of the store. Our Cathlamet Hunter came to inform us that he had killed an Elk. 4 men were immediately sent off, who returned with the Meat towards evening. 3 Men sick.[138]

---

[136] Communicating among the various tribes could be difficult, as their separate languages were quite different. The coastal tribes and the traders had already begun to evolve a kind of trading pidgin, known as Chinook, which had started to incorporate English words and phrases, especially those commonly used by sailors. However, a trip into the interior, such as was being planned for Stuart, would need an interpreter.

[137] James Lewis was the clerk who accompanied Alexander McKay on the last voyage of the *Tonquin*.

[138] McDougall does not specify the purpose or destination of the *Dolly*, but judging by her return on December 26th with a cargo of timber, the Cowlitz was the likely destination. The carpenter was probably Michel Laframboise, who is not mentioned in the log while the *Dolly* is away. Eleven days in irons for the Belleaus was not an especially severe punishment for desertion. McDougall may well have felt that he could not feed idle hands and that those who stood security for the deserters would be certain they stayed around.

6th. Friday. Clear wea: Wind S. E. People employed as yesterday. Jeremy sent Mr. McDougall a Letter, apologizing for his past conduct, & promising to behave well for the future; on the strength of which he requested his release, but was refused. Sick-list as yesterday.[139]

7th. Saturday. Clear wea: Wind N. E. People employed as yesterday. In the morning our Iroquois Hunter arrived with the meat of 3 Elk. One Man sick.

8th. Sunday. Wet cloudy wea: Wind N. E. Sick-list as yesterday.

9th. Monday. Mild & pleasant wea: Wind S. W. People employed as yesterday; 4 men sawing; Mathews joining the floors of the store. The Sandwich Islanders gathering Moss, & Mr. Mumford cutting Logs behind the Fort. One Man sick.

Decr. 10th. Tuesday. Clear Wea: Wind N.N.E. People employed as usual. Visited by some of the Chinooks, who brought us 45 Smoked salmon. One Man sick.

11th. Wednesday. Cloudy wea: with some rain. People employed as usual, viz., sawing Plank, clearing behind the Fort, getting out Saw Logs, etc. Two men sick.

12th. Thursday. Rainy Wea: Wind N. E. People employed as yesterday. This morning our Cathlamet Hunter arrived with the meat of a young Elk. He having killed another requested assistance to fetch it. Accordingly, 6 hands were sent off for that purpose. Sick-list as yesterday.

13th. Friday. Wind & Wea: as yesterday. People employed as usual. Toward evening, the 6 Men who were sent off yesterday returned with the meat of the Elk. Sick-list as yesterday.

14th. Saturday. Rainy Wea: Wind S. W. People employed felling trees behind the Fort. Visited by a few Natives who brought us some fresh & smoked Salmon, with a few Beaver skins. Towards evening our Iroquois Hunter arrived with the meat of 3 Elk. Sick-list as yesterday. Jeremy let out of Irons, but could find no security.

15th. Sunday. Clear, mild Wea: Wind W. S. W. Our Iroquois Hunter returned to his house in the forenoon. Calpo arrived with 5 Swan & 2 Geese. Visited by Kamaquiah, who brought us some wapatoes. 1 Man sick.

16th. Monday. Clear Wea: wind N. E. Set 4 hands to fell trees behind the Fort, who very negligently left a tree almost felled, when called to breakfast. During their absence, it fell on the smoke house and killed one of the

---

[139] Jeremy may have interpreted McDougall's release of the Belleaus as a kind of amnesty, but he found that it did not extend to him. See below, December 14th, for his release.

breeding Sows, which was in at the time. Mathews making a stair-case for the Store. Mr. Mumford caulking the store. Sick-list as yesterday.[140]

17th. Tuesday. Cloudy with some rain, wind N. E. People employed as yesterday. Jeremy hewing a frame for a Shed to build the Barges, etc., in.

18th. Wednesday. Rainy Wea: Wind S. W. People employed as yesterday. Some Chinooks arrived from up the River, and reported that the Natives about the Rapids were dying very fast of (as we suppose) a kind of Pleurisy. Sick-list as yesterday.[141]

Decr. 19th. Thursday. Cloudy wet Wea: Wind N. E. People employed as yesterday, the Black Smith repairing tools, etc. 3 Men sick.

20th. Friday. Clear, pleasant Wea: Wind N. N. E. People employed much the same as yesterday. We were obliged to take in about 25 Bushels of Turnips left in the garden; one of them measured 33 Inches round, & weighed 15½ lbs. One Man sick.

21st. Saturday. Rainy Wea: with thick mist. Wind S. W. People employed as yesterday. Visited by a Wakaicum who brought us 24 Salmon. Sick list as yesterday.

22nd. Sunday. Clear Wea: Wind N. Towards Noon the weather cleared up. Sick list as yesterday.

23rd. Monday. Cloudy wet Wea: Wind N. E. 4 men employed sawing plank for Barges, floors, etc.; 4 Sandwich Islanders clearing a road to haul out timber. Black Smith mending tools. Mr. Mumford caulking the store. 2 men sick.

24th. Tuesday. Cloudy with incessant rain. Wind variable. People employed as yesterday. Sick list as yesterday. Calpo and William (Sandwich Isldr) who had been sent a hunting with him arrived with 9 Swan, 2 Geese, & 2 Ducks.

25th. Wednesday. Cloudy wet Wea: Wind W. S. W. This being Christmas, all hands had a holiday & were treated with Grog on the occasion.

---

[140] This accident reminds one of the very real dangers relatively simple tasks such as clearing the area behind the post could pose to the unwary. Recall the loss of life during the time of first clearing in the spring; see above, pp. xxiii, 14.

[141] The Indians' susceptibility to various minor illnesses of the Europeans is well known; this illness, apparently a form of pneumonia, may have been brought among them by the Astorians. In 1830, Captain John Domins of the ship *Owhyhai* brought what was apparently a viral pneumonia to which the natives were especially susceptible. Thousands died, among them Comcomly; some of the smaller tribes were possibly wiped out by it. Ruby, Brown, *Chinooks*, chap. 11, passim.

Visited by a Clatsop from the Rapid, who informed us that the Dolly was on her way down. Sick list as yesterday.[142]

26th. Thursday. Cloudy with intervals of rain. Wind W. S. W. All hands employed as usual. About 3 P. M., the Dolly arrived with a cargo of Timber. All well. Sick list as yesterday.

27th. Friday. Cloudy wet Wea: Wind N. E. Tried to unload the Dolly, but could not effect it on account of the Swell in the Bay. People employed as follows, viz., Mr. Farnham & the Sandwich Islanders clearing a road for hauling out timber; two saws going; Mr. Mathews & the Carpenter laying the floor in the lower end of the Store. In the afternoon, our Iroquois Hunter arrived with his family having met with no success, all he brought was a young Bear Cub. Sick list as yesterday.

28th. Saturday. Cloudy Wea: with a few showers of rain. Wind N. E. People employed as usual. Farnham and McLennan cutting trees. Visited by a few Indians, who brought some Matts to trade. Sick list as yesterday.

29th. Sunday. Mild, cloudy Wea: Mr. Farnham, our Iroquois Hunter & 3 Sandwich Islanders were sent up the River to hunt. Traded a few Beaver. Sick list as yesterday.

30th. Monday. Cloudy with thick mist. Wind S. E. Unloaded the Dolly; Sawyers & Carpenters at their respective works. Sick list as yesterday.

31st. Tuesday. Clear, pleasant Wea: Wind N. E. People employed at different jobs. Carpenters preparing timber for partitions, sawing keels for Barges. All hands allowed the afternoon to cut fire wood, etc. Sick list as yesterday. [Radishes that were left in the garden even today in full blossom.][143]

1812

Jany 1st. Wednesday. Ushered in a pleasant sunshine with white frost. Wind N. E. At sunrise, the Drum beat to arms and the colours were hoisted. Three rounds of small arms & three discharges from the great Guns were fired, after which all hands were treated with grog, bread, cheese & Butter.

---

[142] The grog was apparently in addition to the usual liquor ration. The men were also treated to small servings of bread, butter, and cheese. These meager treats "delighted" the men, according to Franchère, for they had been eating dried fish for nearly two months, "which was very poor food." Franchère, *Journal*, p. 108.

[143] The words in brackets were written in pencil, under the day's entry.

A good Dinner & grog were served out to all hands. At sun down 3 big Guns were fired & the colours taken down, after which we had a dance, and retired about 3 A. M.[144]

2nd. Thursday. Pleasant wea: with white frost. Wind N. E. All hands were allowed this day to recover of last night's fatigue. Jeremy has undertaken to cure Tuannan of the Venereal, & altho he has only prescribed for a few days, his patient looks considerably better.[145]

3rd. Friday. Clear, pleasant sun shine. Wind N. E. People variously occupied: 4 men Sawing; 3 squaring Saw logs; the Carpenters working at the partition; the Sandwich Islanders clearing a road to haul timber out of the Wood, 2 men sick.

Jany. 4th. Saturday. Clear, pleasant Wea: Wind N. E. People employed as yesterday. Messrs. McLennan & Mumford & Jeremy hewing a shed frame. Sick list as yesterday.

5th. Sunday. Wind & Wea: as yesterday. The Natives mostly all affected with Colds that carry them off in great numbers. 3 Men sick.[146]

6th. Monday. Mild & pleasant Wea: Wind N. E. People employed at various jobs. Uncovered the coalpit, but found it almost all consumed. 2 Men sick.

7th. Tuesday. Wea: as yesterday, wind East'y. Making up the Coalpit anew. Mr. Mumford clearing away Brush; Olivier & Laframboise making a Pig Pen, the other being employed as Coal House; Carpenters laying the floor of the store; the Black Smith making Locks for the Store Doors. Three Men sick.

8th. Wednesday. Clear, pleasant Wea:, wind North'y. People employed as usual. Visited by some Cathlamets, who traded a few Beaver skins. 4 men sick.

9th. Thursday. Clear, sunshine, Wind N. E. People hauling out timber.

---

[144] New Year's Day was celebrated with a good bit more vigor than New Year's Eve and, as much as circumstances permitted, feasting and drinking. The Americans looked for this as much as the French Canadians, as Lewis and Clark gave their men the day (or two) to celebrate; Ronda, *Astoria*, p. 218.

[145] Aside from a drastic (and self-explanatory) treatment later, McDougall does not specify just what Jeremy is doing for the hapless Hawaiian. Venereal disease was treated by mercury, most often in an ointment. It had been used by the Arabs for various skin diseases and was applied soon after the disease first appeared in Europe; see William Allen Pusey, *The History and Epidemiology of Syphilis* (Springfield, Illinois: Charles C. Thomas, 1933), p. 37. Later, when McDougall runs out of mercury ointment, he makes his own; see below, February 22, 1813.

[146] This probably refers to the same illness as McDougall noted above, December 18.

The Coal pit, being finished last night, was immediately set on fire & Mr. McLennan attending it. Hauled out a few Saw Logs. Sick list as yesterday.

10th.—say Friday.[147] Wind & Wea: as yesterday. People variously employed. Towards evening got another Saw Log. Carpenters framing the Shed. Sick list as yesterday.

11th. Saturday. Cloudy with some rain. Wind W. S. W. The sudden change from frost to rain has affected the most of our people in a very serious manner, particularly the Sandwich Islanders. A canoe of Clatsops passed the Fort on their way home from up the River and informed us that they heard Mr. Robert Stuart & his party were on their way down, and that our hunters up the River had killed some Elk. 8 Men sick.[148]

12th. Sunday. Cloudy with partial showers of rain. Wind W. S. W. Sick list as yesterday.

13th. Monday. Cloudy, wet wea:, wind variable. People employed as usual. Sawing; framing the Shed; clearing land, etc. The Black Smith making Locks, etc., for Store Doors. Sick list as yesterday.

14th. Tuesday. Cloudy wet wea:, wind variable from S. to S. W. People employed as follows: 2 Men Sawing; 3 framing the Shed; 1 attending the Coal pit; 3 cleaning Muskets; Taylor & Black Smith at their respective works. Visited by some of the Wakaicums, who traded a few Beaver. Sick-list as yesterday.

15th. Wednesday. Wea: as yesterday, wind South'y. People employed as usual. 7 men sick.

16th. Thursday. Rainy with thick mist. Wind N. W. People at different jobs: the Carpenter getting out timbers for Barges; the Cooper Splitting & dressing Staves for Kegs; the Black Smith mending axes; 4 Men sawing & 2 clearing away brush. 7 men sick.

17th. Friday. Cloudy with partial showers of rain. Wind S. W. People employed much the same as yesterday. John Belleau (one of the Sawyers) unfit for duty, as also the Cooper. The Carpenters still framing the shed. Mr. McLennan & Antne. Belleau getting timbers for Barges. 2 men clearing away Brush. Sick list as yesterday.

18th. Saturday. Dull, cloudy Wea: Wind N. E. People employed as yesterday. About breakfast time Mr. Farnham, our Iroquois Hunter & the

---

[147] Immediately before this, the clerk had written "Thursday," then crossed it out with diagonal slashes.

[148] It should not be surprising that the Hawaiians suffered severely from the cold, damp coastal Oregon climate; see below, p. 134, for a time when all of them will be laid low with various colds, etc.

three Sandwich Islanders arrived with the meat of 6 Elk, having gone as far as the entrance of the Cowlitsk River. About 5 P. M. we were agreeably surprized by the arrival of Messrs. Donald McKenzie, Robert McLellan & John Reed (clerk), with 8 hands, viz.:

> William Cannon
> Joseph L'Andrie
> Andrez Dufresne
> Etienne Leucier
> Michel Samson
> Andrez Vallé
> Prisque Felax
> Guillaume Le Roux, dit Cardinal,

in two canoes, they having left Messrs. Hunt & Crooks with 36 men on 2nd November last, on this side * the R Mountains, among the Snake nation. [They separated from the party to search for horses, but being unable to bring them any assistance they continued on their way here.] They encountered considerable hardships, and suspect that should the latter Gentlemen pursue their route this Winter, they must seriously suffer for want of provisions, etc. 6 men sick.[149]

---

[149] As described in the introduction, the Astorians were divided into three parties, those on the *Tonquin*, a group that traveled overland from St. Louis, and those on the *Be⸻ ⸻hich* left New York City in October 1811 under the direction of one of the partners, John Clarke, and arrived at the Columbia in May 1812. The overlanders were under the direction of Wilson Price Hunt, a New Jersey native who was in the fur trade in St. Louis. Owing to several misjudgments by Hunt, nominally the senior partner under Astor (partly because of his American citizenship), the party experienced severe hardships and, in November, separated into several smaller parties. When they had left the Arikara Indians on the upper Missouri in mid-July, there were sixty-four in the party. Along the way, five either turned back or were separated from the main party and five were killed. Eventually fifty-four overlanders arrived at Astoria in several parties. See Rollins, ed., *Stuart's Narrative*, p. 312, n. 44 for a list of the overlanders; and J. Neilson Barry, "Astorians Who Became Permanent Settlers," *Washington Historical Quarterly*, 24, No. 3 (July 1933), 221–31 and No. 4 (October 1933), 282–301; Kenneth W. Porter, "Roll of Overland Astorians," 1810–1812, *Oregon Historical Quarterly*, 34, No. 2 (June 1933), 103–12, 286. Barry should be used with care. At the asterisk, several words have been heavily crossed out and "side the R. Mountains among" written above. The bracketed words are a marginal addition. McDougall, already facing a difficult time with provisions, must have experienced mixed feelings, pleased to have the additional hands, especially the nominal superior, Hunt (who arrived February 15), on whom some of the responsibility of the post could be placed, but anxious about feeding and sheltering the additional men. Donald McKenzie and Robert McLellan were partners. Portions of Hunt's journal for the overland trip (now lost) are printed as Appendix A in Rollins, ed., *Stuart's Narrative*, pp. 281–308.

19th. Sunday. Flying clouds & a strong gale from N. E. This morning we fired 3 rounds of small arms & 5 big Guns, the Colours hoisted, etc., to welcome our friends. The People were indulged with liquor, etc. 3 Men convalescent and four still sick.[150]

20th. Monday. Wind and Wea: variable. People employed as usual. 5 Men sick.

21st. Tuesday. Cloudy wea:, wind N. E. People employed between Sawing, cutting trees & Brush, Packing furs, etc. Got up the Shed. The Black Smith making Augers, etc. 5 Men sick.

22nd. Wednesday. Wea: as yesterday. Wind S. W. People employed as usual; the Cooper clearing the cellars; sick people cleaning arms; the Carpenter preparing timbers for Barges. 3 Men sick.

23rd. Thursday. Cloudy, rainy wea:. Wind W. S. W. People employed as yesterday. In clearing the Store & Cellars, we found a pipe of Brandy in a very leaky state; started it into another pipe. 3 Men sick.[151]

24th. Friday. Cloudy wet wea: Wind W. S. W. People employed much the same as yesterday. In the morning, Messrs. McLellan & Farnham went out a'hunting with 4 Men. Ignace with two Sandwich Islanders left the Fort for the same purpose. Sent 3 more Men to hunt swan, etc. 5 Men sick.[152]

25th. Saturday. Cloudy with some rain, wind S. S. W . People variously employed. Sick people cleaning arms. 4 Men sick.

26th. Sunday. Cloudy, wet wea: Wind S. S. W. Visited by a few Indians who traded a few Beaver Skins. Sick list as yesterday.

Jany. 27th. Monday. Cloudy with incessant rain; Wind W. S. W. About noon, Mr. Stuart & his party arrived, having left Mr. Bruguier, Joseph Lapierre & Peter Pahia (a Canaka) hunting Beaver. He gives a very satisfactory account of the country, as abounding in Beaver, etc., particularly the upper parts of the River. He traded upwards of 100 Beaver from the Natives, whom he found very peaceable & generally honest. They are exceedingly ill off for provisions, being unable or too indolent to kill Beaver or Deer at this Season, & no fish frequenting their waters since the fall to the

---

[150] Symptomatic of the low state of the post's provisions and the additional demands now being placed on them, the celebration of the first overlanders' arrival seems to have been a decidedly low-key affair.

[151] A pipe is a large cask; if the word was being used strictly, it meant four barrels or 126 wine gallons. Liquor was shipped on board the *Beaver* in containers of that size; see Porter, *Astor*, I, 503: "Invoice of merchandise shipped on board the *Beaver*."

[152] Ignace is the Iroquois hunter who arrived with Robert Stuart, October 5, 1811.

beginning of March. Our people employed as usual. The 3 hunters that were sent up the River arrived towards evening having killed nothing. Five Men sick.[153]

28th. Tuesday. Cloudy, wet wea: wind S. W. People employed about mooring the Dolly, taking one of her Cables into the Store, Rigging, etc. Sent out 3 Men a'hunting. Carpenter unwell. 6 Men sick.

29th. Wednesday. Cloudy [and misty] mist.[154] Wind South'y. People employed much as usual, between Sawing, clearing land, covering the shed & cleaning arms. Towards evening Messrs. McLellan & Farnham with their party having met with very little chance. They brought the meat of an Elk & wolf. 6 Men sick.

30th. Thursday. Thick fogg but mild Wea: calm. People employed as yesterday. After Breakfast dispatched Messrs. Reed & McLennan for the seashore to make Salt with 2 men. Sent likewise Messrs. McGillis & Pillet with a Sandwich Islander to hunt Beaver. 8 men sick.

31st. Friday. Rain by intervals, with a strong S. W. wind. People employed as usual covering the shed, cutting Brush, cleaning Arms, etc. The Carpenter getting better. 3 Sawyers unfit for duty. Seven men sick.

Feby 1st. Saturday. Begins with rain, but clears up about 9 A. M. Strong S. W. wind. People employed much the same as yesterday, cleaning the Fort & Store. The Carpenter resumed his work. 6 men sick.

2nd. Sunday. Cloudy with Wind South'y. One of the Sawyers getting better. The Natives, who have been lodged for 3 Months past in the bay below the Fort have departed for the upper part of the River to catch Uthel-chans* which entered the River a few days ago. Our Hunter arrived this morning, having killed nothing. Sick list as yesterday. *or small fish resembling smelts[155]

3rd. Monday. Cloudy with partial Showers of rain. Wind S. by W. After breakfast Messrs. R. McLellan, R. Stuart, & R. Farnham with 5 Men left this, the two former with 4 Men to hunt, & the latter with one Man to catch Sturgeon & Uthelchans. People employed as usual; the Carpenters laid the keel of the Whale Boat. In the afternoon, Mr. Bruguier arrived, having

---

[153] Robert Stuart's party was the one that left the fort on December 5, 1811, for an exploratory venture up the Cowlitz River.

[154] The bracketed words were written above the line; under them the words "with Scotch" were lightly crossed out with diagonal slashes.

[155] As noted previously, "uthlecans" were a variety of herring, sometimes called candlefish because of their high fat content. McDougall inserted the asterisk and added the explanatory note at the end of the entry.

catched 28 Beaver after Mr. Stuarts departure from the Cowlitsk River. His success displeased the Natives, who obliged him to leave the place. Sent Cardinal & Vallée to Hunt Swan. 3 men sick.

4th. Tuesday. Pretty clear with partial showers of rain; wind S. W. People employed about different jobs. Got the Coal out of the Kiln, but found a very small quantity, say 25 Bushels. All hands convalescent, 3 men still unfit for duty.

5th. Wednesday. Cloudy. Wind S.W. 5 men cutting trees, etc., for another Coal pit. The two Sandwich Islanders who were with Ignace came home, he having had no success & was left starving. 2 men were immediately dispatched with a small supply of fish & Rice. Sick-list as yesterday.[156]

6th. Thursday. Cloudy, with heavy rain all day. A heavy gale of wind from the S. W. People employed cleaning arms. Two Men sawing boards. The Black Smith, Carpenter, & Cooper at their respective works. Sick list as yesterday.

Feby 7th. Friday. Cloudy with incessant rain. Wind W. S. W. People employed as yesterday. 5 men cutting wood for Coal-pit, but were soon obliged to desist on account of the rain. Sick list as yesterday.

8th. Saturday. Cloudy with intervals of sunshine. Wind S. W. People employed at different jobs—cutting wood for coal pit; sawing; clearing Brush, etc. Carpenters, Cooper and Blacksmith at their respective works. Two Men sick.

9th. Sunday. Clear & pleasant wea:, with a light Breeze from E. N. E. Visited by Watatchum who brought us a few <u>Uthelchans</u>, the first we have seen this year. The Indians begin to catch them in abundance. 1 Man sick.[157]

10th. Monday. Clear Wea: Wind N. E. People employed at the Coal pit (say 8 Men). Mr. Mumford clearing away Brush, Olivier squaring a saw log, 2 sawyers at work; all others employed as yesterday. 1 Man sick.

11th. Tuesday. Clear, with a violent gale of wind from N. W., accompanied by hail Stones. People employed as yesterday. Towards night the two Sandwich Islanders who were sent to Ignace arrived with the meat of an Elk. 2 Men sick. [Today we saw the first snow this season.][158]

12th. Wednesday. Cloudy with showers of rain. Wind South'y. People employed as yesterday. In the morning Mr. Farnham arrived from the Chil-

---

[156] Recall that Ignace was now living apart from the main party, on Young's Bay, with his family; see October 28, 1811.

[157] Watatchum is the "Cathlamet hunter." On April 25, 1812, he will bring in three geese for the post.

[158] The bracketed words were added in pencil.

wits Village, with 9 Sturgeon & 1 Bushel of Uthelchans. Sent two Men to Ignace, our Iroquois Hunter. Two men sick.

13th. Thursday. Clear & pleasant Wea:. Some snow fell during the night. Wind S. E. Sent off Mr. Farnham with two Sandwich Islrs to catch more Fish, as we are very short of provisions. Sent Lapierre to join Cardinal & Vallée, in order to get Cedar timbers for Barges. People employed finishing the coal-pit; set it on fire about noon. Towards evening, Ignace arrived, having accidentally cut his foot very bad. Visited by a few Chinooks who brought us a few Beaver Skins. 3 Men sick.[159]

14th. Friday. Clear sunshine. Wind N. E. People employed as yesterday. Several canoes of Clatsops went down, laden with Sturgeon & Uthelchans, but they would not dispose of them on any account what ever. 4 Men sick.

15th. Saturday. Mild & agreeable wea: Wind N. E. People employed as usual. Towards noon, Messrs. McGillis & Pillet arrived, having killed 2 Beaver only. Visited by Comcomley, who brought 40 to 45 Beaver. One of the Cathlamets presented us with about 2 Barrels of Uthelchans. About 2 P.M. we were agreeably surprised by the arrival of Mr. Hunt with 30 Men, a Woman & 2 children, in 6 Canoes. They met with Mr. Crooks, but were obliged to leave him & 5 Men with the Snake Nation, they being too weak to proceed. Mr. Hunt thinks it probable that they will winter thereabout. 4 Men sick.[160]

---

[159] On February 3, Cardinal and Vallée had been sent to hunt swan, locale unspecified. There was no further note of their return or where they might have been sent for cedar. Although it was not specifically noted, it seems a fair inference that Farnham was sent back to the Chilwits village near Oak Point from which he had just returned. See below, March 1 and 3, 1812, for his shipments of sturgeon and a deer.

[160] This is the second group of overlanders to arrive at Astoria. Ramsay Crooks did winter over with the natives, arriving May 11 with John Day. Ramsay Crooks was a partner; John Day, a Virginia-born hunter who joined the party at the Nodaway camp on the Missouri. See Stella M. Drumm, "More About Astorians," *Oregon Historical Quarterly*, 24, No. 4 (December 1923), 350. The woman and two children were the family of Pierre Dorion, the son of Lewis and Clark's interpreter; Irving, *Astoria* (Rust ed.), pp. 97–99. The remainder of the party arrived January 16, 1813. McDougall now had thirty-four additional mouths to feed, but with Hunt having been given primary authority by Astor, it was his problem. However, with the arrival of the *uthlecan*, it was not as much of a problem. As Franchère noted: "The arrival of so great a number of people would have embarrassed us had it taken place a month earlier. Happily, the natives now brought us fresh fish in abundance." *Journal*, pp. 110–11. One change that might have been expected did not apparently occur. There is no sign in the log of Hunt's taking over the post. To judge only from the log, McDougall continues to supervise affairs. Within a little more than a month of Hunt's arrival, however, the Astorians mounted their most ambitious effort into the interior; see below, March 21, 22. Hunt may have been primarily responsible for this burst of energy. Ronda, *Astoria*, pp. 238–42. With the arrival of the *Beaver* in May, Hunt was distracted from affairs at Astoria by concern for

16th. Sunday. Wind & Wea: as yesterday. About noon Messrs. R. Stuart & R. McLellan with their party returned, having met with very little success, and brought us the meat of a small Deer, with a few Uthelcans. About dusk Kanakers arrived with a canoe load of Uthlecans. Sick list as yesterday.

17th. Monday. Clear, pleasant wea: Wind N. E. The old hands of Astoria were allowed this day to welcome their new friends. 2 Men attending the Coal pit. 5 men sick.[161]

18th. Tuesday. Cloudy, with a Strong gale of wind at S. W., accompanied with hail & Snow. People at their usual work, except the Blacksmith. 3 men sick.

February 19th. Wednesday. Clear, pleasant Wea: Wind N. E. People employed as yesterday. Visited by a few natives, who brought us some Uthlecans. Sick list as yesterday.

20th. Thursday. Wind and Wea: as yesterday. People employed much the same also. In the morning B. Jones went out, and returned about noon, having killed an Elk. Six men were immediately sent after the meat, & 4 of them returned with part of it, the two others having lost their way through the wood. Mr. McGillis was sent over to the sea Shore to take Messrs. Reed & McLennan's place. Benjamin Roussell was likewise sent up the River to join Cardinal & Vallée to procure some cedar timbers for Boats, etc. * 3 men sick.[162]

21st. Friday. Clear pleasant wea: Wind East'y. All hands were allowed to rest and feast with their new friends. In the morning 3 men were sent after the remainder of the meat that had been left in the wood yesterday, who

---

another area of the Pacific Fur Company, the opening of a steady and profitable relationship with Count Alexander Baranov and the Russian-American Company post at New Archangel (Sitka) in Alaska. He left Astoria in June for what was to be a short trip to Sitka. He did not return until August 1813, by which time his authority had effectively been transferred to McDougall, McKenzie, and the other partners who had remained at the post. Ronda, *Astoria*, pp. 285–92.

[161] It seems odd that McDougall did not take advantage of Hunt's arrival on Saturday to make Sunday the holiday and try to get everyone back to work on Monday. And, like that for the first party's arrival, the welcome seems to be rather low key. It may also be noted that "Astoria" is used here for the first time in the log. However, Alexander Ross notes the name being given on May 18, 1811, shortly after the arrival of the *Tonquin* in the Columbia. *Adventures*, p. 81.

[162] Benjamin Jones was one of the new arrivals; a Virginian, he had been recruited by Hunt near the Omaha villages on the upper Missouri in May 1811; Drumm, "More About Astorians," 355. At the asterisk, "4 men went after the remainder of the meat" has been crossed out. This was probably a task McDougall intended to have done on the 20th, but could not get around to it. See below, February 21, for the securing of the meat.

returned about 3 P.M. without it not being able to find the place. At dusk Cardinal & Vallée arrived not being able to find the timbers they had been sent after. They brought down a few Uthlecans & some axe handles. Messrs. Reed & McLennan likewise arrived from the salt works, with what little salt they had made (say about 2 Bushels). 3 men sick.

22nd. Saturday. Cloudy wea: with some rain. Wind S. W. In the morning B. Jones went out with 3 men to get the remainder of the meat. They all returned with it about noon. Sick list as yesterday.

Feby 23rd. Sunday. Cloudy with partial Showers of rain. A heavy gale of wind from the Westward. 3 men sick.

24th. Monday. Cloudy by intervalls. Wind S. W. People at their usual labor (say) the old hands; only the Blacksmith unfit for work. 3 Kanakers who were comming down the river with a canoe load of 11 Sturgeon were unfortunately upset in a ripple opposite tongue point, and narrowly escaped with their lives. Those were disagreeable news as we are very short of provisions and a great many people about us. Sick list as yesterday.

25th. Tuesday. Cloudy wet wea:. Wind South'y. The old hands employed as usual. Sayers putting their Saws in order. One of the men was last night taken very ill with the pleurisy. Visited by a few Indians who traded some Sturgeon & 2 Beavers. 4 Men sick.[163]

26th. Wednesday. Cloudy with incessant rain all day. Wind South'y. About 9 A. M. 3 Canoes were sent up the Cowlitzk River to hunt Beaver, they having Messrs. McLennan & Thomas McKay to superintend them. 3 more Canoes were sent after Saddle trees, Boat Knees, & Sturgeon. 4 men were sent a hunting. One of them returned about dusk without success. People employed hewing Saw-logs, sawing plank for Boats, etc. L. Labonté, one of the men who came with Mr. Hunt (a carpenter by trade) began today to assist Mr. Mathews. 5 men sick.[164]

27th. Thursday. Cloudy with intervalls of rain. Wind South'y. People employed as usual, 8 Men hewing saw logs, 2 men working at a canoe, 4 men Sawing, 2 at the coal pit, etc. About 10 A. M. Mr. Farnham arrived with a timely supply of 9 Sturgeon requesting a canoe to be sent with him as

---

[163] McDougall certainly meant sawyers. As noted previously, "pleurisy" probably referred to a form of viral pneumonia.

[164] Wood for saddle trees and for boat knees would, ideally, be shaped in such a way as to require little additional work to suit them for the curves needed for the pack saddles. Boat knees were braces for the angles between the hull of the boat and the thwarts or cross members. The confused syntax should not obscure the fact that LaBonté was the carpenter, not Hunt.

he had about 30 more on hand. He had not met the People sent him yesterday. 5 men sick.

28th. Friday. Cloudy with a few Showers of rain. Wind variable from S. to N. W. In the morning sent off a canoe with 3 men, to fetch over Mr. McGillis and his party as the salt making wont answer this season, owing to the scarcity of dry wood, etc. People employed as yesterday. Sick list the same also. Visited by a few Indians who brought us some Uthlecans to trade.[165]

29th. Saturday. Cloudy with partial showers. Wind N. People employed as usual. Sick list as yesterday.

March 1st. Sunday. Ushered in a fine pleasant wea: Wind N. E. About noon the men that had been sent with Mr. Farnham arrived with 29 Sturgeon. The remainder of the day was cloudy and rainy. Sick list as yesterday.

2nd. Monday. Flying clouds with frequent showers of hail, wind S. E. People hewing and hauling out saw logs. Opened the coal pit. About 10 A. M., B. Jones & his party arrived with the meat of an Elk. The men that had been sent over for Mr. McGillis returned having had their canoe Broken by the violence of the surf, on landing at the Chinook village. Calpo & Gassacass brought them over. 3 men sick.

3rd. Tuesday. Rain & melted snow all day. Wind S. W. People employed making hoe and axe handles. A Canoe arrived from Mr. Farnham with 17 Sturgeon & a small Deer. Mr. Mathews unwell. Labonté getting better. 3 men sick.

4th. Wednesday. Rain & Snow all day, with Thunder. People employed as yesterday. The Blacksmiths making trading axes. A Canoe was sent to Mr. Farnham but the wind & wea: compelled them to come in again. 4 men sick.[166]

5th. Thursday. Cloudy with frequent showers of hail. Wind S. W. In the morning, Jones went out a hunting, and returned about 2 P. M., having an

---

[165] The cool, rainy climate of coastal Oregon obviously ruled out salt-making by evaporation. The Astorians had now discovered that it also made boiling sea water difficult, at times, impossible. Later they will preserve fish by both pickling and drying, the preferred native method, but this was also made difficult by the climate.

[166] Trade axes could be almost any type of that ubiquitous tool. However, "French" axes, referring to style, and not where made, tended to be the most popular. See Russell, *Firearms*, pp. 268–75, for descriptions and illustrations of common types. Chapter Five, "The Ax on America's Frontiers," is a general description of the history and development of the tool. Since three of the blacksmiths at Astoria, Roussel, Leclerc, and Michel Sanson were French Canadian, their product probably resembled Russell's examples of French axes.

Elk. People employed as usual between hewing, Sawing, cutting down trees, etc. Sick list as yesterday.

6th. Friday. Clear wea: Wind N. E. In the morning, sent out 4 men with Jones to fetch the meat of the Elk he killed yesterday. People employed at different useful jobs, making hogpen, cutting down trees, hewing saw logs, etc. Mr. Mathews yet unwell. About sundown Mr. McGillis & his party arrived with the salt they had made. He was on his way to the Chinook village after provisions when he received the letter sent him by Gassacass who came over with him. About Dusk, Jones and the men that had been sent with him arrived with the meat, they fell in with a gang of Elk & he killed five of them, three only of which he could find. 4 men Sick.

7th. Saturday. Cloudy with frequent Showers of rain. Wind South'y. People employed as usual. Falling timber, hewing saw logs, Sawing planks, etc. Sick list as yesterday. In the morning sent out 8 men for the meat of the three Elks, who all returned with it about Sundown.

8th. Sunday. Cloudy, rainy wea: Wind S. W. Mr. Mathews well. 4 men Sick.

9th. Monday. Cloudy wet wea: Wind S. W. People employed as usual. In the afternoon, the men that had been sent after saddle Trees arrived with a number of them & 60 axe handles. 4 men Sick.

10th. Tuesday. Cloudy wet wea: Wind N. E. People employed as usual. Mr. Pillet left this early this morning with 3 Kanakers to relieve Mr. Farnham. 3 men sick.

11th. Wednesday. Cloudy with intervalls of rain & hail. Wind S. W. People employed cutting wood for another coal pit. Hewing, sawing, etc. 3 men Sick.

12th. Thursday. Cloudy wet wea: Wind South'y. People employed as usual making pack Saddles, preparing canoes for a voyage up the river etc. Visited by Comcomley who brought us 10 Beaver skin; also by Calpo who brought us 41 Beavers & 3 Sea otter. 3 men Sick. Ignace, our Iroquoi hunter getting better.

13th. Friday. Cloudy with partial Showers of rain. Towards noon it cleared away. Wind South'y. People employed as yesterday. About 11 P. M., Mr. Farnham with 2 men arrived with 14 Sturgeon having left another canoe with 16 more aground on a sand bank in Gray's bay. It being a dark night, they could not get off. Sick list as yesterday.

14th. Saturday. Cloudy, wet wea: Wind S. W. In the forenoon, the Canoe Mr. Farnham had left behind arrived with the Sturgeon, People employed as usual. Visited by Comcomley who brought a few Beaver for trade. 5 men sick.

15th. Sunday. Fine, clear, pleasant wea: Wind N. E. Preparations making for Mr. R. Stuart's departure, and the People going for the goods Mr. Hunt left in Cache this side of the Rocky mountains. Sent 2 men up the river for Sturgeon. Visited by a few Indians who brought some Beaver & a few hats. Sick list as yesterday.

16th. Monday. Clear and pleasant wea: Wind N. E. People employed as usual. Visited by a few Cathlamats & Chinook Indians who brought some beaver, clemels & Dried fish. Sick list as yesterday.

17th. Tuesday. Cloudy wet wea: Wind S. W. People employed as usual, between finishing the coal pit, hewing saw logs, preparing & mending canoes, Packing up goods & Provisions, etc., making pack saddles. 2 men sawing, the 2 other Sawyers being sick. Visited by a few Chinooks who brought some matts, hats, etc., for trade.[167]

18th. Wednesday. Wet disagreable wea: Wind South'y. People employed hauling out saw logs, finishing the coal pit, etc. Towards noon, 2 men arrived with a load of hoops for the Cooper. Sick list as yesterday.

19th. Thursday. Wind & Weather much the same as yesterday. People employed much the same also. Last night 2 men arrived with a load of 9 Sturgeons. 4 men sick.

20th. Friday. Cloudy, Wet Wea: Wind South'y. People making axe handles, Sawing plank, finishing & covering the Coal pit, etc. In the afternoon it cleared away. 2 Sawyers still sick. 6 men unfit for duty. Visited by a few Clatsops who traded some Beaver.

21st. Saturday. Cloudy with thick haze; towards noon it cleared away. About 3 P. M., 3 Canoes manned by 9 men left this with Messrs. McGillis & Farnham, who are both going to the Cache in order to fetch down the goods, etc., that were left there.[168] In one of the canoes (which is laden with goods, etc., for Messrs. D. & R. Stuart), Mr. Bruguier (who is to accompany the latter) took his passage. 6 men sick.

22nd. Sunday. Cloudy, disagreeable, wet wea: Wind S. W. About 3 P. M. Messrs. R. Stuart, R. McClellan, J. Reed, B. Jones & 2 Canadians left this to join the canoes that went up yesterday which were to wait for them at

---

[167] Both the "matts" and hats are likely to be examples of the woven reed work for which the natives, especially the women, were known. They were probably used as rainwear, but could also serve as interior partitions, etc.

[168] Hunt had cached (i.e., hidden, usually by burying) his trade goods near present-day Lake Walcott on the Snake River in south-central Idaho. Ronda, *Astoria*, p. 186.

Chilwits village. Mr. R. Stuart with his canoe is to proceed to Mr. D. Stuart's establishment & Mr. Reed with a small assortment of goods & small supply of provisions for Mr. Crooks is to proceed (accompanied by Mr. McClellan, B. Jones, & 2 Canadians, A. Vallée & Fr. Leclerc) down the Missouri to St. Louis and from thence with some dispatches he is entrusted with proceed to New York. 5 men sick.[169]

23rd. Monday. Cloudy wea: Wind South'y. People employed as usual hauling out timber, clearing away & cutting logs. The coal pit being now ready, set it on fire. Visited by a few Chinooks & Tshichilish who brought a few beaver to trade. 6 men unfit for duty.[170]

24th. Tuesday. Rainy, disagreeable wea: Wind S. W. People employed as usual. Found one of our young sows had pigged in the wood. 8 young ones were dead and one alive was taken in the Pen with the sow but soon died also. After Dark one of the Kanakers that had been sent after Sturgeon arrived, having left the 2 others above Tongue Point, which they could not double, having a load of 30 Sturgeon. Five men sick.

25th. Wednesday. Tolerable clar. Frequent showers of Hail & Snow, with a heavy gale at S. W. Last night the shed of the saw pit was blown down by the violence of the wind. The Dolly likewise parted with her hawser. People employed hewing the frame of a house, clearing land, etc., our invalids getting better. 5 men sick.[171]

26th. Thursday. Cloudy, mild wea: Wind variable from N. to S. W.

---

[169] After all the planning and preparations, little will result from this expedition. Going through the Dalles, a series of rapids requiring a long portage, was always a problem for the Astorians. The local tribes, Wishram and Wasco (of the Penutian linguistic stock), considered it their right to charge tolls, i.e., rob groups moving through of as much as possible. As Alexander Ross put it: "To say that there is not a worse path under the sun would perhaps be going a step too far, but to say that, for difficulty and danger, few could equal it, would be saying but the truth." *Adventures,* p. 109. The dispatches for Astor with which John Reed was entrusted were sealed inside a shiny metal box that caught the eye of some Wishrams, who assumed that it must hold valuables. In the fight that followed, Reed suffered a serious wound from a hatchet, two Wishrams (possibly more) were shot, and the box was lost. Franchère describes the fight, *Journal,* pp. 112–14. Stuart took the party on to the post near the confluence of the Columbia and the Okanogan, supplied it, and then returned to Astoria on May 11. Since the reason for Reed's journey was lost and he was badly hurt, he returned as well. One fortunate event did occur during the trip. While returning, the Astorians ran across Ramsay Crooks and John Day, making their way down the river. Robert McClellan was a Pennsylvanian, experienced on the frontier, who had accepted a partnership, possibly from Hunt at the Nodaway camp. As soon as he arrived at Astoria with the first group of overlanders, he decided he wanted no more of the enterprise and would go home at the first opportunity. That came in June, when Robert Stuart left with dispatches for Astor. Ronda, *Astoria,* pp. 136–37, 239–40.

[170] As noted above, n. 71, the Tshichilish were probably Chehalis Indians.

[171] The house will be the second one built; it was made even more necessary by the recent arrival of the overlanders and the hoped-for coming of a supply ship with additional workers.

People employed as yesterday. In the morning sent a canoe to get the sturgeon at Tongue Point, who all returned about noon. Visited by two or three canoes of the Chinooks, who brought us a few Beaver & some dried Uthlecans. About dusk, Messrs. McLennan & Thomas McKay arrived with one Man from the Cowlitzk. The Hunters had met with little success as yet, having caught no more than 11 Beaver, which he Brought with him. Sick list as yesterday.

27th. Friday. Incessant rain all day. Wind S. W. People employed as follows: 2 Men sawing, 2 ditto attending the coal pit, Blacksmith's making axes, preparations making for Mr. McKenzie's departure on a voyage up the Wolamat, Carpenter mending canoes, etc. Our Invalids getting better. 5 men still unfit for duty.[172]

28th. Saturday. Cloudy, wet wea: Wind South'y. People employed much the same as yesterday, between hewing, sawing, etc. In the morning, sent three Kankers up the river after Sturgeon. Sick list much the same as yesterday.[173]

29th. Sunday. Fine mild wea: Wind Variable from N. E. to N. W. but mostly calm. This being Easter Sunday, all hands were treated on the occasion with flour, Grog, & Molasses. Visited by Comcomley, who brought between 30 & 40 Beavers to trade; also by Kamaqhiah, who brought us some Uthlecan. Sick list as yesterday.[174]

30. Monday. Cloudy with some rain, wind S. W. People employed hewing, Burning coals, clearing land, making an inclosure in the garden to plant some turnips, mending canoes, etc. About 1 P. M. Mr. McLennan, T. McKay & B. Rouselle left this in order to proceed up the Cowlitzk to fetch down some of the hunters. 4 men sawing. 4 men sick.

31. Tuesday. Cloudy wea: but mild. Light wind at S. W. People employed much the same as yesterday. About 10 A. M., Messrs. McKenzie & Matthews, with 6 men & 2 canoes, with a small assortment of goods & provisions left this on a voyage up the Wolamat river in order to explore that part of the Country. Visited by several natives who brought some Beaver & 1 Sea Otter to trade. 4 men still unfit for duty.

April 1. Wednesday. Fine mild wea: with intervals of Sun Shine; wind West'y. People employed as usual putting the Store in order, etc. Visited several canoes of Chinooks who brought Uthlecans for sale & a few Beaver.

---

[172] "Wolamat" is an alternative spelling for Willamette; the river was also referred to as McKay's River, presumably in honor of Alexander McKay, the partner lost with the *Tonquin*.

[173] "Kanker" is yet another spelling of Kanaka, a name for a native Hawaiian.

[174] Obviously, it is still short rations at Astoria, if Easter Sunday is celebrated with the sparse repast mentioned here.

Towards evening, Mr. Mumford arrived with the three men that had been sent up the river after Sturgeon, informing us that they could not catch any more. They brought with them a load of dried Uthlecans & Sturgeon. 4 Men sick.[175]

2. Thursday. Cloudy wet wea: Wind West'y. People occupied clearing the Stores, lower cellar, etc.; a party preparing timber for wheel barrows. A number of Indians about us. Traded a few fathom of <u>Uthlecans</u>. Sic list as yesterday.[176]

3rd. Friday. Fine clear wea: but cold with white frost. Wind East'y. People at their usual work. 2 party hewing the frame of two Houses. 2 men attending the coal pit. In the morning Calpo arrived with 3 Geese, having had the misfortune of upsetting his canoe, by which he lost thirteen others, etc. Traded a few Beavers, etc. 3 men sick.[177]

4th. Saturday. Fine clear wea: with white Frost in the morning. Wind N. E., but the afternoon a fresh breeze from the S.W. People employed as yesterday. Sent out 4 Men a Hunting. Visited by a few natives who brought us some uthlecans & a few Beavers. 3 Men sick. The shop being finished, took in the goods into it this afternoon.[178]

5th. Sunday. Wind & wea: as yesterday. About 10 A. M. two of our hunters arrived, having killed a Goose, a Duck, & a dozen of Plovers. The other two arrived about noon but had not killed any thing. Visited by some Chinook Indians who traded some beaver and Uthlecans. 3 men sick.

6th. Monday. Wind & weather much the same as yesterday. People employed between hewing, sawing, preparing Plank for the upper Floor of the Store, etc. Roussel, the Blacksmith unwell. Sent two men up the river to hunt Geese, etc. Visited by a few Indians who traded some Uthlecans & Beaver; also by some Chilwits who brought a letter from Mr. Pillet informing us that he had a suply of 30 Sturgeon on hand. 3 men sick.

7th. Tuesday. Pleasant Clear Sun Shine; wind West'y. People occupied much the same as yesterday. Early this morning sent out 3 men in a canoe to get Sturgeon, sent likewise a Kanaker with Cannan to hunt Elk in young's

---

[175] McDougall doubtless means that the post was visited *by* several canoes of Chinooks.

[176] This is the first reference to a common way of "packaging" uthlecans, i.e., by stringing them through the body and selling or trading them by the fathom, i.e., the length of a man's outstretched arms, five to five and one-half feet.

[177] "2 party" presumably means that two men were working at the task for preparing frame timbers for a dwelling house.

[178] At this time, "shop" was generally used to indicate a place where buying and selling or, in this context, trading, took place. The "store," referred to below on April 6, was where goods were stored. That one building, however small, was devoted to trading indicates that Astoria was developing into a substantial complex.

bay. Visited by a great number of the surrounding tribes who brought some Beaver & dried Fish. After dark two hunters that had been up the river after Geese returned having killed only two. 3 Men sick.

8th. Wednesday. Cloudy; Wind N. W. People occupied as usual. Visited by a number of Indians who brought some Beaver, Otter (Land) and Fish to trade; also the meat of two Elks, which they say are in great numbers on the Clatsop Point. 3 Men Sick.

9th. Thursday. Cloudy, wet wea: Wind S. W. People differently occupied about the Buildings—clearing one end of the Store to lay the upper floor. About noon, Cannan returned having killed nothing. Towards evening Mr. McLennan returned with Brousseau. He Brought us 15 Beavers & an Otter from our hunters. There was a report at the Chelwits that the 3 Canoes with Mr. Stuart had been cut off by the Indians at the First Rapids, and that they were all killed—without exception. The people that had been sent after sturgeon arrived with 19 of of them, 4 of which were entirely destroyed. 4 Men sick.[179]

10th. Friday. Cloudy Morning, rainy. Wind East'y. People employed the afternoon only, hewing etc. In the morning sent out 3 Kanackers up the river after Sturgeon & Hoop poles. We understood this morning by some Indians who came down from the Cathlakamaps that only a skirmish had taken place between our people & the Indians at the rapid, when the latter were put to flight. However, this ought to make us well aware of their bad intentions, and no Small party should attempt to pass there without being well armed and on their guard. Sick list as yesterday, with the addition of Martial, who feels as if he would have another fit of the appoplexy.[180]

11th. Saturday. Clear wea: Wind S. W. People employed much the same as yesterday. Visited by Comcomley who traded a Sea otter & a few Beavers. In the forenoon, Mr. Dorion & family with J. Lapierre returned as they could catch no beaver. Sick list as yesterday.[181]

12th. Sunday. Cloudy wea: calm. This being the anniversary of our landing at this place to form the establishment, all hands were treated with grog,

---

[179] The trouble reported by the Chelwits is a garbled version of what had happened at the Dalles; see above, pp. 78–79, for the departure of the parties; for what had actually happened, see below for successive reports, starting April 10, each painting the incident in less dire terms than the preceding report, until the return of the parties on May 11, 1812.

[180] Hoop poles probably refers to thin poles which could be bent into circles and used as barrel hoops. Cathlakamaps were probably the Cathlakamass, one of the Upper Chinook tribes clustered about the mouth of the Willamette River; see Ruby, Brown, *Guide*, pp. 25, 26, 32. François Martial's "appoplexy" may have been a form of epilepsy.

[181] Pierre Dorion is the guide and interpreter mentioned earlier; see above, n. 160.

etc. Visited by Several canoes of Chenokes in one of which was <u>Stachum</u>, a chief, who was presented a Hat and some trifling articles, after which he and his attendants traded a Sea otter, a few clemels & about 36 Beavers. Sick list as yesterday.[182]

13th. Monday. Cloudy wet wea: Wind S. S. W. Carpenters employed laying the upper Floor of the Store. The greatest part of the People fixing the upper part of the Shed, lodgings, etc., as the house is too small to contain them all. 4 Men Sick.[183]

14th. Tuesday. Cloudy with rain in the Morning. About noon it cleared up. Wind South'y. People employed hewing, etc., others clearing land; carpenters laying floors, Blacksmiths making axes, etc. Visited by a few Clatsops, who brought two indifferent sea otters, one of which they traded. 5 Men sick.

15th. Wednesday. Cloudy morning with a few showers of rain. Towards noon it cleared up & the remainder of the day was tolorable. Wind N. W. People employed much the same as yesterday. At noon Gardépie, Lavaleé & Thomas McKay arrived, as they found little or no beaver to catch. Soon after Brugere & Delome arrived with a load of Hoops & three Kanakers, also with 12 Sturgeon & a load of Hoops. Visited by a few Indians who brought us Some Small Fish to trade. 5 Men sick.

16th. Thursday. Clear by intervalls with a few light showers; wind S. W. People employed much the same as yesterday. Mr. Mumford painting the barge, 2 Men making oars for ditto. Visited by a few natives who brought a few beaver & some dried fish to trade, etc. 5 Men sick.

17th. Friday. Cloudy, with partial showers. Wind South'y. People employed much the same as yesterday. Visited by a few Chinooks who trade about 18 Beaver and Otter skins and the meat of a young Elk. Sick list as yesterday.

18. Saturday. Cloudy wet wea: Wind South'y. People employed indoors, viz. Making Barrows, fixing the upper part of the Store, etc. Towards noon, Lavalle returned with Wm Karimou & Powrowie, but brought no sturgeon, as they had not caught any since 12th instant. 2 Men likewise came for provisions for the Hunters Dorion & Ignace. Sick list as yesterday.[184]

---

[182] "Chenokes" is yet another alternative (and inventive) spelling of Chinook. Stachum may have been a chief of one of the villages in the area subordinate to Comcomly. Sea otter pelts were the most valuable ones available in the area.

[183] One of the few references found in the log to what must have been the very crowded conditions at Astoria caused by the arrival of the overlanders.

[184] The "[wheel]barrows" would be for the movement of goods about the post. Karimou and Powrowie were Hawaiians. Apparently Dorion and his family were living away from the post, perhaps at Young's Bay with Ignace, the Iroquois hunter and his family.

Journal
Commencing 19th April 1812
Ending 31st December 1812

April 19th. Sunday. Cloudy, dry, cold weather. Wind S. W. The scarcity of provisions, and understanding from the Indians that there was a good fishery of Sturgeon at the Chelwits, about thirty miles above the Factory, induced us to send a clerk & 2 men to attend lines, etc., at which they were steadily employed from third February last to this day. During which time they supplied the Factory with Sturgeon and [gap] of <u>uthlecans</u> or smelts. 4 men were almost constantly employed during the same time to fetch the Fish. The misfortune of having our only Hunter laid up with a sore foot since last 13th February retarded the progress that would otherwise have been done at the establishment and compelled us to purchase from the natives about [gap] fathoms of dried Smelts at the rate of three fathoms of fish for 1 fathom Gurrahs as also ten or twelve bales of dried Sturgeon, at the rate of one fathom Calico for a Bale containing 10 Pieces of which dried fish we have now a supply for nearly a month, by which time we hope the salmon will be in abundance. The people, too, perhaps owing to the change of diet, are more or less affected, & we have constantly 4 or 5 men on the sick list.[1]

---

[1] The fishery party is the one referred to several times previously, see above, February 3, 1812. The reference to only one hunter is puzzling, as McDougall had hired a Cathlamet to hunt; in addition, the Iroquois, Ignace, and, increasingly, Ben Jones had hunted for the post. Later, McDougall will note that the Cathlamet had failed in his duty; perhaps he was absent at this time. The hunter with the sore foot is Ignace. See above, I, n. 62, for an explanation of fathoms of smelts and gurrahs. Calico was a cheap cotton cloth, originally woven in Calcutta, India. Only a number could be fitted in the gap in the log. McDougall may be under-stating the extent of illness, especially as it could well be scurvy, from which even the Indians suffered at this time of the year. The Hudson's Bay Company had discovered that an ample supply of fresh meat generally prevented scurvy. Fresh vegetables also provided the necessary nutrients and while potatoes and similar vegetables were not as effective as leafy ones, they were usually eaten in quantity and were available through the winter. The wapato referred to above, I, n. 106, was similar to the potato in this respect. See Kenneth J. Carpenter, *The History of Scurvy and Vitamin C* (Cambridge: Cambridge University Press, 1986), pp. 137, 224, 242, for relevant entries. See Coues, ed., *New Light*, II, 859, for Alexander Henry's comment that, owing to the shortage of fish, in late March, early April, the Indians ate quantities of berries, grasses, and the like. "This vegetable diet has the good effect of purifying the blood and clearing them of scabs. I am told that by June, when the salmon come in, they are clear of scabs, from which at present, few, if any, are exempt." Scabs were one of the first

20th. Monday. Clear pleasant wea: Wind variable from N. E. to W. People employed as follows. Ten men hewing, 4 men sawing, 3 men at the coal pit; 2 Men at the Shallop: 5 getting fire wood and other necessary work about the buildings. The Carpenter, Cooper, Blacksmiths, etc., at their respective works. Visited by a few natives, also by Squamaquiah, who brought a few beaver to trade. 4 Men Sick.[2]

April 21st. Tuesday. Fine, clear weather. Wind S. W. People occupied much the same as yesterday. 6 Men clearing down at the wharf. Roussil, the Blacksmith, unwell. In the afternoon Coté, one of our best axe men, cut his wrist very bad. Visited by Calpo, who traded a few Beaver skins. 6 men sick.[3]

22nd. Wednesday. Cloudy, wet wea: Wind South'y. The hewers having finished the frame of two houses last night, sett them clearing the spot which is intended for those buildings. But the bad weather compelled them to turn in doors, making wheell barrows, Boxes for putting lead into, etc. Carpenters at their usual employment. Roussil and Cooper unwell. 7 men sick. Traded 10 Beaver skins from Calpo.[4]

23rd. Thursday. Incessant rain all day, with violent gusts of wind from the Westward. People severally occupied indoors, making Balls, etc. The carpenter putting up a partition in the upper part of the store. Towards evening the three men that had been sent up the river after Boat Knees arrived with 58 of them. 6 Men sick.

24th. Friday. Clear pleasant wea: People Employed Rolling logs, cutting stumps, and clearing away behind the Buildings. Visited by a few Clatsops who brought us about 20 Beavers to trade. In the afternoon Calpo arrived with about 15 Geese. In the morning sent three men up the river after boat knees. About dusk the whale Boat was launched and rowed round the Bay

---

symptoms of scurvy. Franchère referred to the Astorians' consumption of berries, etc., obtained from the natives for their antiscorbutic effect (*Journal*, 97–98, and n. 4). The following winter it was necessary to form a special camp at Oak Point, and send all those suffering from scurvy to be treated there under Franchère's supervision; see ibid., p. 118.

[2] Squamaquiah was probably Kamaquiah, the Chinook headman referred to above, June 12, 1811; see I, n. 58.

[3] "Joseph Cotte" is on a list of Pacific Fur Company employees for the winter of 1813–14; his capacity is given as "M. & Sawyer." See the Appendix. Since he is not listed on the *Tonquin*, he must have been one of the overlanders. This is one of the rare entries mentioning a relatively serious injury in the arduous work of clearing and maintaining a clear area around the post.

[4] The "houses" are dwelling houses for the increased population; see below, May 9th, for the arrival of the *Beaver* with twenty-five more persons for the post.

by 10 Rowers, She appeared to be very smart and does credit to the Builder, it being his first trial. 4 Men sick.[5]

April 25th. Saturday. Clear, pleasant weather, Wind S. W. Part of the people employed Rolling logs, cutting stump, etc. Carpenters, Cooper, Blacksmith. etc., at their respective work. Mr. Mumford & Jos. Lapierre overhauling the Shallop. In the morning Watatcum came in with 3 Geese. Sent out 2 men a hunting. Calpo left this today in order to proceed as far as the Wolamat, to purchase Salmon which they begin to catch at that place, He was entrusted with a letter for Mr. D. McKenzie, informing him respecting the news we had heard about the murder of our people at the Falls, and warning him against the Indians, etc. Traded a few skins. Sick list as yesterday.[6]

26th. Sunday. Cloudy with Frequent Showers of rain. Cold raw wind from the West'd. The two hunters that had gone out yesterday returned about noon without success. 5 Men sick (i.e.), unfit for duty.

27th. Monday. Squally, with frequent showers of Hail & rain. People employed cutting up logs, rooting out stumps, etc. 2 Men cleaning & repairing arms, etc. 5 Men sick.

28th. Tuesday. Weather much the same as yesterday. People employed much the same also. In the morning Mr. Pillet with the two men that had been sent with him as far as the Cathlapootle Nation, in order to bring off an American by the Name of Pelton (which we heard had been detained there on his way down about two months ago) which he effected with a little difficulty. He heard on his trip that a few miles below the falls, Mr. Stuart & his party having engaged some of the natives to transport his bales, etc., over the Portage. The latter after loading their horses ran away. Which Mr. Stuart Perceiving, he ordered them to come back, but they continuing their way to the hills, he told them he would fire, and effectually discharged his piece at them and killed one of their chiefs, after which a skirmish took place in which Mr. R. Stuart Received a wound in the neck but not mortal, as

---

[5] It is unfortunate that the name of the builder is not recorded, but McDougall almost always referred to the craftsmen simply by their trade, not their name. This anonymous craftsman is probably Henry Wicks (sometimes Weeks), who traded places with Johann Kaster (sometimes Koaster or "translated" as Castles), the original shipwright/carpenter retained for the post, when Kaster proved inept with the earliest stages of the *Dolly*'s construction. Kaster died on the *Tonquin*, see above, I, n. 27

[6] Watatcum is the Cathlamet hunter previously hired; see June 7, 1811, I, n. 54. McKenzie left Astoria March 31 on a trading expedition up the Willamette. The "murder of our people" referred to the much-exaggerated story of the incident at the Dalles where John Reed lost the dispatch box; see below, May 11, 1812, for the final report on the incident.

they continued their march the next day. The nations name that committed the robbery, according to what information Mr. Pillet could get, is Chilwits, a powerfull and ferocious tribe. The three Kanakers that had been sent after boat knees likewise returned with a load of them.[7]

Visited by 3 Canoes with the chief of the Chelwits, who traded (as well as a few Kelemooks) about 38 Beaver skins and a small Sea Otter, some dried sturgeon & Seal oil. 5 Men sick. In the morning 2 Men arrived from our Hunters with the meat of 3 Elks. Our Cathlamat Hunter also came in with the meat of a young Elk.[8]

29th. Wednesday. Clear, pleasant wea: Wind S. W. People employed cutting up logs, rolling, clearing, etc. Carpenter finishing wheel Barrow. Cannan repairing muskets. Blacksmiths mending axes. Convalescent People making Balls, etc. In the morning 2 of our hunters came in, having killed 5 Geese only. An Indian brought in the meat of a small Deer. 5 Men sick.

30th. Thursday. Wind & weather as yesterday. People employed cutting & carrying out Poles for garden fence. Carpenter making a gun carriage. Blacksmiths fixing wheel Barrows, etc. Visited by Comcomly and a chief of the Cathlapootles. The former brought a few beaver skins for trade. 2 men employed making a Seine. 6 men sick.[9]

May 1. Friday. Clear, pleasant weather. Wind S. W. People employed carrying out fence Poles. One party enclosing the garden, 2 men clearing

---

[7] The Cathlapootle were identified above, I, n. 79. Archibald Pelton was a native of Northampton, Massachusetts, who went trapping as a member of a party employed by Manuel Lisa of St. Louis. His experiences, during the winter of 1810–11 after he had become separated from his associates, deranged him. He found his way to the Nez Perce and was living with them along the Clearwater when he was discovered by Donald McKenzie's segment of the Astorian overlanders. They brought him to Astoria. When the former Pacific Fur Company employees left Fort George, formerly Astoria, in the spring of 1814, he stayed behind with the North Westers. Sometime later, while tending a charcoal pit away from the post, he was killed by a Clatsop who mistook him for a white who had done the native an injury. The Clatsop was tried by a court composed of North Westers and Chinook elders of both sexes. See Alvin M. Josephy, Jr., The *Nez Perce Indians and the Opening of the Northwest* (New Haven, Conn.: Yale University Press, 1965, pp. 46–47, and n. 12; hereafter, Josephy, *Nez Perce*, and J. Neilson Barry, "Archibald Pelton, the First Follower of Lewis and Clark," *Washington Historical Quarterly*, 19 (1928), 199–201. Pelton's conduct was so erratic that his name came in time to mean crazy or drunken conduct in the Chinook trade lingo of the lower Columbia; see Ruby, Brown, *Chinook*, p. 150. The reference to Mr. Stuart's fight is to the trouble Robert Stuart and party had moving through the Dalles. This was first reported above on April 9; see also below, May 11, when some of Stuart's party returned.

[8] The Chelwits were identified above, I, n. 19. The chief was Ka-las-kan; see I, n. 68. The "Kelemooks" may have been an alternative rendering of clemels, the elk skin armor referred to above; see I, n. 96.

[9] The name of the chief is unknown.

and preparing the earth to receive the seeds, 2 Men making a Flag Staff. The tradesmen at their usual occupations. 5 Men sick.[10]

2nd. Saturday. Cloudy weather. Wind S. W. People employed in the forenoon putting up a flag staff, the remainder of the day making fence, carrying out poles, for ditto, etc. Visited by a few Chinooks who traded 10 Beavers. Sick list as yesterday.

May 3rd. Sunday. Cloudy with partial showers of rain. In the morning a thick mist, which was dispelled by a fresh West'y Breeze, about noon. Some of our invalids getting better. 5 Men sick.

4th. Monday. Pleasant with a few light showers of rain. Wind West'y. People employed carrying out fence poles. 2 men making fence, 4 Men sawing, [2 Men busy refitting the Dolly.] In the morning, sent out 2 men a hunting, so that we have now 6 Men out after provisions. Tradesmen at their usual occupations. 4 Men sick. Visited by Cassacass (Comcomly's Son) who brought a few Beavers to trade & some dried Queenhalt salmon, which he also traded.[11]

5th. Tuesday. Wind and weather much the same as yesterday. People employed in the same manner also. In the afternoon, the fence having been completed, a party were set rooting out stumps, another cutting down timber for a wharf, etc. Visited by a few Wakaicums who brought us 24 Fresh Salmon Trout. Calpo arrived from the Cathlacamaps and confirmed the news brought by Mr. Pillet with some little difference. But to all appearance the party (with the Exception of Mr. Stuart) are gone on safe. He likewise adds that they met Mr. Crooks & party above the Falls. who are gone back with them. Mr. McKenzie to all appearance is gone on safe and has caught some beaver. 5 Men sick.[12]

6th. Wednesday. Cloudy with frequent showers of rain and violent gusts of wind from the Westward. People employed hauling out Timber for a Wharf. 7 men clearing a spot to plant Turnips, etc. 6 Men sick.

---

[10] Although McDougall had not been specific, last summer's garden had apparently been productive. Certainly, the effort being put into this summer's would indicate that, especially enclosing the area.

[11] The bracketed words are a marginal addition. Queenhalt salmon were a variety of salmon taken by the Quinault Indians on the central Washington coast; see above, I, n. 53 for an identification of the tribe.

[12] The wharf will provide a safe place to moor the *Dolly* and the expected supply vessel; it was needed because of the difficulty of anchoring safely near the post. Robert Stuart had gone on to supply the post on the Okanogan. Crooks is Ramsay Crooks, a partner and one of the overlanders who was accompanied by John Day. Donald McKenzie was trapping and trading on the Willamette.

May 7th. Thursday. Clear pleasant wea: Wind S. W. People occupied rooting out stumps, making a Wharf, Fixing and Painting gun carriages repairing canoes etc. After Breakfast, Messrs McDougall, McLennan, Thomas McKay, & 4 Hands went over the river in order to asscertain the truth of a report that a vessel was laying outside, which we saw from this place in the afternoon. They all returned about Dusk. Sick list as yesterday, with the addition of William the Kanaker. By Mr. McDougall's report the vessel was seen (from a promantary near Comcomly's house), Passing and repassing from Cape Disappointment to Point Adams, and apparently sounding or trying the channel. He adds that they saw the Smoak and heard the report of a Gun. In this manner did the vessel appear and disappear alternatively 3 or 4 times.[13]

8th. Friday. Clear pleasant weather. Wind S. W. Seven People employed framing a Wharf, making a platform for the big guns, etc.; a party cleaning a spot for a Garden, clearing the square inside of the Buildings, etc. Early this morning the Sail we had seen yesterday made its appearance going to and fro from Cape Disappointment to Point Adams. She fired three guns, which we answered with as many. We expected to see her come in with the evening flood Tide but were disappointed. After breakfast, Messrs. McDougall, D. McLennan, Thomas McKay with 5 hands took a little provisions & a swivel in order to proceed to the Cape and try to prevail on some Indians to go out to the vessel if she neared the river, or if this was impracticable to make them signals, as they seem to be in expectation of our sending out a pilot, &c. Got the sails of the Dolly bent. 5 Men sick.[14]

May 9th. Saturday. Mild pleasant weather. Wind S. W. In the morning, People employed sinking a pier for a Wharf, etc. Saw the vessel about noon attempting to come in, which she seemingly effected and got to anchor off Cape Disappointment. Being fearful that she was agground the Dolly was sent to her aid, in case she should stand in need of assistance. About dark, Mr. McDougall returned in the Barge, accompanied by Messrs. John Clark

---

[13] This is the first sight the Astorians had of the long awaited supply ship, *Beaver*, which had left New York in October 1811; in addition to supplies, she brought John Clarke, a partner, five clerks, and twenty-one mechanics and French Canadian laborers; see Jones, ed., *Astorian Adventure*, Parts 1 and 2 for clerk Alfred Seton's record of the journey out. Seton and the others had heard of the *Tonquin*'s loss during their stopover in Hawaii. The master of the *Beaver*, Cornelius Sowle, was as fearful of the bar at the Columbia's mouth as Captain Thorn had been, but he was more considerate of the safety of his men. He will run the bar on the 9th and bring the vessel into Baker's Bay the following day.

[14] The platform is for the large naval cannon shown in front of the post in an illustration following p. 142.

(proprietor), Alfred Seaton & G. Ehnenger with a Canadian & an American having succeded in getting outside of the bar, accompanied by Comcomly in his large canoe and getting safe on board the Beaver. This relieved our anxiety and apprehensions with regard to the safety of the vessel. 6 men sick.[15]

10th Sunday. Wind & weather much the same as yesterday. About 8 A.M. had the satisfaction of seeing the Beaver getting to anchor in Bakers Bay. Sent the Barge with Mr. Pillet to fetch the live stock up to the Factory. About 4 P. M. Mr. Rhodes, first mate of the Beaver, with Mr. Mumford, came up sounding the channel from Baker's Bay to the Factory, which they found very shallow. Sick list as yesterday.[16]

11th. Monday. Clear pleasant weather. Wind S. W. Early this morning we were agreeably surprised with the arrival of four canoes from Mr. David Stuart's Establishment, having been compelled to come back owing to the robbery committed by the Indians at the Falls. They having taken two bales of goods, and after wounding Mr. Reed, robbed him also of a small package which unfortunately contained the material papers intrusted to his care. This occasioned their return. Mr. D. Stuart had upwards of one thousand Beaver skins at his establishment, which he left in charge of Messrs. A. Ross & McGillis. On their way down they met Mr. Crooks and John Day, who had both been robbed of the little property they were possessed of, and were living among the Indians. Messrs. McKenzie & Mathews returned from the Wolamat, of which river they give a very satisfactory account, having caught Beavers and traded [gap]. The Banks of the river abounds in game of all kinds. Deer are very numerous. About 1 P.M. the Barge returned from the vessel with the live stock, consisting of 3 She & he Goats, 2 fowls, viz. Hens, 2 Geese, and 2 ducks. Soon after, the Dolly anchored in the bay, having the following passenger Settlers on Board. Messrs. Nichols, Halsey & Cox, clerks; Mr. Wadsworth, Master of Shallops and a Sandwich Island woman; 8 Labourers and tradesmen & 3 Sandwich Islanders. They sounded the channel comming up, but found it shallow as before.[17]

---

[15] As noted, Clarke was one of the partners of the North West Company; Seton was a clerk, George Ehninger was supercargo of the *Beaver*; he was Astor's nephew, the son of his sister, Catherine.

[16] Rhodes was Benjamin Rhodes. The livestock, acquired in the Hawaiian Islands, are described in May 11's entry. Clarke had also, according to Seton, hired ten natives as laborers. In addition, three of the clerks, Seton included, were allowed to take a boy along. At Astoria, the boys are not differentiated from the adults. See Jones, ed., *Astorian Adventure*, p. 81.

[17] Charles A. Nicoll ("Nichols"), John Halsey, and Ross Cox are clerks. William Wads-

12th. Tuesday. Wind & weather much the same as yesterday. People employed much the same as usual preparing the garden, planting potatoes. In the morning, Messrs. McLennan & Wadsworth with 4 Hands went out to sound the Channel in the Barge and returned about noon, with the same old news. After dinner, they again departed (accompanied by Messrs. Ehnenger & Seaton) in the Dolly. Towards evening she was seen agground on a Shoal inside of spit bank. Our Hunters Dorian & Ignace returned without having killed anything. Sent out 2 More up the river. 6 Men sick.[18]

13th. Wednedsday. Fine clear weather. Wind S. W. People occupied at various usefull jobs. All the men come on Shore for the Establishment set at work. In the evening, received a visit from Captain Sowle, on which occasion a Salute of 5 Guns was fired and the Colors hoisted. 7 Men sick. N.B.: Mr. B. Clapp came to stay on shore.[19]

May 14th. Thursday. Fine Pleasant weather, and the warmest we have had this season. Light wind at N. E. Early this morning, Capt. Sowle left us in order to sound the channel down to the vessel. He told us last night that he could not think of bringing the vessel opposite the Factory on account of the shoalness of the water, but the channel being good on the opposite side of the river, he would fetch her as near as possible. Set a party of men cutting and piling wood to make Coals. Sent out 4 Hunters this morning in Young's Bay. Sick list as yesterday.

15th. Friday. Cloudy with thick Haze. People employed at different jobs. A party cutting & piling wood for a coal pit. In the morning St. Amant, one of the best men, cut his foot very bad, having separated it through & through, the whole breadth of the axe. Carpenters busy fixing the stores, all the young gentlemen putting the store in order, as we intend soon to take an inventory. 8 men sick, Jones & his party came in, having killed an Elk, a Goose, & a Beaver.[20]

---

worth was an American ship's officer who, because of a disagreement with his captain, had come ashore on Hawaii, where he was hired by Clarke; he apparently insisted on bringing along a woman as a condition of employment, not being used "to live in a state of single blessedness." Cox, *Columbia*, p. 45. As "Master of Shallops," he replaced the difficult Mumford, but only for a time; he probably left on the *Beaver* in July. Donald McKenzie and William Mathews's report on the Willamette was so favorable that a post was established on the river, near Salem.

[18] I have not been able to locate "spit bank," other than to note the obvious: that it apparently was within sight of the post. In that area, the Columbia is very shoaly, something which should be obvious by now. It could be any one of several areas indicated in a map ("estuary") following p. 142.

[19] This was Captain Sowle's first visit to the post; hence, the ruffles and flourishes. Benjamin Clapp was one of the clerks who came out on the *Beaver*.

[20] St. Amant's injury sounds crippling, and McDougall notes on May 31 that he will

16th. Saturday. Fine, clear weather, wind South'y. People employed much the same as yesterday. In the evening the Dolly arrived from Baker's Bay, having on Board Messrs. R. Stuart, G. Ehnenger & D. McLennan, & 5 men including 3 Kanakers. About noon Gardipie returned unsuccessful, after dark. Dorion likewise returned without success. 8 men unfit for duty. Set the coal pit on fire. Captain Sowle intends to come up tomorrow if the wind and weather permitt.[21]

17th. Sunday. Wind & weather much the same as yesterday. After Break-fast Mr. Hunt and some of our young gentlemen with a few men went over to the Chinook villages, where he was very hospitably entertained. Mr. Crooks with another party went to view Capt Lewis & Clarke's house up netut creek. Visited by a party of the Celemax nation who are on their way to the Chelwits on a war excursion, Sick list as yesterday.[22]

18th. Monday. Fine, pleasant weather. Wind South'y. People employed burning coals, rolling & piling timber, finishing the wharf, hoeing the gar-den, etc. The tradesmen at different usefull Jobs. 7 men sick. Visited by a few of the Clatsops, who traded about 18 or 20 Beaver Skins. Sent out 7 Men hunting.

19th. Tuesday. Fine mild weather, wind westerly. People employed Piling wood for another coal pit, cutting & carrying out timber for the Wharf, rolling & piling timber to clear land, etc. Tradesmen variously occupied. About sun down 4 of our hunters returned with the meat of an Elk. 7 Men sick.

20th. Wednesday. Fine Clear Weather, Wind southerly. People occupied much the same as yesterday. In the morning, a party with the whale boat went down to Bakers Bay. The men that had come with the meat of the Elk sett off again this morning. 8 Men Sick.

21st. Thursday. Cloudy weather; Wind variable from N.E. to S.W. Peo-ple employed variously, hewing and hauling out Timber for the wharf, a party working at the coal pit, the Kanakers hoeing and sowing the garden. Carpenters, cooper, Blacksmiths & Taylors all employed at their respective trades. Sick list as yesterday.

May 22d. Friday. Cloudy, wet weather, Wind Southerly. people employed in doors, Packing furs, making wheel Barrows, axe-handles, etc. In the

---

probably be on the sick list for a long time. Although McDougall does not note any further treatment, St. Amant is accompanying hunters on July 13th.

[21] Jean Baptiste Gardipie was a hunter hired during the overland trek; Ronda, *Astoria*, p. 135 and Appendix, No. 63.

[22] Netut Creek is known as the Lewis and Clark River today; it is west of Astoria.

morning, Mr. Hunt with [gap] Men went down to the vessel. This evening, all our hunters returned with the meat of an Elk. 9 Men Sick.

23d. Saturday. Cloudy weather, Wind W.S.W. People variously employed Piling, rolling & Burning logs, covering the Wharf, etc. About noon the Dolly arrived with a cargo from the Beaver. Soon after, Mr. Hunt returned with intelligence that Captain Sowle had determined not to come up, as the Shallop would unload her as fast where She Laid, as if he came opposite the factory. Mr. Hunt left a man to chop fire wood for the Ship. Out of the number of men intended for the Settlement, 4 Kanakers & 4 White men are yet on Board. Weeks, our Ship carpenter has been constantly employed on Board the Beaver Since the 12th Instant. 8 Men Sick.

24th. Sunday. Fine agreable weather, Wind Westerly. In the morning, Messrs. Farnham & Cox with 4 men left this in order to proceed to some of the villages above to purchase canoes. Mr. McDougall went down to the Ship and returned about sun down. Sick list as yesterday. Visited by Kamaquiáh and the Chief of the Cathlapootles, who brought us some fresh and dried Salmon, Sturgeon, Wapatoes & Beaver to trade.[23]

25th. Monday. Fine, Clear wea: wind S. W. People occupied rolling off logs, clearing land, & Two carpenters making a dormant window in the Store. Began taking the Inventory. About 1 P.M. the Dolly arrived with a cargo from the Beaver. She returned immediately. Mr. Hunt went down in her. Mr. D. Stuart went down to the clatsops to purchase canoes. 8 Men Sick.[24]

May 26th. Tuesday. Fine Clear Weather; Wind Westerly. People occupied as yesterday. In the morning Messrs. Farnham & Cox returned without success. About 2 P.M. the Dolly arrived with a load, having on board Mr. Hunt & Mr. Rhodes, the first mate, who returned immediately. Towards evening, sent Messrs. Wallace & Halsey with 4 men in the barge to get some axe handles which are already cut opposite Pugets Island, 7 Men Sick.[25]

27th. Wednesday. Fine, Clear weather, Wind as yesterday. People occupied, chopping, taking out coals, clearing land, Carpenters, Blacksmiths, Taylors & Cooper all busily employed at their respective trades. [N.B.: The Dolly came up with a load and returned immediately.] Towards evening

---

[23] Note that the Astorians are now purchasing canoes from the natives, although they will continue to build them themselves.

[24] "Dormant window" is an antique usage for dormer window.

[25] Pugets Island is identified by Philip Ashton Rollins as present-day Deer Island, about six miles down river from St. Helens, Oregon; see Rollins, ed., *Stuart's Narrative*, p. 31, n. 42. Their destination was probably modern Puget Island, about twenty miles above Astoria.

Dorion & Ignace came in with the meat of 2 Elk. Jones, Day & Montigny & Baker went out a hunting. Visited by a few Kelemax who traded a few Clemels & Beaver. 8 Men Sick.[26]

28th. Thursday. Wind & Weather much the same as yesterday. In the after noon had some rain. People Employed much the same as yesterday. About 3 P.M. the Dolly arrived with a load. Towards sun down, Messrs. Wallace & Halsey arrived with a load of oak axe handles. Sick list as yesterday.

29th. Friday. Disagreeable, wet weather. People for the most part cutting up logs, preparing axe handles, etc. In the morning the Dolly, sailed down, to get another load. Busy Stowing & unpacking goods, etc. 9 Men Sick.

30th. Saturday. Same wet weather as yesterday. People occupied for the most part indoors, the Carpenter & Boat Builder repairing canoes, etc. Visited some chilwit Indians who traded a few Wapatoes & Small Fish. Sick list as yesterday.

May 31st. Sunday. Rainy unpleasant weather, rather cold, with violent gusts of wind from the Westward. Our sick are getting on very slowly. St. Amant & Labonté will in all probability be detained from the nature of their complaints a long time. The number of men actually unfit for Service by ruptures & sores, etc., amounts to day to no less than ten. In the evening, 6 of our hunters returned, having been unsuccessfull owing principally to the bad weather which attended them all the time they were out.[27]

June 1st. Monday. Weather cloudy and quite cool; wind Westerly. Mr. D. Stuart went over to the Chinook Village for the purpose of trading for Canoes. Returned in the afternoon with one only. People employed at rebuilding the Wharf, which was found not sufficiently high for the tides. Carpenter & Boat builder repairing and altering canoes. Patterson making some conveniences for the Store. Other Mechanics occupied as usually at their different trades. Sandwich Islanders clearing the ground back of the buildings. Sick list as yesterday.[28]

---

[26] The bracketed material is a marginal notation. "Kelemax" is possibly an alternative spelling for Tillamooks.

[27] Louis Labonté was one of the overlanders who arrived with Wilson Price Hunt. On February 26, he is identified as a carpenter by trade (see Appendix, No. 87) and recorded as assisting William Mathews at an unspecified task. Though there has been no indication of an injury, McDougall notes him getting better on March 3. Joseph St. Amant was injured on May 15, from a cut by edged tools. These must have been frequent, but they are seldom noted by McDougall. Even more unusual is his note of "ruptures," that is, hernias, and sores, presumably from venereal disease, incapacitating a number of men.

[28] John Patterson was probably a carpenter. He was hired in New York in October 1811 for a salary of $180 a year, which was more than most of the clerks were receiving, and came to Oregon on the *Beaver*. See "Articles of Agreement," Porter, *Astor*, I, 475–78. He left with Wilson Hunt and several others on the *Albatross*, August 25, 1813.

2nd. Tuesday. Clear and pleasant Weather. Wind from N.E. to West. People employed during the fore noon same as yesterday. In the afternoon at Clearing the Land, fixing axe handles and different Jobs. The Dolly arrived from Bakers Bay in the afternoon, where she had been detained for two days in a violent storm of Wind & Rain. Parted both her Cables and narrowly escaped being driven ashore, but fortunately had one of the Beaver's anchors on board, by the assistance of which it was prevented. The Ship likewise was in considerable difficulty and damaged her Cables very much. The Dolly brought up little else besides the Blacksmith's Tools, Forge, Bellows, Anville, etc., on account of the confusion on board Ship.

June 3rd. Wednesday. Weather as yesterday, clear and pleasant. Wind fresh at Westward. Early in the morning B. Jones was sent hunting, who returned in the evening, having Killed an Elk at a short distance of two or three miles from this. People employed at cutting & clearing the land. Carpenters & Boat Builder repairing and altering canoes. Arranged the other Blacksmith's Tools got from the Ship and set him to work. Cooper unwell and off duty. 6 men sick. In the afternoon received a visit from Captain Sowle who remains the night with us. The Dolly, started again for Baker's Bay at 12 o'clock.[29]

4th. Thursday. Wind and Weather as yesterday. Despatched a number of men early this morning for the Elk Killed yesterday, who returned with it in a few hours. Messrs. Matthews, Seton & Halsey with a number of men started up the River to procure some oak Timber for the Ship. Mr. McClellan & B. Jones went out hunting.[30] After breakfast, Captain Sowle returned

---

[29] There were apparently several men skilled or reasonably adept at blacksmithing at Astoria. Augustin Roussel had come out on the *Tonquin* as a blacksmith, along with Giles LeClerc, identified as a silversmith (in the 1813–14 roster, he is reduced to simple laborer; Appendix, No. 103). William Cannon was recruited as a hunter by Wilson Price Hunt at Mackinac Island in August 1810 (Ronda, *Astoria*, p. 121) and arrived with the first overland groups in January 1812. He is identified as a blacksmith by Russell (*Firearms*, pp. 381–82), although there is no direct evidence in the log that he worked as such at Astoria, etc. On the roster of Pacific Fur Company employees referred to above, "William Canning" (No. 34) is listed as a millwright. François DuCharquette (No. 37), Francis William Hodgins (No. 69), and Michel Sanson (No. 157) are listed as blacksmiths, along with Augustin Roussel (No. 150). Micajah Baker (No. 20) signed the "Articles of Agreement" with John Jacob Astor in October 1811 and came out on the *Beaver*. See "Articles of Agreement," Porter, *Astor*, I, 475–78. He is carried on the roster as "Free" and described as a blacksmith. Others worked at the craft without explicit recognition of their status as a skilled worker; for example, John Baptiste Pillon, No. 137, is on the roster as a laborer, yet he was working, along with Baker, Hodgins, and Sanson on April 5, 1813, on the forge. Louis LaBonté, No. 87, is listed as a carpenter, but on several occasions, he was recorded as working at blacksmith jobs; for example, see below, January 26, 1813. See below, note 31, for Daniel Perry ("Purry").

[30] The location of this oak timber is not apparent. Oak Point, at that time located on the south bank of the Columbia, near present-day Crims Island, about fifty miles from the river's

again to the Ship. People employed as yesterday. The Dolly arrived in the afternoon from Baker's Bay, in which came Mr. William Wadsworth & Daniel Purry. The former was engaged at the Sandwich Islands as a Clerk and Navigator, the latter in New York a Blacksmith by trade, having untill now been employed on board the Ship. Mr. McClellan & Jones returned towards evening without success. Three men that had been sent up the River after Oak Timber on Monday returned this morning with a load. Visited by numbers of Indians who traded some Wapatoes, and a few Clemels. Sick list as yesterday.[31]

June 5th. Friday. Morning clear and pleasant with light airs from Westward; afternoon cloudy. Sent three men up the River for Timber. People employed as yesterday. At 10 o'clock the Dolly started down for Baker's Bay. Went in her Mr. William Wadsworth, who is going with the Ship on the Coast. Sent likewise Garopie down to hunt for Capt Sowle. Purchased of some Indians the meat of an Elk and a few Wapatoes. Three men employed all Day fixing the Seine and making other preparations for fishing. The Dolly arrived again in the afternoon with some few goods on board. Sick list as for several days past.[32]

6th. Saturday. Morning cloudy with squalls of fine Rain. Afternoon clear and pleasant with Wind at Westerly. Messrs. Matthews, Seton, & Halsey with their party returned from their jaunts, having succeeded in getting the timber necessary, traded also a number of fresh Salmon, Beaver Skins & Clemels. The Dolly started again for Bakers Bay at 12 o'clock. People variously employed, as for several days past. Sick list the same.

7th. Sunday. Fine pleasant Weather, with the Wind light from Westward. Visited by a number of Indians from whom traded some fresh Salmon. At 2 o'clock the Dolly returned with the few remaining articles that are now to be landed from the Beaver. Messrs. Reed & Cox also returned this forenoon, who had been sent yesterday down to the Clatsop Village for the purpose of trying the new Seine for Salmon. Caught but three.

June 8th. Monday. Cloudy, Calm weather. People variously employed.

---

mouth is a possible location, but this depends entirely on the name of the area. See Franchère, *Journal*, p. 93, n. 2. It is also possible that the timber was obtained from several areas or wherever found.

[31] Purry is yet another blacksmith. He is probably Daniel Perry, who signed on with Astor in New York City in October 1811 and came out on the *Beaver*; see "Articles of Agreement," Porter, *Astor*, I, 475–78. There is no further mention of him. The men who returned with oak timbers are a separate party from those who were sent off on Thursday. McDougall has several parties out for that purpose.

[32] Wadsworth was apparently going on the *Beaver*, anchored for safety in Baker's Bay. After this, he is not mentioned in the log.

Mechanics all employed at their several occupations. Three men working at Making a Tent, oil cloths & Bags, at which they were busy during the last week. A number employed making Paddles & Oars for the Canoes. The remainder, with the Sandwich Islanders, at work clearing away near the buildings. 6 of the men and 2 Sandwich Islanders sick.

9th. Tuesday. Clear and pleasant Weather with fresh breezes from the Northward. John Day went out hunting in the morning. In the afternoon returned unsuccessful. People employed same as yesterday Clearing Land, making oil cloths, Painting Tent, etc, Mechanics busily employed in their respective occupations. For two days past have been laying out Mr. D. Stuarts outfit. The young men Clerks mostly busy in putting up Provisions, etc., for him and the other Gentlemen's Equipments or outfits. Traded with the Natives a number of Beaver Skins and Two Sea Otters. Sick list as yesterday.[33]

10th. Wednesday. Weather as yesterday, Wind fresh at Westward. Men employed clearing away the Land as for several days past. Two making Canoe Sails, one painting Oil Cloths. Two or three making Paddles and Oars. Clerks, etc., all busily occupied in laying out and packing Mr. Clarke's outfit. The Boat with Mr. Reed and six men started for the Ship in the forenoon, but returned soon without effecting it, on account of the fresh breeze and tide against them. Soon after the Shallop attempted going down, but returned also, her sails being much torn and out of repair. The trip was therefore deferred untill another day. In the afternoon, Jones went out hunting. Returned again in a few hours, having Killed an Elk about 4 miles from the Factory. Visited by numbers of Indians, who traded a few Wapatoes, Skins, and 30 or 40 fine Salmon. Sick list same as yesterday.[34]

11th. Thursday. Clear, pleasant weather, wind S. W. Mr. Wallace and 6 men were sent after the meat of the Elk killed yesterday, and returned with it in a few hours. John Day and Ignace went hunting. People mostly employed cutting, Burning, and rolling Logs. Others at different Jobs, making Canoe Sails and other preparations necessary in forwarding things to be got ready for the general departure of our Voyagers. Clerks, etc., busily employed in arranging Mr. Clarke's outfit. Mechanics at their different occupations. At 11 o'clock was visited by Captain Sowle, who spent the remainder of the day with us. Six men sick. Hunters returned unsuccessful.

---

[33] As used here, "outfit" meant the field equipment and trade goods needed for either a trapping or a trading venture into the interior. Obviously, several ventures into the interior are being gotten ready. They will leave on June 29th.

[34] Mr. Clarke was John Clarke, the partner who arrived with the *Beaver*.

12th. Friday. Wind and Weather as yesterday. People employed same as yesterday, principally at burning logs, etc. After Breakfast, Captain Sowle returned in his Boat. The Dolly was also despatched at the same time for the Ship. Still busy in laying out Mr. Clarke's outfit. One of our men (Pelton) whom we released some time since from the Indians above has been apparently deranged at several times, and to day is very troublesome. Some suspicions are entertained that he may feign insanity for some design or other, and was therefore punished and afterwards confined, to try what effect it shall have, and ascertain the reality of his madness. The Dolly arrived again towards evening. Sick list as for several days.

13th. Saturday. Fine pleasant Weather; Winds Westerly. The People variously employed, being now divided or distributed among the Gentlemen for voyaging are fixing canoes and otherwise arranging for their departure; others clearing Land, burning, cutting & rolling Logs, etc. With our Mad man there appears little alteration, none for the better however, and he is still kept confined, the doubts respecting the certainty of his madness are not yet settled. Visited by number of the Natives, who traded great numbers of fine Salmon. Purchased two weighing 83 lbs.

14th. Sunday. Fine pleasant Weather, with Westerly Winds. Visited by numbers of Indians bringing plenty of fresh Salmon. Purchased also a fine Canoe. The Shallop was despatched with several of our Gentlemen on board in the forenoon, who dine with Capt. Sowle on board the Beaver. Returned again in the evening. 5 Men sick.

15th. Monday. Cloudy Weather with violent gusts of Wind from S.W.; continued heavy squalls throughout the day. People variously employed, fixing the Barge, canoes, etc., in which they are shortly to proceed up the River. Occupied in laying out Mr. McKenzie's outfit, which was completed. Our Madman (Pelton) still continuing the same. Sick list as yesterday.

June 16th. Tuesday. First part of the day cloudy with some Rain, afternoon pleasant. Wind Westerly. People variously employed; a number cutting and piling Wood for a Coal Pit, some rolling & burning Logs, others preparing Canoes, Sails, Paddles, etc., etc. Mechanics all busily occupied at their different trades. The Dolly was despatched for Baker's Bay in the forenoon, from whence she returned at evening. Completed the outfits of Mr. McKenzie and Mr. R. Stuart. Pelton continues as for several days past; that he is in reality insane there is now little doubt and has become an object of compassion. 5 men Sick, and 4 Sandwich Islanders.

17th. Wednesday. Cloudy, with intervals of Rain throughout the day. People employed as yesterday. Visited by a number of the Natives, one of whom (a young Lad) was detected in the act of stealing from some of our Sandwich Islanders, and for which had him confined in the Cellar of the Store. Kamaquiah brought back our Cooper's Adze that had been stolen by one of the Indians above some time ago, for which he received a suitable reward. Sick list as yesterday.[35]

18th. Thursday. Cloudy most of the day. Wind Westerly. People employed as yesterday, Cutting and piling Wood for a Coal Pit. Most of them however making preparations for their departure. Carpenters and Boat Builder getting out timber for completing the Bastions adjoining to our enclosure. Blacksmith, Taylors, &c., busily employed at their respective trades. The Dolly was despatched for Baker's Bay in the morning. The young Indian whom we had confined made his escape during the night or early this morning by digging out under the floor, which on examining, we found was easily effected; and that it was necessary to make the place more secure, to prevent any one attempting to find their way in that manner. Visited by great numbers of the Natives in the early part of the day, as was supposed, to enquire after and endeavor to release the prisoner. Tho' they were immediately made acquainted with the circumstance of his having effected an escape. Dorion, one of our Hunters, arrived in the morning with intelligence of having killed two Elk at some distance above Tongue Point. A Canoe with several people was immediately despatched for the meat. Pelton continues as for several days past. Sick list the same.[36]

19th. Friday. Pleasant weather, Wind Westerly. People variously employed. Finished cutting Wood for the Coal Pit. Two men employed digging and placing Logs under the foundation of the Store, from whence our young prisoner made his escape, to make it now more secure. The people that had been sent after the meat of the Elk killed returned this forenoon with one only. The other had been eaten by the Wolves. At 2 o'clock, received a visit from Capt Sowle. Shortly afterwards, the Dolly arrived also from the Ship. Sick list same as for several days.

June 20th. Saturday. Wind and Weather as yesterday. People for the most part employed the same also; the greater part are making preparations for

---

[35] McDougall is stepping up the punishment for the constant pilfering by the natives which had been a feature of life at the post since it was begun. This punishment will, however, be somewhat ineffectual; see the next day's entry.

[36] A bastion is a strong point, usually with firing slits instead of windows, projecting from the wall of a fort to permit an enfilading fire on attackers. Here, the bastions seem to have been placed a few feet ("adjoining to our enclosure") from the walls. See following p. 142 for a suppositious drawing which supports this placement.

their departure—a number working at the Coal Pit, Mechanics all very busy, Carpenters getting out Timber for finishing the Bastions. Visited by numbers of the Natives who brought some few furs. An Indian Woman of the Chinooks was last night at a late hour detected in stealing from one of our Sandwich Islanders. She was immediately brought in and put in confinement, where she continued to be kept during this day. 3 men and 2 Sandwich Islanders sick.

21st. Sunday. Fine pleasant weather, Wind at West. In the forenoon received a Visit from Captain Sowle. Owing to the hurry & anxiety of the Gentlemen to make a start, our Blacksmiths were under the necessity of working to day. Sick list as yesterday.

22nd. Monday. Fine pleasant Weather. Our Indian Hunter came in this morning with information of having killed an Elk. A Canoe and 6 S. Islanders were immediately despatched accompanying him for it, with which they returned in the afternoon. Captain Sowle & John Day went out hunting in the morning and afternoon, but were unsuccessful. Our people that are to remain at this place employed burning a Coal Pit, burning logs, etc. Mechanics at their respective occupations. Blacksmiths hurrying to finish the work necessary for the Gentlemen before their departure, and is the principal cause of their being detained longer than this day, which was the time appointed. 1 Man and 2 Sandwich Islanders Sick.

23rd. Tuesday. Clear pleasant Weather and very warm. Light airs from Westward. Early in the morning Capt. Sowle started to go on board Ship. People employed as yesterday. Three attempts were made to get the Dolly under way for the purpose of proceeding down to the Ship, but were each time prevented owing to the Wind being so light. Received a visit from Comcomly in the early part of the day, who traded a few Skins.

24th. Wednesday. Cloudy, wind very fresh and squally from S.W. People variously employed, attending the Coal Pit, Cutting and Rolling Logs, etc. Mechanics at their several occupations. Carpenters still getting out Timber for the Bastions. The Shallop again struck adrift during the violence of the blow, and was obliged to have her brought farther in the Harbor to make her secure. A regale was given the men this evening as the last previous to their departure. 3 men and 3 Sandwich Islanders off duty.[37]

---

[37] Regale was an informal use of the French noun *régal*, meaning a treat or a delight. Since the Astorians were preparing to send out three trading and trapping parties, as well as another effort to carry letters to Astor in New York, their departure was certainly significant, meriting some kind of a celebration. However, for some unspecified reason, probably the uncompleted work of the blacksmiths, the parties did not depart until June 29th.

25th. Thursday. Fine pleasant Weather, Wind light from Westward. People employed as yesterday. The Dolly with Mr. McLennan and 5 men were
sent down the Ship, which we fear suffered in the blow yesterday, as we
could discover this morning that she had moved to some considerable distance from her anchoring ground. Visited by a number of the Natives who
traded a few Salmon and Beaver. 2 men and 3 Sandwich Islanders sick.

26th. Friday. First part of the day clear & pleasant; latter part cloudy,
Wind light from Westward. Sent two men hunting. People employed cutting, rolling & burning Logs, etc. Some bringing Coal from the Pit. Mechanics severally employed at their trades. Visited by numbers of the Natives,
who traded a number of fine Salmon. Sick list as yesterday. Late in the
evening the Dolly arrived from Baker's Bay, when our anxiety for the safety
of the Ship was eased as it appeared she had experienced no difficulty, nor
drifted at all from her anchoring ground as we had imagined.

27th. Saturday. Pleasant Weather—Wind moderate from Westward. People employed as yesterday. At evening our two men returned from hunting,
bringing in the meat of an Elk. One Man and 3 Sandwich Islanders Sick.

28th. Sunday. Fine pleasant Weather, Wind Westerly. Our Indian hunter
arrived this morning with the meat of an Elk. The Boat was despatched early
for the Ship, for the purpose of having Capt. Sowle come up to Dinner.
About twelve o'clock she returned, accompanied by Capt. Sowle in his boat.
Our Gentlemen being to take their departure early tomorrow, every arrang-
ment was made accordingly. Sick list as yesterday.

June 29th. Monday. Weather fine and pleasant, with light airs from Westward. All hands were stirring early, preparing for the general departure. At
6 o'clock the Goods and Packages were all delivered out of the store and
taken to the Water side, from whence they embark in the Canoes. After
much hurry & bustle, the Canoes, with the young men (Clerks) left here
about 12 o'clock. The necessary Papers not being quite completed, the Gentlemen remained untill afternoon, when all took their leave in Capt. Sowle's
Boat accompanied by him, Mr. Hunt, Mr. McDougall & Mr. Ehninger,
expecting to overtake the party above or near Tongue Point. A handsome
salute was fired from the Battery of our Fortification or Factory, which was
answered from the Boat with three hearty cheers, which altogether had a fine
effect. Our number is now reduced to 38 white persons inclusive, and 11
Sandwich Islanders. At evening, Muskets were given to all hands, and a
watch set during the night, to guard against any danger to be apprehended
from the Indians, tho' we now know of none. 3 men Sick.[38]

---

[38] A total of about sixty men were involved in the various parties. David Stuart, a partner,

It was resolved that Mr. Hunt should embark on board the <u>Beaver</u> to perform the voyage on the Coast, and untill his return in the fall, Mr. McDougall is to take charge of the Factory, when it is intended he will go to winter in McKay's River or Wolamat.[39]

June 30th. Tuesday. Fore part of the day cloudy with some rain, Wind

---

took William Matthews and Donald McGillis, clerks, and several men to his post at the confluence of the Okanogan and the Columbia, thence on to his post in the Shushwaps country, near present-day Kamloops, British Columbia. John Clarke, a partner, took Benjamin Pillet, Donald MacLenon (also spelled McLennon), Russel Farnham, and Ross Cox, clerks, and other men to establish a post near Spokane, Washington, as a direct challenge to the North West Company's post, Spokane House. Farnham and Cox went on to trade with the Flathead Indians, MacLenon among the Coeur d'Alene, and Pillet among the Kootenais. The Flat Heads lived in western Montana, in the Bitteroot Valley; they were Salish-speaking; see Josephy, *Nez Perce*, p. 20. The Coeur d'Alene were also known as the Skitswish, an inland division of the Salishan; they lived about the headwaters of the Spokane River, on both sides of the Washington–Idaho border. The Kootenais (also Kutenai) had a unique language and were possibly related to the Salishan group; they lived along the upper Columbia River and near the river and lake which bear their name in British Columbia and Montana; see John R. Swainton, *The Indian Tribes of North America* (Washington, D.C.: Smithsonian Institution Press, 1952), pp. 411–12, 393–93. Donald McKenzie, partner, took Alfred Seton and John Reed, clerks, to establish a post on the Snake River, among the Nez Perce, thus redeeming a promise made when that tribe aided the overlanders the previous year. After some reconnoitering, McKenzie built his post on the Clearwater, just above where it flows into the Snake, in the area of present-day Lewiston, Idaho; see A. W. Thompson, "New Light on Donald McKenzie's Post on the Clearwater, 1812–1813," *Idaho Yesterdays*, 18, No. 3 (Fall 1974), 24–32. Reed and four men were sent on to Caldron Linn where the overlanders had cached a large store of trade goods during their difficult journey; Caldron Linn was a falls and whirlpool on the Snake River, probably Dry Creek Falls, near present-day Murtaugh, Idaho. Ronda, *Astoria*, pp. 182–86. Reed returned from his assignment in October, reporting to McKenzie that most of the caches had been discovered by the natives and looted; see Jones, ed., *Astorian Adventure*, p. 106. Finally, Robert Stuart and a small party were carrying letters to Astor in New York. Included in the Stuart party were Robert McClellan and Ramsay Crooks, both of whom gave up their partnerships in the company, Ben Jones and John Day, the hunters, and two Canadians, André Vallar and Francis LeClerc. Chittenden, *Fur Trade*, I, 204; also, Irving, *Astoria* (Rust, ed.), pp. 256–61, give some of the rosters of the various parties. Stuart's journey east is described in Rollins, ed., *Stuart's Narrative*. The party accompanying Captain Sowle camped overnight near Tongue Point with those heading for the interior, then returned to the post; see the entry for June 30. McDougall's anxiety about the post now centers on its defense by the much smaller number of men present, rather than food, in spite of his explicit admission that they have no concrete reason to fear the natives.

[39] This decision recalls the dual character of both the Pacific Fur Company and Sowle and Hunt's mission with the *Beaver*. Not only were they to carry furs from the Columbia to market in Canton, but they were also to supply the Russian American Company's post at New Archangel (Sitka), Alaska, with trade and other goods, and carry its furs to market in Canton as well. At this point, Hunt intended to go to Sitka, unload cargo which Captain Sowle had brought along for the Russian post, load any pelts they had, return to the Columbia, load their accumulated pelts, and send Captain Sowle and the *Beaver* to Canton. However, the ship was damaged during its stay in Alaska and Hunt and Sowle agreed that it was prudent to sail to Hawaii where the damage could be repaired, rather than try the mouth of

light from N. W.; afternoon pleasant. Early in the morning, the Boat with Capt. Sowle, Mr. Hunt, Mr. McDougall & Ehninger returned, having overtaken the Party last evening a little way above Tongue Point. Spent the night with them and saw all under way this morning. Immediately on their return preparations were made for the departure of the Ship's Boat & Mr. Hunt, who goes in the Ship on the Coast. At 9 o'clock, all was in readiness. A handsome salute of Eleven guns was fired from the Factory. The Shallop at the same time was despatched for the Ship. Cannan with one man and a Sandwich Islander went hunting. Our Iroquois Hunters Ignace and Dorion with their families went out yesterday to spend some time hunting, accompanied by Thomas McKay and Two S. Islanders. In the afternoon our Indian Hunter Watatkum brought in the meat of an Elk. At evening the Shallop arrived from the Ship for some things Capt. Sowle had forgotten.

July 1. Wednesday. Clear pleasant Weather, Wind N.W. and N.N.W. The Shallop was despatched early for the Ship. Thomas McKay and the Two men arrived with the meat of an Elk from Ignace & Dorion. Greater part of this and the one procured yesterday was sent on board Ship. People mostly employed rolling, cutting & burning Logs & Stumps. Two men attending a Coal Pit. Carpenters getting out Timber for the Bastions. Blacksmiths employed at their Trade. Taylor, etc., on board the Shallop. Thomas McKay and men returned to the Hunters. 3 men & 1 Sandwich Islander sick.

July 2d. Thursday. Clear pleasant Weather, Wind as yesterday. People employed the same also. Cannan and the two men returned unsuccessful. Visited by a number of Chinook Indians who on seeing our manoevering and Exercise with Small arms were very much frightened, and made the best of their way from the place in great haste, which circumstance served to strengthen our belief that they are not friendly disposed towards us, and are conscious of having either a desire to harm us or have already concerted measures to that effect. However it may be, such regulations are now adopted as is to be hoped will effectually prevent any such attempt by them.[40]

---

the Columbia. In Hawaii, Hunt sent Sowle on to Canton, believing he could charter a vessel quickly and return to Astoria. But he was not able to return until August 1813, and control of the post passed effectively to McDougall and McKenzie, in spite of Hunt's nominal status as supervising partner. Ronda, *Astoria*, pp. 283–86.

[40] This passage illustrates the latent distrust in the relationship between the Astorians and the neighboring Chinooks with whom they had the most frequent and close contact. As noted above, because of the smaller number of men at the post, McDougall believes it is prudent to see to its defenses by exercising the men at arms, etc. The Chinooks, probably visiting for an innocent purpose, were understandably alarmed at seeing the martial exercise and left as

3d. Friday. Weather as Yesterday, wind fresh from Westward. People employed as for several days past. In the afternoon the Dolly returned from Baker's Bay, being as we supposed the last trip she will make before the departure of the Beaver, as she is now waiting only for a fair Wind to go to Sea. 3 men and 1 Sandwich Islander sick.

4th. Saturday. Wind and Weather as yesterday. This being the anniversary of the Independence of the United States, The American Flag was displayed at Sun rise, and a salute fired suitable to the occasion.

Our People (who are now few in number) having been for several days occupied in burning Logs, etc., found it necessary to attend to the fires untill 12 o'clock, when all hands broke off and had the usual allowance for a regale given them. The day with us ended as it began, in peace and sociability, the customary salutes being fired at 12 o'clock and at Sun set.

July 5th. Sunday. Morning cloudy with some squalls of Rain. Latter part clear & pleasant; Wind Westerly. Visited in the course of the day by numbers of the Natives, who all however appear very timid in approaching our enclosure. Sick list same.

6th. Monday. Clear pleasant Weather, Wind at N.W. People variously employed, Hewing & cutting Timber, making Coal Pit, burning and Rolling Logs, etc. Labonte making Ladders. Visited by one of Comcomly's Sons (the oldest), who behaved very improperly in the afternoon while our men were exercising with small arms. He wished to be allowed to come within the Gates, which was refused [him]. He then began making much noise, and attempted climbing up the Pickets, after having previously been ordered to go away. He was then driven away, and a number of men sent along to see that he departed in his canoe, which he did with his men. Watatkum came in at evening with intelligence of having Killed two Elk near the Clatsop Village, requesting men might be sent with him in the morning to fetch the meat. Sick list the same.[41]

7th. Tuesday. Weather as yesterday, Wind Northerly. In the morning, sent 11 Sandwich Islanders with Watatkum after the Elk killed yesterday, with which they returned in the afternoon. Thomas McKay and the two S.

---

quickly as possible. Their flight is taken as proof that they intended a sneak attack. In this encounter, the natives would seem to have acted more reasonably than the Astorians. This helps to explain what McDougall was trying to do when he married one of Comcomly's daughters later; see below, July 20, 1813. Presumably, the Chinooks would not attack their chief's son-in-law.

[41] This was probably Gassagass (or Cassagass); the "him" in brackets is lightly erased in the manuscript.

Islanders arrived also in the forenoon, bringing the meat of Two Elk. People employed as yesterday. Visited by great numbers of Indians in the fore part of the day, who traded several Skins. Their behaviour was particularly observed during the time of their stay, in which there was nothing improper or unbecoming, tho' we were under some apprehensions of their having some design by coming in so great numbers at one time. This, however, was soon relieved by their departure. At evening loaded all our Swivels, etc., with Shot. Sick list as for several days past.[42]

8th. Wednesday. Clear pleasant Weather, Wind Westerly. In the forenoon, received a Visit from Mr. Hunt and Capt Sowle accompanied by Comcomly, who had gone on board Ship with a complaint respecting the treatment his son met with here on Monday evening. He was brought here for the purpose of having an understanding concerning it, as it appeared the story had been represented very much exaggerated. The matter however was here explained to his satisfaction, or apparently so. After dinner they returned on board Ship, being anxious to improve the first opportunity for getting to sea, none having yet offered since all was in readiness. Comcomly also accompanied them in the Boat. Our people employed to day as usual: Carpenters, Cannan & Cooper framing the Timber for the Bastions, with which they make considerable progress. Sent one man & Two S. Islanders with Tools, etc., up the River to the Hunters, Ignace & Dorion. Sick list the same.[43]

9th. Thursday. Weather Clear & pleasant and very warm; Wind S.W. All hands employed as usual. Carpenters, etc., at the Bastions, which we are very anxious to have completed as soon as possible. Visited by a few Clatsop & Chinook Indians who traded a few Skins and a number of Salmon. In the afternoon our Hunters, Ignace & Dorion, arrived, having been terribly alarmed the evening before by hearing several large guns fired, or what they supposed to have been guns. From this they concluded the Factory had been attacked by the Natives in the night. To satisfy themselves of what they were already fully convinced in their minds, and to see what the consequence

---

[42] With Captain Sowle and the *Beaver* presumably gone (actually, it was not able to sail until August 3 because of adverse winds), McDougall's fears seem heightened. He takes the large number of natives as an indication of possible mischief on their part. Actually, the natives may have come in larger than usual numbers because they were afraid of these apparently belligerent men with guns, thus reluctant to come alone or in small groups. As before, each side's actions and reactions reinforced their mutual fears and suspicions. Note that the swivels, i.e., small cannons, were loaded against a night attack. See below, July 27, for an increase in the post's armament when Captain Sowle gives several small cannon and balls to McDougall.

[43] The tools were to be used to build a canoe; see below, entry of July 28.

might have been, they started early this morning and walked down, leaving their Canoes, &c., behind. On arriving within sight of the place they remained for some time sheltered from the view of any of the people, in order to ascertain whether any were still alive, and to their great relief soon found all safe. It appeared the report they heard was caused by the falling of several large high stumps of trees during the night, which our people had been burning. However groundless their apprehensions were, the anxiety they experienced from that time untill their arrival must have been extremely unpleasant. 3 men and 1 Sandwich Islander Sick.[44]

10th. Friday. Cloudy weather with Wind at Westward. People employed as for several days, principally cutting and rolling Logs. Two attending the Coal Pit. Carpenters employed at the Bastions; Blacksmith, Taylors, etc., at their respective trades, Four Sandwich Islanders were sent after the Canoe our Hunters had left at their encampment up the River. 4 men and 1 S. Islander Sick.

In the evening between 10 & 11 o'clock, Just after the Watch was set and the remainder all retired to rest, we were dreadfully alarmed by the cry that Indians were Just coming to attack us. The word was sent by Calpo. A number of his slave girls came running into the Factory in a terrible fright with the cry. This alarmed the Watch, who immediately ran within the gates, secured them, and beat a general alarm. All hands were soon to Quarters under arms. Great confusion prevailed through the whole for some time, but by Midnight everything was arranged, the cannon drawn in the square and loaded, as also the Swivels & Cowhorns. One half our number were set on Watch during the remaining part of the night, while the others retired a second time to rest.[45]

11th. Saturday. Cloudy Weather and Cool, Wind Westerly. Not having seen any Indians make their appearance last night, we conclude it must have been a false alarm of Calpo's. On enquiry, it appeared that two Indians only came to Calpo's house, from whom he learned that a great party was on their

---

[44] Obviously, McDougall was not the only one who feared an attack by the Chinooks and other tribes. Ignace's and Dorion's fear highlights their anomalous status. Although they were Indians, they were so closely tied to the Astorians and so far away from their own people that, in the event of real trouble with the natives, they were just as likely to be killed as the whites. Indeed, given that they were usually off by themselves hunting, they could be taken more easily than those in the fort. They also must have feared for their families, frequently left alone. McDougall's awareness of their feelings is a rare example of sensitivity on his part.

[45] McDougall explains the origin of this false alarm in the following day's entry. "Cowhorns" were cohorns, a small bronze mortar, usually mounted with handles, throwing a small ball. They would be particularly useful in the small fort which Astoria had become.

way from the opposite side, instigated by Comcomly's son (Cassagass) coming to attack us. The fright however may prove serviceable by making our people more vigilant in their watch, and observing better the instructions given them. All hands employed rolling Logs, being exceedingly anxious to get the ground clear around the Factory. In the afternoon the 4 men returned with the canoe they had been sent after. 3 men & 1 Sandwich Islander sick.

12th. Sunday. Clear pleasant Weather, wind fresh at Westward. The sawyers, LaFramboise & Belleau kept busy to day sawing Timber for the Bastions. Visited by several Clatsop & Chinook Indians. Sick list as yesterday.

13th. Monday. Pleasant weather, wind N. West & W. All hands busily employed. Carpenters, Boat Builder & Cooper framing the Bastions. Two men sawing. Two attending a Coal Pit. Blacksmiths & Taylor at their respective occupations, the remainder with the Sandwich Islanders at work rolling & cutting Logs, burning stumps, etc., etc. Visited in the course of the day by numbers of the Natives who traded a few Mats, etc. Early in the morning a chief of the Chlewitz, above here, arrived with a number of Salmon and the meat of a small Deer, which he traded, bringing also intelligence of our Company who have gone up the River, which if true is unpleasant news. He informs that the Boat which Mr. Clarke took along, in passing a small rapid or current broke loose and filled, and part of the goods lost, and that they had made a stop on that account to endeavor and find the goods again. From the manner in which he delivered his information we have no reason to doubt the correctness of it. Sick list as yesterday. Our Hunters, Ignace & Dorion, with their families, accompanied by Brugeire & St. Amant with 2 Canoes, went up the River hunting this morning.[46]

14th. Tuesday. Clear pleasant Weather, Wind fresh at Westerly. People employed as yesterday. In the afternoon received a Visit from Mr. Hunt, Capt Sowle, and Mr. Ehninger, from the Ship. Being yet detained by contrary Winds, not one opportunity having offered by which they could with any degree of safety attempt going to Sea. The news of our alarm on Friday evening had not reached them untill their arrival here. We learn that the Indians in the Bay near the Ship have for several days past conducted themselves differently from usual, and in a manner to excite suspicions of their

---

[46] As with the incident involving John Reed, this report of trouble on the way up the Columbia was garbled and exaggerated; see below, July 18 and 28. See Rollins, ed., *Stuart's Narrative*, pp. 34ff., for a description of the canoe upset which was the major event of the passage. Washington Irving, *Astoria, or, Anecdotes of an Enterprise Beyond the Rocky Mountains*, ed. Edgeley W. Todd (Norman: University of Oklahoma Press, 1964), hereafter Irving, *Astoria* (Todd ed.), pp. 257–59, also describes the passage through a difficult portage.

bad designs. For this purpose, a very strict and armed Watch has been kept on board. On examining minutely different circumstances, we have at this time every reason to believe the natives are watching only a favorable opportunity to take advantage of our negligence (if we may be guilty of any) or at any rate when we may be unprepared, and destroy us if possible. Sick list as for several days past.

15th. Wednesday. Cloudy Weather, wind at S.W. People employed as yesterday. Greater part however rolling Logs, etc., being exceedingly anxious to get the ground clear around the Factory. Mr. Hunt, Capt Sowle & Mr. Ehinger started very early in the morning for the ship. Raised the frame of one Bastion last evening. The Carpenters busily employed at the other. Visited by numbers of the Natives who traded a few Mats, etc. Sick list the same.

16th. Thursday. Wind and weather as yesterday, cloudy and gloomy. All hands employed the same also. Visited by several of the Natives who traded some Mats and a few Salmon. Two men and one S. Islander sick.

17th. Friday. Cloudy unpleasant Weather, with some fine Rain. All hands busily employed as usual. Carpenters framing the Bastions. Two men Pillon & LaFramboise sawing. Two attending Coal Pit. Blacksmith and Taylor at their trades. Remainder part rolling and cutting Logs and Stumps, etc. Traded a number of Salmon. Sick list as yesterday.

July 18th. Saturday. Cloudy Weather with light winds from Westwards. All hands employed as yesterday, with the addition of one man attending Coal Pit. This afternoon raised the timber for the cover of one Bastion. The other is delayed on account of sawed Timber, which cannot be procured so fast they use it. By some Indians from up the River who came down for the purpose of Fishing, we learn some further account concerning our Party proceeding up. The misfortune that befel the boat proves by their account to be not so unfavorable as we at first supposed or had reason to believe. They inform also that the party had passed the worst rapids, or that part where we had expected they might meet with difficulty. The natives on their approach, conscious of having acted improperly on a former occasion, all fled, deserting their house, etc., which our people set fire to; and which we hope may prove an example to them in future and shew what they may expect from such behavior as they were guilty of to our former party. Sick list the same.[47]

19th. Sunday. Clear pleasant Weather, Wind W. Visited by numbers of

---

[47] This is an embroidered account of the incident first reported above, on July 13. See there and below, July 28, August 3.

the Natives who traded 40 or 50 Salmon, some Beaver & Clemels. Two men & one S. Islander sick.

20th. Monday. Weather as yesterday, Wind fresh from N.W. All hands variously employed as during the last Week. Began burning the Log heaps, etc., which burned remarkably well, most of them being quite gone by evening. Visited by several of the Natives, from whom we purchased great numbers of Salmon, some Beaver and Clemels, Mats, etc. For the week past and at this time we have purchased a plentiful supply of Salmon for all hands, besides a good number salted. The large Fire and Smoke occasioned by burning Logs caused a general movement of our Hogs, goats, Fowls, etc., from among the Stumps, etc. In the stir appeared a Sow with a fine Litter of Pigs, a Hen with several young Chickens. Besides one of the slut-dogs had Pups under a stump, which unfortunately perished in the Fire before she had time to remove them. Coti, who has been for some time laid up with the Venereal, and was on that account prevented from going up with the Party, resumed his work to day, reducing our sick list to two, viz. Labonté, who has been a long time ill and is now very low, and Tuana the S. Islander, who has also been a long time laid up (with the Venereal) with little prospect at present of recovering entirely. Several others of the men are badly affected with the Venereal, tho they do not break off from their duty.[48]

21st. Tuesday. First part the day, clear & pleasant, afternoon cloudy. Wind at W. and N. W. quite cool. All hands employed as usual. Three burning coal; Blacksmiths, Taylor, & Carpenters employed at their respective trades; the remainder rolling Logs. Raised the body of the other Bastion this forenoon. Our Invalid Pelton absconded himself yesterday, where he cannot be found, tho' we suppose him to be not far off, having several times within these few weeks absented himself for a day or two at once without the knowlidge of any one. Once the Indians brought him back from a little distance above here along shore. Louis Labonté and John Little off duty to day, making our sick list amount to 4 persons.[49]

July 22nd. Wednesday. Forenoon cloudy, with some fine Rain, afternoon pleasant; Wind Westerly. People employed as usual. Two men only working at the Bastions, the other two Carpenters being sick. Mr. Halsey & Thomas McKay went up the River about 4 miles to the Village in hopes of finding Pelton, of whom we have yet heard nothing, nor can imagine where he is.

---

[48] "Slut-dog" is an antique usage for a female dog, a bitch. Venereal disease was probably a very common medical problem at Astoria, but, as noted previously, McDougall seldom indicated the nature of the illness.

[49] In spite of persistent efforts to find him, Pelton will not turn up until August 1.

They returned in the afternoon with out any intelligence of him. For two days past none of the Natives have visited us. Gervais is also sick and our list amounting now to 5.

23d. Thursday. Cloudy Weather and cool, Wind Westerly. All hands employed as usual. Carpenter making the roofs for the Bastions. Visited by some few of the Natives, but for three days past have bought no salmon. Mr. Halsey & T. McKay were sent again in pursuit of our invalid Pelton, but returned without obtaining any account of him. Little, Gervais and Tuana sick.

24th. Friday. Cloudy weather much as yesterday, Wind Westerly. The people for some time employed at rolling logs. Finished the Job this forenoon allotted to them for the week, and have therefore the remaining part as holiday. Others—Mechanics, Sawyers, etc. occupied as usual. Two Carpenters and Cooper at work covering the Bastions; the other (Little) laid up. In the afternoon very unexpectedly, tho' much to our satisfaction, received a Visit from Mr. Hunt, Captain Sowle and Mr. Ehninger. The Ship being still detained by contrary Winds. Being late, spent the night with us. Sick list as yesterday.

July 25th. Saturday. Cloudy, Wind fresh at Westward. Mr. Hunt & Company started very early for the Ship. Mechanics & sawyers occupied as usual. The others having the day to themselves, except the three employed burning Coal. Visited by numbers of the Natives who traded some Mats and a few Salmon. Sick list as for several days.

26th. Sunday. Cloudy with Wind light from the Westward. Cannan & Cooper went hunting in the forenoon, but without success. Traded 20 or 30 Salmon, some Mats, etc. Sick list as yesterday.

27th. Monday. Cloudy as yesterday, Wind same also. All hands busily employed. Three men burning Coal. Three Carpenters employed at the Bastions. Blacksmiths & Taylor at their respective occupations. Two men sawing Boards for finishing Bastions, the remainder of all that are not sick at work rolling, cutting & Burning Logs. Visited by a few Natives, among others Comcomley's young son, who traded a few Salmon. At 1 o'clock received a Visit from Mr. Hunt, Mr. Ehninger and Mr. Mumford in the Ship's Boat, bringing with them for this place two brass three pound Pieces and 20 or 30 round shot. In consequence of the singular behavior of the Indians in the Bay near the Ship and the apprehensions of real danger from them, the Boat came well armed. Mr. Hunt informs that yesterday, while Capt Sowle, himself, and Mr. Ehninger were on shore in the Bay, great numbers of the Indians gathered round them. When he plainly discovered their intention towards them were hostile, They immediately made the best of their way to the Ship, concealing as much as possible any apprehensions or signs of fear. Great numbers of Neweetie Indians are now in Bakers bay near the Ship, where they arrived but a few days since, who it seems are the cause of this extraordinary behaviour. Sick list as for several days, 4 viz., Little, Gervais and the two invalids LaBonte and Tuana.[50]

28th. Tuesday. Clear pleasant Weather, the first for some time. Mr. Hunt & company started early for the Ship. People employed as yesterday, except Cannan who hurt his hands in such a manner yesterday as to disable him from rolling logs. By some Indians from up the River arrived at the Chinook Village, we learn further and more satisfactory accounts of our Party's proceeding in the interior. It appears Mr. David Stuart's large Canoe and not Mr. Clarke's Boat met with an accident, and lost considerable quantity of Goods, which they were prevented from regaining on account of the Waters of the River being too high. Since which time the natives have been employed in search of the things lost, and of which they have procured considerable part, such as Clothes & other dry Goods, Axes, Muskets, etc., things most essential and of greatest value. The account already stated of the manner in which they proceeded with the Natives at the falls differs from the present one in a few particulars, as the circumstance of setting fire to the Lodges is now contradicted, though no doubt the account is in substance correct. Sick list as yesterday. Gervais, one of the number, employed however making Mockasins. At evening our two Hunters with their families, the two men who accompanied them, St. Amant & Bruguiere and the S. Islander Bob arrived, having been absent since 13 Instant up Young's River making a Canoe, which they have completed. But had not help sufficient to get it into the Water.[51]

July 29th. Wednesday. Clear, pleasant Weather, Wind at Westward. All hands employed as yesterday. Three at work at the Bastions, with which they make very little progress, and appear not in the least hurried, notwithstanding the great necessity of having them completed as soon as possible. Sent two men after the Canoe the Hunters left round Point George yesterday on their way home, the wind being at that time too fresh to bring it round. Visited by great numbers of the Natives, who traded plenty of Salmon, some

---

[50] The gathering of natives in the bay was apparently an annual event, connected with the usual pattern of salmon runs. McDougall, of course, suspected the worst. If the unasked-for loan of the small cannon is any indication, so did Sowle and Hunt.

[51] See above, July 8, for the sending of tools to Dorion and Ignace. Obviously, they used them to build the canoe.

Beaver, & Mats. For two or three days past, Salmon has been brought in abundance. Sick list as yesterday, 4 in number.

30th. Thursday. Cloudy Weather, Wind fresh at Westward. All hands busily and variously employed. Little and Gervais resumed their work to day. Carpenters and Cooper covering Bastion; framing a platform to be raised within the Pickets all round, for the sentry to walk on; & making carriages for the two Brass pieces got the other day from the Ship. Two Sandwich Islanders sent to assist the three men already at the Coal Pits, cutting & piling Wood etc. The remainder rolling Logs, cutting & Burning Stumps, etc. From the old Indian who lives about us here, and has no other asylum or home to protect him, being as was mentioned some time ago an outcast from his tribe, the Chinooks, we learn or are warned of the intention of the Indians soon after the ship shall leave this. A large number are to proceed in Canoes up Young's Bay and get opposite to the Southward, where they are to leave their Canoes and proceed through the Woods, arrive in the skirts at evening, and at a signal all to rush into the place at once. Indians from above are to Join at the same time and Massacre the whole of us. The old fellow has not been known to relate such stories without a foundation, but what degree of credit can be allowed this is hard to say. We hope, however, in a short time have our preparations of defence so far advanced as to feel secure of danger from that quarter. One man and one S. Islander sick.[52]

31st. Friday. Clear pleasant Weather. All hands employed as Yesterday, except three Sandwich Islanders sent in addition to the number Yesterday to the Coal Pits. Raised the platform on one side and nearly completed the flooring. Visited by several natives, who traded about 20 Salmon, some Mats, etc. Sick list the same.

Augt 1st. Saturday. Clear weather, & pleasant. All hands busily employed as usual. Three men only at the Coal Pits, having a sufficient quantity of

---

[52] There is no prior mention of this native in the log. The Astorians called him Racoon, fed him, and made certain of his well-being by looking in on him from time to time. On October 26, 1812, he was found dead in his cabin, and buried near the post, see below. As a source of intelligence about the natives' intentions toward Astoria, he was no more reliable than anyone else. McDougall mentioned other information he had given the post; perhaps some of the previous tales in the log had come from Racoon, but without credit. If he was not completely shunned by his people, he may have heard talk of an attack, one which obviously never got beyond the talking stage. If the natives had followed the plan in the log, the Astorians would have been sandwiched between the shore and the hostile Indians. In the entry, "outskirts" is presumably meant instead of "skirts" and, in the last sentence, "to" is omitted before the word "have."

Wood cut and collected for Two Pits. Carpenter, Cooper, etc., employed finishing Bastion, making platform, etc., etc. Pelton, who we had now given up for lost and began seriously to think dead, very unexpectedly made his appearance this evening, after being absent for 12 days, in the woods, as he says, alone, living on berries and the like, which is pretty evident from his appearance, being reduced exceedingly thin. But seems more rational than when he went away. Fired our two Brass Pieces from the upper Bastions by way of experiment, which had a good effect and will answer to our wishes. Sick list the same.[53]

2d. Sunday. Fine pleasant weather, wind fresh from Westward. Received a Visit from Skamaquiah, to whom was advanced the amount in value of a Horse, or two thirds only of the value, the remainder to be paid on delivery of the horse, which is to be in a few days, it being now on the opposite side of the River at Chinook Point. Two men and two Sandwich Islanders sick.[54]

3rd. Monday. Clear pleasant Weather. All hands employed pretty nearly the same as during last week. Carpenters, Cooper & Cannan employed at Bastions and Platform; three men at the Coal Pits. Blacksmiths and Taylor at their respective trades. (Boy Perrault was last week set to work with the Taylor, of whom it is intended he shall learn the trade). The remaining number at work out cutting, burning, and Rolling Logs and Stumps. Two sawing boards. At 8 o'clock this morning had the satisfaction to see the Beaver under weigh, and in a short time over the Bar and out of our sight, after having been laying one-month waiting only an opportunity of getting to sea.[55]

From the numerous reports spread about and some certain circumstances, we are induced fully to believe the natives intend an attack on us now the Ship is off. Great numbers from the tribes above are at this time with the

---

[53] Pelton would continue to behave erratically. He stayed on when the post was sold to the North West Company in November 1813. He is carried on the books during the winter of 1813–14 as "fool"; Appendix, No. 144. Later, he was killed by an Indian; see above, II, n. 7. The "brass pieces" are the three-pound cannons which Captain Sowle lent the post on July 27.

[54] Although the horse could be purchased either for food or for work, it turns out that several more horses are obtained later and used to pull logs up to the fort; see below, August 9, 14, 1812.

[55] The "taylor" was Richard Milligan, who signed on with Astor in New York in October 1811 and came out in the *Beaver*; see "Articles of Agreement," Porter, *Astor*, I, 475–78. He was carried on the 1813–14 roster as a tailor—see Appendix, No. 113—and was mentioned on December 29, 1812, as working on trousers and shirts with Moses Flanagan. "Boy Perreault's" apprenticeship was brief; on September 7th, he was sent off with several others to cut timber.

Chinooks, and who are more daring & resolute than those residing around us, from whom also in conjunction with the others we have most to fear. Every preparation was therefore made to day and every thing put in readiness for an attack. The Ports in both Bastions were cut and guns in them. The platform on the North side was also in part finished, sufficient for the Watch to stand inside in the evening.[56]

This afternoon had the satisfaction also of receiving a Letter from our Gentlemen, by return of the Clatsop Indian who accompanied them, dated above the Grand Falls, 17th July, where they arrived without any molestation, or detention by the natives. On the contrary, were treated by them very civilly. In passing one of the Rapids, Mr. David Stuart's canoe unfortunately upset, lost a few pieces of goods, and recd. considerable damage to the canoe. The loss sustained however was shared by the Gentlemen and made up to Mr. Stuart on the spot.[57]

The circumstance most to be lamented is the case of poor John Day, one of Mr. Robert Stuart's company, who they inform us became delirious the second day after leaving this place, attempted killing himself several times, and was otherwise so troublesome and in fact dangerous that they came to a determination and left him with the Cathaputle Indians, a chief of which was paid for bringing him down, and also a Letter from Mr. D. Stuart, neither of which however have yet reached here. It was with much regret they inform that he was left, particularly on the part of Mr. S. They express also a doubt of the reality of his madness, whether it was not pretended as an excuse from performing the Journey. Tho' of this we must Judge from his future conduct after he shall reach here, which we expect daily.[58]

---

[56] Fear of an Indian attack will never completely leave McDougall, even after Comcomly is his father-in-law. The "tribes above" that he mentions include the Chehalis, who had a reputation for hostile action against traders. Nevertheless, they were probably in the area only for the fishing and had no idea of an attack, especially now that the post was fully enclosed and armed with several cannon.

[57] Until the other parties return to Astoria, this will be the final—and correct—word on Stuart's accident.

[58] John Day's conduct on this occasion cannot be fully explained. What seems likely, however, is that, as he approached the area where he had spent the winter with Ramsay Crooks, he found himself unwilling to continue. Recall that that winter had ended with the two of them being found naked, without even a flint to start a fire, on the bank of the Columbia by David Stuart's party the previous April. Possibly the fear of facing something like that again drove Day into a temporary state of insanity or he feigned it in order to be sent back. Whichever it might be, when he did return to Astoria, his conduct was reasonable. He returned east with the North Westers in the spring of 1814. In 1820, trapping with Donald McKenzie in southern Idaho, he died of natural causes. See Drumm, "More About Astorians," 335–60; see also T. C. Elliott, ed., "Last Will and Testament of John Day," *Oregon Historical Society*, 17, No. 4 (December 1916), 373–79.

The reports given us some days ago concerning the Gentlemen up the River, the loss of a Boat or Canoe, etc., corroborate in many things with this, and was as nearly correct as could be expected from Indians. We were also told three days ago that a man was left above sick, but gave little or no credit to it. These two instances may serve to shew what degree of credit may in general be given to reports of the natives around us, and serves also in the present instance to strengthen the belief of the intended attack on us.[59]

Among other arrangements this afternoon, divided our whole number into six Watches to stand within the inclosure in the Bastions and on the Platforms, which was before in thirteen. Our men begin now also to be sensible of the necessity that such measures should be adopted and attend to them with alacrity. 5 men sick.

August 4th. Tuesday. Clear pleasant Weather, Wind fresh at Westward. All hands employed as Yesterday, except the three who have been burning Coal, being now at work with the others clearing away stumps, Logs, etc. St. Amant, Dorion, and Ignace making a Cedar Canoe, for which they brought Timber from the place where the other was built, in Youngs Bay. Visited by many Indians in the course of the day, with whom traded great numbers of Salmon, some few Hens, Mats, etc. Among others came also Gassagass, Comcomley's son, in disguise, and hid in a canoe for some time untill discovered, when he was immediately ordered away. Set two Sentinels to day, which it is intended shall be done regularly for some time. One constantly at the Gate and to admit no Indians but such as have business, and accompanied by some of our people. One of the Carpenters (LaBonté) sick, making our List 6 in number.[60]

5th. Wednesday. Cloudy, Wind fresh at Westward. All hands employed as yesterday. Visited by a good number of Indians, who traded some Salmon, a few Skins, etc. Six men sick. Two of the number however well enough to be set at work running Balls, which they were employed in during the day.[61]

---

[59] This paragraph is an interesting illustration of McDougall's inability to distinguish between native reports of what had happened up river, reports which often filtered through several parties before reaching his informant, and reports of possible Indian attacks, often stemming, it would seem, from the imagination or misperception of the reporter. Just how the exaggerated reports of Stuart's accident and the garbled but largely accurate news of Day's illness confirmed McDougall's fears of a native attack escapes me.

[60] Gassagass was *persona non grata* possibly because of rude behavior some weeks before; see above, July 6, 1812. Note also the precautions against too many Indians being inside the post's palisade at any one time.

[61] The phrase "running balls" refers to the making of musket balls, a relatively simple operation which most of the men at the fort were able to do.

6th. Thursday. Pleasant weather, Wind Westerly. All hands employed as Yesterday, with the addition of Cannan to the number clearing away stumps, etc. Patterson, another of the Carpenters, sick. Visited by several of the Natives. Skamaquiah, etc., and Samasay, with whom we bargained also for a horse, which he is to bring across the first opportunity in calm weather. Traded a great number of Salmon, Mats, etc. LaBonté resumed his work this afternoon. 6 men sick.[62]

August 7th. Friday. Pleasant Weather, Wind light at Westward. People employed as usual. Visited by very few Indians of late, since our preparations of defence have been so nearly completed. Indians visiting us have made their stay as short as possible, being apparently sensible of our feelings towards them. From our old Indian (Racoon) we were last night informed of the intentions of the Natives to take away the Shallop, which, from circumstances appeared quite probable. One of our large cannon was therefore immediately placed on the platform in front of the inclosure, in readiness bearing upon her in case of such attempt. Sick list as yesterday.[63]

8th. Saturday. Pleasant, Wind Westerly. People employed as usual. Visited by numbers of the Natives trading Salmon, etc., of which we now get a plenty. In the afternoon set the Cooper at work overhauling and examining our Salted Salmon which are found very good. To day Skamaquiah and Samasay brought each a horse. Three men and two Sandwich Islanders sick.[64]

9th. Sunday. Pleasant, clear weather, Wind Westerly. In the morning arrived from up the River our neighbor Calpo & family, having been absent one week. Brought with him a horse and great numbers of Salmon. Traded also with the Cathlatamass for one of the guns our people lost in going up the River. His object in going so far up was for the purpose of trading Horses and bringing down the person left by our company, whom at the time he left here, we did not know to be John Day. He however came down with them and arrived in good health without any appearance of having been crazy as our Letter gave to understand. He relates to us that he had no wish

---

[62] Skamaquiah was Kamaquiah, previously identifed as a Chinook headman from a neighboring village, see I, n. 58. Samasay is probably another Chinook, perhaps also a headman from yet another village. Apparently, both live on the north shore of the river, which had a number of Chinook villages.

[63] As before, McDougall seems to place implicit faith in any report of possible hostile action by the natives. Just what they would have done with the *Dolly*, which had proved too small for ocean use and too ungainly for the river, is something of a mystery. At least the response, sighting one of the cannon on the vessel, is rather slight.

[64] As noted, the horses were to be used for dragging logs to the post.

to return, but that he was treated in so shameful a manner by Mr. McLellan (who also accompanies Mr. Stuart) that he could not possibly endure it. He at length gave way to passion, retorted on McLellan and (as he says) exposed some certain facts and gave his mind freely, on which they endeavored to persuade him he was crazy. He acknowledges he might have acted as a madman as he really was for a while, but occasioned only as mentioned. Mr. Stuart probably foresaw the disagreeable consequences that would attend the Journey should they continue together and left day behind. It appears that the Indian who was paid for bringing him down paid no attention to the promise, allowed him to have most of things stolen and to be taken from among his own people (the Cathlaputles) where Calpo found him. Sick list as Yesterday.[65]

10th. Monday. Pleasant Weather. People mostly employed as during last week. Carpenters covering one of the Bastions and other work about the Platforms, etc. Blacksmiths & Taylor at their respective trades. A number employed making a road to draw out Timber for the buildings. Remainder cutting, rolling, & burning Stumps and Logs. Visited by numbers of the natives, who traded some furs, Salmon & Mats. Two men & two Sandwich Islanders sick.[66]

11th. Tuesday. Cloudy wea: Wind light at S. W. People occupied the most part at clearing a road. 3 men working at a harness & Collars. Sick list as yesterday.

12th. Wednesday. Wind and wea: much the Same as yesterday. People employed much the Same also, one man cutting hay, 2 men attending the coal pit. Visited by a few Clatsops who traded Some Beaver. Sick list the Same.

Augt 13th. Thursday. Cloudy Weather as for several days past. People variously employed. Carpenters, Taylor, and Blacksmiths at their respective trades. Cannon with three men making a Lime Kiln. One making harness. Three at the Coal Pit. The remainder cutting wood for Lime Kiln, cutting hay. Finished road in which to draw out Timber, etc., etc. 3 men sick. Sawyers completed the timber, etc., for Bastions this day.[67]

---

[65] See above, n. 58, for a discussion of John Day's "madness." The Cathlatamass were probably one of the Upper Chinookian tribes clustered about the mouth of the Willamette, possibly the Cathalakamaps. Cathlaputles is a variant spelling for Cathlapootle. The broken promise was probably an agreement by the Cathlapootle to see Day all the way to Astoria.

[66] The road was probably to be used by the newly acquired draft horses when they pulled logs.

[67] Lime was used as an ingredient in whitewash and in tanning. Advanced agriculturalists in the eastern states had begun to use it as a fertilizer, but it is doubtful the Astorians knew of that use. In the event, they failed to make any lime.

14th. Friday. Pleasant calm Weather. All hands employed pretty nearly as Yesterday. The harness being finished, tackled one of the Horses who drawed very well & with little difficulty. Three men with his assistance drew out considerable Timber for the buildings. Two Sandwich Islanders cutting & bringing home hay. Visited by numbers of Indians who traded 4 Beaver, some Mats, Gum, etc. Among others, one arrived from up the River, bringing back the Dog (General) Mr. Clarke lost on his way up. Of this we had been informed by their Letter, but doubted whether we should get him again. Carpenters finished the Bastions to day. Three men cutting & hewing timber for buildings.

15th. Saturday. Pleasant and very warm; Wind Westerly. People employed as Yesterday. Visited by numbers of Indians trading Mats, Gum, etc., etc. Dorion, Ignace, & Bruguiere, working at 2 cedar canoes for some time past, and which will occupy them for some time to come. 3 men sick.

16th. Sunday. Clear pleasant Weather, Wind Westerly; proved a very warm day. Visited early by several of the Natives, traded some Venison (one Quarter), Mats, Skins, etc. 2 men sick.

Augt. 17th. Monday. Hazy, sultry Weather. All hands variously employed. Mechanics at their respective trades, Carpenters commenced framing the building. Two men with the horses drawing out Timber. Cannan & two others burning Lime Kiln, which they set fire to this morning. Three attending Coal Pit. Two or three cutting & bringing home hay. Remainder cutting & hewing Timber, cutting wood for Lime Kiln, etc. 4 men sick. John Day, who went out last evening, returned this forenoon having killed a young Elk, very fat. Sent some men with him for it, who arrived in the afternoon. Visited by numbers of Indians, traded some Gum, Mats, Waltap, etc., etc.[68]

18th. Tuesday. Cloudy, misty Weather. All hands employed pretty nearly as Yesterday. Our horses begin to work very well, and so far answer our

---

[68] If McDougall had ever indicated what the "waltap" was used for, it might have been possible to identify it precisely. It is probably what Ross Cox called whattap, i.e., a tough fibrous root used in sewing bark canoes (*Columbia*, p. 371, n. 3). However, the Astorians did not use bark canoes on the Columbia, because of the absence of the appropriate tree. What they did find was wattap, vessels woven of a tough, fibrous root by the native women; they were woven so tightly that they could hold water and were used to cook, heating the contents with hot stones pulled from a fire. The mats that the Astorians have been trading for some time were probably the same material. They may have used the vessels for dry storage and the root as caulking for the plank canoes and boats they built. It should be noted that the Chinook women, because they made the vessels and probably also dug the roots, were the ones who conducted the trade. See below, August 20, 1812, for an explicit mention of women doing this trading. The gum was also used for caulking canoes and boats.

wishes. Visited by several natives trading Mats & Gum. John Day went hunting again this afternoon. 5 men sick. Received a Visit from Comcomly and his youngest son, who traded a number of Beaver Skins. Brought also a pocket Pistol belonging to Mr. Seton lost on his way up with the party among other things. He told us a long story about his having a number of people out hunting Beaver, and likewise that he would trade all the Guns, found by the Indians above belonging to our party that he should see, for which he has the promise of a suitable reward.[69]

19th. Wednesday. Cloudy and Rainy most of the day. People employed as for two days past. John Day returned this forenoon unsuccessful. Visited by a few Indians with Gum, Mats, and 2 small Beaver. 5 men sick.

Augt 20th. Thursday. Cloudy with intervals of Rain throughout the day. People employed as usual. One man working in the Garden sowing Turnip seeds. During last night a fire broke out among the old logs, Stumps, brush, etc. that has been thrown off the bank adjoining our Garden, and raged at a great rate. All hands were called up, endeavoring to stop it, but could not. Some part of the fence had caught fire, but the whole along the bank was taken down to prevent further mischief. Fortunately the wind at the time was blowing from the Southward and the buildings, therefore in no danger. Two men busy part of the day putting the fence up again. Visited by great numbers of the natives, principally Women, bringing large quantities of waltap, Gum, etc. 6 men sick. John Day, Mr. Halsey & T. McKay went with a Canoe up Youngs River to spend some time hunting.[70]

21st. Friday. Pleasant Weather. People variously employed, as during the Week, Three in the Smith's Shop, Three framing Buildings, 2 sawing, 2 burning Lime Kiln, 8 at the coal Pits, cutting wood, etc.; the remainder cutting & hewing Timber, leveling the ground where the buildings are to stand, etc. Taylor employed during the week making a Tent, Oil Cloths, etc. Cooper, Harteau, Flannagan, LaBonte & Tuanna Sick. Visited by many of the natives trading gum, mats, etc.

---

[69] Comcomly seems to have had three sons: Gassagass, Chalowane, and Shalakal. Their birth order, other than that Gassagass was oldest, is uncertain; see below, September 16, 1812.

[70] The fire is a clear demonstration of the frailty of the post. Had the wind turned and the fire gotten out of control, they could have lost their shelter, food, tools, everything, and been reduced to an absolute dependence on the natives for their shelter and most of their food. It is interesting that McDougall does not suspect the natives of setting the fire or, if he does, does not record his suspicion. It may well have been either from a workman's carelessness or natural. Until the day before the fire, McDougall does not record any rain for the month of August, so the tangle of brush, stumps, etc., was natural tinder.

22d. Saturday. Weather as yesterday. People employed the same also. Visited by several of the natives trading a few Skins, Gum, Mats, etc. 5 men sick.

Augt 23rd. Sunday. Fine pleasant Weather, Wind fresh at Westward. Visited by a few Indians, trading a few Mats etc. John Day & Company returned from hunting unsuccessful. 4 men sick.

24th. Monday. Clear pleasant Weather, Wind N. E. and very warm. All hands variously employed. Burning Lime Kiln, Coal Pits. Cutting hay, cutting wood for Coal Pits. Sawing timber for buildings, framing ditto, hewing timber, levelling foundation, and gathering stone for chimneys. John Day, Thomas McKay & Jeremie went up the River in a canoe to spend some time hunting. Visited by some of the Natives who traded a few fresh Salmon, Skins, etc., etc. Sick list as Yesterday.[71]

25th. Tuesday. Warm pleasant Weather, Wind most of the day from N.E; towards evening changed to N. W. and became very cool. All hands employed pretty nearly as Yesterday. Two hands went yesterday round Point George to cut hay, where they will probably be employed several days. Our hay at home was stacked to day, being very well cured. Clerks employed examing & beating furs. Visited by a few of the natives, who traded a few Skins. 3 men sick.[72]

26th. Wednesday. Cloudy most part of the day with wind from Westward. People variously employed framing, building, cutting & hewing Timber, Sawing, gathering Stone, making Hay, cutting wood for Coal Pits, etc. One man with the Horse drawing Timber. After nine days constant attendance with two men to the Lime Kiln, we are obliged to abandon the project as fruitless. No appearance of lime whatever is to be seen. While overhauling the Furs to day in the store, an Indian was detected in the act of stealing 3 skins, who, after some little resistance, was secured in Irons, not a little to his mortification, being a stranger and had Just arrived from up the River with a Canoe load of dried Salmon. The idea of being put in Irons (or Chick-a-min, as they term it) is a great dread to the natives, but unfortunately in every instance but one before this they have effected means for their escape. At evening the two returned from cutting hay, their provisions being expended. Two men were sent this afternoon at high water to clear a place in

---

[71] Obviously, Jeremie has worked his way back into McDougall's good graces, at least to the extent that he was trusted off the post, albeit in the company of others.

[72] Beating the furs was part of the process whereby they were cleaned, prior to pressing and packing. "Examing" is a mistake for examining.

the little Bay to haul up the Shallop. Two men sick, besides Jeremy, who is with the hunters having a sore hand.[73]

27th. Thursday. Pleasant Weather, fore part of the day cloudy. All hands employed as Yesterday. Visited by Comcomly, Skamaquiah and a good number of Chinooks, who, we understood were coming to redeem our prisoner. It however proved otherwise, as they did not say anything concerning him, more than inquiring the amount of the theft. Comcomly brought about 30 Beaver, a few Clemels, etc. The beaver he had previously contracted & received payment for. The demand for the Ransom of the criminal in confinment was 6 Beaver, which his woman was in some difficulty to procure. However, at evening they were brought, but three only were taken (the number he attempted stealing), and him released. John Day & Company returned from hunting with no better luck than before. Had several shots but could Kill none with the Rifle (Cooper's). He had it carrying too small a ball. Sick list the same.

Augt. 28th. Friday. Cloudy Weather, wind light wind from Westward. People employed pretty nearly as for several days past. St. Amant employed at making a temporary machine for packing our furs, which has occupied his time greater part of the week. Sent two men up Young's bay after Cedar for the Canoes. Received a Mare from Comcomly, which we traded for while on his last visit here yesterday. Visited by several of the natives trading a few Mats, Gum, etc., etc. Cannan & Jeremy getting out Stone, blasting, etc., by the Wharf. Sick list the same.[74]

29th. Saturday. Weather cloudy & unpleasant. For two days past have not done any thing to the furs on account of the Weather. People employed much the same as Yesterday. Sick list the same. John Day went hunting, had two shots at an Elk but lost him. His ill luck in this instance, as in several before, he attributes to the want of a good Gun.

30th. Sunday. Fine pleasant weather, Wind fresh at Westward. Visited by several Indians, who brought two Beaver, some Gum, Mats, etc. Calpo brought here and traded a gun that he purchased from an Indian living up

---

[73] As an example of the way the trade lingo, Chinook, formed, "Chick-a-min" or "click-a-min" was a repetition of the sound of the handcuffs or irons being fastened and locked. In spite of the dire tone of the punishment, McDougall deals rather gently with the thief, as the next day's entry shows. This is not to say that the Europeans were entirely reasonable in expecting the natives to follow their notions of private property, especially when the disparity in possessions is considered.

[74] The machine is a press, for compacting the furs into the smallest possible package for shipping. See Paul C. Phillips, *The Fur Trade*, 2 vols. (Norman: University of Oklahoma Press, 1961), I, 198, for a picture of a fur press.

the river, which had belonged to Mr. Reed and was lost by the party proceeding up. LaBonté & Tuanna, the old invalids only on the sick list. Flannagan is unwell & complaining, but keeps about at light work.[75]

31st. Monday. Clear pleasant Weather, light wind from N. W. All hands variously employed, cutting Wood for Coal Pits, building a shelter for Coals, etc., Cutting Hay, Cutting & hewing Timber, Sawing, getting out Stone. Carpenters at work framing, etc. One man employed with the two hunters making Canoes. Taylor occupied as for some time past making Tents, etc. The two men sent on Friday for Timber returned this morning. John Day, Thomas McKay & Flannagan went in a canoe up the River hunting. Clerks, etc., examining and beating the Furs. Visited by a few Natives bringing Gum, etc. In the afternoon raised the frame of our New House, which was put up without any difficulty whatever. Sick list as Yesterday.[76]

Septr 1st. Tuesday. Pleasant weather as Yesterday, people employed much the same also. Visited by Comcomly, etc. At evening John Day & Company returned, with the pleasing intelligence of having Killed Two Elk about 8 miles above Tongue Point, where he finds good hunting ground. Sick list same.

2d. Wednesday. Pleasant Weather. People variously employed, Getting out Stone, drawing them, making Hay, Bringing hay and assisting in putting up Coal Pits and bringing out Wood for them. Carpenters, etc., at work at the House. Sawyers & other tradesmen at their usual occupations. Visited yesterday by Ashwallax with two Canoes, bringing for trade, Cedar bark, Hoop Poles, etc., who took their departure this morning. John Day & Co. started this morning again hunting, taking 8 men along to bring the meat of the Elk Killed. The men, accompanied by Thomas McKay arrived with it in the evening. Sick list same.[77]

Septr 3. Thursday. Fine pleasant Weather. People employed as Yesterday. St. Amant still employed at making the machine for pressing furs. Mr. McDougall, etc., employed assorting the Skins, having finished beating them on Monday. Three men digging Clay, and a number of Sandwich Islanders bringing Sand in a canoe from a little distance above, preparing to finish the chimneys in our old house, and build that in the new one. Visited by a few Indians. 3 men sick.

---

[75] Reed probably lost the gun in going up river in July, but it could have gone astray during the abortive effort in the spring of 1812; see above, I, no. 169.

[76] The preparation of tents indicates that more visits to the interior are being contemplated. The house is probably the one for which framing was begun in March.

[77] Ashwallax was a Chelwit chief.

4th. Friday. Weather as yesterday. All hands employed pretty nearly the same. Finished assorting the furs, the press not yet completed. Dorion, Ignace & Company finished another canoe this afternoon, being their third. Thomas McKay, with one Sandwich Islander, was sent in a Canoe to the hunting ground where they left John Day, but the wind from N. E. was too strong, and they returned. [Calpo informed us of an accident having happened to the Ship's Boat at Newittie.] 5 men sick.[78]

5th. Saturday. Fine pleasant Weather. People employed as during the Week. Thomas McKay with one Sandwich Islander went to the hunting ground. Visited by a few Indians, who traded a few Skins, etc. 3 men sick. Cannan cut his leg badly this afternoon, but continued his work. Our Sawyers, Pillon & Laframboise finished the Job of timber for the building in considerable less time than was allowed to them, having worked exceeding well.

Septr 6th. Sunday. Cloudy, thick Weather, with appearances of Rain. At evening John Day and company returned with the meat of an Elk. 2 men sick.

7th. Monday. Cloudy Weather as Yesterday. Early in the morning a party was sent off up the river for the purpose of procuring Cedar Timber for Shingles and for building boats. Mr. Wallace accompanied them. The two sawyers, Boat Builder, two men, & Boy Perreault composed the number. Dorion & Bruguiere were also despatched at the same for Timber for Canoes. Cannan & Cooper were set at work building up the old Chimney. The assistance of 4 men was necessary to attend them. Two working at hay. Three at the Coal Pits. Three at different Jobs, preparing to press the furs, etc. Mechanics employed at their respective trades. John Day, Ignace, Thomas McKay with 2 Sandwich Islanders were sent hunting. Sick list as Yesterday.

8th. Tuesday. Cloudy most of the day, Wind from S. and S. W. People employed much as yesterday. Began pressing Furs, the weather proving unfavorable finished only one Pack. During the time of dirt and confusion while building up the chimney, our mess room was changed for one of the upper Bastions. These for many purposes will be a great convenience.

Septr 9th. Wednesday. Pleasant Weather, Wind light from Westward.

---

[78] The "hunting ground" is probably the area eight miles above Tongue Point, which McDougall referred to on September 1. Calpo's information, in brackets, is a marginal note in pencil. Whatever his source, it probably did not alarm McDougall too much, as Hunt was destined for the Russian post at New Archangel (Sitka), on Baranov Island in Alaska. It was very unlikely that he would pause to do any trading along the way, and he did not. "Newittie" (various spellings) was on Clayoquot Sound, on the west coast of Vancouver Island.

People employed as yesterday. Visited by several Indians who traded some Beaver, Berries, Mint, etc. Purchased also from one the meat of a Bear, Just killed on his way down the River. Sick list again reduced to the number of two, Viz., Labonte and Tuanna, both invalids.[79]

10th. Thursday. Fine Weather, Wind light at Westward. All hands variously employed, pretty nearly as usual. Mr. Wallace with most of the party returned from up the River, having met with no success in finding Timber suitable to saw for Boats, etc. Roussel, one Sandwich Islander, and Boy Perreault only remained. They were set to sawing timber for Shingles for which purpose the timber will answer. Dorion and Bruguiere succeeded in procuring their timber for Canoes and arrived along with the others. Visited by several of the Natives, trading, among others Walaly, with the meat of a Bear, but which had been too long killed. Cannan & Cooper finished the chimney in the old House this evening, which unfortunately smokes at such a rate that it must be taken down and again built. Sick list same.

11th. Friday. Cloudy with partial showers during the day. All hands variously employed. 8 men employed at Coal Pits. Cooper & Cannan were set at work pulling down the chimney which smoked so badly as not to be endured. Three men attending & assisting them. Finished packing Furs. Sick list as for some time past.

Septr 12th. Saturday. Pleasant Weather. People employed pretty much the same as yesterday. Cooper only working at the chimney. Cannan unwell & laid up. St. Amant with the horses drawing Timber to the Saw Pit. Visited by several of the natives. At evening Thomas McKay and the Two Islanders arrived from the Hunting ground with Two Elk, leaving John Day and Ignace remaining. 3 men sick.

13th. Sunday. Pleasant Weather as yesterday. Visited by a few Indians, Ashwallax and others from up the River with same Cedar Bark & Hoop Poles. One of our sows had Pigs to day which were all immediately eaten by her and the other hogs, the second instance of the Kind which has happened with them this season. Sick list as Yesterday.

14th. Monday. Pleasant. At evening appearance of Rain. People variously employed as during last week. Cannan continuing unwell. The Cooper is at work alone building the chimney, three men assisting him. 7 at the Coal Pits. Two bringing clay from a little way above. Two sent up the River where

---

[79] Aside from the "working wounded," that is, Cannan who cut his leg on September 5 and Flannagan who was feeling "unwell" on August 30, this is about the smallest sick list since the Astorians first landed. This happy situation did not last long.

Roussel, etc., were left getting out timber for Shingles, one assisting Dorion in making another Canoe. Mechanics busily occupied at their several trades. 3 men sick.

15th. Tuesday. Pleasant Weather, Wind at Westward. Rain during good part of last night, the first of any consequence for a long time. People employed nearly as Yesterday. Sawyers busy sawing Boards, etc., for buildings. Visited by a few Indians. Little was set at work yesterday putting the Shallop in order for a trip up the River, caulking the Decks, etc., etc., it being now near the season she should be gone for the purpose of procuring Provisions: Salmon, etc. Sick list same.[80]

16th. Wednesday. Pleasant fine Weather. People as usually employed. Visited by several canoes of Indians from up the River with Cedar Bark, Wapatoes, etc. John Day & Thomas McKay with the S. Islanders arrived from hunting, bringing the meat of an Elk. Traded one Elk with Samasay and good part of another with Skamaquiah. For several weeks they have been very fat and tolerable plenty, but are now getting poor. Sent two Islanders in a Canoe to bring home Ignace & family from hunting, who all arrived in the evening. 5 men sick. Visited to day by Two of Comcomly's sons, Gassagas & the younger one. The breach with the former was made up. He was very sensible of having acted improperly, and of the disadvantage it was to him to be at variance with us. We have now his promise for better behavior in future.[81]

17th. Thursday. Pleasant Weather. People employed much the same as for some time past. St. Amant with the assistance of Two Islanders repairing the old chimney in the men's part of the building. Cannan & Little off duty. Several occupied for several days past in building a house for Fowls, Hogs, etc. Most of the men except Mechanics, & Sawyers working at the Coal Pits, cutting Wood, etc. An Indian arrived in the afternoon from Baker's Bay with intelligence of having heard Two guns fired off Cape Disappointment, one yesterday evening and one this morning, tho' he could see no sail.

---

[80] John Little is on the roster of Astorians (Appendix, No. 101) as "boat builder." He was one of those who signed on in New York in October 1811 and came out on the *Beaver*; "Articles of Agreement," Porter, *Astor*, I, 475–78. His location is given as *Raccoon*, the Royal Navy vessel which arrived at Astoria shortly after the post had been sold to the North West Company in November 1813. It left in December with Little and Paul Jeremie aboard; see Franchère, *Journal*, p. 135. Jeremie had signed on as a clerk, and Little was being taken to the Hawaiian Islands because of his poor health. He has not been mentioned previously in connection with boat or ship building.

[81] See above, August 18, 1812, for a note on Comcomly's sons. See below, October 2, 26, 1812 for further mention of the other sons.

We strongly suspect it may be the Beaver tho' we do not expect her so soon by 3 weeks. Ashwallax, who is here encamped on our Point with his party of domestics, etc., having brough down Bark, etc., for trade, being detained on account of the loss of his canoes from the wharf, was to day on the Clatsop point in search of them, heard also the report of two guns. Sick list as yesterday.

18th. Friday. Pleasant Weather. All hands employed as Yesterday. Cooper finished the chimney at length, which will answer the purpose wished for. Visited by numbers of Indians, Clatsops, Cathlamats, etc. Purchased a canoe and a number of Beaver. Among others came Watatkum & his wife formerly residing here with us as hunter, and for that purpose was furnished with a musket & ammunition. Some time ago he was taken sick and removed for a while to the Clatsops. He soon recovered and has continued away since during the whole of the best season for Elk, Keeping the musket & ammunition, with which he killed great numbers of Elk, but brought us none. For his misbehavior we now had him put in Irons. Ashwallax & his men returned again this evening after a fruitless search for his canoes. Sick list the same.[82]

Septr 19th. Saturday. Pleasant Weather, wind light at Westward. People employed much as yesterday. Ignace & family with one Sandwich Islander went up the river to spend some time hunting. Our Clatsop visitors yesterday informed us of the destruction of the Beaver and all hands on board somewhere near or at Nootka. The intelligence they said came from people arrived among them far from the Northward. Little credit however was given to the story, as the supposition that the Beaver is now off the Cape is not yet satisfied. Sent two men with a canoe up to where our people are making Shingles. Ashwallax & party went with them, having given over further search for his canoes, and had no other means of getting to his Village.[83]

20th. Sunday. Cloudy thick weather. Two of our men that went out hunting this forenoon in a small canoe returned with a Bear which they killed in the River at Point George. 2 men sick.

21st. Monday. Cloudy, unpleasant weather and considerably cool. People variously employed, four Sawing, seven at the Coal Pits [Two cutting a road

---

[82] See above, June 7, 1811, for the original agreement with this native. The length of his stay in irons is unknown; the next mention of him is on October 1st, when he returns with "the meat of an elk."

[83] McDougall is correct in not crediting the news of the loss of the Beaver, but how it is related to the ship's non-appearance off the "Cape," i.e., the mouth of the river, is a mystery. As Ashwallax's village is about forty miles up the river, the place where the men are cutting shingles must be within that distance.

across to Point George, for the purpose of having our horses pass there to feed in the meadows & marshes.] Cooper at his trade, Cannan employed at guns, etc. St. Amant & one S. Islander with the horses drawing out stone for the chimney in the new house, one man preparing mortar for the same. Mechanics busily occupied at their several trades. Two canoes arrived in the afternoon with shingles from up the River. 3 men sick.[84]

Septr 22d. Tuesday. Cloudy Weather, Wind at N. W. Mr. Wallace and party consisting of seven persons & 3 canoes started early after shingles. People occupied much as yesterday: 4 only at the coal Pit; Cannan & Cooper with 3 men to assist them began the chimney of the new building; Two getting out stones for ditto. Visited by a number of Indians who traded several fine Sturgeon. [We now learn from the Indians that it is Capt. Eayres and not Capt. Sowle that is cut off, etc.] John Day, Mr. Halsey & T. McKay in the forenoon went in a canoe above Tongue Point to spend some time hunting. Sick list as yesterday.[85]

23rd. Wednesday, Pleasant weather. People employed as usual. One of the sawyers laid up with a sore foot, which stops one saw. Mr. Franchere and one man putting a new roof on part of the Blacksmith's Shop. Visited by several canoes of Indians from up the River, with Cedar Bark, etc. 4 men sick.

24th. Thursday. Cloudy, Wind light at N. E. All hands employed as usual. Boat builder making a small skiff to accompany the Shallop, which he has been for 2 days employed at. The new building, Coal Pits and canoes now occupies all hands (except Blacksmiths, Taylor, etc.) in one way and another. Mr. Wallace and party arrived with 3 canoe loads of shingles. At Evening John Day & company returned from hunting bringing the meat of three Elk. Sick list as Yesterday. In this Pelton, our strange fellow, is not ever included, as we can make neither one thing or another of him.[86]

---

[84] The bracketed words are lined out in the manuscript. See below, September 27, for the accomplishment of the task.

[85] The bracketed words are a marginal notation with no place indicated in the journal for their insertion. "Capt. Eayres" is George W. Ayers, captain of the *Mercury*, which was in the area at the time; there is no indication, however, that he had any particular difficulty. In December, he was at Oahu where he did business with Wilson Price Hunt. See Porter, *Astor*, I, 435, 469, 472, 518, 522.

[86] The "boat builder" is presumably John Little. See the next day's entry for the completion of the vessel. Since McDougall notes that he has been working on it for two days, Little finishes the job in three or four days. A skiff is defined variously as a small, light sailboat or a rowboat.

Septr 25th. Friday. Cloudy with some Rain. All hands employed as Yesterday. Ignace & family arrived from hunting, bringing only a few ducks, etc. Boat builder finished the Skiff, and with it took off the anchors, etc., to the Shallop. Made also other preparations for her departure. At evening Comcomly arrived from up the River with considerable Quantity of furs, being too late to trade them. Encamped for the night in the little Bay below us.[87]

26th. Saturday. Weather as Yesterday, rained considerably during the night. Comcomly, after trading to the value of about 90 Beaver, took his departure for Bakers Bay. All hands busily employed as for several days past. 4 men sick.

27th. Sunday. Pleasant, wind N. W. Eleven men were set at work cutting a road through the Wood to Point George for the purpose of having our horses pass there to feed, for which they received a small present each. Had it completed in a few hours. Sick list the same. In a fracas that took place between two of the men on Friday last at the Coal Pit, one was so badly wounded as to be laid up unfit for duty, making 5 men sick.[88]

28th. Monday Cloudy, unpleasant Weather. All hands variously employed between the building, Coal Pits, & Sawing. Four shaving & sawing shingles. One of our Sawyers who has for several days been sick resumed his work to day, when another one is laid up; so that one saw only is going. In the afternoon the two Canoes arrived from up the River with the remainder of the Shingles and men that were left there. Finished arranging the Shallop which is now ready for departure. Sick list as yesterday.

29th. Tuesday. Cloudy with some rain, wind light from the Southward. All hands employed as yesterday. Sick list the same. John Day, Thomas McKay and one Sandwich Islander went in a canoe up Young's River a hunting. Got the articles for trade, etc., put on board the Shallop.

30th. Wednesday. First part the day cloudy, afternoon clear & pleasant, wind light at S.W. All hands busily employed as usual. In the afternoon the Dolly took her departure on a voyage up the River. G. Franchere, Benjamin

---

[87] Comcomly is apparently again (or still) acting the part of middleman between the Astorians and some of the up-river tribes.

[88] Here, McDougall records the performance of the task first put in, and then lined out, on the 21st. Perhaps it was not done then because he underestimated its size and difficulty, as it takes eleven, not two, men to do it "in a few hours" and all receive "a small present." The present may have been in consideration of working on Sunday. He also notes what probably occurred much more frequently than the record of the log shows, fights among the men. Notice that he does not even bother to record either the names or whether the fighters were European or Hawaiian.

Clapp, John Little, Joseph Gervais, Alosy. Flanagan & three Sandwich Islanders on board. 8 men sick.[89]

Oct. 1st. Thursday. Pleasant Weather, wind fresh at N.E. People employed much the Same as yesterday. One man blasting rocks, and one man clearing a road to draw out wood for the coal pit. Visited by a number of the natives who traded a few skins. In the afternoon Watatkum brought in the meat of an Elk. Ignace & family returned from hunting, bringing the meat of half an Elk. At evening Comcomily with two of his sons (Gassagass & Chalowane) arrived from Bakers Bay with a quantity of furs & some fresh Salmon. Being too late to trade them, they encamped in the little bay below us. 7 men sick.

2d. Friday. Pleasant, wind variable from N. E. to S. W. People occupied much as yesterday. Cannan & Cooper with three men working at the chimney in the new house. Visited by a few Chinook Indians who traded 5 Large Sturgeon. Comcomly & his son Gassagass after trading to the value of about fifty Beaver took their departure for Bakers Bay. Chalowane (having offered his services) remained to accompany the shallop up the river. In the afternoon, Chalowane left here in a Canoe for the Dolly which is now laying at anchor in Grays Bay in sight of the Factory, where she has been since the evening she left here, detained by adverse winds. Sent with him Two Sturgeon. John Day & Com. returned unsuccessful. Sick list as yesterday.[90]

3d. Saterday. Cloudy, latter part clear and pleasant, Wind Westerly. All hands employed as yesterday. Visited by a few natives who traded a few skins. Sick list the same. St. Amant & one Sandwich Islander stacking and securing the hay that was blown down some days ago in Youngs Bay. Eight men at work at the Coal pits, building a shelter for the coal, [drawing out wood with the horses] and attending to the pits.[91]

4th. Sunday. Morning, thick hazy weather; afternoon, pleasant, wind fresh at Southward and Westward. Visited by a few Indians trading some skins, etc. Sick list the same.

---

[89] This is the trip contemplated on September 15 when McDougall noted the necessity of getting the shallop ready to send her up river to secure provisions. He may also have been moved to send her off by Comcomly's trading (on September 26 and October 2) about 140 beaver pelts, clearly the result of the old Indian's self-appointed role as middleman between the Astorians and the tribes up river. The *Dolly* returned on October 22 with furs, dried salmon, and oak timbers.

[90] This hiring of Chalowane seems straightforward; however, see below, October 26th, where the pilot seems to be Shalakal. It is hard to believe that McDougall either does not know the difference between the two or has confused their names. Gray's Bay is about ten miles northeast of Astoria, on the north bank of the Columbia.

[91] The words in brackets are lightly lined out in the manuscript.

5th. Monday. Wind and weather as yesterday. People variously employed. Patterson at work at the building. Cooper & Cannan with four men to assist them at the chimney. Two men sawing, 5 at the coal pits. One shaving poles for the canoes, one shaving and sawing shingles. Dorion & one man employed at the canoe. Blacksmiths and Taylor at their trades. John Day, Ignace, Thomas McKay with two S. Islanders started this morning a hunting. Eight men on the sick list.

6th. Tuesday. Clear pleasant weather, Wind fresh at N. E. People employed pretty much as yesterday. Two men boiling gum. St. Amant assisting Dorion & Brugier with the canoe. Visited by several of the natives who traded a few furs, etc. Six men Sick.[92]

7th. Wednesday. Cloudy with some rain. All hands employed as yesterday. Dorion & Co. finished the Canoe this afternoon, being their fourth one. Ignace with one S. Islander arrived from hunting, bringing about 20 ducks. Visited by a few Indians trading skins, mats, etc. 5 men sick. During the night, the men employed at the coal pit had all their tools stolen from them by the Indians.[93]

8th. Thursday. Cloudy wet weather, wind Southerly. People employed as usual. Ignace & family went up the river to spend some time hunting. Lucier, Belleau, Jeramie, LaBonte & Tuanna Sick.

9th. Friday. Pleasant, Wind S.W. People variously employed. St. Amant & Dorion Caulking canoes, Six men attending the masons & making mortar, two gathering stone, two only at the coal pit, One boiling gum, two shaving Shingles, mechanics at their different occupations. At evening John Day and party arrived from hunting, again unsuccessful. Sick list as yesterday.

10th. Saterday. Pleasant weather, wind fresh at Northward. People as usually employed. Sick list the same.

11th. Sunday. Weather as yesterday, Wind Southerly. Visited by a few of the natives who traded six fresh Salmon. Sick list the same. Cannan & Cooper kept busy to day at the chimney. Dorion, St. Amant & Creole finished guming one Canoe today.

12th. Monday. Forepart of the day Pleasant. Afternoon Cloudy, with appearances of rain. All hands variously employed, two only at the coal pit, Four guming canoes, one boiling gum for ditto. At evening Cannan &

---

[92] The gum which the men have started to prepare in some quantity recently is an accompaniment to the canoe building, with the gum (and possibly the waltap) being used to caulk the plank canoes. See below, October 11 and 12, 1812.

[93] See below, March 10, 1813, for the outcome of this incident.

Cooper finished the Chimney. Carpenters, Blacksmiths, & Taylor at their respective occupations. John Day, J. Carteau & one S. Islander went in a canoe up youngs River to spend some time a hunting. Visited by a few Indians trading Salmon, etc. LaBonté who has been a long time ill is fast recovering, and insists that he keeps about at light work, & has been for several days past assisting with the canoes. Roussil laid up with a sore hand, making our sick list amount to 5 persons.

Oct. 13. Tuesday. Cloudy with rain. People variously employed. Cannan & Cooper boaring & pining Shingles; nine men employed at the Coal pits, Cutting Wood, etc.; One man caulking the Store with moss. Visited by a few Clatsops trading a few Clemels, etc. Four men Sick. Two of the number, however, well enough to be set to work Smoking Skins and making mockasons, which they were employed in during the day.[94]

14th. Wednesday. Cloudy unpleasant weather. People employed nearly as yesterday. Cannan & Paterson putting the roof on the new house, Cooper & LaBonté Shaving Shingles, 3 men carrying ditto, 8 at the Coal pits. Ignace & family returned from hunting, bringing about 20 Geese and as many Ducks. Sick list the same.

15th. Thursday. Squally with rain, wind at S. W. People employed the same as yesterday. In the Afternoon our Indian Hunter brought in a few geese. John Day & Co. returned, with no better luck than before. Sick list as yesterday.

16th. Friday. Incessant rain all day. People employed nearly as yesterday. Cannan & Cooper with two men to assist them building a wall on each side of the chinmey in the new house. Bruguiere set to Work with LaFramboise sawing Plank for the building. One man with the horses drawing plank from t' e saw pit to the building. Visited by a few of the natives, who traded several roasted salmon. Ignace & family with one Sandwich Islander went hunting. Sick list the same.

Oct. 17th. Saterday. Wet, disagreeable weather, wind S.W. People Busily employed between the Building, Coal Pits, and Canoes. In the Afternoon, Dorion & Co. finished gumming the canoes. 5 men Sick.

18th. Sunday. Clear, pleasant Weather. Wind fresh at N. E. Sick list the same.

---

[94] Boring and pinning shingles means drilling a hole in the upper portion of the shingle and pinning or fastening it to the roof. The skins which were being smoked were probably deer or elk. Recall the abortive attempt to make lime. If it was wanted for tanning, then smoking could be an alternative method of preparing the skins for use, in this case, "mockasons."

19th. Monday. Wind and Weather as yesterday. All hands variously employed. 8 men at the coal Pits, 2 in the Smith's Shop, 4 Sawing, 3 putting a new roof on part of the shed, 2 men with the horses drawing out timbers. Patterson & LaBonté employed at the building, Cooper laying hearths in ditto. Taylor at his trade. Visited by a few of the natives, trading a few fresh Salmon. Seven men off duty.

20th. Tuesday. Weather clear and quite cool, wind Northerly. People employed nearly as yesterday, Three men building a hog pen, One digging Potatoes, which turn out near Six bushels, and among them were two weighing 3¾ lbs. Dorion & LaBonte employed at the canoes. Sick list as yesterday.[95]

21st. Wednesday. Wind and weather as yesterday. People employed as usual. Cannan blasting rock, 5 men bringing hay from young's bay to the coal pit. John Day with one man went in a canoe above Tongue point to spend some time hunting. Discharged our four large guns, which have been loaded for some time past, and had them painted. Cooper, Macon, Lucier, Belleau, & two S. Islanders Sick.[96]

Oct. 22nd. Thursday. Pleasant. People employed nearly as yesterday. 2 at the coal pit, 2 cutting timber for the saw pit, 4 bringing hay. In the afternoon Ignace & family returned from hunting bringing about 30 Geese. Mr. Clapp also arrived in their canoe, having left the Shallop at anchor on this side of Tongue Point. Wind and tide against him. At evening the Shallop arrived and anchored in the bay below us, with a cargo of Furs, dried Salmon, and some Oak Timbers. (All Well). Visited by a Cathlamet Indian who traded thirty three fresh Salmon. 6 men sick.[97]

23d. Friday. Weather as yesterday. People employed the same also. Got the Shallop alongside of the wharf and unloaded her. Visited by a few Indians who traded a few fresh Salmon. 5 men Sick.

24th. Saterday. Same Pleasant weather as yesterday, Wind northerly. People employed as usual. One man with the horses drawing out wood at the coal pit, 3 cutting wood to build a Shelter for the Goats. John Day returned from Hunting, bringing the meat of a Bear. Afternoon Dorion & Ignace

---

[95] As in December 1811, without explicitly stating it, McDougall seems more than content with the produce of the garden.

[96] Discharging the cannons was a precaution against the charges in them becoming damp, thus making them unreliable in the event they had to be fired in anger. Also, the task of withdrawing the charges, without firing them, was bothersome and dangerous.

[97] The *Dolly* is returning from the trip up river which began nominally on September 30, actually on October 2. The parenthetical "All Well" refers to those on the shallop; as usual, there are five or six men on the sick list.

with their families went in two canoes up the River, to spend some time a hunting. Watatkum brought in 11 Geese. 6 men Sick.

Octr. 25th. Sunday. Weather Pleasant as Yesterday, Wind from N. E. In the afternoon Comcomly and suite arrived with Furs, Salmon, etc., being late encamped near the Factory. Calpo with his whole train also arrived from the opposite side of the River to reside at his old place. Several of the people that went hunting Yesterday evening returned with little success. Sick list as Yesterday.[98]

26th. Monday. Cloudy with appearances of Rain, Wind from Southward. Early in the morning a Canoe with Cooper and 5 men were sent off up the River to cut Oak Timber, having with them a small supply of Tobacco & Gurrahs to purchase Provisions, etc. In the course of the forenoon the Dolly was also despatched up the River on a second trip, with Mr. Franchere and 5 men on board. He is to proceed as far up as before if practicable, for the purpose of procuring Provisions, and on his return bring a load of Oak Timber. Comcomly, after trading a good number of fresh & dried Salmon, besides a quantity of Beaver Skins departed for Chinook. His young son Shalakal, who had remained here since the return of the Shallop (after being well rewarded for his services on board her) went away with him. The old Indian (Raccoon) who has for a long time been fed by our bounty was this morning found dead in his Hut. His remains were decently interred in the little Bay below the Factory. Mechanics as usually employed. 4 men sick. The remainder occupied between the Coal Pits and furnishing the Sawyers with Timber. 4 men sawing.[99]

October 27th. Tuesday. Cloudy with intervals of Rain. People as usually employed. A small canoe arrived from up the River with 18 fresh Salmon which were purchased. At evening a Regale was given to the Sandwich

---

[98] With this entry, a new scribe with strikingly different handwriting takes over transcribing the log. Calpo's stay on the south bank of the river will be a short one; see December 21, 1812, for McDougall's summary removal of his new neighbor.

[99] Recall that when the *Dolly* left on October 2, Chalowane was on board; now, Shalakal is being rewarded for services. Unless the shallop came and went, unrecorded, exchanging the two young men, we are faced with an insoluble (and not very significant) mystery; see n. 89 above. The respect shown the old Indian, Racoon, even to the extent of "decently" interring his body is a touching and relatively rare example of respect by the Astorians for a native. The usual Chinook Indian burial practice was to place the body in a canoe with some possessions and provisions and expose it in a tree or on an island. See Jones, ed., *Astorian Adventure*, p. 183. Since Racoon had been banished, he would probably have been left unburied in his hut, or just thrown in the woods, as was done with slaves and persons of no account.

Islanders, this day being their New Year, much celebrated by their country-men. Sick list as yesterday.[100]

28th. Wednesday. Weather as Yesterday, Rainy. Seven men employed at Coal Pits, four Squaring Timber for sawyers, two men sawing, 4 Sick. Mechanics as usually occupied. Had two of our Horses shod, which employed the Blacksmiths good part of the day, being unprepared for such work. Purchased from the natives near 40 fresh Salmon.

29th. Thursday. Rainy disagreeable weather. People employed pretty nearly as Yesterday. Arranged good part of the Outfit for Wolamut River. Could not complete it on account that some Iron works were not in readiness. 4 men sick.

30th. Friday. Weather as Yesterday, Wind fresh & squally from South-ward. For three successive nights have had violent storms of wind & Rain. Men employed as usual, sick list same.

31st. Saturday Disagreeable weather with intervals of Rain. All hands employed as during the week. Two busy most of this day, covering the outside of the store with Mats. 4 men Sick.

November 1st. Sunday. Rainy greater part of the day, Wind moderately fresh from S. W. During a violent shower of rain last night had unusual heavy Thunder. In the evening Comcomly with three Canoes arrived bring-ing fresh Salmon, etc. Encamped near the Factory. Sick list as for several days past, viz., Antoine Belleau recovering from an illness of the Venereal. Two Sandwich Islanders laid up with colds, and Tuanna, the old invalid.

2nd. Monday. Rainy, almost incessantly as during the whole of the last week. Mechanics variously occupied at their respective trades. The remain-ing number of men employed at the Coal Pit, Sawing and preparing Timber in readiness for Sawyers. Comcomly & his son Gassagass traded upwards of one hundred Salmon, and some few furs. The weather proved so stormy and blustering as to forbid their attempting to cross the river and therefore re-mained with us the day & night. In trying the new Traps made for the Wolamut outfit, near half the springs break, owing to the bad quality of the Steel. One more Sandwich Islander added to sick list, making it now 5 in number.

---

[100] The Hawaiian calendar is complicated. First, there are two. One follows a lunar year of 354 days, with twelve months divided into twenty-nine and one-half days each; the other is sidereal (and solar) with 565 days. They are not synchronized, either with each other or with the Western, Gregorian calendar. Valerio Valeri, *Kingship and Sacrifice: Ritual and Society in Ancient Hawaii* (Chicago: The University of Chicago Press, 1985), "The Calendar," pp. 195–99. This celebration of an Hawaiian new year seems to be the only one observed at Astoria.

3d. Tuesday. Weather as yesterday. People employed nearly the same also. Two men with the Horses drawing out Logs for the purpose of building a shelter for Goats, etc. Two Sandwich Islanders filling with earth beneath the floor of the new house. Comcomly & train took their departure for home, promising to be here again with Salmon in six days. Visited by several other Chinooks bringing Salmon and a few Geese. Sick list as yesterday.

4th. Wednesday. Weather tolerably pleasant, without Rain; Wind fresh at S. W. All hands employed nearly as Yesterday. Three men laying up a house which is to serve as a shelter for the Goats. Sick list same. At evening, Watatkum with one other Clatsop arrived with a few Geese, some furs, etc.

5th. Thursday. Pleasant Weather, Wind N. E. All hands variously employed. Cannan at work with the Carpenters, shaving shingles for repairing a part of the old house, in order if possible to make it comfortable. Finished covering the back part of the store with Mats, which the rainy Weather prevented being done sooner. 3 men sick.

6th. Friday. Cloudy, Wind light from Northward & Eastward. People as usually employed. Ignace & his son arrived here in the afternoon, leaving his canoe at Tongue Point. Some Geese & Swans that him & Dorion had killed were brought by Ashwallax, who arrived shortly after in a Canoe. Dorion & families remained above. Ashwallax traded a few Beaver Skins only. Sick list as Yesterday.

7th Saturday. Rainy, Wind variable. People employed as during the week past. Ignace with Ashwallax started for hunting again. Supplied the latter with a Musket and Ammunition for the purpose of procuring provisions for us. Sick list same.

8th Sunday. Rainy, disagreeable weather, wind at Westward.

9th. Monday. Weather as yesterday. All hands variously employed, pretty nearly as last week. Coal Pits & Sawing occupying greater part besides the Mechanics, that are fit for duty. Nearly all the Sandwich Islanders are laid up on account of the continual Wet & damp weather that now prevails. One of our hogs was attacked to day by a Bear near the Coal Pits, and so badly hurt that it was necessary to Kill it for the meat. The people at work heard the noise, went to it, & fired twice at the Bear, but without effect. Several instances of the like has happened before.[101]

---

[101] The difficulty that the damp, cold weather of the Columbia posed for the Hawaiian natives has been noted before; this is an especially clear example of it. There will be several attacks by bears on the Astorians' livestock, which was generally allowed to forage in the woods for themselves. The bears were probably fattening themselves up for their winter hibernation and were more intent on feeding than during the summer.

10th. Tuesday. As usual, Rainy. Messrs. Wallace & Halsey occupied in arranging & packing their Outfit. No intelligence has yet reached here from the people at the Oaks, who stay much beyond the time intended. In the afternoon one of the hogs was heard to make a great noise in the wood a little below the factory and concluding it was certainly attacked by a Bear, several ran to its assistance; when they found our largest hog killed, and the Bear still upon him, which with much difficulty was killed also. Cannan has again unfortunately cut himself, and laid up. Creole unwell, and all the Sandwich Islanders off duty except three.

Novem. 11th. Wednesday. As Yesterday, Rainy. The few men that are able to work employed at the Coal Pits, cutting Wood, etc. Greater part however are laid up with colds. Mechanics occupied as usual. Visited by some Chinooks from whom purchased upwards of 60 fresh Salmon.

12th. Thursday. Rainy as usual. Finished cutting wood for Coal Pits this season, as the weather compels us to abandon further work of this kind. Two men still employed in burning, having Two Pits yet to complete. Roussel this day finished the Beaver Traps (50 in number) for the Wolamut department, with which there has been much trouble on account of the bad quality of the Steel for Springs. Sick list as yesterday.

13th. Friday. Tolerably pleasant, without rain. All hands employed as usual, cutting & hewing Logs for Sawyers, gravelling within the inclosure, and sundry small Jobs. Mechanics at their usual occupations. Comcomly & suite arrived in the afternoon, bringing upwards of five hundred smoked Salmon and a few furs. Five men sick.

14th. Saturday. Clear & pleasant for a novelty. People employed as usual. In the afternoon, Cooper & party arrived from the oaks, having left there, this morning, at which time also the Shallop had left there, but without any wind, drifting only with the tide. Notwithstanding the continual bad weather, they succeeded in getting out a sufficient quantity of Timber to fill the Shallop. Sick list as yesterday.

15th. Sunday. Weather variable, with heavy showers of hail & rain.

16th. Monday. Clear & pleasant. Mr. Franchere arrived with the Dolly about 12 o'clock in safety, having made a tolerable good trip, tho' performed during the worst of weather; besides bringing a load of Oak Timber. Mechanics occupied at their respective trades. All hands beside employed getting out wood for the last Coal Pit. Cooper putting up provisions, etc., for Wolamut outfit, which is now almost completed. 4 men sick. At evening Comcomly's two sons arrived in a large Canoe on their way up the River, bringing a quantity of dried & fresh Salmon. In coming out of the small river up which they live, their canoe upset in a violent, heavy surf. Good part of the provisions then intended to be brought, besides many things else were lost.

17th. Tuesday. Pleasant, afternoon cloudy. Most of the people employed getting out Wood for Coal Pits, several busy discharging the Dolly. Mechanics occupied as usual. Sick list as Yesterday.

Nov. 18th. Wednesday. Cloudy. Wind fresh from N. E. Completed discharging the Dolly, received and examined the returns of her trip, etc. Several hands employed preparing a place to haul her up for the winter. Visited by some Cathlamat Indians who brought a few Salmon, etc. At evening Watatkum arrived with intelligence of having killed an Elk near Capt Lewis's house, and requesting that men might be sent in the morning to bring it. 5 men sick.

19th. Thursday. Rainy during the day. Four Sandwich Islanders with a canoe were despatched early this morning accompanied by Watatkum for the meat of the Elk he had killed. Returned at evening. All hands employed good part of the day hauling the Shallop into the place prepared for the purpose. Accomplished it at high water with very little difficulty. Sick list as Yesterday.

20th. Friday. Rain most of the day. The party for Wolamut River broke off work to day to prepare for their departure, which at present constitute most of our number beside Mechanics. Two men employed at Coal Pit, four at sawing, remainder at small Jobs. Visited by a few Chinooks bringing some Sturgeon. 6 Men sick.

Nov. 21st. Saturday. Cloudy, unpleasant weather. People employed as during the week. One Sawyer sick, four Sandwich Islanders sick. In the forenoon Dorion & Ignace with their families arrived from hunting, bringing only a few Geese & Swans. Visited by Ashwallax who accompanied the hunters down, brought some swans, etc. At evening a regale was given to the men that are going up the Wolamut, every thing being now in readiness for their departure.

22d. Sunday. Raining almost incessantly throughout the day.

23rd. Monday. As yesterday Rainy, which continued with such violence as to prevent the party from setting out. All hands set to work as usual. Two at the Coal Pit: four Sawing. Mechanics at their different occupations. The few Sandwich Islanders fit for duty employed about the buildings at different Jobs. Cannan, Baker, & 4 Sandwich Islanders sick.

24th. Tuesday. Rainy & disagreeable weather. All hands were assembled and the party detained untill afternoon to Witness an experiment performed on our unfortunate Sandwich Islander Tuanna. Having learned that by killing an animal & placing him immediately in the body of it while warm, would effect a cure, one of our horses was brought and the experiment tryed. At 3 P.M. the party consisting of Messrs. Wallace & Halsay, John Day and the two Indian Hunters with their families, and twelve men took their departure in two canoes, Leaving our number at this place reduced to thirty three inclusive. Sick list as yesterday.[102]

25th. Wednesday. Cloudy without Rain. All hands variously employed. Mechanics at their different occupations. Four sawing, Two at the Coal Pits. Boat builder commenced work at his trade for the first. Sick list as yesterday.[103]

26th. Thursday. Weather as yesterday. Wind at N. W. Carpenters etc. removed from the new house, in one end of which was placed the furs, where also the Mechanics will mess during the winter, the other part being occupied by the Sandwich Islanders. People as usually employed. Two preparing mortar etc. for building a new chimney to Blacksmith's shop. 6 men sick.

27th. Friday. Weather tolerably pleasant during most part of the day. Three or four hands making the chimney to the Smith's Shop which was completed in the afternoon. All hands else employed as usually. Sick list the same. Traded a few fresh Salmon from Calpo.

28th. Saturday. Cloudy with intervals of Rain throughout the day. People employed much as usual. 5 men sick.

Nov. 29th. Sunday. Rainy, disagreeable weather. Labonte, the carpenter, and 4 Sandwich Islanders sick.

30th. Monday. Cloudy and unpleasant. All Hands variously employed. Three Blacksmiths now at work. Cannon set to with Boatbuilder. Two car-

---

[102] Further comment on Jeremie's "remedy," other than to note that it did not effect any improvement, other than temporary, in Tuanna's condition, seems unnecessary; see below December 17th. The clerks in charge of the Wolamut (i.e., Willamette) venture are William Wallace and John Halsey. Day's being sent on the trip would indicate a good bit of confidence by McDougall in his sanity, as he would not entrust a possible madman to two relatively inexperienced clerks. The two Indians refers to Ignace and Dorion, who had an Indian mother. In addition to trapping beaver, the Willamette party would largely be feeding itself, thus relieving the strain on the post, during the difficult winter months, between salmon runs. They would establish themselves near Salem, about fifty miles up river from its mouth at Portland. See Fred S. Perrine, *Oregon Historical Society Quarterly*, 25, No. 4 (December 1924), 310.

[103] Since John Little has been working, McDougall cannot mean that he just started. What may be meant is that he started work on the first example of a certain type, in this case, unspecified. See below, December 10, 1812, for mention of continued work on what is presumably the same vessel. Possibly, his work in refitting the shallop (see above, September 15, 1812) was not thought to require special skills.

penters at their trade. Flanagan employed with the Taylor. Two at the Coal Pits. Jeremie turned Physician and attends to the sick. One man with the few Sandwich Islanders fit for duty, occupied at small Jobs. 5 sick. At evening visited by Skamaquiah, bringing a few fresh Salmon and furs.[104]

Dec. 1st. Tuesday. Rain throughout the day. All hands variously employed, most of the number beside Mechanics at the Coal Pit, getting out and securing the Coal, the last Pit being now finished burning. 4 men sick.

2nd. Wednesday. Snow and Rain during the day. A greater quantity of snow fell to day than had been seen by us here before. People employed as yesterday. Visited by some Cathlamat Indians on their way home from the Clatsops, from whom purchased a deer they had just killed in the water at Point George. Sick list as yesterday.

3rd. Thursday. Weather wet & disagreable. All hands employed as yesterday, in the afternoon completed work at the Coal Pits, having the coals in the house prepared for that purpose and well secured. 4 men sick.

4th. Friday. Rainy. People as usually employed. Having now four Blacksmiths and but one forge, arranged to have that constantly occupied day and night. LaBonte and one man cutting & hewing Timber for Saw Pit. Sick list same.

5th. Saturday. Weather as yesterday. All hands employed as during the week. Sick list the same.

6th. Sunday. Rainy during the day. At evening Calpo brought in a number of Geese & Swans, for which he had been supplied with ammunition. Three Sandwich Islanders sick.

7th. Monday. Rainy, as usual. All hands variously employed. Mechanics at their respective occupations. Two hewing Timber for Sawyers. Patterson getting out Gutters for Store. Sandwich Islanders busied at small jobs. Visited by Comcomly, Two sons and suite, himself on the way up the River for trading, brought a small quantity of dried Salmon. Two Sandwich Islanders sick.

Decr. 8th. Tuesday. Cloudy and unpleasant without Rain. All hands as usually employed. Visited by Kaessnoe, Chief of the Cathlakemacs. Comcomly left here in the forenoon for the Chelwits. Sick list as yesterday.

9th. Wednesday. Tolerably Pleasant Weather. Presented Kaessnoe with a Coat of Blue Lion Skin and a pair of Fowls, after which he took leave for home. Two hands occupied in building an oven.[105]

---

[104] See above, I, n. 18, II, nn. 29, 31, for who the blacksmiths might be.

[105] Kaessnoe's tribe is probably the Cathlakamass; see above, I, n. 180, and below, December 13. "Blue Lion Skin" refers to blue-colored lion cloth, an obsolete French linen fabric

10th. Thursday. Pleasant, without rain. Little & Cannan completed the work of one Boat ready for the Timbers. On examining the Oak sticks here, it is found none will answer. The Boat must therefore remain in this state untill timber can be procured from above. Two Sandwich Islanders sick.[106]

11th. Friday. Pleasant Weather. Little, Cannan, Macon & 3 Sandwich Islanders were despatched early this morning for the Oaks, in order to procure Timber suitable for the Boats. All hands else employed as usual. Flannagan and 2 Sandwich Islanders sick.

12th. Saturday. Cloudy, no rain. Men employed as during the week. Sick list as yesterday.

13th. Sunday. Rainy throughout the day. At evening Comcomly arrived from up the River having accompanied Kaessnoe (Chief of the Cathlakamats) home. Passed the Oaks in the night, therefore did not see our People there. Two Sandwich Islanders sick.

14th. Monday. Weather as Yesterday. All hands variously employed. Little else beside the work of the Mechanics going forward. Four men sawing. The Sandwich Islanders employed to keep things about the place in order. Comcomly after trading to some small amount on credit left us and started for home. 3 men sick.

15th. Tuesday. Cloudy with Rain most part of the day. Carpenters employed getting out the gutters for the store. All hands else as usual. Two Sandwich Islanders sick.

16th. Wednesday. Clear pleasant weather. All hands as usually employed. Blacksmiths divided in Two Watches are at work day & night. Two of them making Nails for Boats, the others making Axes, etc., for the next spring. Much time is spent in hammering the Iron to a suitable size, there being none on hand of the kind necessary for the work. Three hundred small axes are now made. Tuanna only now sick, who is apparently getting better.[107]

Decr 17th. Thursday. Pleasant, moderate Weather. The tides for two or

---

made of hard spun yarn, usually woven in a plain or small dobby weave; see Isabel B. Wingate, *Fairchild's Dictionary of Textiles*, 6th ed. (New York: Fairchild Publications, ca. 1979). Blue seems to have been a preferred color with the natives, blue beads sometimes trading at a premium contrasted with those of other colors.

[106] Presumably, this is the boat begun on November 25.

[107] The Astorians are confidently preparing for another season of trading by getting ready a large number of trade axes and the like. Why the blacksmiths had to work so hard with the wrong size steel is puzzling, considering the quantity shipped on the *Beaver*; see Porter, *Astor*, I, 494, 504 for the inventory entries for iron and steel. Recall also the earlier complaints regarding the poor quality spring steel for the traps for the Willamette venture; see above, July 1, 1811.

three days past & this day have been higher than at any time this season. In the afternoon Little, Cannan, & Company arrived with two canoes loaded with timber, leaving behind ready cut as much more which the canoes could not bring. Carpenters employed at getting out Gutters for all the buildings. The experiment performed on our invalid Tuanna some time since, together with the unremitted attentions of Doctor Jeremy has evidently a good effect.[108]

18th. Friday. Cloudy with intervals of Rain. All hands busily employed. Sandwich Islanders bringing Coal for the Blacksmiths. Tuanna only sick.

19th Saturday. This morning Cannan, Labonté & Macon with four Sandwich Islanders were despatched for the remaining timber at the Oaks, and to cut some more for other purposes. Weather Rainy & disagreeable. Patterson employed fixing Births for the Sandwich Islanders in their part of the house, as he cannot finish the Gutters untill Labonté's return to assist him.

20th. Sunday. Cloudy, with some rain. Calpo arrived last evening bringing a number of Swans & Geese, for which he has been gone up the river several days. Visited by some Cathlamat Indians bringing upwards of fifty fresh Salmon. Learned from them some accounts from Mr. Wallace & party. A number of people of their nation had just returned from the Wolamut River who report that the party passed the falls, or Rapids in safety, and had arrived at their place of destination. Were putting up buildings, and that one person of their number had been killed by a White Bear.[109]

21st. Monday. Cloudy with some Rain. All hands busily employed, much the same as for some time past. Early this morning a number of hands were sent to Calpo's lodge for the purpose of sending all the Girls away. Sick list still reduced to one person only.[110]

---

[108] This improvement will be only temporary; the "experiment" refers to the rather drastic (drastic at least for the horse) remedy tried on November 24, 1812.

[109] The buildings, etc., refer to the post established near the present site of Salem, Oregon. The report of someone's death was incorrect. "White Bear" was a common term for a grizzly bear, irrespective of its actual color.

[110] Calpo seems to have been running a house of prostitution for the convenience of the Astorians. While the Chinooks practiced polygamy, it was unusual for anyone but a chief to have more than one wife, and even chiefs rarely had more than two or three wives. Hence, the "girls" were not Calpo's harem. Owing to the relatively frequent visits of trading vessels, the Chinooks had a reputation for promiscuous morals, because their women had ample opportunity and no qualms about selling themselves. See Ruby, Brown, *Chinook*, pp. 63–65. The Chinooks were actually much closer to most of the other tribes in this respect. Alfred Seton contrasted the chaste behavior of the Nez Perce women with the other tribes he encountered while with the Pacific Fur Company; see Jones, ed., *Astorian Adventure*, p. 105. James Ronda discusses the experience of the "Corps of Discovery" while living near the Clatsops and contrasts it with some of the practices of the Plains Indians; see *Lewis and Clark Among*

22nd. Tuesday. Weather much as Yesterday. Patterson finished the Job of putting up Births and began again at the Gutters. Other Mechanics employed as usual at their respective trades. Sandwich Islanders bringing coal for the Smith's, etc. One man sick.

23rd. Wednesday. Cloudy, calm Weather. Visited by several Indians living a few miles behind us in Young's Bay, who are in pursuit of a woman lost belonging to them. It appears that she was one of a number of Indians that were upset in canoe between our Factory and Tongue Point some days ago. One slave man who was saved reached the Lodges and reported that this woman spoken of was also saved, that he had left her on the shore where they first landed. Now that she cannot be found, they suspect that either Calpo's people or the Whites have made way with her. From circumstances however it would appear the slave man did not tell the truth, and that the woman was drowned.

24th. Thursday. Cloudy, Wind fresh from N. E. People as usually employed. At evening, Cannan & company arrived from up the River, but were obliged to land their Timber above Tongue Point where it was left, on account of having broken one of the Canoes. Tuanna only on the sick list, who is getting much better.

25th. Friday. Christmas. Cloudy, and unpleasant Weather. A suitable treat was given to all hands in order that they should enjoy themselves as well as circumstances would permit. A weekly allowance of Flour has been given to all since the 29 November, and which is still continued for want of other provision.[111]

26th. Saturday. Tolerably pleasant. Wind fresh from Southward. All hands still keeping Christmas.

27th. Sunday. Rainy & unpleasant Weather. Since Monday last, when Calpo's people were ordered to send their Girls away, no difficulty happened with them untill Yesterday, when it was discovered that they had concealed them only, and not sent them off. Calpo was therefore sent for last night and peremptorily ordered to be off with the whole of his people immediately; at wich he took an affront, and refused to accept of a small quantity of Tobacco

---

the Indians (Lincoln: University of Nebraska Press, 1984), pp. 207–10. What is more intriguing is why McDougall feels it necessary to crack down at this point on what had been a thriving trade (to judge from the incidence of venereal disease among the men) ever since the Astorians had arrived on the Columbia. Perhaps he feared even more serious problems during the coming holiday season when drinking would be enough of a problem.

[111] The flour was apparently a supplement to the inadequate rations of salmon, etc., on which the men were subsisting; see below, January 3, 1813.

offered him, but left the house saying he would never again enter it. Visited by one of the Indians living in Young's Bay who informed that the woman spoken of a few days since as lost, was at length found, and all suspicions silenced.

28th. Monday. Rainy, incessantly during the day. The people having kept up Christmas at so high a rate that few of them were able to begin work this morning. Blacksmith's, Sawyers, & the Sandwich Islanders only busy. Boat-builder, Cannan, Cooper, Carpenters, etc., laid up. Labonté attempted work and began to make an armed chair.[112]

29th Tuesday. Cloudy and Raining most of the day. People began work this morning as usual. Two Blacksmith making small Axes. Two making Nails and other work for Boats. Little & Cannan employed at the Boat. Cooper getting out stuff for Kegs. Milligan & Flannagan making Trowsers & Shirts. Four men sawing. Carpenters both occupied at small jobs. Doctor Jeremy employed in his Labratory and collecting roots. Macon & the Sandwich Islanders at different Jobs, a part cutting Brush, etc., behind the factory, bringing coal for the Smiths, etc. One person only sick.

Decr 30th. Wednesday. Tolerably pleasant Weather. Carpenters busied at the Gutters. All hands else employed as Yesterday. Calpo & family yesterday left the Point for Chinook. This morning, persons were sent to the Lodge to destroy the remains of their houses, which was soon accomplished.[113]

31st. Thursday. Pleasant Weather. People mostly employed as Yesterday. Labonté hewing Logs for Saw Pit. Patterson unwell. Sandwich Islanders cutting brush, bringing Coal for Smiths, etc. Tuana only sick, who appears now be getting better.

Thus ended the year 1812.

---

[112] To judge from the length of the hangovers, the increased liquor rations must have had a prodigious effect on the men; this was possibly due to the relatively meager food allowances which they seem to be receiving. Those "laid up" were presumably the ones most affected by the holiday celebrations. LaBonté's "armed chair" was an arm chair.

[113] The Point was Point George, the peninsula on which Astoria was located; Chinook was Comcomly's village, across the Columbia River, on Banker's Bay.

Sketch of a model of the ship *Tonquin*. Built in New York in 1807, the ship was destroyed off the Northwest coast in 1811. Sketch by E. W. Giesecke from the model in the Oregon Historical Society.

Three Chinook Men. Drawing by George Catlin. © Collection of The New-York Historical Society.

Astoria as it looked in 1813. Note platform with cannon. From *Narrative of a Voyage to the Northwest Coast of America* by Gabriel Franchère (New York: Redfield, 1854).

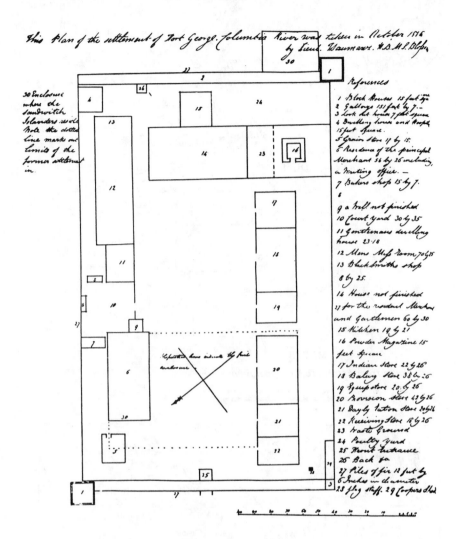

Plan of the Settlement of Fort George. From *The Oregon Country Under the Union Jack* by B. C. Payette (Montreal: Payette Radio Limited, 1962).

MAP I

Route from Astoria to Whirlpool River ············

SCALE IN MILES

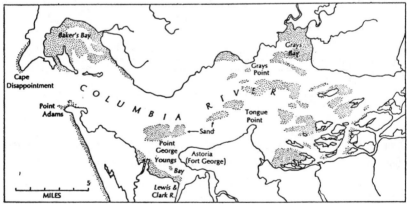

Upper: Map showing activities of the Astorians west of the Rocky Moun-
tains. From *A Voyage to the Northwest Coast of America* by Gabriel Franchère
(New York: Citadel Press, 1968). Lower: Mouth and estuary of the Colum-
bia River, showing shoals (shaded). From *Journal of a Voyage on the North
West Coast of North America During the Years 1811, 1812, 1813, and 1814* by
Gabriel Franchère, ed. by W. Kaye Lamb, trans. by Wessie Tipping Lamb
(Toronto: The Champlain Society, 1969).

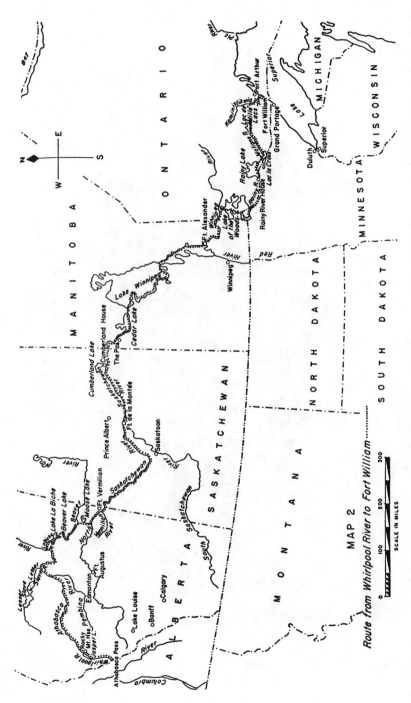

Map showing route of the Astorians to Fort William, on Lake Superior. From *A Voyage to the Northwest Coast of America* by Gabriel Franchère (New York: Citadel Press, 1968).

Chief Concomly. Drawing from Duncan McDougall's Astoria Journal, 1810–1813. Courtesy The Rosenbach Museum & Library, Philadelphia.

Journal
[Jan. 1, 1813—Nov. 20, 1813]

January 1st. Friday. Pleasant Weather. Wind fresh from S. W. Labour of every kind was laid aside and a treat given to all hands, that they might make merry on the New Year.[1]

2nd. Saturday. Being the last day of the week, was allowed to the men as a holiday. Visited by the Chief of the Clatsops and a number of his people for the purpose of trading. Weather fine and pleasant.[2]

3rd. Sunday. Pleasant Moderate Weather. Continue still to give to all hands a weekly allowance of Flour, and have no prospect of doing otherwise untill the season of Sturgeon & Uthlecans shall arrive.[3]

4th. Monday. Weather as Yesterday. One of the Blacksmiths, Cannan, Boatbuilder, Taylor & Flanagan unable to begin work this morning, having kept up New Year at too high a rate. Others at work variously. Two Blacksmiths making Axes. Four men sawing. Labonté hewing Logs for Saw Pit. The Sandwich Islanders cutting Brush. Watatkum arrived early this morning bringing the Meat of a Beaver and word of having Just Killed an Elk near Captn. Lewis' wintering place. One of the Sawyers with four Sandwich Islanders were therefore despatched with him in a canoe for it, and returned successfully at evening.

5th. Tuesday. Pleasant, clear Weather. The nights are now quite cold with pretty severe frosts: the first of any moment we have yet seen this winter. All hands variously employed. Blacksmith as usual. Little & Cannan setting a kettle, & fixing a steam Box. Patterson making a Tool chest for his Tools. Labonté with one man hewing Timber for Saw Logs, Cooper dressing stuff for Kegs. Four men sawing, Jeremy mending & repairing canoes. Sandwich

---

[1] As noted at the beginning of 1812, the new year was greeted most vigorously on New Year's Day, with as much celebration as possible. In Astoria, in 1813, rather little was possible.

[2] By giving the men Saturday off, McDougall was, in effect, giving them a three-day holiday in which to celebrate. See the entry for January 4 for the result. Dhaitshowan was the chief of the neighboring Clatsops.

[3] See below, January 9, for more information on the rations at Astoria. The flour was in addition to the usual fish. This winter, especially the approaching months until the smelts and salmon return in the spring, will be the most difficult the Pacific Fur Company Astorians have on the Columbia.

Islanders cutting Brush, bringing Coal, etc. Visited by two of Comcomly's sons who returned directly again to Chinook. One man only sick.[4]

6th. Wednesday. Weather as for several days past clear & pleasant tho' tolerably cool. People employed as Yesterday. Milligan and Flanagan making trowsers & shirts.

7th. Thursday. Pleasant clear Weather. People mostly employed as yesterday. Labonté and one of the Sawyers at work in the woods getting out Oars for Boats. One Sawyer being sick. Little & Cannan finished their steam Pot and bent their Timbers. Two Blacksmiths making awls the others still at small axes. Two men sick.

8th. Friday. Pleasant and quite cold. All hands as usually employed. Visited by a few Indians, Skamaquiah's people, who brought nothing for trade. Two men sick.

9th. Saturday. Clear cold Weather. People employed as during the week. One saw only going, one of the Sawyers being still unfit for duty. Visited by some Indians from whom we purchased four fresh Salmon, being probably the last that may be seen this season. Two of our people complained to day that they were unable to work on account of the living. They cannot eat fish, and say the allowance of flour is not sufficient alone. Was therefore under the necessity of allowing them a small quantity of Rice in addition. It requires now the greatest economy in giving out our little provisions in order that it shall last untill the season of fish may arrive, which however is not far distant. Two men sick.[5]

10th. Sunday. Hazy Weather and considerably warmer than for some time past. In the afternoon was visited by Comcomly and suite in three Canoes, bringing over a horse, for which he had been paid in part some time before. Being a fine pleasant evening, all returned before dark.

11th. Monday. Clear and pleasant. All hands variously employed. Two Blacksmiths making small Axes, one making Awls, the fourth laid up with a lame arm. Four men sawing. Two cutting & hewing Logs for Boards. Patterson employed with Boat builder. Cooper dressing stuff for Kegs. Sandwich Islanders cutting Brush and bringing Coals. Cannan, with two Sandwich Islanders were sent early this morning hunting in order if possible

---

[4] The "Kettle . . . steam Box" were to be used in bending wood for boat building; see below, January 7, 1813.

[5] In spite of the low number of men on the sick list, it seems that the general state of health at Astoria was not very good. Flour, fish, and occasional meat probably sustained life, but not energy. Later this season, McDougall will note the presence of scurvy among the men.

to kill something that may add to our present living. Jeremy sent in pursuit of Roots, being still attending on Tuana who appears getting better.[6]

12th. Tuesday. Fine Weather. All hands employed as Yesterday. Since the commencement of the New Year the weather has been constantly clear & pleasant, the nights quite cold and freezing to a considerable degree. Our large he-goat had become lame from some cause not known, and was therefore Killed while the meat was yet good. One blacksmith off duty.

Jany 13th. Wednesday. Fine pleasant Weather. People employed much the same as for several days past. The making of awls is given over while one Blacksmith continues sick, the remaining three employed at axes. Jeremy set to work with Boat builder & Carpenter. Sandwich Islanders cutting brush.

14th. Thursday. Weather as Yesterday. Early this morning Watatkum arrived with the meat of one Elk in his Canoe, having left another in the Woods near Captain Lewis's wintering place. Macon, with four Sandwich Islanders were despatched in a Canoe for the meat with which they returned at evening, furnishing us with a seasonable supply. Mechanics as usually employed. Baker resumed his work, Tuanna only sick.[7]

15th. Friday. Cloudy and thick mist, with light airs from Southward. People busily employed much as usual. One saw only going. Belleau laid up with rheumatic pains. In the afternoon Cannan arrived after an absence of near five days. Killed nothing.

16th. Saturday. Weather much as Yesterday. Wind from N.E. Cannan and the two Sandwich Islanders started again this morning for hunting in another direction. People variously employed pretty nearly as during the week. Just at evening were much surprized at the unexpected arrival of Mr. McKenzie with his whole party (except two men who remained with Mr. Clarke) besides the four men left behind by Mr. Crookes on his way across the country, and the two hunters left for the purpose of Trapping; making the number in all Twenty two persons, inclusive. That part of the country in which he had began an establishment did not answer the ends expected, and for this reason left it, securing his goods, etc., in cache. The Goods and other property left in Cache by the party on their way across the country were sent for and brought to Mr. McKenzie's place and deposited with his. The whole of the property belonging to individuals which had been secured separately

---

[6] Various roots were consumed by the natives as part of their usual diet; the wapato frequently referred to could be classified as a root. The vitamins they contained were probably the effective ingredient.

[7] Micajah Baker was a blacksmith; see above, II, n. 29, and below, January 29.

from the Goods, Mr. Reed found had been stolen and destroyed. Mr. Robert Stuart left there an account of his having passed the place on his way to New York in due season and in safety. Mr. M. K. likewise reports favorable of that part of the country where Mr. Clarke is established, whom he visited in person.[8]

17th. Sunday. Cloudy calm Weather. A regal was given to all hands. Our number now amounts to fifty five persons inclusive, a sorry circumstance with our small stock of provisions.

18th. Monday. Pleasant. Wind from Northward. The people being engaged yesterday in frolic, were unfit for work. Two Blacksmiths and the Sandwich Islanders only on duty. Belleau still laid up with the Rheumatism. Tuanna mending slowly.

19th. Tuesday. Moderate Weather. All hands at work variously. Two Blacksmiths repairing axes. Little & Patterson at the Boat, Cooper Dressing Hoops. Milligan & Flanagan employed as usual. Two sawyers at work. Three men cutting and hewing Logs. Cannan employed with Carson, one of the new hunters, making a stock, etc., for Mr. McKenzie's gun. Sandwich Islanders cutting brush, and at other small Jobs. In the afternoon visited by Comcomly and suite in Two Canoes, for the purpose of trading, bring upwards of one hundred & thirty Beaver Skins, and a few dried Salmon. Two men sick.

Jany. 20th. Wednesday. Cloudy calm Weather. People employed as Yesterday. Four Blacksmiths at work, two making Rivets for Boat, the other two at several small Jobs, and at evening began making Traps. Visited by a few Cathlamat Indians, but traded nothing. Belleau getting better.

21st. Thursday. Cloudy with intervals of Rain, and some sleet of hail and Snow. All hands variously occupied. Blacksmiths making Traps and Iron work for Boat. Cooper laid up. Four Sawyers at work. Two men cutting and hewing Logs. Sandwich Islanders cutting Brush and bringing Coal for Blacksmiths. Visited by a few Chinooks from whom we purchased one hundred dried salmon. Two persons sick.

---

[8] See above, June 29, 1812, and II, n. 38 for the departure of McKenzie and others from Astoria. Donald McKenzie ("Mr. M. K.") had been on the Snake River in Idaho. John Clarke was near Spokane, Washington. Ramsay Crooks was accompanying Robert Stuart in his overland journey to New York. See Jones, ed., *Astorian Adventure*, pp. 109–11, for Alfred Seton's description of the process of putting the goods in cache and the journey back to Astoria. The four men left behind by Crooks were Alexander Carson (no. 35), Louis St. Michel (no. 156), Pierre Delauney (no. 50), listed in the 1813–14 roster, Appendix, and Pierre Detayé. Three hunters were left behind to trap: Edward Robinson, John Hoback, and Jacob Rezner; which of them did not come to Astoria is not known. See Irving, *Astoria* (Rust ed.), chap. 31, and Ronda, *Astoria*, p. 179.

22nd. Friday. Pleasant after a stormy night, during which considerable snow fell. Cannan still employed with Carson at Mr. McKenzie's gun. One Blacksmith only at Work. Four men sawing. Patterson and Little at the Boat. Labonte making a chain. Sandwich Islanders as usually employed. Cooper still unwell. 6 men sick.

23rd. Saturday. Cloudy cold disagreeable Weather. People variously employed pretty nearly the same as during the week. Two Blacksmiths making Traps, for the purpose of despatching a party up the Wolamut, as our small stock of provisions will not warrant keeping so many people as we have here at present, unemployed.

700 Tomyhawks are now made, a sufficient number of that kind, as we learn from Mr. McKenzie they are but an indifferent article for trade with the Indians in the interior. Halfaxes do much better. 5 men sick.[9]

Jany. 24th. Sunday. Tolerably pleasant, but cold Weather. Wind from Northward. In the afternoon visited by Comcomly who brought for Trade a Sea Otter, and a few dried Salmon. Since last fall reports at different times have been made known to us by Comcomly, & others of his people concerning a boats crew said to have been cut off to the Northward since the departure of the Beaver from this place but no credit was ever given to it: Again to day he repeated the same, and in which he appears so much interested that we cannot but notice it. He related it in substance pretty nearly as follows, Vizt. A boat's crew, consisting of 20 persons, including some one officer or other person more than ordinary, went on shore from their Ship to trade with the natives at a great distance to the Northward of this for Sea Otter. They were well received, invited into the house of a Chief, and had commenced a trade, without discovering signs of any bad intentions from the people in whose power it appeared they then were. He described particularly the manner in which the white people sat, all armed with Pistols; also how the Chief arranged his men, having two to attack each white man at the same time, when a signal was given to commence a massacre: The Whites succeeded in Killing a good number of the Indians, and among others the Chief, (whom he speaks of as being a very great one,) but were at length Killed, not one escaping. The Indians seeing their chief killed severely regretted his loss, and became desperate. The people on board Ship, anchored at a small distance from shore, hearing the affray, with the help of glasses it

---

[9] See Russell, *Firearms*, chap. 5, passim, for a general discussion of axes on the frontier; pp. 275–84, 89–93 for comments on tomahawks. Russell cautions that both terms, "tomahawks" and "halfaxes," were used indiscriminately.

was supposed saw the event, and immediately cut their cables & put to sea, having a few men only on board. This Comcomly has learned of people coming from the Northward at different times since the transaction took place; the truth of it he does not doubt, but who the persons were, or to what Ship they belonged cannot be properly ascertained. The Indians name Captain Eayres and Mr. Hunt. It is therefore doubtless one or the other, or a party from one of the two Vessels. His oldest son, who is now gone to the Northward, will on his return probably bring further information. The character of Comcomly from the commencement of our establishment untill the latter end of the year past appears not to have been properly understood, notwithstanding he has uniformly and always professed himself friendly to us. He was even suspected during the time of our apprehension of danger last fall, tho' what was learned from his young son who accompanied the Shallop up the River shortly afterwards corresponding so well with what we learned otherwise, as also from circumstances, induced us to believe the old man sincere. He now tells us that the Indians from the Northward, great numbers of whom live with his people during the summer & fall, intimated their designs of destroying us, and that some of his own people had likewise shown an inclination to assist, but that he, well knowing the consequences that would follow, always opposed it; and to day he made renewed avowals of friendship, and wished to impress us properly with his intentions, that whatever the Indians around us might be disposed to do, we could depend on his good offices to quiet them, and assist us on every occasion. After finishing his trade and taking up some small amount on credit, he departed for home.[10]

25th. Monday. Cold unpleasant Weather, Wind fresh from Northward. We are now under the necessity of stopping from most of our men two meals a day, and to break off work. Mechanics kept employed as usual and 4 men sawing, the only people now at work. A good number with 2 Canoes went off hunting, being supplied with ammenition & a little Tobacco in order to support themselves and do otherwise as well as they can. Every encourage-

---

[10] There seems to be no truth to this story of a shoreside attack on a boatload of European sailors at this time. Hunt did not stop to trade on his way to Sitka and Captain George Ayres (Eayres) was not in the area. This entry also marks a striking change of heart about Comcomly's friendship and reliability. From now on, McDougall will pay the utmost attention to the old Indian's statements and rely on his promises. The high point of this "special relationship" will be McDougall's "marriage" to one of Comcomly's daughters; see below, July 20, 1813. The "Indians from the Northward" are probably the Chehalis, who came every year for the Columbia salmon; see above, July 12, 1811, and I, n. 71.

ment is given to the Indians in order to induce them to bring us Salmon, they are even paid in Cloth Blankets, but all does not answer. We cannot purchase a sufficiency to support the people. Events from every quarter wear unfavorable appearances. The news Mr. McKenzie learned from the people of the N.W. Co. directly from Montreal, that War was declared between the U. S. and Great Britain, leaves every reason to suppose that another Ship will not be here next Spring. War was declared in June 1812 and the only hope to be cherished that a Ship shall be here in season is that Mr. Astor may have anticipated the event and arranged accordingly. We have now stoped selling to the people every thing except what may be absolutely necessary for them. A party will in a few days be sent up the Wolamut, which will lessen our number, and every arrangement made that we may consume as little as possible untill spring, when we may know the event which now gives so much anxiety. One Blacksmith & Flannagan Sick.[11]

26th. Tuesday. Cloudy and severe cold Weather. Wind from Northward. Mechanics as usually employed. One Blacksmith still sick. Labonte supplies his place, in order to keep the forge constantly occupied. Little and Patterson finished the first boat and took it outside the square. The Oars are yet to be made, at which they are employed. Sick list as Yesterday.

27th. Wednesday. Weather much as Yesterday. People occupied in the same manner also. The ground is now covered with Snow in the Woods, and frozen so hard that our Hogs, Fowls and Goats are unable to pick up their own living. We have reason however to hope that such weather will not be of long continuance, being a thing so uncommon here. Watatkum came in the afternoon with two Swans, the only game he was able to procure for us.

---

[11] Everything seems to be conspiring against the success of the Astorians. The shortage of food is obviously extreme, and no expedient seems able to secure additional provisions. Cutting down rations at Astoria and sending parties off to forage for themselves at a distance from the post might get them through the next two months until the smelts and salmon appear in the river. McKenzie had learned of the war while visiting John Clarke's post near Spokane; John George McTavish of the North West Company came by with a copy of the declaration and letters from Montreal. The news of the declaration of war, accompanied as it was by news of an armed naval expedition being dispatched from Britain to seize the post as the spoils of war, compounded the poor situation at Astoria. Fearing that Astor could send no help, the partners at the post, McDougall and McKenzie, called "a sort of council of war, to which the clerks of the factory were invited pro forma, as they had no voice in the deliberations. Having maturely weighed our situation . . . we concluded to abandon the establishment in the ensuing spring, or, at latest, in the beginning of the summer" (Franchère, *Journal*, p. 117). In the meantime, they would stop all but the most essential trading and try to accumulate pack horses for the overland journey. See Ronda, *Astoria*, pp. 264–65; also, above, Introduction, pp. xx–xxi.

He saw some of our people above, they had not killed anything, and were living on dogs, that they purchased from the Indians.[12]

Jany. 28th. Thursday. Cloudy and more moderate. Mechanics as usually employed. Carson and Cannan completed Mr. McKenzie's gun, and the latter began stocking one for Mr. Reed. Two Blacksmiths making Traps, in which they make some considerable progress. Visited by a few Indians of the Cathlamats, who brought some skins for trade. We refused to purchase them with such articles as they wished, which very much displeased them. The President's Proclamation of War, a copy of which Mr. McKenzie brought down, leaves us no room to doubt of its authenticity. An Inventory being consequently taken of the Goods and Stores at this place, it was found far short of what would be necessary in the present crisis; it is therefore Judged prudent for the safety of so large a party as we now form in all the Columbia to suspend all trade except what may be necessary for our support, which cannot be avoided. During the last visit of Comcomly he was presented with a Blue Lion Skin Great Coat, handsomely made with large Capes, the whole bound with red binding: after the manner he had expressed a wish to have such a coat. It is mentioned here on account that it was omitted in the proper place. Two men sick.[13]

29th. Friday. Weather as Yesterday. Wind from Northward. The Boat builder & Patterson this morning refused to work, as they said, on account of the living, which is the same now as for some time past. The allowance of flour as given out to all hands for some time past is as follows, Viz., To the four Blacksmiths, who work watch about day and night six pounds a piece. Other mechanics five pounds. The four Sawyers, four pounds, and the remaining number of men, including Sandwich Islanders, three pounds each. The living of the Mechanics is in every respect the same as usual, as it is necessary they should be Kept at work, and without that it could not be expected. Gave ammunition to those two, and they went hunting in order to procure their own living, accompanied by Baker, one of the Blacksmiths, who is unable to work on account of a lame arm. The sawyers broke off work to day and went on one meal a day, having considerable stuff already

---

[12] To modern sensibilities, eating dogs seems a drastic step to take, but one must recall that it was common among the natives, and, when they were hungry enough, Europeans ate them also. Hence, this party may simply have been using an available food.

[13] This gift was presumably given on January 24, 1813. See above, December 9, 1812, for the gift of a similar coat to Kaessnoe, and II, n. 105.

sawed, their work at present will be of no particular consequence untill we are able to procure provision.[14]

30th. Saturday. Cloudy moderate Weather. Blacksmiths & Taylor occupied as usual. Cannan still employed at Mr. Reeds gun, the only people at work. Cooper laid up. One party of our people that went hunting on Monday last returned home, having made out to live very well. Brought with them two Swan & four ducks. At evening Comcomly and suite arrived; being late they encamped for the night.

31st. Sunday. Pleasant and moderate. Traded with Comcomly & his people, who had altogether only One hundred smoked Salmon, after which they took their leave. In the afternoon the remainder of men sent hunting returned, having succeeded in like manner with the others, but brought no game with them. As it was intended the party for the Wolamut should start tomorrow, a treat was given to the men destined for the voyage.[15]

Febry. 1st. Monday. Rainy most of the day. Little work of any kind going forward, the effects of the frolic being not yet over. Cooper & one Blacksmith at their trades. Boat builder repairing Canoes intended for the Wolamut. Cannan, Patterson and four others sent up to the Oaks in the new Boat for Timber. Four men sick.

Feby. 2nd. Tuesday. Cloudy, thick Weather. After considerable bustle, the party for the Wolamut or McKay's River, consisting of Mr. Reed, Seton, Thomas McKay, Two trappers and 13 men set out about 9 o'clock this morning. Visited by a few Indians, and among others Watatkum who has yet killed nothing. Two Blacksmiths began making half axes. One making awls, assisted by Labonte, who still supplies the place of Baker, laid up. Boat builder employed at a second Boat, Taylor at his trade, Cooper sent hunting. Two men sick. Mr. Reed, for McKay's river, took Letters for Mr. Wallace, containing: instructions to suspend trade of every kind for the present.[16]

---

[14] The complaint of the ship carpenters underlines the drastic food situation at Astoria; presumably the rations are weekly and not daily allocations. The *Beaver* had carried 413 barrels of flour to Astoria in the spring of 1812, the last supply received by the post. See Porter, *Astor*, I, 480. The carpenters, Little and Patterson, may have been the ones who were sent hunting. It is about this time that Franchère recorded a daily ration of four ounces of flour and one dried fish weighing about one and a half pounds, per person. *Journal*, p. 117.

[15] Under the circumstances, one would like to know just what constituted a "treat," especially as the effects of the "frolic" were still felt the next day.

[16] As implied, Reed and the others were to join Wallace and Halsey on the Willamette; the latter two had left Astoria on November 24, 1812, the day Jeremie performed his "experiment" on Tuana. Apparently, they had selected a satisfactory site for their headquarters. As Alfred Seton noted, "They were situated in a part of the country, where game was tolerably

3rd. Wednesday. Raining violently most part of the day. People employed much the same as Yesterday. Cooper at his trade. Joseph Lapierre set at work with the Taylor in place of Flanagan, who went with the party. Baker & 2 Sandwich Islanders sick.

4th. Thursday. Weather nearly as Yesterday. People occupied the same also. Blacksmiths not yet began making half axes, being employed repairing Tools and putting their Shop otherwise in order. One of our Sows made her appearance to day with six small Pigs, an uncommon circumstance at this season of the year. Sick list as Yesterday.

5th. Friday. Rainy as Yesterday. The few people at work occupied the same as for several days past. Blacksmiths at small Jobs, arranging their Tools. Visited by a number of Chinook Women who brought a few dried Salmon. Baker & one Sandwich Islander sick.

6th. Saturday. Raining violently all day. In the forenoon the party returned in the Boat with a small load of Timber; were unable to embark all that which was left some time ago above Tongue Point on account that some large Logs had drifted on it. Flanagan, who had been sent with the party for McKay's River, came back with them, Mr. Reed having suffered him to return, contrary to his instructions.

7th. Sunday. Weather as Yesterday, with high winds from Westward. Comcomly with a number of his people came over in a large Canoe in the forenoon, bringing a most lamentable account of the loss of a canoe which came here with Salmon for us on Friday last, and that three persons of the number in it were drowned. His people, relatives of the deceased, he said reproached him for their loss. He having sent them over, promising to follow with his own canoe the next day, which illness prevented. At the request therefore of his people, and to exonerate himself from further blame he had now came, expecting restitution from us. The circumstances related appearing very probable, and as we have no reason to doubt the integrity of the old man, the following presents were made to him in presence of all the Indians accompanying him. Viz. For himself, one blue blanket, one Tomyhawk & three heads tobacco.* For the three that escaped being drowned, each: one Tomyhawk, one fathom gurrahs, & three heads Tobacco; and for the friends of the three deceased, to each; one white blanket 2½ point, one Tomyhawk,

---

plenty, had built themselves a small house to shelter them from the weather, & sent their party in different directions to trap beaver & get their living." Jones, ed., *Astorian Adventure*, p. 112. He had no serious complaints about their situation, which lasted until mid-March when they returned to the post. Not counting those persons sent away on short hunting trips, the second Willamette party's departure left thirty-seven persons still at Astoria.

one fathom gurrahs & three heads Tobacco; making in all, one blue blanket, 3 white ditto, 7 Tomyhawks, 6 fathoms gurrahs & 21 heads Tobacco. Presented the old man also with a Skein of holland Twine, being to complete a net for which a greater quantity had been given him some time before; and after trading 80 dried Salmon, he took his leave apparently well satisfied. Our stock of fish was quite exhausted when we received this supply, which proved tho' small a seasonable supply. The same allowance of flour continues to be given to all hands. Mechanics are fed beside with fish as usual, & kept at work. All hands else receive fish once a day only, and are idle. The return of Flanagan adds one more to the number that have to be fed on rice, making in all three persons. Sick list as Yesterday.[17]

8th. Monday. The morning violently stormy with wind and rain. In the course of the forenoon became tolerably pleasant. Mechanics as usually employed at their respective trades. Patterson began work again with Boat builder, making the moulds and raising a second boat. Blacksmiths making Sturgeon Hooks. Preparations are also making otherwise to be in readiness for fishing in a few days. Baker resumed his work again to day, having been for several weeks off duty. Labonte who supplied his place now employed at small Jobs. Visited by the Chief of the Clatsops (Daitshowan) and several of his people who remained here most of the day: The purpose of their visit being to enquire into & satisfy themselves respecting the loss of those Indians, as mentioned Yesterday. One of them as they informed us was of their nation. After being informed what had been given to Comcomly they departed in the evening seemingly satisfied. Tuanna & Dick sick. Three of our men beside Tuanna are now ill of the Venereal. Viz. Little Milligan & La-Pierre, tho' they are all on duty.[18]

9th. Tuesday. Cloudy with intervals of rain throughout the day. Wind from Northward. People employed as Yesterday. Mr. Franchere preparing to be off tomorrow for the purpose of fishing for Sturgeon. Blacksmiths

---

[17] This is an example of the trust now placed in Comcomly. McDougall hands over a sizable quantity of trade goods on the word of the old man that losses had been suffered while sending salmon over to the post. Previously, restitution might well have been made, if only to stay friendly with the Chinooks, but suspicions would probably have been put in the log. At the asterisk, two lines have been erased, and except for a two-inch gap, written over. In the gap, the words "For the three" can be read.

[18] One of the relatively rare mentions of what was obviously a continuing problem of some seriousness, the aftereffects of the men having sexual intercourse with the native women. Apparently, McDougall's doctoring of them for this problem was reasonably successful, as only Tuanna is incapacitated by it for a long period of time, and he was infected when he came to Astoria with the *Tonquin*.

occupied in the evening & during greater part of the night making a large Sledge. About 2 o'clock the Shop was discovered to be on fire by Jeremy, who fortunately happened to be up at that time. The roof was in a blaze, and would in all probability very soon have communicated to our dwelling house, but that it was hapily extinguished.[19]

10th. Wednesday. Fine, clear pleasant Weather, exceeding any seen since last fall. The party as was intended should have started this morning for the fishing ground, but were detained untill afternoon to build a new chimney to the Blacksmith Shop, the old one being destroyed in the fire last night. At 3 o'clock however they set out, Vizt., Mr. Franchere, Cooper, and 8 men including 4 Sandwich Islanders; in two Canoes, having every necessary to commence fishing, a small supply of provisions for immediate use, and a few articles of Goods, such as gurrahs & Tobacco for the purpose of purchasing more in case they do not meet with early success.

11th. Thursday. Clear & pleasant Weather. Our small number employed as usual, each at their respective trade. Patterson at work with Boat builder, the other Carpenter at small Jobs. Sandwich Islanders bringing coal for Smiths and Two of them sent to pump out the Shallop. Just at evening were visited by Calpo & his wife, who brought upwards of One hundred dried Salmon for trade.[20]

12th. Friday. Weather as Yesterday. Wind light from N. People variously employed. Cannan began work with Boat builder. Patterson complains he cannot live on dried fish and has quit work. Three of the Blacksmiths now at work all day beating Out Iron for half axes. Roussil has a lame hand & cannot work with a hammer, is employed at small Jobs. Calpo & his people took leave this morning for home. In the afternoon Watatkum arrived in a canoe with the chief of the Cathlamats, bringing the meat of an Elk, not quite entire, but however small was very acceptable.

13th. Saturday. Weather exceedingly pleasant & moderately warm. Early in the forenoon were visited by Comcomly in a small Canoe, with 3 persons only beside himself bringing a few Uthlecans, the first seen by us this season, and in fact some of the first taken in the river. As he came over with these immediately on receiving them in order to be the first who brought the Kind to us, and for this he was presented with a wool Hat, a present of no great

---

[19] For all the problems he had caused before, Jeremie redeemed himself with this service; the loss of the dwelling house would have been a very serious matter, especially in February. However, it is doubtful McDougall saw it in quite this light.

[20] This is Calpo's first visit since the expulsion of his "ladies" from the neighborhood of Astoria; see above, December 21, 27, 30, 1812.

value, sufficient however to satisfy him. He delivered us a most sorrowful account concerning Messr Wallace, Halsey & party whom he says are all destroyed by the natives inhabiting that part of the country where they had settled themselves. The news he received by a messenger from the Cathlaka-maps, who live at the mouth of the Wolamut or McKay's river, sent express for the purpose and which he related nearly as follows: The party had arrived at some considerable distance up the river and made an establishment. The natives flocked to see them from every quarter, and from a great distance, the sight of white people being a thing so wholly new among them. They soon however came to a resolution of destroying the whites, the more easy to effect which they were frequent in their intercourse apparently friendly & advised them of certain places at some distance that abounded in furs & animals, with a design that they should send persons for the supposed purpose, and thereby lessen the number at the principal establishment. It succeeded. Parties were sent & the few who remained behind fell an easy prey. The old man with much earnestness assures us 'tis true. He says it came in too direct a manner to be otherwise and that this news, together with accounts of the death of a chief to the Northward, to whom he was related, has kept him crying for two or three days. After spending some time in discourse & receiving a Blanket on credit took his leave, promising soon to bring plenty of fish. Great numbers of Canoes seen passing up the river, proceeding to the fishing place. In the afternoon was also visited by the Clatsop Indian who accompanied the Parties beyond the rapids last spring as interpreter on his way home from the falls. Received by him a note from Mr. Franchere who arrived at the Chelwitz yesterday. He left the small Canoe with 4 men below to fish for Uthlecans and to return here if successful. The Clatsop on his way down learned of the natives at the mouth of the Wolamut some account of the report Comcomly brought us this morning. The two differ widely. The latter did not understand that the party were yet actually destroyed, but that plans had been formed as already related to cut them off. The accounts he said were undoubtedly true and everything would take place as he had mentioned. In either case it leaves us cause of serious alarm. Traded from this man a keg of sugar nearly full, which he got from the natives at the rapids. They saved it among other things lost by Mr. David Stuart last spring. Just at evening our Canoe left, as mentioned in Mr. Franchere's note, arrived with about eight bushels of uthlecans.[21]

---

[21] This long and sorrowful tale has nothing behind it. See below, February 19, 27, March 1, 8, 18, 1813, for further reports and a final confirmation that nothing had happened. The Chelwitz have been previously identified; they lived about forty miles up the Columbia on the

14th. Sunday. Pleasant Weather, much as Yesterday. Allowed the men to take a row in the new Boat as far as Chinook Village, from whence they returned in the afternoon, In the morning despatched the Canoe that arrived last night with the same 4 men to Mr. Franchere, with some few articles he had requested for the purpose of properly arranging his Fishery. Sent him an account of the reports received concerning the first party up the Wolamut, our apprehensions on the occasion, and instructions for him to proceed immediately as far as the Cathlakamap Village in order to ascertain if possible some information more satisfactory, and if in the event there shall remain a probability of the truth of it, engage with the Chief Ka-es-no to send some of his people express in pursuit of Mr. Reed & party, to apprize them of the circumstances, if he shall not already know it, and have them return here as soon as possible. In the afternoon our other large Canoe with Pillon and Coté (two sawyers), Brosseau & one Sandwich Islander arrived, bringing 7 Sturgeon and a considerable quantity of Uthlecans. At the same time a young Cathlamat Indian arrived with a small canoe full of the same kind. He had promised to bring the first he should catch. We therefore received them as a present. He was the first Indian who brought them to the Factory last year and says now that sickness prevented him being the first this season. Gave him in return for his fish a Blue blanket & 1 head Tobacco. We have now for the first in a long time provision plenty for all hands. Further short allowance will be done away. Gave to the Mechanics only their usual allowance of Flour. Patterson was excepted from this, having quit work part of last week and would give no assurance of doing better in future. Two Sandwich Islanders sick.[22]

15th. Monday. Pleasant Weather same as for several days past. All hands set to work this morning. Mechanics employed much as during last week. Cannan & Patterson assisting Boat builder. Labonte at sundry small Jobs. Blacksmiths preparing Iron for Half Axes & making a few Sturgeon hooks to a pattern sent down by Mr. Franchere. Two Sawyers commenced work sawing boards for boats, the remaining number employed with axes cutting fire wood, etc. Sandwich Islanders part of the day bringing Coals. Visited by a few Clatsop Indians on their way to the fishing place. Our supply of provi-

south bank. The sugar was lost in an accident suffered by David Stuart's canoe the previous July, probably while going through the Dalles. See above, July 28, 1812.

[22] For a time, the worst of the food shortage was over. Now, McDougall probably moved to the fore of his concerns the overall situation of the enterprise, i.e., the state of war between the United States and Great Britain, the likelihood of no supply vessels from Astor, and the rumored expedition on its way to take Astoria.

sions is now so plenty that many of the Uthlecans are fed to the hogs, as they would otherwise become good for nothing. Milligan & 2 Sandwich Islanders sick.

16th. Tuesday. Cloudy, calm Weather. People employed as Yesterday. Saw numbers of canoes passing down the river with fish, but were visited by none. Sick list the same.

17th. Wednesday. Weather nearly as Yesterday, afternoon more pleasant. Two Blacksmiths, Taylor, Carpenter & 2 Sandwich Islanders sick. Others employed as usual. Sandwich Islanders cleaning & putting the place in order. Patterson quit work this morning again because he did not receive an allowance of flour, the reason of which is already mentioned. In the afternoon visited by Comcomly, sons and suite. Traded a few dried Salmon, 3 doz. Hen's Eggs, and an old impression of Moore's Practical Navigator of 1801 (brought from the Russian establishment to Northward), articles not included in the general catalogue of trade at our place. Fowls were given to Comcomly by us last year. After this took their leave. Visited also by a few Clatsops on their way home with fish. They traded nothing. 6 men sick.[23]

18th. Thursday. Clear & Pleasant, light airs from Northward, the greater part calm. In the morning despatched the large canoe with Brosseau, Pinolt & 3 Sandwich Islanders to the fishing place, with several small articles requested, and directions for Mr. Franchere to come down on his return from up the river. Patterson was directed to go in the canoe with the number, which he did not relish, & when he was satisfied we were not trifling with him, chose rather to conform as desired & went readily to work. Three Blacksmiths at work; finished beating out Iron and began making half axes. Two men sawing. Three at the boat. One Tayloring. Labonté making spouts to the gutters of the buildings etc. which constitute the whole number on duty, beside two S. Islanders at sundry small Jobs. One Blacksmith, Taylor & 3 Sandwich Islanders sick.

19th. Friday. Pleasant & warm. Wind N. Men employed as Yesterday. Labonté again supplies the place of the Blacksmith who is sick, as they are

---

[23] These were certainly not included "in the general catalogue of trade" at Astoria. Since the hen's eggs probably came from the chickens the Astorians had given the Chinooks the previous year, one wonders if they kept any fowl for themselves, as there has been no mention of any hens, or of their usual produce, until now. The navigation manual, John Hamilton Moore's *The New Practical Navigator: Being an Epitome of Navigation Exemplified in a Journal at Sea*, 14th ed. (London: G. & J. Robinson, 1801), was probably purchased to keep Comcomly happy, not for any real need. It is interesting that its source was known and that it had come more than 1,100 miles, doubtless through a chain of native traders, from Sitka to Astoria.

working by watches regularly. Little, who has for a long time been infected with the venereal, gave up work and prepared himself to go through a course of medicine with which he will commence to night. Baker & Milligan very ill, both have their legs swelled and inflamed with other symptoms of a scurvy. Their diet etc. is therefore adapted agreeably to directions to be pursued for effecting a cure of it. If it shall prove in reality the scurvy we can impute it only to the very bad provisions on which all hands have been for some time past obliged to live, viz., the worst kind of smoked Salmon. At evening the small canoe arrived bringing 6 Sturgeon. Mr. Franchere had been up the river as directed & returned to his place this morning, from whence the Canoe was immediately despatched with the pleasing intelligence that the report as already mentioned, which occasioned the necessity of his trip up is entirely without foundation, and only a fabrication of some of the Indians, of which he received the most positive assurances from Ka-ess-no, chief of the Cathlakamaps.[24]

20th. Saturday. Clear & pleasant. Wind N. Sent the canoe that arrived last night with the same 4 men above Tongue Point to fetch the Timber left there some time ago which is now wanted for the Boat. Cannan & Patterson go on to finish the boat now up, which wants only the Timbers, Gunwale, etc., to be added to complete her. Others employed as during the week. The Canoe returned at evening with all the timber. Sick list as Yesterday.

Feby. 21st. Sunday. Cloudy, Calm Weather. Gave to the Mechanics the usual allowance of flour. 4 men sick.

22nd. Monday. Cloudy & calm as Yesterday. Mechanics employed as last week. Blacksmiths making half axes, rivets, etc., for the Boat. Two men sawing. In the afternoon sent the small canoe & 4 men up to the fishing place. Visited by a good number of Clatsop Indians on their way up the river, from one of whom purchased a large Sturgeon. Baker, Milligan, Little & one Sandwich Islander sick, the two former are treated for the scurvy, of which they have still apparent symptoms. In the case of Little, with the venereal he makes use of Mercurial Ointment. For upwards of twelve months we have been wholly destitute of every kind of medicine necessary for the cure of this disease (venereal) notwithstanding more or less of our number are continually afflicted with it. Mr. Thompson of the N.W. Co.

---

[24] As noted, mercury ointment was the usual treatment for syphilis; see entry for January 2, 1812, I, n. 145. Baker's and Milligan's scurvy was not owing to the smoked salmon, but to the lack of variety in the diet during the difficult times of December and January when they had little more than bread and salmon, with infrequent portions of fresh meat. See entry for April 19, 1812, and II, n. 1 for the treatments for scurvy used at the time.

during his visit here in the summer of 1811 presented Mr. McDougall with a small Jar of Quicksilver intended for making an artificial horizon, for the purpose of astronomical observations, etc. This may be considered a fortunate circumstance, as the ointment can be made from it with ease, and serves now as a substitute for medicine better prepared and adapted.[25]

23rd. Tuesday. Cloudy with mist and rain. Men employed as usual. Two S. Islanders bringing gravel & Coals. 5 men sick.

24th. Wednesday. Rainy most of the day, with a thick fog. Wind light from Northward. Cannan added to the sick list of Yesterday. Patterson alone working at the Boat. Others as usually employed. Jeremie mending a canoe, as beside the two attending the fishery, we have not another fit for use. Toward evening Mr. Franchere arrived in the large Canoe with 5 men bringing 5 Sturgeon only, and a small quantity of dried Uthlecans. He did not come down sooner, waiting for more Sturgeon, but to no purpose as scarce any have been caught for several days past. It is yet too early in the season for them to be taken in Plenty.

25th. Thursday. Cloudy, calm Weather, with intervals of Mist and rain. Patterson ailing, with appearances of the scurvy, so that work at the boat is wholly stop'd for to day. Labonté repairing Canoes, while another supplies his place in the Blacksmith Shop. Others employed as usual. 5 mechanics and 2 S. Islanders sick.[26]

26th. Friday. Cloudy, with intervals of Rain & Sunshine. Wind light at S.W. In the morning Mr. Franchere took his departure for the fishing place in the large Canoe, accompanied by Brousseau and 4 S. Islanders, besides Baker and Patterson, two invalids and Pelton, the latter to remain during the fishing season being of no service whatever here. The two others to remain untill they shall get better of their complaint. Cannan resumed his work at the boat. Labonté employed with him. Pinot filling his place in the Blacksmith Shop.[27]

---

[25] Mercury ointment was the most common form of treatment for syphilis at the time, as noted above. What is perhaps surprising here is the apparent ease with which McDougall turned the mercury which Thompson had given him into a medicinal ointment. There were several forms of fat or grease available which could be used as the carrying agent for the mercury; the trickiest part of the operation was probably mixing the "quicksilver," which well deserved its name, with the chosen agent.

[26] In its earliest stages, scurvy shows itself in a general weakness and an apparent lassitude or unwillingness to exert oneself, often mistaken for malingering. The mechanics especially may have been experiencing these symptoms.

[27] This may have been the camp that Franchère recorded himself as running during this winter for some suffering from scurvy. *Journal*, p. 118.

27th. Saturday. Most of the day pleasant. Wind S. W. Visited in the forenoon by Comcomly & his followers, who traded a few Eggs & took a Blanket on credit. The principal object of his visit it appeared was to give us some further accounts relating to Wallace & party, which he obtained from one of his people Just returned from up the river. The former account he allows to have been incorrect. The present story states: It so happened at the establishment of the party that all hands were sent out to bring in meat of Elk and Deer (of which they had Killed great numbers) leaving only two S. Islanders in charge of the store. During their absence the natives near at hand, in considerable numbers (whom he denominated Calapoyas) visited the place & finding only those two to guard it, rob'd and took away all the principal goods, as Blankets, Cloths, etc., etc., without offering any violence to the 2 S. Islanders, who probably being overpowered in numbers made no resistance. On the return of Wallace & party he, with most of his number repaired immediately to the lodges of the Indians in order to secure the goods, who, instead of offering to return them, were all assembled with Bows & arrows ready for an assault. On discovering this movement, the whites proceeded instantly amongst them, seized some and broke their bows or cut the strings, wich brought on a general scuffle. Wallace's party it appeared had taken the precaution to load their Muskets with Powder only, and on perceiving the extremity to which they were reduced fired among the Indians which instantly frightened & dispersed them, and greater part of the goods were obtained. Ka-es-no, chief of the Cathlakamaps, hearing of what had taken place repaired immediately to the Calapoya, harangued them, pointed out the great impropriety of such conduct & the consequences that would follow, told them in what manner himself & other chiefs on the river treated the whites & the goods effects arising from it, and exhorted them without delay to return the remaining articles stolen. After hearing him, they followed his counsel, the things were all brought, and him (Kaesno) charged as mediator to return them & make up the breach. For which services Wallace had rewarded him with 2 fathoms Blue Cloth, 2 Wool Hats, and two Blankets. This it would appear has been performed by Kaesno & the news reached Comcomly, since Mr. Franchere was up to his Village. Sick list same as for several days past.[28]

---

[28] The Calapoya (also Calapooya or Kalapuya) spoke the Central Kalapuyan dialect and lived along the Willamette in west central Oregon. The tribe where Wallace and Halsey located was the Yamel, a sub-division of the Kalapuya; see Ruby, Brown, *Guide*, pp. 10–11. See above, February 13, for the original report; see also: February 14, 19, March 1, 8, 1813

28th. Sunday. Rainy most of the day, with heavy squalls from S. W. Intended sending the small canoe up to the fishing place, but the bad weather prevented it. 4 men sick.

March lst. Monday. Wind fresh from Westward. Weather tolerably pleasant. Early in the morning sent off 3 men in the small Canoe to Mr. Franchere, with directions for him to go up a second time to the Cathlakamaps, and ascertain the truth of the report received from Comcomly on Saturday, and whether true or not endeavor to engage Kaesno to go to Wallace's place with a Letter, that he may bring back some written account that will satisfy the anxieties entertained for the safety of the party. Mechanics etc. employed as last week. 3 S. Islanders at different Jobs. 4 men sick, beside the invalid Tuanna, who is not generally included in the list.[29]

2nd. Tuesday. Squally unsettled Weather, with frequent showers of hail & rain. Wind Westward. Jeremie & 1 S. Islander assisting Cannan & Labonté at the boat. 2 S. Islanders bringing Coals, cutting Wood, etc. Blacksmiths & Sawyers as usually occupied. In the forenoon visited by Comcomly, 2 sons & suite who traded two or three hundred smoked Salmon & a few fresh Uthlecans. After spending good part of the day with us, started for home. Sick list the same.

3rd. Wednesday. Flighty Weather, with intervals of sunshine & snow squalls. There was more snow fell during the latter part of the night & early this morning than has been seen before by any of us at this place. Mechanics etc. employed as Yesterday. Sick list continues the same. Visited by a few Clatsop Indians on their way home with fish, of which they would trade none.

4th. Thursday. Weather still unsettled, wind variable, with some showers of rain. S. Islanders employed most of the day cutting & clearing away Logs that had drifted round the wharf, which hindered hauling up Canoes at the usual place. Roussil laid up with a sore hand. At evening set Jeremie to work with one of the Blacksmiths, in order to keep up the watches, that the forge may be constantly occupied. In the forenoon the new Boat which was anchored in the bay with a small grapnall parted the line & went ashore. No

---

for further reports. On March 18, 1813, there was a final confirmation that there had been no conflict whatever between Wallace's party and the natives.

[29] It is interesting to see that, despite all the protestations of faith in the integrity and candor of Comcomly and apparent good relations with Kaesno, McDougall wanted confirmation directly from Wallace of his party's safety. Considering the quality of the bad news received from the natives, it was not surprising to see that he did not trust the good news either.

damage however was done to it and to prevent the like happening again had it hauled ashore and secured. Just at evening the youngest of our she goats was found in the Wood with 2 little ones, both alive & well.[30]

5th. Friday. Weather as Yesterday. Wind S.W. All hands employed as usual. Roussil still unable to work. No account from our Fishermen above from which we conclude they catch no Sturgeon. All hands here have been for several days been living on the few Uthlecans that were Salted. Near a hogs head of these were cured in this manner, when we first received them. Sick list as for some time past.[31]

6th. Saturday. Weather as for 2 or 3 days past. Frequent showers & Snow squalls. All hands employed as during the week. Visited by a few Clatsop Indians on their way up the river for fish. Sick list continues the same.

March 7th. Sunday. Tolerably pleasant for most part of the day, a few squalls of snow & hail. Wind light & variable. Cannan went as far as Point George in the forenoon hunting, and returned in a few hours with 2 geese. Sick list as for some time.

8th. Monday. Weather as Yesterday, squally & unsettled. Early in the morning Mr. Franchere with 4 men arrived in the small canoe bringing 2 Sturgeon. Left the large Canoe and 4 S. Islanders behind on the way down with 10 Sturgeon more. These arrived in the afternoon. Mr. Franchere was up to the Cathlakamaps last week. The story last received from Comcomly proves wholly without foundation. Kaesno knew nothing of it. We suspect some artful Indians, seeing how well Comcomly is now with us, has imposed upon him by a relation of such stories as he brought us. Kaesno would not engage to go to Wallace's place, not knowing the distance. It appeared that when he acquainted Mr. F. on his former visit of the distance to them being so short, it was to Mr. Reed's party, on their way up, who had encamped at some place to hunt a while, from whence Indians had brought accounts of them. Mechanics as usually employed, except Cannan who is fixing his gun. Patterson arrived in the Canoe & was set to work at the Boat alone. Labonté at small Jobs. 2 men here sick, & one above with Cooper at the fishing place besides Roussil, who is still laid up with a sore hand.

9th. Tuesday. Flighty Weather as for several days. People variously em-

---

[30] A "grapnall" (spelled grapnel) is a metal rod ending in several hooks arranged at different angles to the shaft, for grasping or holding. In this case, it was being used as an anchor for a small craft.

[31] The tight situation with regard to the provisions may be contrasted with the plenty of only a few weeks back. At this time of the year, especially before the salmon run began, both sturgeon and smelts were uncertain.

ployed. Those arrived Yesterday busy part of the day clearing out the square, other part cutting brush, etc. Visited by Comcomly & followers, who on account of the bad Weather remained the day & night with us. Took 4 Blankets on credit to be paid in smoked Salmon, which we have been able to purchase with Blankets only, since the commencement of this year. Delivered the old man also a Blanket, a fathom Calico & 5 heads Tobacco as a present for Joseacha, the Indian who was on board the Tonquin at the time she was lost, to be given him provided he will come to this place and give us the account himself. In which case he is also to be presented with a suit of clothes and several small articles named to Comcomly. Delivered likewise a Blanket, a fathom Calico and 3 heads Tobacco for the Chief of the Queenhilt, where Joseacha lives. Both these presents are to be given by Comcomly in case Joseacha will accompany him here. Otherwise all to be returned. Sick list as Yesterday. In the afternoon sent Antoine & 2 S. Islanders in the small canoe up to the fishing place, the weather was so bad as to prevent their setting out earlier in the day.[32]

10th. Wednesday. Weather squally & unsettled. Wind Southerly. People employed much as Yesterday, at sundry Jobs, putting the place in order, etc. Visited in the afternoon by a few Chinook Indians sent by Stachum, a chief, to return the tools stolen last October from the Coal Pit by his slaves, Viz., a shovel, a spade, a large axe, & two hoes. An iron rake & a brass Kettle is yet wanting, the latter of which they gave some assurances of returning. The other has been destroyed & made use of. Gave 2 heads tobacco to these men bringing the Tools & sent 3 more to Stachum with word he should be treated well if he came here now the things were returned. Traded with them 60 smoked Salmon, after which they left here for home. Comcomly & his people returned early this morning. One of the S. Islanders (Peter) ill with symptoms of the scurvy. Jeremie also laid up.[33]

11th. Thursday. Rainy most of the day. People were employed as usual. Mechanics at their several trades. 2 Sawing, the remainder putting the place in order, bringing gravel, etc. 6 men sick.

---

[32] The natives seem to have sensed the changing situation at Astoria and apparently raised the price for provisions substantially. As noted above, I, n. 88, Joseachal was the Quinault Indian interpreter hired by Captain Thorn while on his trading trip north in 1811. He was the only survivor from those on board the *Tonquin* and hence the only source for what happened. Joseachal arrived at Astoria on June 15; see the entries for June 15 and 18, especially the latter, for transcriptions of his testimony. His name is usually spelled with an "l" at the end. "Antoine" could be either Pepin or Plante; see Appendix nos. 145 and 139.

[33] These tools were stolen on October 7, 1812. There does not seem to be any explanation advanced for the delay in returning the tools.

12th. Friday. Weather as Yesterday. People employed nearly in the same manner also. Little, Milligan, Baker, Roussil, Jeremie and 2 S. Islanders sick.

13th. Saturday. Weather rainy the forepart of the day, afternoon tolerable clear. Wind from Eastward. People employed bringing up gravel & cleaning about the place. Towards evening Baker & 2 S. Islanders arrived from the fishing place, bringing 2 small Sturgeon only, being all they had caught since 8th Inst. Baker informed us of a report which was in circulation among the Indians of some white men being on their way down the river, and who it appears had broken their canoe, & were either repairing it or making a new one. They also add that they have been pillaged by the natives at the falls, & on account of which the whites threatened them with immediate death if they did not instantly restore the stolen effects. This so frightened the natives that they durst not venture near their camp. Sick list as Yesterday.[34]

14th. Sunday. Fine, clear Weather. Wind N. E. Finding it impossible to feed all hands here, and not having any pressing work, the Timbers for Boats being now all in readiness, it was thought proper to despatch two canoes this morning with 10 men, which with the six employed at the Fishery reduces our number to Twenty three, which we hope to be enabled to maintain. Visited by a Canoe of Chinooks who traded one hundred & forty dried Salmon. 3 men sick.[35]

15th. Monday. Weather squally. Wind variable from N. W. to N.E. Baker resumed to day his usual occupation in the Blacksmith's Shop. Roussil still unwell. In the morning Cannan went out a hunting and returned about noon without success. Labonté at different little necessary Jobs. Two S. Islanders fetching Coals etc. Two boys attending sick people. Mr. Clapp indisposed and confined to his room. Ouvré was to day taken with violent pains in his breast & sides, which indicates a pleuretic habit. 7 persons unfit for duty. On examination to day found that our stock of flour was so far gone that we were under the necessity of reducing the Blacksmiths allowance to one half.[36]

---

[34] Just who, if anyone, was having trouble with a broken canoe is not clear. If it was Astorians, McDougall has not noted it elsewhere. Some North Westers were on the Columbia at that time, but very far up. There is no incident recorded at this time which corresponds with Baker's report of a confrontation. Difficulties at the falls between natives and European parties moving through were common and this may be a blending of several previous incidents.

[35] Inferentially, the ten men were sent up to the fishery, somewhere near Oak Point, or at the mouth of the Cowlitz River.

[36] J. Bte. Ouvré's illness was so brief (see March 16) that it is doubtful it was any form of pleurisy; it may well have been some kind of a sprained muscle.

16th. Tuesday. Fine clear Weather. Wind S. W. Mechanics employed as usual. Two S. Islanders cleaning about the buildings and getting fire Wood. Ouvré getting better. 7 men sick. Visited by some Chinook Indians who traded 120 dried Salmon. At evening Watatkum brought in the meat of an Elk.

17th. Wednesday. Morning pretty clear, afternoon cloudy. About breakfast time 3 S. Islanders in a small canoe arrived from the Chelwits with 8 Sturgeon, a timely supply. They brought information that two of our lines had been taken by the Cathlamat Indians, and that they had beat one of our fishermen, Aswalacks, who found them in the act of stealing. Mr. Franchere was in consequence immediately despatched with three men in order to recover the lines etc. Visited by some Indians who traded a few Uthlecans. Sick list as Yesterday.[37]

18th. Thursday. Cloudy rainy Weather. Wind from S. E. Mechanics employed as usual, excepting Baker who is again on the sick list. In the evening Messrs. Reed, Seton & party returned from McKay's River, after an absence of 6 weeks, they left Messrs. Wallace & Halsey at their wintering grounds (about one hundred miles above the falls) all well on the 13 Inst. The present party who were sent up merely to live made out very well, as the country abounds in Elk & Deer, that is to say some parts of it, only as a good hunter could some time supply the party by hunting only a few hours. The river has some Beaver. Messrs. Wallace & Halsey with a S. Islander were the only persons remaining at the house when the party reached their place. They live upon very amicable terms with the natives, who visit them daily & trade roots (their only articles of trade) for meat. Indeed, they seem so far from having a wish to pillage their goods that they seemed to look with more desire upon the contents of the provision store than that of the goods, where the Bales still remain in the same state as when they took them in. The hunters say those they heard from had as yet caught but few Beavers, owing chiefly to the frequent rising & falling of the River, which overflows its banks almost with every shower. Towards night the large canoe came down with 23 Sturgeon. Sick list as yesterday. Visited by Gassacass.[38]

19th. Friday. Cloudy, rainy Weather. Mechanics at their divers occupations. Towards evening Mr. Franchere returned bringing 4 Sturgeon. He

---

[37] See below, March 19, 1813, for Franchère's return and report on this incident.

[38] This is the final report on the supposed looting of Wallace and Halsey's stores which had originally been reported by a tearful Comcomly on February 13, 1813. The expedient of sending some of the men up the Willamette to hunt their food and thus relieve the pressure on the stores at Astoria had worked admirably.

found on his arrival at the Chelwits that Aswalacks had recovered the lines, but 4 hooks had been cut loose by the Cathlamats. 8 men sick.

20th. Saturday. Morning cloudy with a few showers of rain. Mechanics only employed. In the morning Mr. McKenzie with 17 men in the boat went down to the Clatsop Village in order to purchase a canoe, and to recover a piece of Oak Timber (the Keel of the 28 feet Shallop) which the natives found on the beach adrift about 20 months ago. They all returned about noon with the piece of Timber, that is to say about 18 feet of it, as the natives had cut about 10 feet off for their use. Were unable to procure a canoe, having them all employed at the Uthlecan fishery. Mssrs. Seton & Franchere accompanied Mr. McKenzie, the former of whom relates a conversation which took place between him & one of the natives while there, to the following purport: Intimating their disbelief of a Ship coming in the river for us, and the destruction of Tonquin & Beaver by the Indians to Northward, and in case of a ship not coming in, what should we do? Casting up thereabouts the whole number of whites, and then shewing a contempt for such a small number which observations Mr. S. refuted & bantered in suitable manner. Samson, one of the Blacksmiths unwell. 8 men sick. Visited by Calpo.[39]

21st. Sunday. Fine Clear Weather. Wind Eastwardly. Visited by Stachum, who brought one hundred & seventy dried Salmon and a few fish rose. Several canoes of Clatsops passed last night loaded with Uthlecans, which they now catch in abundance. Samson better, 7 men sick.[40]

22nd. Monday. Pleasant. Wind N. E. In the morning Mr. Reed set off in the barge with 10 men, including 2 sick, Roussil & Baker. Sent likewise the small canoe with 5 men. Mr. Reed goes up to supercede the cooper at the Fishery as he's wanted here to pickle Sturgeon, of which we have more than we can consume, and likewise to prepare kegs for Mr. McKenzie's departure; 2 S. Islanders cutting brush. 2 men, Maçon & Coté cutting down trees, etc. LaFramboise, Lapierre & Pillon employed in the Blacksmith's shop. 9 men sick.[41]

---

[39] The oak timber in question must have been for a second shallop; its loss "about 20 months ago," i.e., the summer of 1811, explains the references at that time to "shallops," when only one such craft, *Dolly*, seems to have been built. Alfred Seton, the clerk who "bantered in suitable manner" with the Clatsop, left behind a reasonably copious journal, *Astorian Adventure: The Journal of Alfred Seton, 1811–1815*, but he did not record this conversation. It shows a fairly accurate appreciation of the plight of the Astorians at that time.

[40] The "fish rose" are undoubtedly fish roe, or eggs. The coming of the uthlecans in abundance has again eased the food situation at Astoria for a time.

[41] The cooper was either George Bell who came out on the *Tonquin*, or William Wilson; see Appendix. Donald McKenzie's departure refers to a trip to the interior to retrieve the

23rd. Tuesday. Morning clear with violent wind from N. E. which shifted towards evening to S. E. accompanied with rain. People employed much the same as Yesterday. Labonté and Patterson employed for Mr. McKenzie's departure. Visited by a few Clatsops who staid best part of the day, the wind being too impetuous for them to proceed. 9 men sick.

March 24th. Wednesday. It rained all last night, but this morning, the wind veered again to N. E. Cold raw cloudy weather. People employed as yesterday. About 1 P.M. the boat arrived with the Timber that was at the Helwits and 14 Sturgeon, having left the canoe on its way down with 5 more. Sick list as Yesterday.[42]

25th. Thursday. Fine clear Weather. Wind very fresh at N. E. People employed as follows, Viz., Mechanics at their usual employments, 4 men clearing a spot to haul the barges & canoes, 4 men boiling & cleaning sturgeon. The cooper pickling fish & preparing Kegs for Mr. McKenzie. The fishery supplies us now with more than we can consume & having no salt are under the necessity of boiling the fish & put it in Vinegar, of which we have a tolerable supply. About noon 3 men in the small canoe arrived with 6 Sturgeon. Sick list as Yesterday.

26th. Friday. Tolerable fair with flying clouds. Wind from S. E. Sent off this morning 7 men with the boat to get a supply of Sturgeon and fetch down Mr. Reed and men who are destined for Mr. McKenzie. The remainder of the men employed as usual. Visited by 2 Chinook Indians who traded a few dried & smoked salmon. 9 men still sick.[43]

27th. Saturday. Fine clear Weather. Labonté & Patterson preparing Timber for Boats. Cannan repairing gun Locks. Blacksmith at their usual work. Sick list as Yesterday.

28th. Sunday. Squally, Wind Southerly, accompanied with rain best part of the day. In the evening Mr. Reed and party arrived in the boat with 50

---

trade goods left in a cache at his post on the Clearwater, near its confluence with the Snake, in the vicinity of present-day Lewiston, Idaho; see below, March 31, 1813. This was to be taken as part of the plan to cut back Pacific Fur Company activity in preparation for abandoning Astoria and traveling back by land, a plan formed in consequence of the news of the declaration of war and the sending of an armed vessel by the North Westers to seize the post; see above, January 25, 1813, and, below, June 3, 1813. Why McKenzie, who should have left as soon as possible, lingered until now to leave is unexplained. The return east is postponed and then abandoned for 1813; see below, July 1, 1813.

[42] The "Helwits" refers to the Chelwits, the tribe that lived near Oak Point on the south bank of the Columbia; see above, I, n. 19.

[43] "destined for Mr. McKenzie," i.e., to be assigned to accompany McKenzie on his trip to the Clearwater.

Sturgeon, having left about 40 more on our line. He informs that the Indians don't catch them so plenty as some days past. Sick list always the same.

29th. Monday. Fine pleasant Weather. Wind S. W. Three men employed fetching up Coals. Mechanics at their usual labor. Preparations making for Mr. McKenzie's departure. 7 men sick. 4 men boiling & cleaning fish for the Pickle. In overhauling the cellar found that the cask, containing only a few days before Eighty gallons Brandy was entirely leaked out, the dampness of the cellar having rotted the hoops, & for we found they had given way at one end.[44]

30th. Tuesday. Fine pleasant Weather. Strong wind at S. W. People employed much the same as Yesterday. We have now about one hogshead of pickled Sturgeon, which if we succeed will last about one week. Sick list as Yesterday.[45]

31st. Wednesday. Cloudy with light Wind at S. W. Early this morning sent off the Boat with 7 men for a load of Sturgeon. After breakfast Mr. McKenzie left this for his wintering grounds, accompanied by Messrs. Reed & Seton in 2 canoes manned by 17 men, forming a total number of 20 Persons. He goes up light, having only provisions & very few articles of trade. Visited by 2 canoes of Clatsops and 2 of Chinooks, in one of the latter came Calpo & his wife. About noon Watatkum came in with the meat of an Elk. The party now remaining here consists of 31 souls including those employed at the Fishery. Say 4. 6 men sick.[46]

---

[44] The alternation of feast and famine, at least as regards fish, continues at Astoria. Mc-Dougall does not specify whether or not any brandy remained after the unfortunate loss recorded here. Apparently, no brandy was shipped to Astoria on the *Beaver* (although it did carry ten casks for the Russian post on Sitka); the men would have to be content with ale, wine, rum, whiskey, and gin. Sixteen barrels of vinegar had also come on the *Beaver*; hence, McDougall's "tolerable supply" (March 25). See Porter, *Astor*, I, 480, 499, 502.

[45] How much pickled sturgeon there would be in a hogshead is not easy to determine; of the cargo shipped on the *Beaver*, a hogshead of tobacco contained about 1,000 lbs., one of coffee, 628 lbs., and a hogshead of molasses, about 100 gallons; see ibid., 487–89, 499.

[46] As previously noted, the purpose of McKenzie's trip was to retrieve the trade goods cached near Lewiston, Idaho, in December 1812–January 1813. On their way up the river, McKenzie's party met John George McTavish and two canoes of North Westers on their way down to Astoria, where they were disappointed to find that the armed vessel *Isaac Todd* had not arrived. When McKenzie arrived at the caches, he found that the natives had looted them. Reed and another man were sent to inform Clarke at Spokane of the loss and deliver instructions from McDougall. During April and May, McKenzie, Seton, and their men went through the Nez Perce villages in the vicinity, retrieving the goods, often at the point of a gun; see Jones, ed., *Astorian Adventure*, pp. 112–15, and Appendix A for Seton's description of these events.

April 1st. Thursday. Cloudy Weather with fine rain all day. Mechanics only at work. Sent one of the cooks after coals. Our sick on the recovery. Roussil resumed his work. 4 men sick.

2nd. Friday. Fine clear Weather. Wind S.W. People employed much the same as Yesterday. Cannan repairing a canoe. Visited by Gassacass, who brought some few dried Uthlecans and 20 Eggs for trade. Also by Skamaquiah, from whom we purchased a horse, which he's to fetch down in a few days. Towards evening the boat arrived with 15 Sturgeon, 7 or 8 only of which were good. Baker & Flanagan came down, the former's health being entirely re-established, at least to all appearances. Mr. Clapp resumed his occupation. 2 white men and 2 S. Islanders still sick.[47]

3rd. Saturday. Fine clear Weather. Wind S. W. Blacksmiths & Carpenters at their usual work. 3 men cutting wood for a coal Pit. Roussil still unable to work. 3 white men & 4 S. Islanders sick. Visited by a few Chinooks, who traded some dried fish.

4th. Sunday. Morning rainy, remainder of the day pretty fair, with a fresh gale from Westward. Watatkum came in with the meat of an Elk. Mr. McDougall unwell. 8 persons unfit for duty.[48]

5th. Monday. Fine clear Weather. Wind S. W. People employed as follows: Baker, Sanson, Hodgens & Pillon at the forge. Labonté & Patterson making Boxes, etc. Jeremie cutting wood for Coals. 2 S. Islanders carrying out coals. Sent off in the morning Cannan, Laframboise & Macon, who are to take the Cooper & Antoine in order to proceed to the Cathlakamaps to procure a Rifle that the Chief has traded from the natives at the Rapids, and to cut 300 Ash saddle crutches. Sick people cleaning arms. 6 men unfit for duty.[49]

6th. Tuesday. Weather squally. Wind S. W. People employed as Yesterday. Set Sanson making Blanket Capots for the Indian trade, as Mr. McKenzie informed us that the Indians of the interior do not like the 2½ point

---

[47] Baker had been sent up to the fishing camp which Franchère was supervising on February 26, 1813, apparently suffering from scurvy.

[48] This is one of the few explicit mentions of McDougall's being sick. Several of those at Astoria record him as frequently being too ill to administer the camp.

[49] Sending off the five craftsmen and laborers to retrieve the rifle indicates that McDougall was too ill to go himself and that he did not have a clerk to take charge of the party. "Saddle crutches" are, specifically, that part of the saddle tree which supports the pommel, or front, of the saddle. They may have been used more generally here simply to indicate saddle trees, for, on April 13, the party is recorded as having returned with "Saddle Trees." Also, the saddles in question were probably for pack horses, and would not have a pommel.

Blankets & will not trade them, they finding them too small. 6 men still unwell.[50]

7th. Wednesday. Weather much the same as Yesterday. People employed the same. About 9 a.m. our small canoe came down from the fishing place with William & Peter, two S. Islanders, bringing all the implements which had been in use, and the necessary account of fish received, sent by Cooper, whom Cannan met a little below the Chelwits village. Wobaloma & Ashuallacks, two of the fishermen, arrived also at the same time to receive their payments. With very little difficulty settled with them, but deferred paying them untill tomorrow. 7 men sick.

8th. Thursday. Squally Weather, Wind S. W. People employed as usual. 4 of those unable to do duty set to cleaning fire arms. Satisfied Wabaloma & Ashuallacks for the amount of Sturgeon furnished by them, which amounted to near two hundred, or, in value, three hundred & ninety five Beaver taken since 13 February. Of these, one hundred & Sixty were consumed at this place (save 5 Barrels that were pickled, and are now in the Store), the remainder were eaten by the people employed at the fishery, or spoiled from the impossibility of conveying them here in season. As it would have taken too great a share of our small articles to satisfy for so large an amount, were under the necessity of paying a good part in Cloth & Blankets. Of the first they receivd 24½ Yds (Lion Skin) and of the latter 15 of 2½ pt. For the remaining part they recd. small axes, knives, scissors, hats, etc., etc. and were in the end apparently perfectly well satisfied. Traded also from Wobaloma for 3 Blankets of 2½ pt. a large Canoe which we are to bring down by the first opportunity. Visited by a few Chinooks, who brought some dried Uthlecans & Salmon for trade. Sick list same.[51]

---

[50] Michel Sanson was carried on the books as a blacksmith; he must have been a versatile craftsman; Appendix, No. 157. The capot was a hip-length jacket, often with a hood, made usually out of blanket material. This was a way of getting some value out of what was proving to be unsalable merchandise. See above, I, n. 54, for the approximate sizes of these blankets. Europeans frequently contrasted the short, squat build of the coastal natives with the tall, usually thin physique of the plains Indians. Considering that the former spent much of their time in canoes and other river craft, rowing or paddling, and were relatively sedentary, while the latter either rode or walked and moved their camps frequently, the physical differences should not be surprising.

[51] This entry is an unusual glimpse, for this log, at the manner in which much of the trading must have been carried on. Notice the use of beaver as a medium of exchange, much like modern currency. Obviously, the items available for trade bore more or less standard prices stated as so many pelts, or a portion of a pelt in the case of small items, much like 2½–point blankets. Arriving at a settlement, then, was no more complicated than adding up a shopping list in a modern store. This is probably overstating the convenience of the process, but it is removed from the barter-type exchange usually thought of in connection with fur

9th. Friday. Weather mostly fair. Wind S. The few hands now here employed as usual. Jeremie having cut his foot Yesterday is laid up. In the afternoon sent 2 S. Islanders to cut wood at the Coal Pit. Sick list as Yesterday.

10th. Saturday. Pleasant. Wind fresh at Westward. Four men cutting wood for Coal Pit. Others occupied as during the week. In the forenoon visited by Comcomly & Sons, in a large Canoe bringing for trade four hundred Queenhilt Salmon, for which they had previously been paid in Cloth Blankets. The old man returned but 2 or 3 days since from the Northward, and brought with him here to day the things intended for Joseacha & the Queenhilt chief, in case the former should accompany him here, as mentioned in our Journal some few days since. He had left home here for the northward on Comcomly's arrival at Queenhilt, who in consequence missed seeing him. Towards evening discovered a large cloud of smoke proceeding from a fire on the summit of Cape Disappointment, which we supposed to have been made by the Indians as a signal to some vessel in the offing. The fire was observed to continue bright till late in the evening.[52]

11th. Sunday. Incessant rain during the fore part of the day. Afternoon high wind from S. W. & Cloudy. The rain completely extinguished the fire on the Cape, & that, together with the storm of wind accompanying dampened further expectations of seeing a sail. At 10 0'clock were much surprized by the Arrival of Mr. J. G. McTavish, Mr. Laroque, Michael Bourdon & a party of 18 men in two bark canoes, from the establishments of the N. W. Co. on this side the Rocky Mountains, who encamped in our little bay below the Factory. Mr. McTavish (the principal) was received by us with every civility reasonably to be expected in like cases, and his object & views in coming here were immediately made known to us. He has an establishment in the neighborhood of Mr. Clarke, which place he left on the 2d Inst. &

---

trading and the like. "Lion Skin" is the linen cloth mentioned above, II, n. 105. Astoria is running low on trade goods, not a surprise, considering the cargo lost on the *Tonquin*, as well as that carried away from the various caches by the natives. Even so, there will be a considerable inventory when the post is sold to the North Westers in November 1813; see "Inventory of Sundries delivered to the North West Company, Astoria, October 1813," in "Message of the President of the United States [James Monroe] Communicating . . . documents relating to an establishment at the mouth of Columbia River." House Document 45, 17th Congress, 2nd Session. Jan. 27, 1823, 1–80.

[52] "Queenhilt Salmon" (Quinault) is another form of what is commonly called Chinook salmon. The mention of Comcomly's return of various trade articles refers back to March 9 when McDougall recorded an attempt to bring the sole survivor (Joseachal) of the *Tonquin* tragedy to Astoria so he could be questioned and as accurate a narrative of the event as possible be compiled. Joseachal will come to Astoria on June 15, 1813.

handed us a note open from Mr. C. of that date, containing merely a request that a few articles of iron works for his barge might be sent up by Mr. McKenzie, otherwise only complimentary. We have accounts from Mr. D. Stuart also, who it appears has established himself on the waters of Fraser's river, to which place he had penetrated last season. Mr. LaRoque had been established in opposition along side of him. On their way down saw that the barge belonging to Mr. Clark had been broken in pieces by the Indians. Fell in with Mr. McKenzie & party 10 miles above the Falls on the 7th Inst. who had passed thus far in safety. Acquainted Mr. McK. with the accounts they had received above from the Indians, that his <u>caches</u> were robbed; which from circumstances of their having seen Indians with Scarlet Cloth, fine Shot, etc., from the direction of his place & offering to sell to them, is no doubt correct. From the accounts brought by Mr. McKenzie on his arrival here in January last, we had expected Mr. McTavish & party down in all March, but had this time given them over. That they were coming here formidable in Opposition, to await the arrival of a Ship from London on account of the N. W. Company, equiped with everything necessary & adapted to Indian trade, arranged by men possessed of experience & a thorough knowledge of the business, we had also heard, but gave little credit to that part.[53]

12th. Monday. Weather Squally & unsettled, intervals of rain & Sun Shine, Wind fresh at S. W. & Westward. This being the anniversary of our first landing at Astoria, a treat was given to all hands suitable to the occasion. Liquor was also given to the men of Mr. McTavish's party, that they might make merry here with their Countrymen on their meeting. Work of every Kind was therefore laid aside for the day. Visited by a great number of

---

[53] With the arrival of McTavish and the large body of North Westers, the situation has obviously changed dramatically for the worse. Although McDougall knew of the declaration of war, he apparently did not take too seriously the story of the rival company's vessel having been dispatched for the Columbia. Now he did. The gentlemen's agreement not to compete too strongly and the division of territory arrived at with David Thompson in July 1811, when a partial merger of the Pacific and North West companies was thought to be in the works, was now set aside. There is no certain evidence as to just what McTavish might have told McDougall regarding "his object & views in coming." Since the decision to abandon the post and return east via the overland route had already been taken (see above, January 25, 1813, and n. 11), the practical effect of McTavish's arrival was to confirm that decision, although it would prove impossible to execute that year. The events and decisions that followed have been described briefly in the Introduction; for a detailed treatment, see Ronda, *Astoria*, pp. 263ff. Clarke had established himself near present-day Spokane, while David Stuart was near Kamloops, British Columbia.

Clatsop Indians, who remained most of the day out of curiosity to see the strangers. 5 men sick.[54]

13th. Tuesday. Cloudy with fine rain most of the day. All hands still engaged in their frolic, & no work going forward. Visited by numbers of the natives who traded some dried Uthlecans. We value them at the same rate as last year, but find we cannot purchase them with articles of the like kind, and are now under the necessity to pay for them with knives, files, small axes etc. At evening, Cooper, Cannan & party arrived with Saddle Trees in two Canoes, bringing with them the one purchased from Wobaloma, of which we informed Cooper by letter. He had been to the Cathlakamaps, but found them in possession of the Musket lost by Mr. McKenzie's party, & not a rifle. This he traded and brought down. Shortly after them Kalaskan, Chief of the Chelwits, & the last of our Fishermen to be settled with, arrived with his party in a large Canoe, brought three fresh Sturgeon & some dried Uthlecans, encamped below the Factory. Sick list as Yesterday.[55]

14th. Wednesday. Fine rain throughout the day. All hands variously employed. Mechanics at their several occupations. One man assisting Blacksmiths, in place of Roussil, who is still laid up with a lame hand. Others at sundry small Jobs within doors. Settled with & paid Kalaskan for his Sturgeon amounting in all with those of Yesterday to Eighty Beavers in value. Paid 36 Beavers in Cloth & Blankets, the remaining in small articles, which he was pleased with. Made him, as well as the other two settled with before, some trifling presents, having all behaved well as regarded the Fishery, & to our people who remained among them. The old man, as chief of the Village behaved exceedingly well. Mr. McTavish's party employed in putting up a

---

[54] McDougall has been criticized for his hospitality to McTavish and the North Westers, most elegantly by Irving (*Astoria*, Chap. LIV). This has been interpreted as part and parcel of his presumed disloyalty to Astor and taken as a forerunner of the favoritism supposedly shown in the terms of sale which he negotiated later with the North West Company. The details of that transaction can stand separate from his hospitality to McTavish and his men. Recall that both had been in the North West Company, that a good number of the men of both companies had known each other and worked together in the past, that both the Astorians and the North Westers had a majority (in the latter, all) of Scots and French Canadians in their groups, with only a minority of United States citizens in the Astoria contingent. It would have been surprising if McDougall had not treated the North Westers as he did. It was both good manners and good sense for the small number of Europeans to cooperate with each other in the face of their situation on the Columbia in 1813.

[55] The cooper, George Bell, and others had been sent up river for the saddle trees on April 5, 1813, as well as to secure the weapon referred to here. McDougall paid Kalaskan in the same way he paid Wobaloma and Ashwallax, April 8, 1813.

small shelter for their Baggage etc. in the little bay below us, where they first encamped. He requested an Iron Staple & hasp for a lock to the door, which was made for him.[56]

15th. Thursday. Rainy the whole day. Wind S. W. All hands employed. Mechanics as usual. Several cutting wood for a Coal Pit, but make little progress in the constant rain. Carpenters making Gun Cases, etc. Visited by Comcomly, 2 Sons & a great number of his people. Some for the purpose of trade, others through curiosity to see the strangers. Purchased from the old man & his people 180 fathoms dried Uthlecans, for which we were under the necessity of paying in part small axes, knives, & files. Received from Mr. McTavish a small Bale of goods, comprizing his whole assortment, for which we shall account to him the value in provisions. Arrangements having been formed between Mr. McDougall & him that the latter shall not attempt trading provisions this spring, which would only in that case cause it to come much higher than the present extravigant price, which we are under the absolute necessity of paying. He is neither to give out any intimations to the natives that a Ship is coming for him, or that he is in any manner opposed to us in disputing a trade, until she actually arrives, and it can no longer be hid. From such measures, under present circumstances it is thought will result mutual advantage. Our sick on the recovery. Roussil still laid up.[57]

16th. Friday. Tolerably pleasant most of the day with some few Showers of rain. Wind fresh at Westward. Visited by Calpo & his wife & many other Chinook Indians. Traded with the former 180 fathoms dried Uthlecans & 110 pieces dried Sturgeon, in the same manner as the fish traded yesterday, amounting in value to 71 Beaver. Traded with others 93 fathoms Uthlecans & a few dried Salmon. Watatkum came in at evening with the meat of an Elk. People occupied pretty nearly as Yesterday. Cannan making a turning Lathe, Cooper at his trade. Sick list the same.

17th. Saturday. Fine clear Weather. Wind Westerly. Five men cutting

---

[56] The building of a shelter, apparently fairly substantial, for his baggage and stores indicates that McTavish has settled in for a relatively long stay. He will leave Astoria on July 5, 1813. During this time, relations between the two groups are apparently cordial and relatively close, with a good bit of sharing of game, tools, canoes, etc.

[57] The agreement outlined here illustrates two things. First, the close relationship between the two groups mentioned in the previous note; the sharing of trade goods and provisions, certainly indicates a mutual trust. Second, the desire to hide the fact of their separate and competitive character from the natives underlines the need the Europeans felt to show a solid front. Although it is justified here as a way of keeping prices from going even higher than they had, it may also have been seen as a defensive tactic against the always feared attack by the natives.

wood for Coals, Mechanics as usually employed. Visited by several Canoes of Chinooks, from whom we traded one hundred & thirty four fathoms dried Uthlecans. Comcomly was of the number & had about 50 fathoms. After the trade was over presented him with a Blanket for good behaviour. Towards evening the women about the place were all ordered off. Cooper unwell. 5 men sick.[58]

18th. Sunday. Cloudy without rain. Wind fresh at Westward. Being Easter Sunday gave all hands a small treat. Visited by several Chinook & Clatsop Indians. Our Chinook hunter brought in an Elk. Traded also 20 fathoms fish. Sick list as yesterday.

19th. Monday. Pleasant, with a moderate breeze from Westward. Mechanics severally employed at their trades. Roussil resumed his work in the Shop, but is unable to use the hammer. One man employed to assist the other three Blacksmiths, same as for some time past. One Carpenter making Gun Cases, the other repairing & putting in order Wheel Barrows, & other tools about the place. Little, Milligan & 2 S. Islanders sick. Visited by numbers of Indians who traded a considerable quantity dried fish.

20th. Tuesday. Cloudy, Wind fresh at Westward. People employed as Yesterday. Jeremie unable to chop, set him at small Jobs grinding knives, etc. 5 men hauling out wood for a Coal Pit. Cooper resumed his work. 5 men sick. Visited by 2 Chinooks in a small Canoe, from whom we traded the meat of an Elk.

21st. Wednesday. Rainy throughout the day, & mostly calm. All hands variously employed as for two or three days past. Sent Mr. McTavish a large Canoe for the purpose of bringing home meat. One of his hunters having Yesterday killed 3 Elk at no great distance from the factory. On the return of the canoe he sent us several pieces of meat, comprizing nearly a whole animal, in return for what we had sent him of the like kind during the week past. Visited by numbers of the natives from whom traded 76 fathoms fish. Sick list as yesterday. Observed several flocks of pigeons flying over to day.

22nd. Thursday. Heavy rain all day. Mechanics as usually employed. Other hands at different small Jobs within doors, most of the number picking the stalks out of Tobacco & preparing it for manufacturing. Sick list the

---

[58] Just why the women were ordered away is puzzling. Obviously, from the incidence of syphilis and the frequent references to trading "waltap," etc, they were often at the post. Whether their numbers had become bothersome, whether the presence of the North Westers had caused some competition in the sexual commerce that went on, McDougall does not note. Equally interesting is why they are so seldom ordered away (assuming a complete record in the log), as their presence must often have been distracting.

same. Little continues very weak, apparently no better than two or three weeks ago, having been constantly bathing almost every day for some time to get the Mercury out of his system, which has very much reduced him. Milligan getting better. He was enabled Yesterday to speak for the first time in upwards of twenty days. The mercury had a surprizing effect on him, altho he made use of but a small quantity, owing evidently to the remains of the scurvy, with which he had been affected previous to using it. 4 S. Islanders laid up with Colds. Two boys attending the sick.[59]

23rd. Friday. Clear most of the day. Wind strong at Westward. Several hands at work getting wood for the Coal Pit. Cannan & two Carpenters at various necessary Jobs. Other Mechanics as usually employed. Flanagan making shirts. Sick list as yesterday.

24th. Saturday. Rainy greater part of the day. Wind fresh from Westward. Visited by 2 Canoes of Chinooks, bringing over a few Geese & Ducks. The weather too bad to send people to the Coal Pit. Employed them at several small jobs about the house, securing our dried fish, etc. of which we still expect to purchase more. Mechanics employed as during the week.

25th. Sunday. Squally from S. W. with intervals of pleasant Weather. Several Canoes of Indians, principally Clatsops about all day & were suffered to remain on account of bad Weather. Purchased a few fathoms of Uthlecans. 5 men sick.

26th. Monday. Cloudy with strong wind from W. & S. W. All hands variously employed. Four Blacksmiths & Pillon at work in the Shop. Two filing Axes & Knifes, the others beating out Iron for half axes. In giving out iron for half axes we find there is not more on hand than for about 3 hundred. The remainder of the Iron is all too small. One carpenter at work, three hands arranging & securing fish. S. Islanders hoeing the garden. Patterson & Cannan sick. Little & Milligan getting better. Three S. Islanders unfit for duty.

27th. Tuesday. Cloudy, afternoon rainy, at evening violent gusts of wind from S. W. Saw great numbers of geese flying to Southward & Eastward. Mechanics severally employed. Most of the hands occupied as yesterday. Two men repairing garden fence, one preparing the garden for planting & sowing. Macon is made Gardener. Sick list the same. Visited by Calpo's wife & several of her people; traded some fish.

---

[59] The "manufacturing" of tobacco probably refers to chopping it so that it could be smoked in pipes, the most common manner of consumption at the time. McDougall's homemade mercury ointment seems to have had drastic effects on Little and Milligan; "bathing" may refer to internal purgatives as well as external bathing.

28th. Wednesday. Cloudy, with fequent squalls of Rain, hail & snow. Cold & uncomfortable. People at work as Yesterday several cutting wood at coal Pit. Patterson at work. Cannan getting better. Visited by a few Indians, but had no trade. In the forenoon one of Mr. McTavish's canoes that had been sent with a party of men on a hunting excursion a short distance up McKay's river, returned loaded with fresh venison. The Weather had been too unfavorable to admit of their drying any great quantity. He sent us the meat of near two Deers. 6 men sick. Sanson began putting up the Coal Pit, while another man fills his place in the Blacksmiths Shop.

29th. Thursday. Disagreeable Weather, frequent squalls of Rain, hail & snow as Yesterday. Visited by several Canoes of Chinook Indians, from whom purchased a good number of Geese. Sent a part to Mr. McTavish. At evening visited by Ka-las-kan chief of the Chelwits, who brought for trade 5 fresh Sturgeon & some dried fish. Sent Mr. McT some fresh Sturgeon also. 5 men sick.

30th. Friday. Clear & pleasant for the first in several weeks. 5 men employed at the Coal Pit, putting it up and bringing out wood. Others employed as usual. Macon unable to do duty & is cutting & preparing potatoes for planting. Traded with Kalaskan & other Indians that came about for several fathoms dried fish. Having now almost a sufficient supply on hand, cannot longer afford to pay any Iron works for them. If we purchase more it must be for such articles as we chuse to offer. Traded also some Geese from a Chinook who has taken up hunting for some time past. Has killed & brought us two Elk & so far behaved himself very well. Sick list as yesterday.[60]

May 1st. Saturday. Clear & pleasant. Wind westerly. All hands employed as during the week. Macon commenced planting Potatoes. Calpo brought us 10 Geese; visited by several other Indians, but no trade. Sick list the same, most of the number recovering slowly.

2nd. Sunday. Cloudy, but moderate Weather. Wind at S. W. and towards evening has some rain. A party went down to the Sea Shore on the Clatsop side in the forenoon in our barge, consisting of Messrs. McDougall, McTavish, LaRoque & Clapp & 9 men. All returned in the afternoon. Visited by some few Indians and purchased one fresh Salmon, the first we have seen

---

[60] McDougall's note as to the scarcity of iron goods, i.e., half-axes and the like, and that the natives would have to accept "such articles as we chuse to offer," emphasizes the small inventory of trade goods the Astorians had left at this point. He may also have been thinking ahead to the acquiring of horses for the trip east and been hoarding trade goods against that eventuality.

this season. Sick list the same. Little continues very low & weak. Milligan recovering fast, went out to day for the first time since his illness. Dick, the S. Islander very ill with the Scurvy. Two S. Islanders (Boys) still attending the sick at which they have been constantly employed upwards of two months.

3rd. Monday. Clear & pleasant. Wind raw from Westward. All hands busily employed. Mechanics as usual. Macon and 3 S. Islanders working in the Garden planting Potatoes etc. Two hands assisting the Blacksmiths, Sanson & 2 others at the Coal pit, which in the afternoon they finished & set fire to. Visited by some few Indians but had no trade. Cannan resumed his work with the Carpenters. Sick list now 4 in number.

4th. Tuesday. Pleasant & moderate. Wind at N. W. Hands disposed as Yesterday. One only with Sanson. 4 S. Islanders digging out a large Stump in the garden. One Blacksmith Sick. The others with 2 men to assist finishing off Knives & Axes. Macon planting the garden. Mr. McDougall accompanied Messrs. McTavish & LaRoque on an excursion to the Chinook village in a canoe belonging to the latter for the purpose of obtaining a view at Sea from the high land at Chinook point. All returned at evening accompanied by a canoe with three Indians, who brought over a fine fresh Salmon. These Indians would not sell the Salmon at home & allow the whites to cook it on account of their superstitious notions, noticed during our first year here, but came over on purpose to cook it for us themselves. They were unwilling absolutely to deny the fish to Mr. McDougall, but it was on these conditions only he could obtain it. Little, Milligan, Hodgens & 2 S. Islanders sick.[61]

5th. Wednesday. Fore part of the day cloudy with some showers of rain, afternoon clear & pleasant. Wind Westerly. People occupied as Yesterday. Number of sick the same. Visited by Stachum & several other Chinook Indians, two of whom brought the small boat belonging to the Shallop, which he had observed to be missing for some time, untill Mr. McDougall saw it during his visit to Chinook Yesterday. Traded a few fresh Salmon, partly dried, which came from the rapids, & some dried Uthlecans. Mr. McTavish's hunters killed an Elk, of which he sent us part. They were unlucky— shot three but could get only one.

6th. Thursday. Tolerably pleasant. Wind moderate at Westward. People disposed as Yesterday. Visited by a number of the natives who traded a few

---

[61] See I, n. 52 for a brief description and a reference for the ritual surrounding the first salmon of the spring run.

fresh Salmon half dried. Sent a few of them to Mr. McTavish. Watatkum came with the meat of an Elk, the first he has killed for several Weeks. Little, Milligan, Baker, Patterson & 2 S. Islanders Sick, <u>beside</u> Tuanna.

7th. Friday. Weather as Yesterday. Men employed in much the same manner also. Set Tuanna at work with Macon in the garden, as he appears now active & strong, much better than he has ever been here. Jeremie at small jobs in the Store. Visited by a few Indians. Our Chinook hunter brought two ducks, the only game he had killed. Samson & Antoine Belleau attending Coal pit. 5 men sick.

8th. Saturday. Clear & pleasant. Wind fresh at S. W. & Westward. People employed as during the week. Blacksmiths very busy finishing off their work. Visited by some Clatsop Indians who brought the meat of an Elk to trade. 4 men sick.

9th. Sunday. Cloudy moderate Weather. Wind light at Westward. Visited by several Canoes of Indians. In the forenoon Gassacass brought over a horse, which we traded. In the afternoon a Chinook Indian from Baker's Bay arrived with the meat of an Elk, and at evening Watatkum came in with words of having also killed an Elk at some considerable distance up Young's bay. Traded also about 50 Salmon trout.

10th. Monday. Clear most of the day. Wind at S. W. Weather unsettled. Early this morning sent off a canoe and men for the Elk of Watatkum's, he accompanying them in a small canoe. Two men of Mr. McTavish's were of the number. They all returned at evening with the meat, which was at a great distance from here. Visited in the forenoon by Comcomly & a number of his people, who traded a few dried fish. One of his slave men while here was troublesome to some of our people at their work, and when they ordered him away, the rascal drew his knife upon them, which they let pass unpunished. Shortly afterwards he had the assurance to come into the houses but was immediately kicked quite out of the place as he deserved. All hands employed in the same manner as during last week. Three Blacksmiths & 2 hands to assist finishing off axes. Two Carpenters at sundry small work. Cooper at his trade. Cannan making Saddles. Two at Coal pit. One gardening, one tayloring. S. Islanders at sundry Jobs. Ouvré set to work with other hands. Sick getting better, the list is now reduced to three. Milligan attempted working to day but can do little yet. Traded with Comcomly during his visit for a very good Fowling gun, which we gave him two old Muskets for of little value.[62]

---

[62] From the day McTavish and his North Westers arrived, there was a good bit of sharing

11th. Tuesday. Cloudy with frequent showers of rain. Weather moderate. People disposed in the same manner as Yesterday. In the afternoon were visited by Ashuallax & three other Indians from the Helwitz, with two or three ducks & a few dried fish for trade. Ashuallax informs us of a story he has learned from the Indians of the Cowlitzk river who have communication through to the Sea at some distance to the Northward, that on a visit to the Sea about a month since, they saw a Ship at anchor in some harbor, trading with the natives. The people of which informed them they were coming into this river in two months. The story at any rate if true can be of no interest to us, as there is no probability that the *Beaver* should be there, or, if there, not trading Beads, etc. as the report says, because they have none suitable. This, however, is the second time within a week or two that we have heard a story of the kind. Flanagan sick, making the number 4.[63]

12. Wednesday. Clear & pleasant. Wind N. W. People variously employed. Patterson, Labonte, Cannan & Laframboise at Carpenters work, making a small gate for the garden and other jobs. Two at work in the garden, with the S. Islanders levelling the walk in front of the Picketing, gravelling it, etc. Blacksmiths finished off all their work on hand, allowed them the afternoon, & gave each a small quantity of liquor, of which they were well deserving, having wrought hard. Ashwallax remained all day with us. Visited by a few Chinooks, but had nothing for trade. Cooper employed in the Store examining our powder in the Magazine. Many Kegs were found in bad order, tho' none of consequence damaged. Arranged the whole, put such in new Kegs as required it, and stowed it away in good order. Three men sick. Milligan much better. Little, our Boat builder recovering slowly. Last night he recd. a most unlucky blow by accident with a stick in the face, which knocked out three of his teeth. He has now been confined since 19 February last and have at this time no hopes of his being able to do duty again for a long time. Instead therefore of having 6 boats completed by the middle of June as we had good reason to expect, we have one only in the water & one unfinished.[64]

and exchange between the two parties. The joint party to retrieve the elk carcass may be an advance on that cooperation or simply McDougall's accounting for what all of his people were doing. The conduct of Comcomly's slave was extraordinary, and it is curious that the old chief's reaction to it is not recorded also.

[63] "Helwitz" is probably a miswriting for Chelwitz. The trading vessel, if it existed, was probably in Willapa Bay, about thirty miles above Cape Disappointment on the Washington coast. It never came to the Columbia.

[64] McDougall is probably referring to whaleboats or their equivalent. See below, May 15, 1813, for his comment that, because of Little's illness, cedar canoes will have to be substituted.

13th. Thursday. Weather as yesterday. Mechanics employed as usual. All hands else sent to carry out Wood to Coal Pit. Blacksmiths repairing axes for use, arranging the Shop, and completing some small jobs. Sick list the same.

14th. Friday. Fore part of the day pleasant, afternoon cloudy with appearances of rain. All hands employed same as Yesterday. One Carpenter & Cannan unwell, making six men Sick. Visited by numbers of Indians of whom we purchased the meat of a small Elk and a Beaver. Sent Mr. McTavish a part of the Elk. His people now occupied making Cedar Canoes.

15th. Saturday. Pleasant. Wind Westerly. People employed as during the week. Sanson & Antoine finished the first Coal pit, which made upwards of 140 Barrels. Preparing to send off a party on Monday for Cedar Timber to build Canoes, which we must now do through necessity, as we cannot longer indulge a hope that our Boat builder will be able to do any work in season. 4 men sick.

16th. Sunday. Pleasant as Yesterday. Visited by <u>Stachum</u> & a number of his people from whom we traded the meat of 2 Elk & 2 Beaver. Sick list the same. Last evening killed our old Black Goat (Billy) which made a mess for all hands to day. He was last spring deprived of the means of being longer useful in his line, and has been since only a pest to the other Goats.

May 17th. Monday. Fine pleasant Weather. Wind Westerly. A party was this morning despatched in order to procure Cedar Timber. Viz. Mr. Franchere, Cannan, Labonte & 2 others. Cooper & one hand went also with them in the boat to assist & cut hoop poles. Two men at the Coal pit beside 4 S. Islanders carrying out Wood. Mechanics employed as usual. Blacksmiths making half axes, for which they have all the iron prepared that will answer. Near as much labor is expended in beating out the iron to a proper size as is afterwards required in making up the work. 4 men sick beside Tuanna. All on the recovery. 3 of them picking Tobacco. Jeremie & Pelton manufacturing ditto.

18th. Tuesday. Weather as Yesterday. People disposed much in the same manner also. One S. Islander only with the 2 men at the Coal pit. The wood being all brought out, they are now putting up the second pit. Visited by several of the natives, and among others our Chinook hunter, who brought us the meat of an Elk. Watatkum also came in at evening but had killed nothing. Purchased a fine fresh Salmon caught above here which was presented to Mr. McTavish. Sick list the same.

19th. Wednesday. Weather squally with showers of rain. Wind Southerly. All hands employed as usual. Three S. Islanders bring Coals & at other small jobs about the place. Visited in the forenoon by Comcomly, his youngest son and a number of his people, bringing a report that they saw a Vessel in the offing last evening & this morning, & that she fired 4 guns. To satisfy any doubts of the truth of this, respecting which all are so anxious, Mr. McTavish despatched a party of his people in a Canoe for the Chinook shore to obtain a sight of the Vessel. Fired three guns as a signal for Mr. Franchere to return immediately with the boat, as much credit is given to the report of the Indians, that a Ship is at hand & in which case the boat will be required here. Comcomly brought near 60 Beaver & 3 Clemels, for the amount of which he has been credited, & after trading returned immediately. 4 men sick. Three of the number however at small work. Little still confined to his bed but recovering. Tuanna at work.[65]

20th. Thursday. Cloudy. Wind light & variable from Southward & Westward. People employed in the same manner as Yesterday. Mr. McTavish's people returned this forenoon without seeing any Vessel, tho' this does not do away our hopes, or credit in belief of the Indians report, as the Weather was too unfavorable to admit of their having a view at any great distance, or of a Vessel, standing in near the land with safety. No Indians came about except a small canoe with 2 Clatsops fishing near the bank early this morning, one of whom came ashore to tell us that he saw a Ship Yesterday from Clatsop point. Sick list as yesterday.

21st. Friday. Weather unsettled, greater part of the day however tolerably pleasant. Wind variable. In the forenoon Mr. Franchere & party returned with a boat load of Cedar & hoop poles. Did not hear our guns. People variously employed in the usual manner. The boat was immediately despatched on a second trip for Cedar with the same number as before except Mr. Franchere & Cooper. It was not thought necessary to detain her here, as the weather would not warrant a Vessel to make her appearance now, if actually off the river. Visited by several Chinook Indians, Skamaquiah, Calpo, etc., none of whom had seen any Vessel. Skamaquiah tells us that one Indian only of the Chinooks saw one. He said she came to anchor off the Cape for a short time & then stood out again. Finished covering the Coal pit & at evening fired it. One S. Islander remains with Sanson to attend it. Antoine went up in the boat in place of Michel who remains here to be

---

[65] Both McDougall and McTavish were thinking about the report of an armed vessel having been dispatched to seize the Pacific Fur Company post on behalf of the North West Company and the British government. For the next week, McDougall frets in the log about the sightings, reports, etc., of a ship, then stops writing about it. However, the anxiety he displays now probably played a role in the decision recorded in the June 3 entry.

otherwise employed. Sick list the same. William one of the number smoking deer Skins. Milligan doing a little at his trade.

22nd. Saturday. Flying Clouds. Wind S. W. & Southerly. Latter part mostly calm. Cooper, Patterson & LaFramboise set to work dressing Cedar & spruce boards for Canoes. Those intended for Boats will answer for this purpose but require dressing down thin. All hands else as usually occupied. Several of Mr. McTavish's people, as also the Indians encamped near them heard a gun this morning, which appeared evident was fired from a ship. Mr. Clapp accompanied by Mr. LaRoque was in consequence sent over to Chinook in an Indian Canoe in order to obtain some information concerning it, and if he should there learn or discover anything satisfactory to proceed as far as Cape Disappointment, and there at the proper time make the signals agreed on with Captain Sowle & Mr. Hunt of the Beaver, to satisfy them, if it should prove to be their Ship, that we were still living, or, if a strange Vessel, that there were white people here. Visited by a Canoe from the Cathlakamaps with the wife of <u>Kaessnoe</u>, the chief & some of his people, and received from him as a present 8 fresh Salmon & a few partly dried. Sent him in return a present suitable, as well for this as his uniform good behaviour towards us, and gave his wife & people also some trifling things for their trouble. Sick list the same.

May 23rd. Sunday. Clear & pleasant Weather. Wind Westerly. Messers. Clapp & LaRoque returned in the forenoon, having been no further than Chinook. They could there learn nothing respecting the firing heard Yesterday, nor could they discover any thing from the high land near the village Yesterday evening or this morning, & therefore did not deem it necessary to proceed further. The Indians still insist that they saw a sail which we are induced to give credit to, but from every account they would make it out to be a Brig. It is most certainly provoking if we shall at last be disappointed & see no sail, & such it would now seem, or at least we fear will be the case. Sick all recovering.[66]

24th. Monday. Fine Pleasant Weather. Wind Westerly. All hands busily employed. Three dressing out stuff for Canoes. Blacksmiths as usual, Jeremie at small work making Bags. S. Islanders at different Jobs, one with Sanson at the Coal Pit. Visited by some few Indians trading gum & 2 Beavers Just Killed. Every encouragement is given to them that they may

---

[66] McDougall seemed to be dismayed that the mysterious ship, if the natives' observations were correct, was a brig, that is, having two masts. This was owing to the fact that the *Beaver* was ship-rigged, that is, three-masted. Thus, if there was a vessel outside the Columbia, it was not the *Beaver*.

procure gum for us. Bargained also with one to day to bring a quantity of Cedar Boards, of certain dimensions, as our great hurry is now to have canoes completed in season, which unless we make exertions cannot be done. Dick recovered of the Scurvy & resumed his occupation. Two men only sick: Little & Milligan, & those fast recovering.[67]

25th. Tuesday. Most of the day pleasant. Toward evening cloudy with fine rain. Wind variable. Men disposed as Yesterday. Visited by numbers of Indians, with Gum for trade. Just at evening 3 Chinooks arrived with intelligence that a Ship was seen a little to Northward of Cape Disappointment, this morning. One of these three say they saw it for some time. He was far in Baker's Bay, beyond Chinook Village & heard first several Guns, which attracted him to the Sea Shore, where he had a sight of her. Sick list as Yesterday.

26th. Wednesday. Pleasant. Clear Weather. All hands variously employed much in the usual manner. Commenced taking an Inventory to be completed by 1 June. In the forenoon the Boat returned loaded with Cedar Timber & a few hoop poles. Purchased also from an Indian 70 Cedar Boards, which were delivered also this forenoon. No confirmation of Yesterday's report. Calpo & family came over on their way up the River on a trading adventure. Purchased from him a horse, to be brought over in a few days. Furnished him likewise with the means of purchasing the Rifles now in possession of the natives at the rapids, and some fresh Salmon, to bring us on his return down. Milligan resumed his usual occupation. Little recovering very fast. Watatkum came in this forenoon with the meat of an Elk, & her fawn only a few days old for which we gave him a trifle. This animal completes the number that he agreed last Winter to bring us, when he was promised if he attended steadily to hunting and behaved himself well, beside being paid the usual price, he should receive as a present a suit of Clothes & hat which was given to him to day.[68]

27th. Thursday. Weather fine as yesterday. People all busily employed. Blacksmiths finishing off work in their Shop, to have all on hand completed by 1 June, when the Inventory will be closed. Cooper, Cannan, Labonté, Patterson & Antoine working at Cedar stuff, with which they begin to make considerable progress. In all our hurry for Canoes we have not one man

---

[67] Owing to the switch from whale boats to canoes, McDougall was probably planning for a greater number of the smaller craft; hence, he needed proportionally more gum for caulking their seams.

[68] By "number he agreed," McDougall is probably referring to the renegotiation of the initial agreement of June 7, 1811, which occurred on September 18, 1812.

among us who understands making them, are therefore guided, or rather, we copy after those made by Mr. McT's people. Two attending Coal Pit. Milligan & Flanagan employed Tayloring, making Shirts etc. in readiness for the arrival of parties from the Interior. Jeremie & the other hands working at Tobacco, making it in plugs, pressing it, etc. Little recovering very fast, & is now the only man sick.[69]

28th. Friday. Weather as Yesterday. All hands busied in the same manner. S. Islanders only working at Tobacco. Jeremie making Bags, etc. One man smoking Deer Skins. Visited by great numbers of Indians trading gum. Bargained with Comcomly for a quantity of Cedar Boards to be furnished in a few days. Purchased also the meat of an Elk. Sick list as yesterday.

29th. Saturday. Pleasant. Wind Westerly. Lent the boat to Mr. McT. to bring over Cedar Timber from the opposite side of the river. Three of our men were also sent along, in return for the services of some of his People on a former occasion. Our canoe makers employed bending Timbers most of the day. Visited by some few Indians trading gum. Watatkum also came in but had killed nothing. Still busied at the Inventory. Last evening Mr. McTavish had stolen from his Tent a number of valuable things: a fine Pistol, Silver Snuff Box, etc. Little only on the sick list.

30th. Sunday. Cloudy, rainy Weather. Wind Southerly. Visited by numbers of Indians trading Gum. Brought also a few Raspberries, for the first this season. Mr. McDougall examined the Papers entrusted to his care by Mr. James Lewis, & such as were Judged could be of no service to his friends were burned, as also the letters sent for him by the <u>Beaver</u>, after being opened merely to see if anything should be enclosed in them, and not perused. Two letters addressed to Captn Jonathan Thorn, and not opened were also burned at the same time, in presence of Messrs. Franchere & Clapp. The boat returned this morning loaded with Cedar Timber for Mr. McT., the wind blowing too fresh last night to attempt crossing.[70]

---

[69] See Rollins, ed., *Stuart's Narrative*, pp. 51–52, for Robert Stuart's disparaging comments about the quality of the canoes made by the Astorians. McDougall's complaint in this entry would seem both to explain and to confirm Stuart's judgment.

[70] Raspberries were probably one of the berries prized for their antiscorbutic value. In the light of the decision taken on June 3, 1813, the inventory and the burning of the documents belonging to James Lewis and Jonathan Thorn, kept long after *Tonquin's* destruction had become a certainty, take on the character of clearing the decks before a final action. It may have been at this time that McDougall decided to keep Lewis's notebook, a small (3¼″ by 4½″) leather-bound memorandum book. It contains notes various and sundry, e.g., business transactions, details of Lewis's ancestry, personal reflections, and, with no explanation, names. Only one aspect of it is intriguing—on one of the marbleized endpapers, the word "murder" can clearly be seen. It is now at the Rosenbach Museum and Library with the McDougall journals.

31st. Monday. Cloudy, with some rain. Wind, variable. People variously employed. Weather would not admit of working out at Cedar Timber. Two Carpenters employed at it in the shop. Cannan repairing Guns. Blacksmiths & Taylor at their trades. The few hands else making Bags & other small work. S. Islanders assisting Jeremie at the Tobacco. Little & Ouvré sick. Visited by numbers of Indians trading gum, & one with a small quantity of poor Cedar boards, which were also traded. Lent the boat again to Mr. McT. to bring over the remainder of their timber which was returned at evening. Cooper employed arranging the Bastions & putting the guns & Swivels all in order & furnishing each with Cartridges, Wads, & every thing necessary for action. At 6 O'clock gave every man a Musket & allowed time to put them in complete order. Completed the Inventory of all.

June 1st. Tuesday. Rainy throughout the day. Wind from Southward. People employed same as Yesterday. Cooper unwell. Visited by great numbers of Indians. Skamaquiah brought over the horse purchased from him & the one purchased from Calpo. Traded some Wapatoes & gum.

2nd. Wednesday. Weather as Yesterday. People disposed in the usual manner. Great numbers of Indians about us all day, detained on account of the Weather. Traded some gum & a few Wapatoes. Toward evening were surprized by the arrival of Messrs. Wallace & Halsey & party, from Mc-Kay's River, forming a number of 26 persons including hunters & families, in three Canoes, bringing with them all the Goods, etc. on hand, beside the proceeds of their trade & hunt, amounting to 17 Packs Beaver & 19 Bales dried meat. Mr. Wallace explored the river for a good distance almost to its source, but could learn nothing of importance more than that it abounds in Beaver, more or less in its whole course. The inhabitants throughout are a set of poverty-strick beings, totally ignorant of hunting Furs & scarce capable of procuring their own subsistence. Labonté & Little sick.[71]

3rd. Thursday. Fine pleasant Weather. All hands were allowed liquor last night after the arrival of the Party, no work therefore of consequence going forward to day. Blacksmiths, Taylor, Cooper & Carpenters only employed

---

[71] William Wallace and John Halsey, along with a number of men, had been up the Willamette, in the vicinity of present-day Salem. The report on the relative poverty of the natives there, probably the Kalapuya tribe, is misleading, as they got along well on natural, seasonal crops and resources; see Ruby, Brown, *Guide*, pp. 274–75. What neither Wallace nor Mc-Dougall (or any other Astorian, probably) considered was the effect their hunting might have had on the natives' sustenance. In January 1814, Alfred Seton recorded the hostile complaints and threats of several natives because of the exhaustion of game in the area; see Jones, ed., *Astorian Adventure*, pp. 144–45. Notice the complaint, made earlier about other tribes, as to their ignorance because they did not trap beaver, i.e., serve the Europeans' needs.

to account. Examined the Bales, Packs, etc., from McKay's river & exposed them to the sun. Several Indians about in the course of the day, but had no trade. Comcomly's oldest son informed us that a Vessel was seen a day or two since off the river, no credit, however, was given to the story. It is now too late to flatter ourselves longer with the hope seeing a Ship. Our views & expectations are bent in different direction. The arrival of one for us would serve to facilitate business, but would not in the present crisis alter arrangements. The arrival of Mr. McKenzie in January with the news of a War in the U. States & the unpromising prospect in the interior of the country, gave a decisive blow & left no alternative but to decide upon such measures as are now soon to be put in execution, & for the forwarding of which every exertion has been made & suitable precaution used at this place to save property. Viz., That we decamp with every thing valuable if possible by the 1st July & make the best of our way to St. Louis. The Gentlemen of the Interior by return of Mr. McK. were apprized of the state of things here, from which, with their knowledge of the Interior they will arrange accordingly. At 6 O'clock this evening all hands were assembled & made acquainted with our determination. The necessity of such steps was explained, and the line of conduct pointed out necessary to pursue as regarded the natives around us, the consequences to be apprehended from the natives, should a disclosure of it take place, and likewise what exertions we should now expect from every man of them.[72]

4th. Friday. Pleasant. Wind Westerly. All hands began work this morning with vigor, every one appears ambitious as they see the necessity of exertions being made. Mechanics employed as usual. Viz., Blacksmiths, Taylor & Cooper. Carpenters with most of the other hands at Canoes. Sanson & one S. Islander still at the Coal pit, of which being the last they make a long job. Some few Indians about but had no trade of consequence. Purchased two or three fresh Salmon. None are now disposed to be sick. Little turned to with the others to day, & attempted work but is yet too weak to do much.[73]

5th. Saturday. As Yesterday. Pleasant Weather. People employed in the

---

[72] Here, McDougall is informing everyone of the decisions made the previous January (see above, January 25, 1813 and n. 11), although by now the possibility of a general movement east by land was fading fast. One of the more remarkable aspects of this notice is that, in spite of the presence of the clerks at the January meeting, apparently the news of the decision made then did not become general knowledge around the post.

[73] The willingness of the men to work and the disappearance, except for John Little, of the sick list is a striking illustration of how dispirited the men had been about the future of the post. Even the decision to undertake the arduous overland trek east must have seemed preferable to staying at Astoria.

same manner. Skamaquiah brought over some Cedar Timber already bargained for. He started from the opposite side with upwards of one hundred pieces, but unluckily in crossing his canoes filled with water and good part was lost.

6th. Sunday. Pleasant. Wind fresh at Westward. Mr. McTavish's hunters killed 3 Elk Yesterday of which he sent us the meat of one this morning. Visited by Comcomly & his youngest son in the forenoon, who brought a few Cedar boards. He has a good number more at home, but it appears brought these few as an excuse only for coming over to see what shall be going forward with us, as by some means or other the natives are already apprized of our determination to leave the country, at least they strongly suspect it, if we may Judge from their enquiries. The old fellow made a singular proposal for recovering the property stolen from Mr. McTavish. Viz. That we should put him in Irons in presence of his People, who would return with the account to his village, and that he should be detained prisoner untill the property was restored. His eldest son only to be made acquainted that it was a voluntary project of his own. We could not but believe the old man sincere in his wish to serve us, but did not, however, think proper to join with his notion. At evening Calpo & family returned from the Rapids with a quantity of Salmon partly dried, traded for us. He purchased also one rifle, which in order to make of much consequence, knowing we were anxious to have it, he sent over to Chinook.[74]

7th. Monday. Cloudy. Wind strong & squally from S. W. raw & uncomfortable. All hands busily employed, most of the number at Canoes & boats & preparing boards etc. for them. Blacksmiths & Taylor as usual. Carson employed stocking guns. Two still at the Coal Pit. Jeremie at tobacco & other small work. S. Islanders variously employed at different jobs. We have indeed full employment for every person in some way or another. Traded with Calpo for a good number of Salmon, & the rifle which was brought across the river this morning. Were obliged to pay for this 5 Lion Skin Blankets & some trifles beside. He had much difficulty & paid a great price to procure it. It is however at this time a good bargain. Visited by several other Indians but traded nothing.[75]

---

[74] One hardly knows what to make of Comcomly's bizarre offer. Suspecting, as he apparently did, the imminent departure of the Astorians complicates the question more. One possible explanation is that the chief wished to ingratiate himself as much as he could with the Astorians, believing it would improve his position as middleman, no matter what result their departure would have. The items referred to were those stolen from McTavish's tent on May 29, 1813 described as "valuable things."

[75] What made the rifle a good bargain "at this time" may have been McDougall's expectation that before long the Astorians, heavily burdened with furs, trade goods, and provisions,

8th. Tuesday. Wind fresh at S. W. Weather unsettled and cool for the season. People employed as usual. Visited by numbers of Indians. Purchased from one Chinook upwards of 100 pieces Cedar for Boards, which with the quantity Comcomly is to furnish will be near or quite enough for the canoes we wish. Completed the Boat so long unfinished & put it in the water. Every thing was in readiness for building another immediately which we had hoped might be done. But Little, the builder, informed us this evening that he would not be able to finish another in time. He is only able to keep about and assist at light work, but cannot by any means do duty yet. Every assistance therefore must now be given towards forwarding Canoes.

9th. Wednesday. Cloudy with Rain good part of the day. Wind Southerly. All hands as usually employed. Visited by numbers of Indians trading Berries & Wapatoes. Watatkum came in bringing a young Elk alive, apparently about 10 days old. He had given it a blow on the shoulder joint in the chase, but it is otherwise well & very tame. A Chinook Indian also arrived from Baker's Bay with word that he had seen a Ship this morning very near in with the land, which was his only errand here. No dependence however is to be placed upon their stories about Ships; they have already too often excited our anxiety to no purpose. John Day went out hunting; returned in the afternoon having killed an Elk not far behind here near Young's Bay. Too late to send for the meat. Completed the first Cedar Canoe.[76]

10th. Thursday. Cloudy & fore part rainy. Weather still unsettled. Despatched a number of hands with John Day for the Elk killed yesterday, with which they returned early. The wolves had fallen in with it, but done no great damage. Greater part of the People employed at the second Canoe & preparing Timber for others. Nearly completed it to day. They begin now to understand the work better than in the beginning & make greater despatch. The present one is altered considerably in dimensions from the first & some improvement made in the workmanship. Sanson at length finished work at the Coal Pit & left the place this evening to be employed with others here. Visited by some idle Indians & traded a few Wapatoes. Patterson one of the Carpenters ill, with a kind of Dysentery.

11th. Friday. Cloudy, unpleasant Weather. People busily employed as

---

would be moving through the area where Calpo had obtained it. Rifles in the hands of possible hostile natives would not be welcome. Carson was Alexander Carson, listed on the 1813–14 roster as gunsmith; see Appendix. He was an experienced hunter and trapper, hired by Hunt on the upper Missouri, along with Ben Jones; see Ronda, *Astoria*, pp. 149, 279.

[76] "Better never than late" might be said about the Astorians' finally coming to distrust the natives' reports of ships off the mouth of the Columbia. McDougall's comment about finishing the "first Cedar Canoe" suggests that the ones made previously were of oak or another wood. The natives generally used cedar for their water craft.

usual. Completed the second Canoe. Shaving & bending Timbers for others, at which greater part are employed. Patterson at his work again.

12th. Saturday. Cloudy, with rain most of the day. Early this morning the parties from the interior made their appearance in a brigade of 6 Canoes & 2 Boats, consisting of Messrs. D. Stuart, McKenzie & Clarke, with most of their people & 4 Indians, forming a number of 53 souls inclusive, with 116 packs Beaver, Baggage, etc., etc., met with no accident of note in coming down. The boat of Mr. Clarke's was found entire; that of Mr. McKenzie's much damaged and barely served to arrive here. Mr. Clarke while encamped where he embarked in Canoes after leaving his place had several things stolen from his Tent in the night by an Indian, a stranger among the tribe where he was. On the day following several were sent in pursuit of him but to no purpose. In the evening he came again to his encampment, stole a canoe & was caught by the watch in the act of stealing a second time. The things stolen were recovered but as an example to others Mr. C. had him hanged. This afterwards turned to the disadvantage of the parties at the Wolawola river, their place of meeting, where the natives refused to sell them provisions on account of it. What effect it may in the end produce we pretend not to determine, but apprehend no good will arise from it. The arrival of so great a number here will make havoc with our little provision remaining, and reduce us all in a short time to a state of absolute dependance on the natives and on our own hunting. Our own people employed at their respective work.[77]

13th. Sunday. Rainy throughout the day. Visited by several Indians. Watatkum brought in the meat of an Elk & her young one alive. We have little hopes of raising this, being much younger than the one brought a few days since which died last night.

14th. Monday. Cloudy, without rain. Weather yet unsettled. Our people

---

[77] David Stuart had been at his post on the Fraser River at Kamloops, British Columbia, McKenzie on the Clearwater, and Clarke at Spokane House. Clarke's precipitate action in hanging the Indian did indeed have repercussions, at least one of which was much more serious than a refusal to sell food. During the winter of 1813–14, John Reed, Pierre Dorion and his family, and others wintered in southern Washington state, among the Shoshone Indians. In January, all of the party, except for Dorion's Indian wife and their children, were killed by natives. She remained hidden in the mountains with her children for some months, eventually finding a friendly band of Walla Walla Indians, who delivered her to a mixed party of former Astorians and North Westers going up the Columbia on their way east in the spring of 1814; Franchère attributes the attack to Clarke's hanging, as does Ross Cox. See Franchère, *Journal*, p. 153; Cox, *Columbia*, pp. 151–54. See also Josephy, *Nez Perce*, pp. 50–51, 52ff. Presently, McDougall will deal with the problem of feeding so many by sending several parties out, not only to trap, but also to feed themselves.

busied as usual, greater number at Canoes. Blacksmiths & Taylor at their respective trades. S. Islanders with Jeremie working at Tobbaco. Carson steadily employed stocking & putting in order Rifles etc. J. Lapierre laid up with the Venereal.

15th. Tuesday. Cloudy, Wind fresh from S. & Westward. In the forenoon despatched our Two Boats & the one of Mr. Clarke; with Messrs. Matthews, Ross, Farnham & Halsey & most of the men that arrived from the interior, on trading excursions up the river. Messrs. Ross & Halsey with one boat to the falls of McKay's river. Messrs. Matthews & Farnham with the other two as far as the rapids, all to be absent about a fortnight. The other hands remaining of the parties set to work with ours, greater part at Canoes. Three making a small press for Furs.[78]

Visited by Comcomly, his young son & suite, bringing with them Joseachal the Queenhilt Indian who was on board the ship Tonquin when destroyed, and whom we have so much wished to see for the purpose of learning from himself the particulars respecting the transactions that took place on board before and at the time she was destroyed. He appeared quite an intelligent Indian, and by means of Comcomly's son as an interpreter & his own knowledge of Chinook with a smattering of English made us acquainted with many little circumstances respecting the proceedings on board. But throughout was only in matter a confirmation of what we had learned long before.[79]

Mr. McKay was first seized, thrown overboard and instantly despatched by the Indians in Canoes. Captain Thorn with only a Clasp Knife defended himself for some time, killed 4 Indians (among whom was the son of the principal Chief, & instigator of the proceedings) and was in a fair way to drive others before him off the decks, when he was cut down by a blow with a war knife, or club, from behind. The manner in which the Ship was blown up he explained fully. They were at the commencement of the difficulty getting under weigh and many of the Sailors aloft. These during the first attack found means to get between decks & with muskets killed many Indi-

---

[78] With these parties, although McDougall is not specific as to numbers, the pressure on the food supply at Astoria is certainly lessened considerably. Ross and Halsey went up the Willamette, Mathews and Farnham continued up the Columbia to either the rapids at the foot of the Cascade Mountains or to the Dalles. Part of their trading will be for provisions as well as beaver pelts.

[79] This paragraph gives an unusual and interesting look at the difficulties of communication in the Pacific Northwest at the time. Notice that McDougall's interview apparently involved using Chinook, i.e., the trade jargon of the area, the native Chinook language, and "a smattering of English."

ans; among these were the Boatswain, two or three other whites & some S. Islanders.

The decks were soon cleared of the crew & filled with Indians. The men below strewed Powder along between decks, then watched an opportunity when that part was crowded & blew it up, which killed best part of a hundred. This explosion set fire to the Ship but did not destroy her. The quarter deck & after part remained entire, & consequently the magazine. While the few Indians on board were endeavoring to extinguish the fire about the Ship three of the crew took to the boat from the Cabin window, & three swam ashore.

Those in the boat he says passed three nations to the Northward along the sea shore, but were at length Killed, we suppose at the Straits of De Fuca; the three that swam ashore were immediately killed.

The Indians continued flocking on board after the Ship was on fire, apprehending no danger, when the crew were all killed or had left her but she at length blew up with a great on board & around near in Canoes, most or all of whom perished. He informs us also that he warned both Mr. McKay & Capt. Thorn that the Indians had a design upon them, but they would not listen to it, allowed as many to come on board as wished, expressed a contempt for the power of the Indians to hurt them, and were even entirely unarmed in the midst of them after he had apprized them of the danger. He may very well be credited in this particular, as he was considered by the natives there an enemy, and but for the circumstance of having a Sister married among them would also have been killed.

The cause that gave rise to this unhappy event is already detailed in our Journal of 1811. To see this man afforded a satisfaction, as there is no question but that he actually witnessed it. Gave him a suitable present as was promised and to the Queenhilt Chief who accompanied him. Rewarded Comcomly also for his trouble.[80]

16th. Wednesday. Weather continues cloudy and unpleasant. People all busily employed as for several days past. Finished the third Canoe & began another. Finished also the small press for furs. One man boiling gum & preparing it for the Canoes. Received two Elk from Mr. McTavish, his hunters having killed 6 Yesterday.

Comcomly left Joseachal & his young son to remain for a few days with

---

[80] This transcription is supplemented by a more systematic presentation of the first portion of Joseachal's story (up to the death of Captain Thorn and Mr. McKay) in the entry for June 18. He was questioned on several occasions by different people at the post between the transcribing of this version and the "revised edition" given below.

us, while he is gone up the river to procure fresh Salmon for us. One man sick.

17th. Thursday. Fore part of the day pleasant. Afternoon cloudy with appearances of rain. People mostly employed as usual. Set 6 hands at work cutting wood for another Coal pit.

18th. Friday. Pleasant. Wind Westerly. All hands variously employed, making Canoes, cutting wood for Coals, preparing gum, etc., etc. Mechanics as usual. Visited by great numbers of Indians. Purchased near 40 fresh Salmon & some Wapatoes. Comcomly arrived at evening but had no Salmon for us. J. Lapierre & Cooper sick. Joseachal took leave of us to day for Queenhilt after being handsomely rewarded for his trouble. As we may probably not have an opportunity of seeing him again it is thought proper here to make further mention of his story in a manner more connected than before, for which purpose he was separately examined at different times by several of us.

The first account we received of the loss of the Tonquin was about the latter end of June 1811, but it was not then thought credible, or noticed in the Journal untill some time in August, after being repeatedly told to us. Hopes were not even then given over for her return untill late in the fall. Time, however settled all doubts, & the fact is now but too well established.

This Indian went on board of her to Northward of Gray's harbor, at or near Destruction Isle, from a fishing canoe, on the promise of Captain Thorn or McKay, or both, that he should be well rewarded for his services, & returned at that place or in this river on the arrival of the Ship in the fall.[81] He had performed already two voyages on the Coast with Captn Ebbets & Captn Brown, & on account of his knowledge of the languages, trade, etc., could render himself serviceable.[82]

The Ship proceeded to Wicanninishes, where they came to anchor toward evening for the purpose of trading Sea Otters. Numbers of the natives were immediately around & on board, but being late Captn Thorn did not commence a trade. Mr. McKay proposed for himself & this Indian to go ashore, which he objected to as not being safe. At length, however, Mr. McKay prevailed upon him to go in an Indian Canoe, while 6 of the natives remained

---

[81] Gray's Harbor is on the Pacific coast of Washington state, about forty miles above the mouth of the Columbia River; Destruction Island is about forty miles above that, at approximately 47°, 40' North, 124°, 30' West, three miles off the coast.

[82] John Ebbets was frequently employed by Astor; see Porter, *Astor*, passim; in 1811, writing from Macao of his voyage to the Pacific Northwest, he mentions a "Capt Brown," but gives no details; John Ebbets to John Jacob Astor, January 11, 1811, ibid., I, 448.

on board as hostages untill their return. Mr. McK. arrived soon on board without any difficulty happening to him, the natives were set at liberty, and we do not learn that any trouble or disquiet was the consequence of it. It is probable his only view in going ashore was to advertise the Indians that they had come to trade with them.[83]

The day following commenced the trade. The natives about the Ship & on board of her were very numerous, had plenty of Skins, but would not trade them at the rate Capt. Thorn wished. He offered them 2 Blankets of Cloth, or Lion Skin, a quantity of Beads, hooks, and Vermillion for each skin, and they would think of taking nothing less than 5 Blankets.

The Chiefs of the Villages ashore were Wicanninish and his two sons (the younger of whose name was Shee-wish), Nook-a-mis & Sid-da-kum, two elderly men. The principal trader or oracle for the day among them was Nookamis. Great quantities of Cloth, Blankets, etc., were brought on deck, the cloth unfolded & laying loose during the long debates about trading. Captn. Thorn alone took upon himself this task. Mr. McK. during the arguments with the natives was sitting on the Taf'rel of the Ship. Captn. T. in his walks about deck had some words with him, probably about the trade. This Indian enquired of Mr. McK. the subject of their dispute, but was told it was about the Sails of the Ship or some such like answer.

They were in this manner engaged in debates about trade untill past mid-day when Capt. Thorn got in a passion with Nookamis (who was continually following him about decks & pestering him to trade) kicked way his Skins, struck him with one across the face, damned his eyes & began preparing to get under weigh. It was after this had happened that the discourse mentioned took place between him & Mr. McKay. The Ship was at this time full of Indians, the decks lined with them on each side. This Indian observed their proceedings after the affront given to the Chief, and apprized both Capt. Thorn & Mr. McKay that they were meditating an attempt to destroy them.

---

[83] "Wicanninishes" is Clayoquot Sound (today, Kyoquot), on the upper west coast of Vancouver Island, about forty miles south of Nootka Sound. Wikiananish, and his father of the same name, ruled the tribes in the area and influenced those throughout the west coast of the island. Both had a history of taking whatever umbrage there was to be taken when dealing with European traders. See Frederic W. Howay, "The Voyage of the *Hope*, 1790–1792," *Washington Historical Quarterly*, 11, No. 1 (January 1920), 3, 23–24, 25–26 for skirmishes between the elder chief and Captain Joseph Ingraham. Later, Captain Robert Gray, the discoverer of the Columbia River, had similar experiences; see John Boit, "A New Log of the Columbia," edited by Worthington C. Ford and Edmond S. Meany, ibid., 12, No. 1 (January 1921), 8, 20–28, 43. *The Dictionary of Canadian Biography*, IV, 767–68, has an article on the elder Wikinanish; the spelling is theirs.

Capt. T. would not listen to it at all, nor would believe them capable of hurting him. In addressing Mr. McK. before this Indian, pointed to the guns & number of arms below seemed to defy them. He continued on deck wholly unarmed, giving orders for getting under weigh, without taking the precaution of making the natives leave the Ship during the confusion of preparing for sea. Mr. McKay was also entirely unarmed. Respecting this, as also of the Captain's being unarmed he was questioned closely.

After the affront offered to Nookamis, time enough was allowed them to consult upon measures to take revenge. The young son of Wicanninish, Shee-wish made himself busy in this, had been ashore & returned with a number of his people. This was not noticed by Capt. Thorn on account of the confusion on board. They were getting up the anchor & loosing the Topsails when the Indians offered a second time to trade. They offered their Skins for 3 Blankets & a knife each which was given. A brisk trade was carried on untill all the Indians sitting round on the decks of the Ship were supplied with a knife a piece.

This was narrowly observed by Joseachal, but probably by no one else on board, as it appears they were not sensible of the danger. He mentions in a particular manner this circumstance, how they concealed the knives in their Blankets, which was thrown off their shoulders laying before them.

The proceedings after this were as related on Tuesday last, with very little difference. The chief mentioned as killed by Captn. Thorn was <u>Shee-wish</u>, not killed but badly wounded in the thigh, fell down the hatch way, and was there either despatched by some of the crew or was blown up with others. Both Mr. McKay and Capt. Thorn after being killed had the head severed from the body, that stripped of every thing & thrown into the sea. When Capt. Thorn received the blow that despatched him, he was seized by an uncommonly strong Indian, brother to Wicanninish.

The whole number of Indians destroyed on the occasion amounts to near two hundred, by the account of Joseachal. He was in the mizen chains trembling for his life during the proceeding of the natives, untill the first explosion when he Jumped in the water & swam ashore.[84]

---

[84] Since Joseachal was the only known survivor of the *Tonquin*'s last voyage, these two transcriptions constitute the most complete and reliable description of the climax of that voyage. All other versions are derived either from what is recorded here or from other conversations that the native interpreter may have had with Europeans. None of the other versions, however, was taken down with the concern for accuracy and completeness evident here. See F. W. Howay, "The Loss of the 'Tonquin'," *Washington Historical Quarterly*, 13, No. 2 (April 1932), 83–92, for a discussion of the provenance and quality of the *Tonquin* narratives then available. To Howay's list should be added Alfred Seton's rendering of the tragedy, derived

June 19th. Saturday. Pleasant as Yesterday. All hands occupied nearly in the same manner also. Finished another Canoe. Watatkum brought in the meat of an Elk. Many Indians constantly about us. Purchased a few Salmon & Wapatoes.

20th. Sunday. Pleasant. Wind fresh at Westward. Visited by great numbers of Indians. Ashuallax & Wabaloma from the Chelwits brought near a hundred fresh Salmon, which are now being taken by the natives in abundance.

21st. Monday. Pleasant. People variously employed much in the usual manner, making Canoes, cutting wood for Coals, etc. Mechanics at their respective trades. Carson employed still at Mr. Clark's gun. John Day & Gervais with 4 men went hunting yesterday in a canoe above Tongue Point. Many Indians about, but traded nothing.

22nd. Tuesday. Pleasant. Wind Westerly. Men employed as usual. An old Chinook Indian brought over a new Canoe of ours that had been missing for near a month, and was as we suppose stolen by some of his nation. Very probably himself had a hand in it. We entertain little better opinion of the best of them. 2 men sick. Toward evening the hunters returned by land without success, the men with the Canoe arrived at near the same time. The Indians are now about the woods hunting with their dogs. No hunter need therefore hope for success near where they may be.[85]

23rd. Wednesday. First part of the day Cloudy, afternoon clear & pleasant. People busied as usual. Cutting wood for Coals, working at Canoes, furs, etc. In the forenoon Messrs. Matthews & Farnham with their party in 2 Boats returned from the rapids, bringing about 400 dried Salmon, 8 Deer Skins, some Wapatoes and the meat of an Elk killed by Mr. Farnham yesterday. Met with little success in trading as most of the Indians living at the rapids had left their villages in pursuit of roots, the waters of the river being yet too high to take Salmon in great abundance. Sent the hunters out a second time equipd as before. In the afternoon began giving out the Equipments due to all hands. Purchased from our Chinook hunter two young Elk.[86]

---

during the stopover of the *Beaver* in Hawaii, April 1812, and from the interviews at Astoria given above. What role, if any, Seton played in questioning Joseachal is not known. See Jones, ed., *Astorian Adventure*, pp. 72, 91–93.

[85] Throughout the journal, this is the only reference to natives hunting with dogs.

[86] The "Equipments due to all hands" possibly refers to a bonus of a musket, etc., given to all the men prior to winding up the affairs of the company at Astoria. Since no one will leave until late August (six aboard the *Albatross*, including the hapless Tuana); see below, August 26, 1813), this distribution, if that is what it is, seems premature.

24th. Thursday. Pleasant. Wind fresh at Westward. People as usually employed. Preparing to pack the furs. Visited by many Indians. Comcomly brought over a horse & a quantity of Cedar boards, which were purchased.

June 25th. Friday. Cloudy, with appearances of rain. Wind fresh from Southward. All hands as usually disposed. Five men with Mr. Reed packing furs. S. Islanders beating skins. Received the meat of an Elk from Mr. McTavish. Purchased also during the day from several Indians the meat of 4 more. We are now enabled to purchase nearly a sufficiency of fresh Salmon for all hands, but it will keep for so short a time only during the warm weather that the supply is very irregular & uncertain.

26th. Saturday. Clear & pleasant. In the afternoon Messrs. Ross & Halsey with their party arrived in the boat from their excursion up McKay's river. Brought but few Salmon on account that they are not yet properly cured & will keep but little time; could have procured almost any quantity but did not on that account. Traded 17 Clemels and about 50 Deer Skins. Obtained from Kaessnoe at the Cathalakamaps the other rifle so long ago spoken of, for which they were under the necessity of paying the same extravigant price as to Calpo for the one he purchased, Viz. 5 Blankets. The hunters arrived also this evening, again unsuccessful.[87]

27th. Sunday. Pleasant & very warm. Good numbers of Indians about, but no trade. One man sick.

28th. Monday. Pleasant as Yesterday. All hands disposed in the same manner as last week, making Canoes, Packing and Pressing furs, etc. Delivered Mr. Stuart's outfit for this year. Visited by several Canoes of Indians, of whom we purchased a few Salmon.

29th. Tuesday. Cloudy with some rain. People busied as usual. Completed the sixth & last Cedar Canoe for the present. Packing & Pressing furs. Delivered Mr. Clarkes Outfit. Visited by some few Indians, but traded nothing. Two men sick.

30th. Wednesday. Rain throughout, a few hands pressing furs. Little work else beside that of the Mechanics going forward. Preparing Outfit, Canoes, etc., for despatching a hunting party up McKay's river tomorrow. Visited by Comcomly in the forenoon, who traded two Sea Otters. Three men sick. Sent Two white men & 3 S. Islanders in a Canoe hunting.

July 1st. Thursday. Weather as Yesterday. Rainy. Wind N. E. Mechanics busily employed as usual, little else doing. Finished packing the furs. Messrs. Seton & Wallace with a party consisting of 3 hunters, 9 men & one boy

---

[87] See above, June 6, 7, 1813, for Calpo's purchase of the first rifle.

(Perreault) set out this morning in one Canoe for McKay's River to spend the season of hunting & await the arrival of Mr. McKenzie in a few weeks.[88] The determination formed some short time since of abandoning this place on the 1st Instant has since the arrival of parties been changed; from the knowledge those Gentlemen communicated of the interior of the Country, and the trade of Horses, which is our greatest object of solicitude, with some other circumstances, it was judged at this advanced season wholly impracticable to make the attempt this year. The arrangements and preparations however, made here for that purpose were not ill timed. It has been finally agreed upon to abandon the country altogether; the arrangements for the year are therefore calculated accordingly. Parties are all to take their departure from the forks of the Columbia on the lst June next.

Mr. McTavish has now given over further hopes of seeing a Vessel for him, and is to leave us in a few days. An agreement has been formed with him on the part of the N. West Co. to avoid a Competition in the upper Country during the present season; the post of Spokan House is given over to them, and they are to abandon wholly the trade of the Columbia and flat-head Country. He receives from us a small quantity of Goods amounting to upwards of Eight hundred Dollars, for which he is to render payment next spring at the forks of the Columbia in any manner that shall best suit our purpose. He has also consented to forward by their winter express a few despatches from us to Mr. Astor at New York.[89]

Mr. Stuart winters at his old place, Mr. Clarke in the flat-head country. Mr. Reed with a small party is sent among the Snake nation; All with such assortments as our small stock would furnish, for the purpose of trading

---

[88] As before, this expedient is being taken in order both to lessen the pressure on provisions at Astoria and gather more beaver as well as dried meat against the winter. The Willamette has proven to be one of the most productive hunting areas available to the Astorians.

[89] This is a substantial, but inevitable alteration of the earlier plan to start east on July 1st, 1813. Recall that Donald McKenzie, who was to carry news of the January decision to pack up and travel east overland, to David Stuart and Clarke in the interior, lingered at Astoria until late March. By that time, it was too late for effective preparations for a spring departure. Even July, in view of the time needed to get over the Rockies, was very late. Now, not only is the Astorians' departure postponed for almost a year, but McDougall and McTavish have arrived at what might be called a market-sharing agreement, with the Pacific Fur Company post at Spokane being surrendered to the North Westers, while the latter abandoned the Columbia and the Nez Perce country in western Oregon and Washington, eastern Idaho. Further, McDougall sold McTavish up to $800 in trade goods to permit them to continue working in the area left to them. Events, however, soon brought about even more of a change. All these arrangements and agreements were spelled out in several documents and entered in the Pacific Fur Company's letter book; see T. C. Elliott, "Sale of Astoria, 1813," *Oregon Historical Quarterly*, 33, No. 1 (March 1932), 44–46.

prime Beaver & procuring Provisions & horses for the voyage across the country in the spring.[90]

Mr. McKenzie winters in McKay's river whither a party is already sent before him as mentioned. He has concluded to remain at this place until the return of that Canoe in the latter part of August, when with an additional number of men he will go up for the winter. While at this place we have only to employ a few mechanics to the best advantage, guard against the treachery of the numerous tribes around us, and live in the best manner we may be enabled to do.[91]

Under present circumstances it has been agreed that two or three Clerks in our employ should be at liberty to engage themselves to the N. West Co., there being a greater number with us than necessary in any case with only the few men we now have. A discharge from the employ of this company was given to Mr. Ross Cox, after which he formed an engagement with Mr. McTavish and goes with him from hence. As we should require more Goods above in the spring than circumstances might admit at that time of our carrying, a quantity will now go up with Mesrs. Stuart & Clarke to form a Depot at the place of one of those Gentlemen, sufficient to complete the loading of all the Canoes.[92]

2nd. Friday. Same rainy Weather as Yesterday. Blacksmiths, Carpenter & Taylor busily employed at their respective trades, preparing to despatch parties for the interior. Laid out the Goods for Depot above. Several hands employed putting them up. Visited by a few Indians of whom we traded some fresh Salmon.

3rd. Saturday. Weather same as Yesterday. Rainy throughout almost incessantly. People variously employed in making preparations for the different Outfits. Visited by numbers of Indians. Traded with Comcomlys eldest son and another 2 small good, & 2 indifferent Sea Otters.

---

[90] David Stuart's "old place" is Kamloops on the Fraser River in British Columbia; Alexander Ross went to the post near the confluence of the Okanogan and Columbia Rivers; John Clarke went among the Nez Perce, and John Reed was sent along the Snake River. Both Clarke and Reed were primarily to trade for horses for the trip east. Any horses acquired would be left with the natives until needed in the spring.

[91] With all these parties being sent to their various posts, when McKenzie leaves, the roster at Astoria will probably number fewer than twenty-five men, lessening the provision problem substantially. "McKay's River" was the name the Astorians often gave to the Willamette ("Wolamat") River; it was also called the Multnomah sometimes. Today, that name is restricted to a channel between the south bank of the Columbia and Sauvie Island, just below the present site of Portland.

[92] Cox is the first of several Astorians who will go over to the North Westers. In a statement dated June 25, 1813, he, Donald McLennan, and Donald McGillis were given permission "to engage elsewhere." See Elliott, "Sale of Astoria," 45.

4th. Sunday. Weather Clear & pleasant. Being the Anniversary of Independence it was observed only as we had not the means of making it a day of festivity. Our Flag was displayed at Sunrise and 3 guns fired. The same repeated at 12 o'clock & Sun set, the only show or parade made on the occasion. Gervais & Michel who were sent hunting on Wednesday arrived in the afternoon, having been two days from their encampment lost in the woods.

5th. Monday. Clear & tolerably pleasant. Wind fresh from Westward. About 11 O'clock, Mr. McTavish & party took their departure in 3 canoes for the N. W. Co. establishments in the upper parts of the Country, having been at this place for near three months, Viz., since 11th April. Mechanics busied as usual. Little else going forward beside preparations of parties for the interior. Numbers of Indians about, traded a few Clemels. Lamasey came over bringing a number of Beaver Skins for the purpose of making up the difference between himself & us, on account that he made an improper use of some articles furnished him last summer to build a canoe with. We had sent him word to bring a number of Skins, and all should be well again. 2 men sick.[93]

6th. Tuesday. Pleasant. Mechanics, etc., at their usual employments, hurrying work to despatch the parties. Visited by some few Indians, through curiosity only. Preparing to despatch a boat for McKay's river tomorrow for the Purpose of trading provisions. Sent Cannan & Gervais with 3 S. Islanders in a canoe hunting.

7th. Wednesday. Pleasant. Wind N. E. The warmest day with us this season. Every thing was bustle & confusion this morning with the parties to be off. Despatched Messrs. Halsey & Thos McKay, with 8 men for McKay's river in a Boat early. At 12 o'clock all was in readiness to load the Canoes, and the Goods taken out of the Store, but the tide not answering it was deferred untill another day, except with Mr. Reed, who took his departure about 1 P.M. with one Canoe only.[94]

8th. Thursday. Pleasant & very warm, wind tolerably fresh all day from Eastward. Early this morning the parties all took leave in 7 Canoes. Hoisted our flag & fired them 3 guns on the occasion. All hands remaining set at

---

[93] The arrangments just made between McDougall and McTavish should have settled the relationship between the two companies through the winter. However, fast-moving developments brought McTavish back to Astoria on October 7, 1813. "Lamasey" was the mixed-race Chehalis Indian Jack Ramsay, previously identified; see I, n. 130.

[94] The boat took the party headed for the Willamette; the canoes would have taken the other parties headed for the interior had they been able to get away.

work putting the place in order. Towards evening Mr. Matthews returned in a small Canoe of Mr. Stuart's, leaving parties encamped a short distance below the Cathlamat Village. The canoe in which he came down was one of those brought from the interior & too small for the present occasion. Came therefore for another in place of it. Cannan & Gervais with their party returned from hunting with the meat of a female Elk & her fawn. After dark another canoe from the parties above arrived for gum; the Canoes were all leaky & the small quantity of gum taken with them for use was insufficient to repair them. Ashuallax from the Chelwit Village arrived bringing upwards of 30 Salmon for trade. Set a watch to night for the first this season.[95]

9th. Friday. At dawn the two Canoes for the parties above set off with the gum necessary. Sent also a part of the Elk received Yesterday & some fresh Salmon. Our few hands here variously disposed. Four sent to put up a Coal pit above here. The place below made use of last season is now destitute of Timber. This wood was cut some days ago while all hands were here about one mile above this. Patterson employed fastening & securing doors, windows, etc. of the new house. All hands living there have removed for the summer within the picketing. Blacksmiths & Taylor at their trades. Cannan repairing guns. Gervais & Martial with 2 S. Islanders sent hunting. Visited by Wobaloman from the Chelwits Village bringing about 50 fresh Salmon. Purchased also a few from some Chinooks. J. Lapierre & Tuanna laid up with the Venereal, both making use of Mercury. One other S. Islander also slightly affected with the same disease, making 3 men sick.[96]

10th. Saturday. Pleasant. Hands disposed as usual. Visited by numbers of Indians but had no trade of consequence. Purchased 3 or 4 Salmon only.

11th. Sunday. Pleasant & warm. Visited by several Canoes of Chinooks. From one purchased the meat of an Elk. Traded with Comcomly a few fresh Salmon.

12th. Monday. Cloudy, moderate Weather. Wind light at Westward. All hands variously disposed. Mechanics at their trades. Others at Coal pit. The

---

[95] The canoe that proved too small was probably made by natives while the leaky ones were Astoria-made. The latter may have needed gum because of changes in them brought on by their first steady immersion. McDougall has again become fearful of the natives, presumably because of the smaller numbers at the post now that the interior parties have left.

[96] Note the necessity of the Astorians going as far as one mile for wood for charcoal. Also, from McDougall's comment about removing everyone inside the picketing, one assumes that the new house was built outside the palisade of the post. See the diagram of the post following p. 142; for the description of its buildings given by Robert Stuart, see Rollins, ed., *Stuart's Narrative*, p. 4.

two Carpenters sent in search of Timber for Gun Stocks. Hunters arrived in the afternoon without success.

13th. Tuesday. Pleasant Weather. Light breeze at Westward. People occupied as Yesterday. Cannan employed at Guns. Visited by some of the natives who traded a few fresh Salmon. One man cutting Grass for covering Coal Pit.

14th. Wednesday. Cloudy with rain good part of the day. Men employed as usual. Visited by one Indian only during the day, from whom we traded a few Salmon. The Salmon purchased for the week past, except what was immediately eaten, we have attempted drying after the manner of the Indians, and with which we are likely to succeed. In the afternoon had unusual heavy Thunder. Patterson, Lapierre & 2 S. Islanders sick.[97]

15th. Thursday. Cloudy, with partial showers during the day. People as usually employed. Building a new Shed for the purpose of drying Salmon under it. Numbers of Indians about. Traded a few Salmon. Sick list the same.

16th. Friday. Weather as yesterday. Rain good part of the day. In the forenoon Messrs. Halsey & T. McKay with the party arrived in the boat from their excursion up McKay's river after an absence of 10 days. Had tolerable good success in procuring Provisions, tho' it is yet too early in the season. Brought down 240 dried Salmon, a few Elk Skins dressed, some fresh Salmon, etc. Did not see any of the parties on their way up the river except Mr. Reed, with whom they were some time in company.

17th. Saturday. Weather the same, rainy most of the day. Wind from Southward. All hands variously disposed as usual. Finished a new Shed & removed all the Salmon into it. The wet weather is much to our disadvantage & hinders any progress being made in drying Salmon. Great numbers of Indians about, among others Calpo & his wife. Purchased a few fresh Salmon & the meat of a small Deer. 4 men sick.

18th. Sunday. Much as Yesterday. Wind fresh from Southward & Showery. Toward evening appearances of better weather. Visited by Comcomly & suite in the afternoon, who returned after a short stay. Traded nothing. Presented him with 2 Small hogs, which had been some time ago promised him.

19th. Monday. Pleasant. Wind Westerly. People variously employed. Greater number beside Mechanics at Coal Pit, cutting wood, etc. Began examining the remainder of furs & preparing them for packing. Two making a Tent, etc. Cannan employed repairing Guns. Visited by a few Chinook

---

[97] This is apparently the first effort by the Astorians to employ one of the common ways the natives preserved; the results will be mixed.

Indians, of whom we purchased 3 or 4 Salmon. 4 men sick, Viz. Lapierre & 3 S. Islanders.

July 20th. Tuesday. Pleasant & warm. People as usually employed. S. Islanders cleaning Salmon & preparing it to dry. Visited by Wobaloma from the Chelwits of whom we purchased upwards of 70 Salmon. Jeremie with one or two S. Islanders preparing tobacco for manufacturing. For some time past have been in treaty with Comcomly for a female branch of his family to remain at this place; a proposal flattering to the old man, and, as we conceive will be the means of securing to us his friendship more effectually than any other measure that could be adopted, and for which purpose only it was proposed. In the afternoon received a visit from him for the purpose of finally settling the agreement spoken of. The female was brought, and the presents agreed on delivered; after which his people took leave without out further ceremony.[98]

21st. Wednesday. Weather unsettled. Frequent showers of rain during the day. Wind Southerly. No Indians about us. Several hands employed as usual at the Coal Pit, being the only work of consequence going forward beside that of the Mechanics. 5 men sick.

22nd. Thursday. As Yesterday, unsettled Weather. People disposed in the same manner also. Great numbers of Indians about. Traded several fresh Salmon. 6 men sick.

23rd. Friday. Pleasant. Wind Westerly. Visited by Ashuallax from the Chelwits, with near a hundred fresh Salmon for trade. Some few Chinooks also about. 5 men sick.

---

[98] McDougall's acquisition of a Chinook bride is presented by him as done solely for the benefit of the company, and so it may have been, although one could question the necessity of the step. To judge from the log entry, Irving's comment that the Scot regarded the marriage "as a high state alliance and great stroke of policy" is somewhat exaggerated. *Astoria* (Rust ed.), p. 328. Alexander Henry, who also had an Indian wife, recorded the purchase price for this lady, who was either "Ilchee" (i.e., Moon Girl) or simply, "The Princess." She took rather seriously her position as the wife of the chief and not only insisted on her prerogatives, but also tried to direct the post's operations from time to time. McDougall downplays the event, but it is possible that a rather elaborate ceremony was followed on the occasion. There is no further mention of the lady in the log. When McDougall left the Columbia in 1817, he did not take Moon Girl along. Some time later she married a Chinook, Cazenove, who succeeded Comcomly as chief when he died in 1830. The union itself was not unique. Any number of Europeans took native women as their wives or companions, in some few cases bringing them back east to Fort William, Winnipeg, or even Montreal. See Irving, *Astoria* (Rust), Chap. LVI; Coues, ed., *New Light*, pp. 890–94, 901; Santee, "Comcomly and the Chinooks," 276; Ruby, Brown, *Chinooks*, pp. 143–45; Brown, "Old Fort Okanogan and the Okanogan Trail," 17; Jesse Douglas, ed., "Matthews' Adventures on the Columbia," *Oregon Historical Quarterly* 40, No. 2 (June 1939), 106; "Alexander Ross," *Dictionary of Canadian Biography*, VIII, 765–68.

24th. Saturday. Pleasant & very warm. People busied as during the week past. Mr. McKenzie with four S. Islanders in a canoe went round to Fort Clatsop, Captns Lewis & Clarke's wintering place, having never been there. Visited by several Canoes of Indians from the Chinook Village. Purchased the meat of a very fat Deer and some fresh Salmon. Skamaquiah also visited us in the afternoon. 4 sick.

25th. Sunday. As Yesterday. Pleasant & very warm. Messrs. McDougall & McKenzie went over to the Chinook Village in a Boat, the latter never having having been there. Returned early in the afternoon. Several Clatsop Indians here, traded 2 Sea Otters. Watatkum brought in the meat of a small female Elk.

July 26th. Monday. Weather the same. People variously occupied, greater part at Coal Pits. Mechanics at their several trades. Preparing Boat etc. for Mr. McKenzie's departure tomorrow. Visited by numbers of Indians. Purchased a few Salmon. 2 men Sick. Lapierre & Tuanna.

27th. Tuesday. Pleasant. Wind Westerly. People as usually employed. Began beating the remainder of furs not yet packed. At 10 o'clock Mr. McKenzie with his party set out on a trading and hunting excursion up the river, consisting of Mr. Halsey, 2 hunters, 2 Canadians & 4 S. Islanders, leaving our number here reduced to 29 persons. Sick list the same.[99]

28th. Wednesday. Pleasant. Wind S.W. Towards evening cloudy with appearances of bad weather. People variously employed as usual. Two Carpenters getting out timber for Oars. Purchased a number of fresh Salmon & 2 Sturgeon.

29th. Thursday. Cloudy with some rain. Wind S. W. Visited early by a number of Cathlamat Indians, who brought near a hundred Salmon. Traded a part of them only which were good. We considered there was no kind of obligation on our part to take more, as it is only when they have more of provision kind than they can possibly consume, that we are benefitted by any of this nation. Visited by several canoes of Chinook Indians also. Traded from them a few Salmon. Comcomly brought over forty Salmon as a present, on account of the late arrangement with him. People as usually employed. Several S. Islanders occupied most part of the time curing fish & taking care

[99] McKenzie's destination does not seem to have been the Willamette. He returned on August 6, having killed nothing. About the same time, Alfred Seton was on the Willamette with William Wallace; in a month, they secured thirty-three bales of dried deer and elk meat; see Jones, ed., *Astorian Adventure*, p. 116, and below, entry for August 6. McKenzie had probably gone up the Columbia.

of it. 3 men sick, Viz., Little, Lapierre & Tuanna, the former of whom is now apparently little better fit for work than he was two months ago.[100]

30th. Friday. Pleasant. Wind S. W. and cool for the season. People employed same as usual. Visited by a small Canoe with Indians from the Clatsops, with whom traded 2 Elk skins.

31st. Saturday. Morning cloudy, with showers of rain. Remainder of the day pleasant. Visited in the afternoon by some Clatsop Indians, who traded the meat of an Elk. 3 sick.

August 1st. Sunday. Some rain in the morning, remaining part pleasant. Visited by some of Comcomly's people, bringing twenty Salmon as a present. Watatkum brought in the meat of an Elk. Sick list the same.

August 2nd. Monday. Pleasant & warm. Wind Westerly. People employed as usual. Two beating furs, three preparing & curing Salmon, others at Coal pit. Mechanics as usual at their trades. Two Carpenters getting out Oars. Little began work regularly for the first since his illness, employed in doing some repairs to the old Boat used by Mr. McKenzie last season, which has been bargained to Comcomly for 2 Horses. Visited in the afternoon by Comcomly & a number of his people. Traded some Beaver. We trade now prime Beaver only at the rate of 9 for a white Blanket. 2 men sick.[101]

3rd. Tuesday. Most of the day Pleasant. At evening thick, cloudy weather threatening heavy rain. Two men only at the Coal pit, attending it. S. Islanders curing Salmon. Other hands beating furs. Visited by numbers of Indians in the course of the day from the Chelwit, Chinook & Clatsop Villages. Purchased three Salmon only, as it appears very few are caught now. Traded a few Elk Skins and one small Sea Otter. One of our Horses that has for some time past been occasionally brought up to ride, etc., for the purpose of breaking him properly, came in this evening of his own will, badly wounded with bites & scratches from the wolves, which are very numerous about us. We cannot but notice this as singular. Having been cured in a former case by our attention, probably induced the animal to come in now in this manner.[102]

---

[100] Just what this "late arrangement" was is not clear. The most recent agreement between Comcomly and McDougall was, of course, the latter's marriage to the chief's daughter, but just why that should oblige him to supply the post with free salmon is not apparent.

[101] The reference to a "white blanket" was probably to a 3-point blanket, white with a single dark stripe at each end, the most common trade blanket of the time. See Hanson, "Point Blanket," 7, and, above, I, n. 54. Assuming the old rule of one beaver pelt per point, McDougall has substantially lowered his offering price, reflecting the plans for a departure overland in the spring when more beaver pelts could be a burden rather than an advantage.

[102] It is surprising that the horses were apparently allowed to roam at will when they were not being worked.

4th. Wednesday. Rained considerably during last night & this morning. The day tolerably pleasant. Wind Westerly. Began packing furs, at which 6 men are employed. Mechanics at their several trades. S. Islanders at different necessary Jobs about the place, bringing Oars out of the woods, etc. No Indians about. 2 men sick.[103]

5th. Thursday. Pleasant. All hands disposed as usual. Three S. Islanders cutting wood at Coal Pit. Mechanics at their trades. Others packing furs. Visited in the morning by a large party of Clatsop & Clemax Indians in 7 Canoes, on their way up the river to make War on the Cathlakamaps, of which the Indians around have been for some time past telling us. One Blacksmith off duty. 3 sick.[104]

6th. Friday. Pleasant Weather. Men employed in the usual manner. Carpenter repairing Boat. Little again unable to work. In the morning Mr. McKenzie & party arrived from up the river much sooner than was expected. Met with no success in hunting. His trade however, much exceeded what was calculated upon, having in this short time traded 1200 dried Salmon, all which arrived here in good order, being more than the whole amount of trade during two trips of the Shallop up the river last year for that purpose. Visited by Comcomly, his eldest son & a party of warriors in two Canoes on their way up the river to witness the battle to be fought at the Cathlakamaps as mentioned Yesterday. The old man is going as peace maker, being connected in his family to the chiefs of both parties. Despatched one of our Canoes at the same time for the village of the Cathlakamaps, with Mr. Franchere, T. McKay, Gervais, Harteau & three S. Islanders. Mr. F. goes up to witness the battle, settle with Kaessnoe for four horses already bargained & to return with J. McKay and one S. Islander immediately after. The other four men accompanied by a young son of Comcomly are to proceed with the Horses & join the party in the Wolamat, with instructions to them not to send a canoe down untill October, & by this means, with the additional help of men & horses improve the whole hunting season. Very unexpectedly at evening Mr. Seton with 5 men in a Canoe reached here from the Wolamat, laden with 33 Bales of dried meat. Their party in one

---

[103] "Bringing oars out of the woods" sounds as if the oars were hidden in the forest, but in the absence of any reason to hide the oars, that could hardly be the meaning. McDougall might have assigned some of the Hawaiians the presumably easy task of carving oars from suitably sized and shaped logs. Such a task may even have been something they frequently did in the islands.

[104] This does not seem to have anything to do with the quarrel which McDougall tried to mediate shortly after the Astorians landed. That was between the Chinooks and the Clatsops and Clemax; see May 16–18, 1811.

month had killed 117 animals, mostly Deer & made the quantity of dried meat mentioned. They were not by their instructions to have sent a canoe down sooner than the 25th, but as they had no fixed residence, were changing camp often, with many of their men sick, & so many Bales to carry from one place to another, could make no progress in hunting. Concluded therefore to send down the quantity on hand.[105]

7th. Saturday. Pleasant. Wind fresh at S. W. Early in the forenoon Mr. McKenzie & Halsey with a party in a Boat started up the river on another trading voyage. Hurried away sooner than intended for the purpose of stopping the men sent Yesterday to take horses up the Wolamat, the arrival of Mr. Seton from that place rendering it unnecessary. The men are to remain with Mr. McK. in the boat. Our people employed as during the week.

8th. Sunday. Weather unsettled, frequent showers of rain during the day. Wind Southerly. Visited by some Chinook Indians, but had nothing to trade. We have purchased no Salmon since Sunday last 1st inst. The Indians catch none.

9th. Monday. Heavy rain in the morning. Wind Southerly, with showers through the day. S. Islanders sent to assist getting out Coals, Sanson having finished the second Pit. Other hands packing Furs. Mechanics variously employed as usual. Visited in the afternoon by Gassagass on his return from the War party. He was too late to see the battle, could not therefore learn much concerning it from him. Saw also several Canoes of the Clatsop & Clemax indians, of the party passing down on their way home, but were visited by none. Lapierre, Little & Milligan sick. Tuanna kept employed.

10th. Tuesday. Pleasant. Clear Weather. Wind Westerly. Early in the forenoon Mr. Franchere arrived from the Cathlakamaps having left Mr. McKenzie there Yesterday morning. He was sent up some days ago in company with Comcomly to be joint mediator with him between that tribe & the Clatsops, who were going to War against each other in consequence of the former's having killed a chief of the latter about twelve months ago. But unfortunately arrived too late either to interfere or witness the battle, which was over when he reached the Warriors Camp Saturday night. On their arrival there, Comcomly hearing that he had been traduced by the former (altho' his relation) made an animated speech, & proposed making common cause with the latter, who were encamped on a large Island, which lies at the

---

[105] McDougall seems to be acting the part of an amateur anthropologist. Given the Astorians' plans, their interest in the future balance of power among the natives could hardly be strong.

lowermost entrance of the Wolamat river & forms a small channel on the
south side.[106] Their Camp could not be more than two, or three muskets
shot from the enemy's village, who probably having heard of Comcomly's
arrival, sent a Messenger during the night who informed him of their having
received a reinforcement of 70 Warriors from some of the neighboring tribes,
and which was announced but a short time before (as is customary among
them) by loud shouts & firing of musketry. These were immediately answered by the Clatsops, who having come off the field of Battle without the
loss of a single man (while several of their enemies were wounded) accompanied their shouts with threats of destroying the rest & burning their houses &
property, and appointed the next day at noon for renewing the attack. The
shouts, threats & firing of musketry continued alternately during the whole
night. By daylight, however, sunday morning they raised their Camp, under
a pretence of proceeding as far as the Cathlapootles village for breakfast, but
were seen gliding down the stream without any noise. Being now left
alone, & not doubting of their returning by mid-day Mr. F. hastened to the
Cathlacamap Village & assured the Chiefs that the whites took no part whatever in their quarrels, except that of conciliating the parties. He was very
hospitably entertained, but had not been long in the chief's house before a
scout having given the alarm, he thought it prudent to retire to an island
opposite the Village to witness the battle which he expected would soon take
place. After waiting however several hours he returned to the Village at the
entreaties of the chief. During the day they were on a constant look out, but
were relieved from their anxiety by the arrival of Mr. McKenzie towards
night, who assured them he had met the Clatsops as far down as the Chelwits, notwithstanding their great boasting.

   Contrary to the Indians' mode of fighting, which is generally by surprize,
these give notice to each other & fight in open day, as can be seen by the
following account of Yesterday's Battle. The Clatsops & their allies, to the
number of Eighty men, in eight canoes having landed in a small Prairie
about 200 Yards below the enemies' village, advanced about 50 Yards, when
the others met them. Having made the demand for the satisfaction of their
chief's death, the Cathlakamaps produced a few Clemels, or War garments,
and Hayquias, but the former demanding slaves, the presents offered were
with drawn & the battle immediately commenced. The latter fired the first
shots, which threw the Clatsops into confusion & made them retreat to their
canoes, from whence they kept a steady fire of arrows & musketry for the

---

[106] The island is Sauvie Island, at the confluence of the Willamette with the Columbia.

space of about an hour, shielding themselves from the arrows of their enemies by heeling their canoes so much to one side as to present part of their
bottom, (while the Cathlakamaps remained exposed to their fire on the
plain.) Having however, received two Bullets through one of them, they
were so much alarmed that they immediately paddled to an Island on the
opposite side of the channel without receiving any other injury. The Cathlakamaps had on their side one man mortally wounded by an arrow which
pierced him through the body. Another was slightly wounded in three places,
and a third had his side grazed by a bullet. Considering their stock of ammunition & the small number of arms among them (the Clatsops having only
four muskets, & the Cathlakamaps three) a great number of shots must have
been fired, as the gable-end of one of the houses was all pierced with bullet
holes.

Thus terminated this petty war without more bloodshed. The Clatsops &
their allies were no doubt frightened by the reinforcement their enemies had
received, and thought it prudent to return to their home, having in a manner
satisfied themselves by the death of one of the enemy's men.[107]

All hands employed here as Yesterday. Purchased a small Sturgeon.

11th. Wednesday. Tolerably pleasant. Wind Westerly. Six men employed
at Coal pit, putting up a new one, bringing out Wood, etc. All hands else
occupied at the Furs, Pressing, Packing, & beating them. Visited by several
canoes of Indians. Purchased 6 Sturgeon & 26 Small Salmon Trout, the first
of Salmon kind had here since 1st inst. 2 men sick. Taylor at work again.

12th. Thursday. Pleasant. Wind Westerly. People employed as Yesterday.
Mr. Seton preparing to set out tomorrow for the Wolamat. Visited by Comcomly & a good number of his people in a large Canoe, bringing a few
Salmon Trout. Took away with him the Boat bargained some time since for
two horses. 2 men sick. Lapierre recovering.

13th. Friday. Weather as Yesterday. All hands employed between Coal

---

[107] This description agrees with most descriptions of conflicts among the Chinooks, when
they did not concern serious matters. The implicit rules by which war was waged seemed
designed to keep the bloodshed low. However, native wars could be serious. In the 1780s, a
contest between the Upper and the Lower Chinooks over clam beds was quite bloody, with
the Upper tribes suffering many casualties. At that time, Konkomis, father of Comcomly, led
the victorious Lower Chinooks; see Ruby, Brown, *Chinook*, p. 17. Note the almost complete
absence of firearms on either side. Franchère's description of the battle is in *Journal*, pp.
104–105. Robert Stuart witnessed a similar battle; see Rollins, ed., *Stuart's Narrative*, pp.
22–23. Irving's description of a Chinook battle borrows from this entry in the log; see *Astoria*
(Rust ed.), pp. 242–43. "Hayquias" are probablyn hyquoas, an ornamental shell, much prized
by the natives; see I, n. 65.

Pits & pressing furs. The people for the Wolamat preparing themselves. Their departure is put off another day. Visited by several Indians. Purchased a few Salmon and the meat of a small female Elk. Sick list the same.

14th. Saturday. Weather as Yesterday. All hands employed as during the week. Mr. Seton with a party of seven men set out for the Wolamat at 11 o'clock. Broke the press last evening. 2 hands repairing it, which occupied the whole day. Visited by 2 of Comcomly's sons and several other Chinook Indians. Purchased several fresh Salmon & the meat of a Beaver.

15th Sunday. Fine pleasant Weather. Wind Westerly. Early this morning Mr. McKenzie & party arrived in the Boat having been again successful in trading. Brought down 2200 dried Salmon, all in excellent order & 30 fresh ones. Went no farther up than the Village of Multnomah's. Several Canoes of Indians about. Purchased 9 fresh Salmon.[108]

16th. Monday. Cloudy with some Rain. Wind S. W. All hands variously employed. Mechanics as usually. 6 men building a house to contain Coals at the Pit, one with Sanson burning Coals, others pressing furs, beating them, etc. Cooper & Patterson repairing Boats. Cannan handling Knives, repairing & arranging Guns, etc. Lapierre & Little, the two sick both able to do a little. Tuanna at work with others. Visited by several Indians, from whom traded 2 large Sturgeon.

17th. Tuesday. Pleasant. People variously employed as usual. Finished the house for coals. Completed pressing the packs made. S. Islanders beating furs. Visited by Comcomly and a number of his people but had no trade. Sent Cannan out hunting alone.

18th. Wednesday. Morning cloudy with some rain. Latter part pleasant, wind light at westward. Early in the forenoon Mr. McKenzie with the same party as before set out on a third trip up the river trading. All hands were employed much as usual. Arranging & pressing Furs, two repairing Boats, two making Boat Sails, etc. Cannan returned from hunting unsuccessful. Visited in the afternoon by two canoes of Chinooks & the chief of the Queenhilts trading a few Beaver. Comcomly sent us a large Sturgeon.

19th. Thursday. Pleasant. People employed much as Yesterday. Lapierre nearly recovered, employed him making blanket capots. Visited by several canoes Indians. Purchased the meat of an Elk.

20th. Friday. Pleasant weather, wind Westerly. People busied as usual. Visited by numbers of Indians with Sturgeon, etc. At 1 o'clock Gassagas

---

[108] The Multnomah were part of the Clackamas division of the Upper Chinookans; they lived on Sauvie Island, the scene of the battle described above. See Ruby, Brown, *Guide*, p. 142.

came over in great haste to inform us that a Ship was off the mouth of the river, & that 2 Canoes had gone out to her this morning. Mr. McDougall with a party immediately Set off in the Boat to ascertain the truth of the Story, but to our great satisfaction the Ship was soon seen coming in over the Bar, and before he had reached the opposite shore above the Chinook Village had anchored opposite the factory. At Sun set the boat returned with Mr. Hunt, Capt. Smith and Mr. Demester on board. The Ship <u>Albatross</u> Capt. Smith of Boston Mr. Hunt had chartered at Woahoo for the passage to this place, being left there from the <u>Beaver</u> in December last. Mr. Demestre passenger in the <u>Albatross</u>. By an arrival from the United States Accounts and papers have reached Sandwich Islands to 18th Feby last. The <u>Beaver</u> reached Canton in safety, having made a good voyage. Accounts reached Mr. Hunt at Woahoo from Captain Sowle in Canton, etc., etc.[109]

21st. Saturday. Forenoon cloudy with some Showers and Squalls of rain, latter part pleasant. Sent our Boat early to the ship for the live stock. Returned loaded about noon. Sent a second time to assist in bringing the Ship over to the factory. Toward evening the Ship arrived and anchored without difficulty directly abreast & a Short distance only from us. Dispatched One man in Comcomly's Canoe with a letter in pursuit of Mr. McKenzie.

22nd. Sunday. Pleasant & warm. All hands busily employed receiving Provisions, etc. from Ship. Were not able to complete the whole to day. The Ship as well as our place swarming with Indians.

23rd. Monday. Weather as yesterday. All hands occupied as yesterday receiving Articles from the Ship except two Blacksmiths making some Iron works for Capt. Smith. Two men at Coal pits as usual. Indians about very numerous. Traded several fresh Sturgeon. At evening visited by Comcomly from the Chelwits from which place he dispatched his people with our man after Mr. McKenzie. The old man repeated to us what the Indians had told him aloud, that the parties of Messrs. Clarke & Stuart were cut off, but refered us to Mr. McKenzie when he shall arrive for better information.[110]

---

[109] See above, entries for June 29 and August 3, 1812, when Hunt and the other partners decided he should take the *Beaver* to Sitka, thus executing the other part of Astor's plan for Astoria. Because of damage to the vessel there, Sowle and Hunt took it to Hawaii where Hunt stayed while Sowle took the ship and its cargo of furs on to Canton. Hunt intended to return to the Columbia on the supply ship Astor was sending. Learning of the outbreak of war between the United States and Britain, Hunt chartered the *Albatross* for a brief trip to Astoria, carrying provisions as well as himself. He had been absent a little more than a year, and control of the post had passed to McDougall, with McKenzie's support. In spite of his nominal status as supervising partner, Hunt was reduced to little more than an errand boy. See below, August 26, 1813, for future action.

[110] See below, August 24, for a fuller report and September 3, 8, and 16 for McDougall's restrained and skeptical response to this report. Exactly what, if anything, happened is not clear in the log.

24th. Tuesday. Warm pleasant weather, all hands employed as yesterday. About noon Mr. McKenzie & party arrived having been up as far as the Cathlacamaps, and traded 1500 Dried Salmon. He brought intelligence of a report among the Indians, that all the whites who formed the party, that left this last July had been cut off in the night, with the exception of one man, whom they described as being left handed, and wearing a brace of Pistols. He was seen in the woods a little above the falls. Visited by a great number of Indians trading Clemels, Beavers and Sturgeon, of the latter great quantities are now brought, for which they receive Beads. Our Supply of Salt enables us to put this up in barrels, etc., which will make valuable provisions for the ensuing season. Salting some for the Ships use.

25th. Wednesday. Fine pleasant weather. All busied as Yesterday. Ships preparing for their speedy departure, taking in water, Ballast, Spars, etc., at which a part of our people are assisting. Great number Indians about us trading as yesterday. Sent on board Ship Six barrels pickled Sturgeon. Came on Shore to remain Joseph Aston a Seaman, he was engaged by Mr. Hunt, to serve as an Interpreter Among the Russians; He belonged to the Crew of the Brig Chatham when Lieutenant Broughton Surveyed the river. Spicer, Reveau & Patterson obtained their discharge from the Service of the Company, and engaged with Capt. Smith.[111]

26th. Thursday. Weather much the same as yesterday. Most of the hands busy for the Ships departure. Mr. Hunt takes his passage on board for the purpose of Chartering a vessel, to be at this place in the month of February or March next. Mr. Clapp received his discharge and goes on board the *Albatross* a passenger in hopes of getting a Situation at the Sandwich lslands. As all hopes of curing Tuana of the venereal was given over, a passage to the Islands was procured him, as well as a boy Sacks. Everything being on board and the Ship ready for Sea. She weighed Anchor about 11 A. M., & with a favorable breeze, was seen off the bar in a few hours. On her departure a

---

[111] The *Chatham* was a tender, attached to George Vancouver's *Discovery*, during his 1792 voyage. In the fall, several months after Robert Gray had entered the river on *Columbia*, she was sent into the river under the command of Lieutenant William Broughton. Broughton took his vessel up above the present site of Portland where he claimed the country for Great Britain. It was he who named Baker's Bay, Young's River, Tongue Point, Oak Point, Puget's Island, and Mounts St. Helens and Hood. See Dorothy O. Johansen, *Empire of the Columbia*, 2nd ed. (New York: Harper & Row, 1967), pp. 44–47. Joseph Ashton remained at Astoria through the winter of 1813–14; see Appendix, No. 1. Henry Spicer, John Reveau, and John Patterson had signed on in New York in October 1811 and come out on the *Beaver*; Patterson was a carpenter (II, n. 28); since the other two were paid salaries close to Patterson's, they also may have had some kind of a skill to recommend them. See "Articles of Agreement," Porter, *Astor*, I, 475–78.

Salute of 9 Guns was fired from the factory. Visited by Indians trading Beaver, Sturgeon, etc.[112]

27th. Friday. Fine pleasant weather. Wind Westerly. Most part of the people employed raising the Shallop in order to repair her. Cooper pickling Sturgeon. Blacksmiths off duty, making our sick list 4 persons. Visited by several families of Chelwit Indians who encamped in the bay below the factory, to dry berries. Traded a few Skins from them.[113]

28th. Saturday. Warm & pleasant. People variously Occupied, 3 repairing Shallop, 7 Chopping wood for Coal Pit, 2 Burning Coals, 3 making packs, mechanics at their different occupations. Watatchum brought in the meat of an Elk. 2 men sick.

29th. Sunday. Same pleasant weather as yesterday. Visited by a few the natives, but traded nothing.

30th. Monday. Weather the same, all hands busily employed, mechanics as usual, 11 men cutting and carrying wood at the Coal pit, 5 pressing packs, 2 Beating furs. Visited by a few natives who traded 14 Sturgeon.[114]

31st. Tuesday. Pleasant and very warm weather, wind N. E. People employed as yesterday. In the afternoon, visited by several Canoes of Chelwitzes trading Dried Salmon, Beaver, etc.

---

[112] Hunt very much disapproved of the decision to abandon the post but, at a partners' meeting on the 25th, with Hunt, McDougall, and McKenzie present, he allowed himself to be outvoted. Citing the poor state of trade on the northwest coast and the interior, the partners reaffirmed the philosophy implicit in the earlier decisions, the first loss was the best loss. In order to avoid any further expense, Hunt was to try to charter a vessel in Hawaii which would remove the furs and the Hawaiian natives, taking the latter home, and the former to market in Canton. The possibility of a sale to the North West Company was also to be explored. Finally, in the event of a delayed return by Hunt, "it is left solely with Mr. McDougall to finally conclude any arrangements we may be able to make with . . . the N. W. Co." Elliott, "Sale of Astoria," 46–47; see also Ronda, *Astoria*, pp. 285–86. Benjamin Clapp got to the Marquesas Islands, where he encountered Commodore David Porter, United States Navy, on a commerce-destroying mission; he signed on with him as a midshipman and, after a number of adventures, including captivity by the British, returned to New York where, after some exchanges with the Navy Department over his pay, he dropped out of sight; see J. Neilson Barry, "What Became of Benjamin Clapp?" *Washington Historical Society Quarterly*, 21, No. 1 (January 1930), 13–17. Note also the end of Tuana's story.

[113] Just what repairs the *Dolly* might have needed are not apparent. She was hauled out of the water on November 19, 1812; there was no further mention of her until February 11, 1813, when McDougall assigns two Hawaiians to pump her out. Although she was believed beyond the reach of the river in November, especially high water may have flooded her, as McDougall notes the necessity of "raising" the vessel. Aside from the seasonal variation in the flow of water, the Columbia is tidal at Astoria and water levels were difficult to predict. By "repair," McDougall may have meant fitting the vessel out for a season's (or what there would be of it) work.

[114] "Pressing packs" probably meant pressing the beaver pelts into uniformly sized packages. Beating the pelts was part of the cleaning process.

Septr 1st. Wednesday. Wind and weather as yesterday. People employed much the same also. Visited by a number of Indians from bakers bay, from one of whom traded the meat of an Elk. 3 Men Sick.

2nd. Thursday. Cloudy. Wind fresh at N. W. People variously employed. 8 at the coal pit, 2 beating furs, 2 packing Salmon, 1 Cutting Grass for Coal pits, 4 carrying out canoe poles from behind the factory. Cannan and cooper employed at Small jobs. Sick list the same.

3rd. Friday. Pleasant. Wind fresh at westward. People occupied much as yesterday. Six men bringing hay from Point George to the Coal pit. Harteau painting Oil cloths, etc. Visited by Calpo & family on their return home from up the river, having been as far as the lowermost entrance of the Wola-mat. They confirm the report of the parties up the river having been de-stroyed, and had they waited two days longer their informers (who came by the Wolamat) offered to bring some of our people's clothes and arms. They likewise say that one man who by Chance was a sleep in a canoe got safe and made his escape into the woods, where he has been seen. They represent him as being left handed and having two dogs following him. This accident happened a short distance above the falls, and it appears that none escaped, even Mr. McTavish and party who were to have gone a head, when ever they would have passed the falls, were also cut off. This story and the manner in which it is related appears highly incredible, that the whole party should have been off their guard is impossible. We fear however that some accident may have befallen Mr. Reed and party after they separated to proceed up Lewis River. Traded 30 Beaver Skins and a few Sturgeon. In the afternoon visited by Comcomly and his followers.[115]

4th. Saturday. Weather pleasant, wind westerly. All hands busily employed as usual. Visited by few the natives trading Beaver, Clemels, dried Salmon, etc. 2 men Sick.

Septemr 5th. Sunday. Pleasant. Wind westerly. At evening Watatkum arrived with the meat of an Elk.

6th. Monday. Cloudy with light rain. Mechanics at their respective Occu-pations. 3 men at the Coal pit, 3 packing furs, 5 Picking Oakum, one caulk-ing Shallop decks. After dinner Mr. McKenzie & Halsey with seven men left this in one of the boats on a trading voyage up the river, they intend to

---

[115] This is an "improved version" of the story which first came to the Astorians on August 24, via David McKenzie. See below, September 8, 16, for more mentions. Nothing of the kind happened, but the matter is not resolved in the log. Ironically, Reed and others would be killed by natives in southwestern Idaho in the winter of 1814–15; see Cox, *Columbia*, p. 152, n. 13.

proceed as far as the rapids to asscertain the truth of the report in circulation, and if true to try and engage the natives to fetch the man, which they say is in the woods. 2 men Sick.

7th. Tuesday. Weather Cloudy. Wind fresh at N. W. All hands busily employed. Sawing Gun Stocks. Caulking and preparing the buildings for the approaching wet season. Salting Sturgeon, etc. Lapierre & Little still unfit for duty. Macon also laid up since yesterday noon, making our sick list three Persons.

8th. Wednesday. Morning foggy, latter part the day pleasant. Wind N. W. People variously employed. Visited by Gassagas and Seven Canoes of Multnomah People trading Beaver, dressed Deer Skins, and dried Salmon. The former told us that our people had not been killed as was first reported, but had been robbed of Several Articles, in passing the falls. Among other articles he mentions a bale of Blankets and several fathoms of Blue Cloth. Traded from him a fowling piece lost last year in Mr. David Stuart's Canoe. Sick list the Same.[116]

9th. Thursday. Rainy disagreeable weather; wind Southerly. People employed in doors, Stowing Salmon, packing furs, etc. Visited by a great number of Chelwits trading Beaver & dried Salmon. Sick list the same.

10th. Friday. Fine clear weather. Wind S. W. People employed much the same as yesterday. Great number of Indians about us from the upper Chelwits and even from the Cathlanaquoi & Cathlaminimen Villages. Such is their eagerness to possess our light blue beads that they offer everything they have in in exchange for them, and we have already traded here more dried Salmon than ever we got by Sending the Shallop up the river. Watatkum brought in the meat of an Elk. 3 men Sick.[117]

11th. Saturday. Cloudy weather. People employed making packs, Stowing Salmon, etc. 2 men gumming Canoes, as it will be almost impracticable when the rainy season sets in, having no shelter for them. Trading as usual. During this week we lost five large pigs, which appeared to have been poisoned, four of which were of those landed from the Albatross.[118]

---

[116] These losses are not reported anywhere else. Perhaps the goods in question came from the upset of David Stuart's canoe the previous year when the fowling piece was lost; see above, July 28, 1812.

[117] The Cathlanaminimin have already been connected with the Upper Chinookan tribes clustered about the mouth of the Willamette; see I, n. 67. The Cathlanaquoi were probably from the same area. This is their only mention in the log.

[118] McDougall seems to be resuming his customary paranoia, even toward his in-laws. Just why the natives would poison hogs is not known. Recall that the hogs customarily foraged for themselves in the woods. It is possible that these newly arrived animals either ate some-

12th. Sunday. Rain throughout the day. Visited by a few Indians trading Berries, etc. One of our breeding Sows appeared this morning with a litter of young pigs. 3 men Sick.

13th. Monday. Tolerable pleasant. Wind Strong at Westward. People employed at various Jobs, Gumming a Canoe, packing furs, etc. Mechanics at their usual occupations. Visited by numbers of Indians from the upper part of the river, trading Dried Salmon, roots & a few Beavers. Our Indian hunter brought in the meat of an Elk. Sick list the same.

14th. Tuesday. Fine, but rather cold weather. People occupied as yesterday. Visited by Gassagas & a number of Chinook Indians, who traded 21 Beaver Skins. Sick list as yesterday.

15th. Wednesday. Pleasant. Wind North East. People employed at different useful Jobs about the factory. In the morning Messrs. Wallace & Seton arrived from McKay's River in three Canoes, they having heard of the arrival of a vessel in the river induced Mr. Seton to embark with three men in a Small canoe to asscertain the truth of the report, when he met Mr. McKenzie about Deer Island, who informed him of the whole, and bid him return, and order all hands down. The hunters for some time back did but very little beside feeding the party, Owing chiefly to the great number of Indians, which over run the Wolamat at this season of the year. They brought about 600 lbs. dried meat and a small bale of tallows. Visited by Indians as usual trading Salmon, roots, etc.[119]

16th. Thursday. Rainy disagreeable weather. The men employed much the same as yesterday. About 11 A.M. Mr. McKenzie and party arrived having been as far as the rapids, but traded few salmon, the Indians having mostly all removed from the river into winter quarters. Gained no intelligence respecting the fate of our people. Purchased a new musket and a Jockey Cap from the natives at the rapids, and an old double barrel gun from the Cathlaminmin Chief. Brought 400 dried Salmon. 2 Men Sick.[120]

17th. Friday. Stormy weather, the wind which was from the south blew a

thing which seriously disagreed with them or, because of the rainy weather noted, caught cold. Astoria was not Waikiki, as the Hawaiians could have told the hapless animals.

[119] Recall that McKay's River is the Willamette. Seton recounts this incident in his journal; see Jones, ed., *Astorian Adventure*, pp. 123–25. Tallow is practically any form of animal fat. Since Seton's party brought down 600 pounds of dried meat, they had had access to a good bit of fat, but just how this might be put into "a small bale" is not clear. Perhaps a tallow was a string or rope saturated with the fat so that it might serve as a kind of wick or lighter.

[120] Dodilcham was the Cathlanaminimin chief. He was the one who bargained vigorously for a large reward to return Jeremie and the Belleaus; see above, November 24, 1811. His name was also spelled Tootilichum; see below, September 23, 1813.

gale, and tore off a part of the roof of the New house, carried away several pieces of bark off the roof of the shed, and blew down several trees. Were under the necessity of removing our canoes, which were under Shelter of some large trees in the woods, to place them in security from the falling of branches, etc. Cooper making kegs. Two blacksmiths off duty making Our Sick List 4 Persons.

18th. Saturday. Same unpleasant weather as yesterday. People employed in doors making paddles, mockasins etc. 3 men Sick.

19th. Sunday. Cloudy with some rain. Another of our breeding Sows was found yesterday with a litter of young pigs. Sick list the Same.

20th. Monday. Weather pleasant, wind westerly. John Day & Carson with 8 men left here in a Canoe to spend some time hunting above Tongue Point. Mechanics at their different occupations, remainder of the people employed cutting and carrying out timber for building a shelter for the goats. Four men Sick.

Septemr. 21st. Tuesday. Pleasant. People employed much the same as yesterday. 8 men building a shelter at the Coal Pit, for the coals. Finished the house for the Goats. Visited by a number of the natives trading Matts, berries, etc. 3 men Sick.

22nd. Wednesday. Cloudy with fine rain. All hands Occupied as yesterday. Finished the house at the coal pit. Little gumming Canoes. In the afternoon a canoe with four men arrived from the hunters, bringing the meat of three Elks. One of our Indian hunters also brought in the meat of an Elk. Visited by Gassagas and a number of indians trading matts, etc. Sick list the same.

23rd. Thursday. Pleasant. People variously employed, 2 gumming Canoes for Mr. McKenzie, 1 Painting Oil Cloths. Mechanics at their different ocuppations. Sandwich Islanders making mortar, remainder at the coal pit cutting and carrying out wood. Visited by Tootilichum, chief of the Cathlaminmin nation, who traded a few Beaver, Clemels and dried Salmon. This morning the four men returned with the canoe to the hunting ground. Sick list as yesterday.

24th. Friday. Incessant rain. All hands employed as yesterday. Tootilichum took his departure after receiving as a present Three Pigs and two fowls. In the afternoon John Day and party returned from hunting bringing the meat of Two Elks. Visited by several Chinook Indians one of whom traded the meat of a Small Deer. 4 men Sick.

25th. Saturday. Tolerable Pleasant. People employed as for several days past. In the afternoon sent a canoe with four men a little distance above tongue point to get a load of hoop poles. Visited by Comcomly & followers, who traded a few Beaver Skins. Supplied Lamasay with a musket, Ammunition & a small canoe for the Purpose of procuring provissions for us. 3 men Sick.[121]

26th. Sunday. Pleasant. The four men arrived with a load of hoop poles. John Day with the same party as before went in a canoe hunting. Visited by Gassagas and a number of Chinooks. Traded the meat of an Elk and some Wapatoes. At evening Lamsay returned with one Swan & a Seal. Sick List the same.

27th. Monday. Forepart cloudy with rain, latter part pleasant. Wind Easterly. People variously employed. Preperations making for Mr. McKenzie's departure for the interior. 8 men Gumming canoes. 1 making a canoe Sail. Cooper making kegs. Labonte making Boxes. Blacksmiths & Taylor at their trades. S. Islanders pounding and grinding Tarro. Visited by a number of the natives, but traded nothing of any consequence. Sick list same.[122]

28th. Tuesday. Fine pleasant weather, Wind N. E. All hands employed much the same as yesterday. 8 men with the two boats bringing hay from Point George to the factory. Visited by a number of Chinook Indians Among them Calpo who traded the meat of three Elks.

29th. Wednesday. Pleasant. Wind Easterly. People busily employed as usual. Cooper with two men building an additional wall to the forge, for the purpose of introducing another pair of bellows's. Jeremie with the two boys covering the outside of the Store with matts. Carson & Cannan came in from hunting, having killed Two Elks near the factory. Sent Five men with them in a canoe to bring in the meat. In the afternoon John Day with the Six men arrived with the meat of Five Elks. Visited by a number of the natives trading Cedar Bark, Wapatoes, etc. Three men Sick.

Septmr 30th. Thursday. Weather pleasant. Wind Westerly. People employed as for several days past. Cooper Salting and putting up meat for Mr. McKenzie, Baker with 3 men employed at the forge. Ashton at work at the Shallop. Carson & party arrived with the meat of the two Elk killed yesterday. In the afternoon John Day, Carson and Cannan with Six men went in a canoe up young's Bay hunting. Visited by Indians trading as usual. Macon resumed his occupation. Little, Milligan, Gervais and 2 Sandwich Islanders, Sick.

Oct. 1st. Friday. Pleasant. Wind S. W. People variously employed. Prep-

---

[121] Hoop poles were probably slender saplings or branches which could be bent into hoops to go around barrels.

[122] Tarro, also spelled taro, is a tropical plant, cultivated for its sweet tuberous root, which was a staple of the Hawaiian diet. Wilson Price Hunt probably brought some for the Hawaiians who had not seen any since the arrival of the *Beaver* in April 1812.

erations making for Mr. McKenzie's departure tomorrow. Six men employed rebuilding the wall of the forge, which yesterday fell down when near finished. Visited by the Chief of the Chelwits and a number of his people who traded some Beaver, Wapatoes, etc. 5 Men Sick.

2nd. Saturday. Cloudy with rain. After dinner Mr. McKenzie left this for the Interior, accompanied by Messrs. Wallace, Seton, & T. McKay in two canoes manned by 12 men forming a total number of 16 Persons. He goes up for the purpose of bringing down the packs and Sandwich Islanders. Mr. McDougall in a light canoe with 5 men Accompanied them. The hunters returned unsuccessful. Traded the meat of an Elk from a Chinook Indian. Sick list the Same.[123]

3rd. Sunday. Squally blowing weather, with rain from N. W.

4th. Monday. Fine pleasant weather. People busily employed as usual. Finished the chimney to the forge. In the afternoon, Mr. McDougall returned, having been up the river as far as the Chelwit Village, and parted with Mr. McKenzie yesterday noon. Visited by a number of the natives trading wapatoes, matts, etc. Three men Sick.

October 5th. Tuesday. Pleasant, wind Easterly. All hands variously employed, putting a new roof on a part of the blacksmiths Shop, Gumming Canoes, etc. 3 Men Sick.

6th. Wednesday. Same pleasant weather as yesterday. People employed the same also. Visited by several of the natives, trading Bark, Hoop poles, roots, etc. Sick List the Same.

7th. Thursday. Weather the same as yesterday. At 9 o'Clock were much surprised by the arrival of Messrs. McKenzie & Clarke in a light canoe, and Mr. McTavish, Mr. Bethune, Mr. McMullen & a party of 16 men in 2 Bark Canoes, from the establishments of the N. W. Company. They encamped in the bay below us. Mr. McKenzie met with Messrs. Clarke & McTavish tuesday afternoon, a little distance above point VanCouver, where he left Messrs. Wallace & Seton with the goods, etc., and Mr. John Stuart with 7 Canoes of the N. W. Co. on their way down for this place. Messrs. McTavish & Stuart with their People and packs, have come down to wait the arrival of their ship, the Isaac Todd, which left England, the latter end of March last, in Company with the Frigate Phoebe.

---

[123] McKenzie's purpose was to bring provisions to the posts in the interior, i.e., Stuart and Clarke, and tell them to send down all their furs and any Hawaiian natives who might be with them. This was so that, when Hunt returned with a ship, the furs and the natives could be sent to their respective destinations.

Sent 5 men in a Canoe to meet Messrs. Wallace & Seton. At evening Calpo arrived with the meat of an Elk.[124]

8th. Friday. Fine pleasant weather. People variously employed. Two digging a vault in the garden to put wapatoes in. Labonte making a door for the blacksmiths Shop. Early this morning Messrs. Wallace & Seton arrived having left the N. W. Brigade encamped at the mouth of the Wolamut River.

Mr. McTavish proposed purchasing the goods and Furs belonging to the company, here (as well as in the Interior) for cost and charges, excepting Articles damaged and in use.[125]

9th. Saturday. Warm and pleasant. Wind Easterly. People as usually employed. The hunters returned in the afternoon having killed a Small black bear. Visited by a great number of Chinooks and Chelwit indians, trading as usual.

10th. Sunday. Fore part of the day pleasant. Afternoon Cloudy. Wind Southerly.

11th. Monday. Cloudy. People occupied Gumming Canoes etc. Blacksmiths & Taylor at their trades. Clerks employed arranging the Store, etc. John Day with Six men went hunting. 4 men Sick.

12th. Tuesday. Weather Cloudy. Mechanics employed at their different

---

[124] This entry marks a drastic change in the fortunes of Astoria and the Pacific Fur Company. In July, the North West partners at Fort William, on Lake Superior, the headquarters of the wintering partners, had received definite news of the sailing of the armed letter of marque ship, *Isaac Todd*, in company with H.M.S. *Phoebe*, for the northwest coast. They immediately sent John George McTavish and others to Astoria to use the threat embodied in the news to strike the best bargain they could with the Astorians. On the way, they stopped at the post on the Okanogan and lured John Clarke into the North West ranks. McTavish seems to have expected McDougall to fall down, play dead, and surrender the post. Instead, having been stung before by news of the imminent arrival of force, the Astorians decided to wait and see. This made McTavish's situation a good bit more precarious than expected. Facing winter and short of time, shelter, and provisions, his options were to retreat, attack, or negotiate. This is not to say that the Astorians' position was strong. McTavish brought along an excerpt of the letter received at Fort William; it threatened that the *Isaac Todd* had orders "to take and destroy every thing that is American on the N. W. Coast." For the moment, the ball was in McTavish's court. Point Vancouver was named by William Broughton; it is on the north shore of the Columbia, above Reed Island, on the eastern edge of Portland. See Ronda, *Astoria*, pp. 287–88; Elliott, "Sale of Astoria, 1813," 47–48. The North Westers are identified in W. Stewart Wallace, ed., *Documents Relating to the North West Company* (Toronto: The Champlain Society, 1934), Appendix A: "A Biographical Dictionary of the Nor' Westers"; they are also listed in the 1813–14 roster given here as the Appendix.

[125] Now the ball was back with McDougall. If he sold now, some of the loss would be made good. On the other hand, if the enemy vessels did come and seize the post, all would be lost. He started talking with McTavish.

occupations. S. Islanders digging Potatoes. Sent Six men in a canoe for John Day and party to return from hunting.

Came to an understanding with Mr. McTavish respecting the disposing of the whole of the Company's goods, Merchandise & Furs to the N. W. Company, and securing a passage to the former to Canada.[126]

At evening Mr. John Stuart with 5 Clerks in Seven Canoes, and 92 Packs, Arrived, being the remainder of the N. W. Co. brigade. They encamped with Mr. McTavish in the little bay below the factory. Visited by several Clatsops, who traded 4 Sea Otters and 10 Beavers.

14. Wednesday. Weather the same. People employed the same also. John Day and party Arrived, with the meat of an Elk.

Notwithstanding the preliminary Arrangements settled with Mr. McTavish respecting the prices of the goods and Furs, those Gentlemen now expect a deduction on the same. It would seem that it is principally Mr. Stuart who objects to them. It being however our determination to accept of nothing less than what would be considered as fair prices, by disinterested persons, our Conference was at an end and additional precautions were taken about the fort that they should take no advantage of the hopes we before entertained, of coming to an amicable settlement with them.[127]

14th. Thursday. Cloudy. Wind Westerly. Six men with the Sandwich Islanders carrying out timber & laying up a house for themselves to live in during the winter.

Visited by Messrs. McTavish and Stuart and finally settled upon the terms the property would be disposed for and the time of receiving payment.[128]

15th. Friday. Weather the same. Settled with the Sandwich Islands and gave them to understand that the business was given up and that Mr. Mc-

---

[126] The laconic entries for October 9 through 12 hid what was certainly both a tense and a busy time for the Astorians as they waited to hear what their fate would be. On Sunday, the 10th, Seton noted the North Westers' "haughty mann[er]. . . . They display 2 British colours, while on our side this is the first Sunday that our flag has not been displayed; it is indeed unfortunate that Mr. Hunt is absent." Jones ed., *Astorian Adventure*, p. 127. He seems to have thought that Hunt would have upheld Astor's interests (and, inferentially, American honor) more firmly. Despite McDougall's statement, the two sides did not yet understand each other.

[127] While this statement about metaphorically battening down the hatches may not have reflected McDougall's sentiments, it does seem to have reflected those of the young American clerks; see Jones, ed., *Astorian Adventure*, pp. 127–29. On the other hand, perhaps McDougall was genuinely angry, as he used the incorrect date for this entry; it was actually October 13. The correct date was used for the next day.

[128] While the terms may have been settled on the 14th, the actual agreement was not signed until the 16th, doubtless because of the preparation of copies, etc.

Tavish became responsible for the amount due them, and that they were at liberty to engage with him 'till Spring, when those that wished to return to the Islands, would be sent home in one of the N. W. Co. Ships. Gave to each of them as a present One New Musket, 1 Powder horn, 3 lbs. Powder, 8 lbs. lead, 10 Gun flints, 1 half axe, 1 Tomyhawk and 3 lbs. Leaf Tobacco.[129]

16th. Saturday. Cloudy with light rain, Wind Southerly. Mr. McDougall employed discharging and settling the Mens Accounts. Signed the agreement with the N. W. Co. made out in duplicate.[130]

17th. Sunday. Pleasant. Clerks employed arranging the Stores, etc. St. Amant, Hearteau and Lucier left this for the Wolamut river, having made arrangements to trap for the N. W. Co.[131]

18th. Monday. Cloudy with rain. Commenced taking an Inventory and delivering the goods etc. to the N. W. Co.

19th. Tuesday. Weather the same as yesterday. Wind S. E. John Day, Carson, Cannan, Baker, Martial & Flangan left this for the Wolamut, having received their discharge and made arrangements with the N. W. Co. to trap till Spring up that river.

20th. Wednesday. Same unpleasant weather as yesterday. Employed the same also. Mr. McTavish and party removed from their encampment into the fort.

21st. Thursday. Weather as yesterday. Employed taking the Inventory, etc.

22nd. Friday. Cloudy. Finished the Inventory and delivered the keys of the Store to Messrs. McTavish & Stuart.

---

[129] McDougall certainly meant the Sandwich Islanders at the beginning of this entry.

[130] The text of the agreement is in Elliot, "Sale of Astoria, 1813," 46–50. In *Astoria*, Irving claimed that the North Westers paid about one-third of the actual value of the furs, merchandise, and equipment at the post, receiving a little less than $40,000. (Rust ed.) p. 344. Astor called the agreement "the supposed fraudulent above mentioned arrangement" when describing it to Secretary of State James Monroe in August 1815; Porter, *Astor*, I, 585. See Ronda, *Astoria*, pp. 288–91, 298–301, and Haeger, *Astor*, pp. 165–67 for recent treatments of the sale. Wilson Price Hunt returned to Astoria in February 1814 with *Pedler*, a ship he had purchased in Hawaii. Finding the agreement signed and the inventory and valuation of furs, merchandise, etc., complete, there was little he could do except secure from the North Westers a draft on their Montreal agents for the balance due. He signed a codicil to the agreement on March 10, assuming equal responsibility with McDougall and changing a provision regarding John Reed, then trapping along the Snake and unaware of events at Astoria. He left there with several of the remaining clerks early in April and sailed to Sitka, where he did some further business with Count Baranov, the governor of the Russian-American Company's post.

[131] As the new arrangement is implemented, at least twenty of the Pacific Fur Company people sign on with the post's new owners; see the Appendix for these three and those mentioned below on October 19 and 23.

23rd. Saturday. Pleasant. Mr. Franchere engaged with the N. W. Company. Also several of the Men, Viz. Lavalle, Trepagnes, Peyette, A. Belleau, Morice Pillon, Laframboise, Brugiere, Labonté, Plante, Gervais & Macon.

24th. Sunday. Weather Tolerable Pleasant.

28th. Thursday. Fine pleasant Weather. In the afternoon Mr. John Stuart and Mr. McKenzie left this with 5 Canoes for the Interior. Mr. McKenzie goes up Passenger to deliver the goods and Settle the business of the Interior.[132]

Novemr. 14th. In the Afternoon were Surprized by the Arrival of Messrs. Alex. Henry, Alex. Stuart & Keith, with a Party of 16 Men, in two Bark Canoes, from Fort William, which place they left the 19th July last. They brought Papers from Canada as late as the 12th June.[133]

Novemr. 30th. The British Sloop War Raccoon Captn. Black Arrived in the River, having on board, Mr. John MacDonald (of the N. W. Co.) with 3 Canadians and a Small Supply of Dry Goods. This Vessel was ordered by the Admiralty at Rio Janario to take on board Mr. McDonald and Sail in Co. with the North West Company's Ship Isaac Todd for this Place. They Parted Company in a gale of Wind of River Plate.[134]

---

[132] Having signed over responsibility, along with the post and its stores of furs and merchandise, etc., McDougall allows the log to lapse, making only two further entries recording the arrival of more North Westers and the Royal Navy sloop *Raccoon*.

[133] Alexander Henry and Alexander Stuart were partners in the North West Company; George Keith was a clerk. See Appendix.

[134] Finally, the much anticipated and feared show of force by the British had arrived in the guise of a sloop of war. The *Isaac Todd* had proven to be an outrageously slow sailer and had been separated from the H.M.S. *Raccoon* and H.M.S. *Cherub* accompanying H.M.S. *Phoebe* from Rio de Janeiro, while rounding the Horn. Despairing of the *Isaac Todd*, and hearing of the raids by the American captain David Porter on British whalers in the Pacific, James Hillyar transferred the North West partner, James McDonald, to the *Raccoon*, ordered it to Astoria, and went in pursuit of Porter. On arrival, Captain William Black of the *Raccoon* expressed his contempt for the collection of miserable buildings masquerading as a fort, took possession of the country in the name of Great Britain, and left soon afterward. See Barry M. Gough, "The 1813 [British] Expedition to Astoria," *The Beaver*, Outfit 304.2 (Autumn, 1973), 44–51. MacDonald took control of the post, which had been renamed Fort George. The *Isaac Todd* finally reached Astoria in April 1814, having taken more than a year to sail from London; see Franchère, *Journal*, p. 148. Franchère also gave a good description of the *Raccoon*'s arrival, in ibid., pp. 131–32.

Appendix

List of People on the Columbia for Winter 1813/14. Viz:

X—People whose time expires in Outfit 1813 & of course
are Free Summer 1814.
√—P. F. Co. People w. whom we have no Agreement whatever.[1]

	Party		Capacity	Engaged	Years
1. Ashton, Joseph	P. F. Co.		Sailor & Workman	19 Oct. 13	1
2. Belleau, Antoine	d″		Baker & Milieu	18 Oct. 13	1
3. Brugier, Pierre	d″		Gouvernail[6]	22 Oct. 13	1
4. Bernier, Julian	NWC	X	Devant[8]	Mont. 11	0
5. Bellart, Alexis	d″	X	Milieu	Mont. 11	0
6. Boisvert, Augustin	d″	X	Milieu	Mont. 11	0
7. Bellanger, Andre	d″	X	Devant	Col. 13	0
8. Bercier, Pierre	d″	X	Milieu H.K.[12]	Col. 12	0
9. Boucher, Charles	P. F. Co.	X	Milieu	23 Oct. 13	0
10. Belleau, J. Bte.	P. F. Co.	√	Milieu		
11. Brousseau, Bazile	″	√	Milieu		
12. Bell, George	″	X	Cooper	1 Nov. 13	0

[1] The document bears many marks, some of which appear to be stray checks made for different purposes from those stated here. I have been careful to put X and √ only where they seem to be clearly indicated and I have probably missed some of the Pacific Fur Company employees who did not sign any agreement with the North West Company.

[2] The North West Company used the livre, a French unit of money, to calculate the wages of those below the rank of clerk. It was seven-eighths of an English shilling, in decimal value, .875. Using Ashton's 600 livres as an example, something like a modern value can be derived. Multiplying Ashton's 600 livres by .875 produces 525 shillings, or £26.25 (525 divided by 20). This sum multiplied by $4.44, an accepted equivalent for the pound in the early nineteenth century, gives $116.55. Using the ratio between the consumer price index (base = 1860) for 1813, 192, and that for 1991, 1,629: 8.48 yields $988.34 in 1991 value. One should recall that a margin of at least 10 percent either way in such conversions should be allowed. Also, this sum did not include food, the "equipment," or shelter. Use of these values and procedures will yield a similarly rough modern equivalent for any of the wages given here. See Gordon Charles Davidson, *The North West Company* (New York: Russell & Russell; 1918, repr. 1967), pp. 202, n. 25, 228–230, hereafter Davidson, *North West;* and Robert Gourlay, comp., *Statistical Account of Upper Canada Compiled with a View for a Grand System of Emigration* (London: Simpson & Marshall, 1822), p. 217 for the Canadian values; John J. McCusker, "How Much Is That in Real Money?" *Proceedings of the American Antiquarian Society*, 101, Part 2 (October 1991), 312, 326, 332.

[3] "Equipt." means equipment, or the yearly supply of clothing, etc., given to each employee. A milieu engaged for the year received two blankets, two shirts, two pairs of trousers, and ten pounds of tobacco. Devants and Gouvernails received the items listed above, fourteen pounds of tobacco, and "some trifling articles," presumably an axe, knife, etc. Davidson, *North West*, pp. 228–230, treats this as well as the compensation for other ranks.

1st Year[2]	2nd Year	Equipt[3]	Station	Where & When Free
600	"	Milieu[4]	Ft. George[5]	at Ft. George 19 Oct 1814
450	450	"	Ft. Geo.	at Montreal same as N.W. C° men
300	P. Post[7]	Gouvernail	Ft. Geo	at Montreal same as N.W.C.
500	P. P.	D.	T. River[9]	at Montreal Feb. 1814
350	P. P.	m	Willam.[10]	at Montreal Feb. 1814
450	P. P.	m.	Ft. Geo.	at Montreal Feb. 1814
700	"	D	Ft. Heads[11]	at Montreal Feb. 1814
350	350	m	Spok. H.[13]	at Montreal Feb. 1814
180	"	0	Spok. H	at Montreal
			Willam.	
			Willam.	
300	"	0	Ft. Geo	at Ft. George 1 April 1814

[4] "Milieu" is French for, among other things, "middle" and apparently derived as a label for those who were middle paddlers in the large freight canoes used on the eastern rivers and lakes.

[5] Fort George is the name the North Westers gave to Astoria.

[6] *Gouvernail* is a French word meaning, when used in a nautical context, "rudder"; thus, the *gouvernail* was the tillerman or steersman in the stern. Both this position and that of *devant* (see below, n. 8) required more than ordinary skill and, hence, were usually compensated accordingly.

[7] "Post" (or P. P.) is probably a reference to a North West Company practice similar to that of the Hudson's Bay Company. The latter's "Standing Rules and Regulations," 1835, #21 specified that, lacking a definite agreement on wages, they would be the "prix du Poste" (literally, the price of the post), the wages of the district to which the person is attached. In all cases, "where engagements are to be renewed in the country, the wages of the District" would be paid, that is, "P. Post." Douglas MacKay, *The Honourable Company: A History of the Hudson's Bay Company* (Indianapolis: Bobbs-Merrill, 1936), p. 364.

[8] *Devant* is a French word meaning, when used in a nautical context, "bow" or "forepart"; thus, the *devant* was a bowsman, helping to steer the canoe from the bow.

[9] Thompson River, probably David Stuart's (spelled Stewart on this list) post at Kamloops, British Columbia.

[10] Willamette River, i.e., the post established near present-day Salem.

[11] Flat Heads, that is, among the Flat Head Indians in present-day northern Idaho and northwestern Montana.

[12] These initials are not used elsewhere in the manuscript. They may stand for "Horse Keeper."

[13] Spokane House, that is, the North West post near present-day Spokane, Washington.

	Party		Capacity	Engaged	Years
13. Bowithick, Joseph	NWC	X	D & Hunter	1 Aug. 13	0
14. Bethune, Angus	"		Clerk		
15. Bourdon, Michel	Free		Interpreter	27 July 13	2
16. Bellaire, Registe	Free		Freeman & H[15]		
17. Boucher, J. Bte.	NWC		Interpreter		
18. Bostonnais dit Page A.[17]	Free		Hunter		
19. Boullard, Michel	NWC	X	Summerman[18]	10 Feb. 10	0
20. Baker, Micajah	Free		Blacksmith		
21. Cayalle, Antoine	NWCo		D & Milieu	Ft. Geo.	1
22. Cotte, Charles	NWC		M	Mont. 12	1
23. Cotte, Joseph	"		D & Milieu	Mont. 13	1
24. Cotenoire, Michel	"		M.	Mont. 13	2
25. Choput, Charles	"		Carpenter & m	L.L.P.[19] 13	1
26. Cire, Joseph	"		M.	Mont. 12	1
27. Chevrette, Charles	NWC	X	M.	B. d. l. R.[20]	0
28. Cone, George	P. F. Co.	√	Gouvernail		
29. Cotte, Joseph	P. F. Co	X	M. & Sawyer	20 Oct. 13	0
30. Connor, Patrick	NWCo	X	Tailor & M.	Atha.[21]	0
31. Cartier, Joseph	d"	X	Guide	Ft. W.[22]	0
32. Cox, Ross	P. F. Co	X	Apr. Clerk	Col. 13	5
33. Clark, John	P. F. Co	√	Proprietor		
34. Canning, William	P. F. Co	√	Millwright		
35. Carson, Alexander	P. F. Co	√	Gunsmith		
36. Cawanarde, Pierre	NWCo	X	D & Milieu	B. d. l. R 12	0
37. Ducharquette, François	P. F. Co.		Blacksmith & M.	16 Oct. 13	1
38. Desmarais, Louis	NWCo		D.	Ft. Wm. 13	2
39. Desmarais, Joseph	d"		Milieu	Ft. W. 13	2
40. Duchesne, Benj	"		Carpenter & m	Mont. 12	2
41. D'Eon, Timothe	d"		D	Mont. 12	2
42. Dupuid, Francois	N.W.Co	X	Milieu	B. d. l. R. 12	0
43. Delauney, Joseph	P. F. Co	√	Milieu		
44. Dubreuil, J. Bte.	P.F.Co	√	Milieu		

[14] Fort des Prairies, one of those guarding the "portage des prairies," off the Assiniboine River.

[15] Hunter.

[16] New Caledonia, a contemporary name for the northern portion of the Oregon Country. In this context, it may mean Kamloops, the post on the Thompson River in present-day British Columbia established by David Stuart in 1811.

[17] Bostonnais was the French Canadian label for all United States citizens; so A. Page was presumably an American.

[18] "Summerman" presumably meant someone hired for the summer to move freight on the Great Lakes and the eastern freight routes going out of Fort William. In that case, just what

1st Year	2nd Year	Equipt	Station	Where & When Free
600	"		Willam.	at F. D. Prairies[14] 1 Aug. 1814
			Ft. Geo	
700	700	clerk	Ft. Heads	Columbia 27 July 1816
			Willam.	
			N. Caled.[16]	
			Ft. Heads	
400	400		T. River	at Montreal same as N.W.C.
			Willam.	
PP	PP	D or M.	Willam.	at Montreal Feb. 1815
PP	PP	M.	T. River	at Montreal Feb. 1815
PP	PP	D. or M.	Ft. Geo.	at Montreal Feb. 1815
350	PP	M.	Willam.	at Montreal Feb. 1816
450	PP	M.	Ft. Geo.	at Montreal Feb. 1815
PP	PP	M.	Willam.	at Montreal Feb. 1815
PP	PP	M.	T. River	at Montreal Feb 1814
			Ft. Geo	
120		0	Spok. H.	time expires 1 May Free Mont.
500	500	M.	Ft. Geo	at Montreal Feb. 1816
		G.	Ft. Geo	at Montreal Feb. 1816
£100 for 6 Y.		Clerk	Ft. Heads	at Montreal Feb. 1819
			Ft. Geo	
			Willam.	
			Willam.	
400	PP	D. or M.		at Bas de la Riviere
450	450	M.	Ft. Geo	at Montreal same as N.W. Co
600	600	D.	Ft. Geo.	at Montreal Feb. 1816
450	450	M.	Ft. Geo	at Montreal Feb. 1816
450	450	M.	Ft. Geo	at Montreal Feb. 1816
600	PP	D.	Ft. Geo	at Montreal Feb. 1816
450	450	M.	Ft. Head.	at Montreal Feb. 1814
			Ft. Geo	
			Ft. Geo	

Boullard was doing at Kamloops, from which post he certainly would not get back to Montreal to watch the leaves fall, is not clear.

[19] L. L. P. is Lac La Pluie, a North West post in the Athabasca Department.

[20] Bas de la Rivière was a North West post at the foot of Lake Winnipeg, Manitoba Province, Canada.

[21] "Atha." was Athabaska River Department, in northern Saskatchewan Province, Canada.

[22] "Ft. W." is Fort William, the western headquarters of the North West Company and the residence of the "wintering partners." It was at the northwestern end of Lake Superior in Ontario Province, Canada.

	Party		Capacity	Engaged	Years
45. Delorme, J. Bte.	"	X	Milieu	23 Oct. 13	0
46. Denille, Louis	"	√	M		
47. Dufresne, Andre	"	√	M.		
48. Deslard, Pierre	NWCo	X	Gouvernail	Atha.13	0
49. Day, John	P. F. Co.	√	Hunter		
50. Delauney, Pierre	"	√	Hunter	17 July 11	3
51. Dorion, Pierre	"	√	Interpreter	25 June 13	
52. Ens, dit Canada, Frs.	NWCo		M	Col. 13	0
53. Finlay, Jac. Rap	NWCo	X	Clk & Interpreter	Col. 12	0
54. Finlay, Rap., Jun	"	X	Interp. & Hunter	Col. 12	0
55. Finlay, Thorburn	"		M & Hunter	3 Jany 14	2
56. Finlay, Bonhomme	"	X	M. & Interpreter	Colª 12	0
57. Fleurie, Antoine	"		M.	L. L. P. 13	1
58. Felix, Prisque	P. F. Co.	√	G.		
59. Flanagan, Moses	"	√	Bookbinder		
60. Franchere, Gabriel	"	X	Clerk	20 Oct. 13	0
61. Farnham, Russel	"		Clerk		
62. Gallioux, Joseph	NW Co		G.	Ft. Wm. 10	1
63. Gardepied, J. Bte.	P. F. Co.		D. & Hunter	27 Jany. 14	2
64. Gervais, Joseph	"		M. & Hunter	15 Oct 13	1
65. Guerin, Morise	"		M.	10 Oct 13	1
66. Gregoire, Francois	Free	X	Interpreter	5 Jany 13	0
67. Gauthier, Francois	NWCo.	X	M.	F. D. P. 12	0
68. Henry, William			Clerk		
69. Hodgins, Frs. Wm	P. F. Co		Blacksmith & M.	18 Oct 13	1
70. Halsey, J. Cook	"	√	Clerk		
71. Henry, Alexander	NWCo		Proprietor		
72. Hoole, Louis Capois	Free				
73. Jeremie, Paul Den.	F. P. Co.				
74. Jacquette, Charles	"		M.	22 Oct 13	1
75. Keith, James	NWC		Clerk		
76. Landreville, Charles	NWC	X	G.	Colª 13	0
77. Lefevre, Laurent	"	X	M.	Mont. 11	0
78. LeCourse, Pierre	"		M.	Colª 14	1
79. Laforte Michel	"	X.	M.	Colª 12	0

[23] "Kootenees"—The Kootenay River flows south from British Columbia into northwestern Montana and northern Idaho, then north again across the border, until it flows into the Columbia through Lake Kootenay. An Indian tribe of that name lived in northern Idaho and northwestern Montana. The North Westers had a post, Kootenay (here, Kootenees) House, near Lake Windermere in southwestern British Columbia.

1st Year	2nd Year	Equipt	Station	Where & When Free
180	0	0	Kootonees[23] Ft. Geo. Willam.	Time expires 1 May. Free Montreal
700	0	G.	Ft. Geo Willam. snakes[24]	at Montreal Feb. 1816 Free man at St. Louis 17 July 14
(900)			snakes	Free on arrival at St. Louis
450	"	M	T. River	at Montreal Feb. 1814
1800	1800	Clerk	Spok H.	at Spok. Ho. 1 April 1816
300	450	M, & H	Spok. H.	at Spok. Ho. 28 Nov. 1814
450	450	M. & H	Ft. Geo	at Spok. Ho. Feb. 1816
250	400	M.	Spok. Ho.	at Spokane Ho 28 Nov 1814
450	PP	M.	Ft. Geo. T. River Willam.	at Montreal Feb. 1815
1200	"	0	FT. Geo. FT. Geo.	Times expires Spring 1814
PP	PP	G.	Willam.	at Montreal Feb. 1815
600	600	D.	FT. Geo.	Time expires 27 Jany 16 Free Mont.
600	600	M.	FT. Geo	at Montreal same as NWC
450	450	M.	Ft. Heads	at Montreal same as NWC
500	500	Clk	Okanan[25]	at Columbia 1 Jan 1814
450	450	M.	Ft. Geo. Willam.	
600	600	D.	Spok. H. Ft. Geo Ft. Geo Ft. Heads Raccoon[26]	at Montreal same as NWC
225	450	M.	Spok. H. Ft. Geo.	at Montreal same as N. W. Co.
700	"	G	Ft. Heads	at Montreal Feb. 1814
300	PP	M.	Ft. Geo.	at Montreal Feb. 1814
450	450	M.	Ft. Geo.	at Montreal Feb. 1815
450	450	M.	Ft. Geo.	at Montreal Feb. 1814

[24] Snakes, that is, the Shoshone living along what is now called the Snake River in western Washington, eastern Idaho.

[25] "Okanan.," that is, the Okanogan River, a tributary of the Columbia in western Washington State.

[26] *Raccoon*, that is, the Royal Navy vessel that visited Astoria in December 1813.

	Party		Capacity	Engaged	Years
80. LaGosse, Charles	"	X.	D.	Col.ª 12	0
81. Latrielle, Antoine	"	X	Gouvernail	Mont. 12	0
82. Landrie, Joseph	P. F. C.	√	M.		
83. Lassier, Charles	"	√	G.		
84. LeCompte, Alexis	P. F. C.		M.	16 Oct. 13	1
85. LaLiberté, Louis	"	√	M.		
86. La Valle, Louis	"		Gouvernail	16 Oct. 13	1
87. LaBonté, Louis	"		Carpenter	16 Oct. 13	1
88. Lafantessie	"	√	M.		
89. LaBonté, J. Bte.	P.F.C.	√			
90. LaPierre, Joseph	"	√	M.		
91. Laframboise, Michel	"			15 Oct. 13	1
92. LaPlante, Louis	NWC		G.	Mont. 12	1
93. Latour, François	"		M.	Ft. W. 13	2
94. Landrie, François	"		M.	Ft. W. 13	1
95. LaPrade, Alexis	"		M.	Mont. 13	2
96. Lussier, Bazile	"		G.	Mont. 13	2
97. Langton, Étienne	"		G.	Mont. 13	1
98. LaVallée, Louis	"		M.	Mont. 12	2
99. Lussier, Étienne	P. F. C.		Hunter		
100. Loyer, Charles	NWC.		M.	Col. 13	1
101. Little, John	P. F. C.		Boat Builder		
102. LeChapelier, And.	"		M.	St. Louis 11	3
103. LeClerc, Giles	"		M.	Berthier[27] 10	5
104. Landrie, François	"		M.	Michc.[28] 10	5
105. Mackay, Jno. And.	NWCo		D &c.	Ft. Geo. 13	2
106. Macleod, Jack	"	X	M.	Ft. Wm. 11	0
107. McTavish, J. Geo.	"		Proprietor		
108. McMillan, James	"	X	Clerk	Ft. W. 11	0
109. McDonald, Finan	"	X	Clerk	Col.ª 11	0
110. Methode, François	"		G.	Col.ª 13	1
111. Mousseau, Louis	"	X	M.	Col.ª 12	0
112. Montour, Nicholas	"		Clerk	F.D.P. 12	1
113. Milligan, Richard	P. F. C.	√	Tailor		
114. Masçon, Alexis	"		M.	Oct 13	1
115. Montigny, Ovid	"	X	G. & Interp.	Dec. 13	0

[27] "Berthier" does not seem to have been a post of the North West Company. It may refer to Berthierville, about thirty-five miles down river from Montreal, which could have been LeClerc's hometown. In any event, he would not see it again as he was a member of John Reed's party which was killed by Indians while trapping among the Shoshone in western

1st Year	2nd Year	Equipt	Station	Where & When Free
600	600	D.	Ft. Geo.	at Montreal Feb. 1814
PP	PP	G.	T. River	at Montreal Feb. 1814
			Ft. Geo.	
			Ft. Geo.	
450	450	M.	Kootenees	at Montreal same as NWC
			Ft. Heads	
600	600	G.	Ft. Heads	at Montreal same as NWC
600	800	D.	Ft. Geo.	at Montreal same as NWC
			Ft. Geo.	
			Willam.	
			Ft. Geo.	
450	450	M.	Willam.	at Montreal
600	PP	G.	Ft. Geo.	at Montreal Feb 1815
450	PP	M.	Willam.	at Montreal Feb 1816
450	PP	M.	Ft. Geo	at Montreal Feb 1815
350	PP	M.	Ft. Geo.	at Montreal Feb 1816
600	P.P.	G.	Ft. Geo	at Montreal Feb 1816
600	600	G.	Willam.	at Montreal Feb. 1816
450	P.P.	M.	Ft. Geo.	at Montreal Feb. 1815
			Willam.	
400	400	M.	Ft. Heads	at Ft William 1815
			Raccoon	
450	450	M.	Snakes	
500	500	M.	Snakes	at Montreal
450	450	M.	Snakes	
700	700	D. & c.	Ft. Geo.	at Montreal Feb 1816
450	450	M.	Ockinan[29]	at Montreal Feb 1814
			Ft. Geo.	
1200	1200	Clk.	Ft. Heads	
1200	1200	Clk.	T. River	at Montreal Feb. 1814
600	600	G.	Kooteness	at Mountain Port. 1815
450	450	M.	Ft. Geo.	at Montreal Feb. 1814
600	900	Clk.	Kootoness	at Montreal Feb. 1815
			Willam.	
200	450	M.	Willam.	at Montreal
150		0	T. River	Time expires 1 May Free Mont

Washington State in the winter of 1813–14; see III, n. 77.

[28] "Michc." is Michilimackinac, a fur-trading center on an island in the channel between Lakes Huron and Michigan. Landry was also with Reed's ill-fated party.

[29] "Ockinan," i.e., the Okanogan River.

	Party		Capacity	Engaged	Years
116. McLennon, Donald	"		Clerk	Col. 13	4
117. McGillis, Donald	"	√	Clerk		
118. Mathews, W. W.	"		Clerk & Archt.[30]	1 Feb. 14	2
119. Mackay, Thomas	"		Clerk & Interp.		
120. Monique, Nicholas	NWC	X	G.	Ath. 11	0
121. Majeau, Louis	"		G.	L.L.P. 13	1
122. Majeau, Pierre	"		M.	L.L.P. 13	2
123. Moineau, Ant.	"		M.	FT. Wm. 12	1
124. Mochomau, Joseph	"	X	Hunter	Col. 13	0
125. McGillivray, Joseph	"		Clerk	Mont.	
126. McDonald, John	"		Proprietor		
127. McKenzie, Donald	P. F. C.		Proprietor		
128. McDougall, Dun.	"		Proprietor		
129. Martial, François	"		M & Sawyer		
130. Ocanasawaret, Thomas	NWC	X	M	Mont. 11	0
131. Owayaissa, Étienne	"	X	M.	Mont. 11	0
132. Ouvre, J. Bte	P. F. C.	X	M.	20 Oct. 13	0
133. Proveau, J. Bte	NWC	X	M.	L.L.P. 12	0
134. Parrault, Louis	NWC		M.	Mont. 11	1
135. Perrault, William	P. F. C.	√	(Boy)		
136. Pacquin, Louis	NWCo	X	G	Col.ª 12	0
137. Pillon, J. Bte	P. F. C.		M	17 Oct 13	1
138. Payette François	"	X	M.	17 Oct 13	0
139. Plante, Antoine	"	X	M.	23 Oct 13	0
140. Pion, Louis	"		Carpenter		
141. Piccard, André	NWCo		M.		
142. Piccard, Maurice	"		M.	Ft. W 13	1
143. Pembrilliant, Ant	"		M	Ft. W 12	1
144. Pelton, Joseph	P. F. C.		Fool		
145. Pepin, Antoine	"		M.		
146. Pillette, Benj.	"		Clerk		
147. Quesnal, Amable	NWCo	X	M.	Ft. W. 11	0
148. Rivet, François	Free		Interpreter	Col. 13	1
149. Roy, Olivier	P F C		M.		
150. Roussel, Augustine	"		Blacksmith	16 Oct 13	1
151. Robert, François	"		M.	16 Oct. 13	1
152. Ross, Alexander	"		Clerk	6 Jany. 14	3
153. Roussele, Benj	"	√	Shoemaker		

[30] Clerk and archivist.

1st Year	2nd Year	Equipt	Station	Where & When Free
240	240	Clk.	T River Willam	at Montreal Feb. 1818
1500	1500	Clerk	Ft. Geo Willam.	FT. George 1 Feb. 1816
600	600	G.	FT. Geo.	at Montreal Feb. 1816
600	600	G	Willam.	at Montreal Feb. 1815
450	P.P.	M.	FT. Geo.	at Montreal Feb. 1816
P.P.	P.P.	M.	Willam.	at Montreal Feb. 1815
600	"	D. Clk.	Willam. Okenan. FT. Geo. FT. Geo. FT. Geo. Willam.	Columbia 4 Sept 1816
300	P.P.	M.	Willam.	at Montreal Feb. 1816
300	P.P.	M.	Willam. FT. Geo.	at Montreal Feb. 1816
400	450	M.	Willam.	at Montreal Feb. 1816
P.P.	P.P.	M.	FT. Geo. Willam.	at Montreal Feb. 1815
600	600	G.	Ft. Geo.	at B d l R Summer 1814
450	450	M.	Kootenees	at Montreal same as NWC
200	"	0	Ft Geo.	Time expires 1 May Free Mont
180	"	0	T. River Spok. Hs. N. Caled.	Time expires 1 May Free Mont.
450	P.P.	M.	Willam.	at Montreal Feb. 1815
P.P.	P.P.	M.	FT. Geo. FT. Geo. FT. Geo. FT. Geo.	at Montreal Feb. 1815
300	P.P.	M.	Willam.	at Montreal Feb 1814
600	600	Interp.	Ft. Heads FT. Heads	Columbia 1 Nov 1815
1000	1000	D.	FT. Geo.	at Montreal same as NWC
450	450	M. Clk.	Spok. Hs. FT. Geo. Ft. Geo.	at Montreal same as NWC at Montreal same as NWC

	Party		Capacity	Engaged	Years
154. Reid, John	"	√	Clerk	Michc. 10	5
155. Shatackoani, Jacques	NWCo	X	D.	Mont. 12	0
156. St. Michel, Louis	P. F. C.	√	M.		
157. Sanson, Michel	"	X	Blacksmith	23 Oct. 13	0
158. Seton, Alfred	"	√	Clerk		
159. St. Martin, Joseph	NWCo		D.	Mont. 13	1
160. Saganakei, J. Bte	"	X	D.	F. d. Pr. 13	0
161. Salioheni, Ignace	"		G.	Colª 13	1
162. St. Amant, Joseph	P. F. C.	√	G.		
163. Stewart, Alex	NWCo		Proprietor		
164. Stewart, John	"		Proprietor		
165. Stewart, David	P. F. C.		Proprietor		
166. Trenchemontagne, Frs.	NWCo	X	M.	Col. 13	0
167. Trepagnier, François	P. F. C.	X	G.	22 Oct. 13	0
168. Tewhattahewnie, Geo	NWC		D. & G.	LLP 13	2
169. Turcotte, J. Bte.	P. F. C.		M.	Mont 10	5
170. Umfreville, Canotte	NWC	X	D.	Col. 13	0
171. Vallade, Rehene	"	X	M.	Col. 12	0
172. Wilson, William	P. F. C.	X	Cooper	26 Nov. 13	0
173. Wallace, William	"		Clerk		
177. Hobaugh, John	"		Freeman Hunter	Missouri 11[31]	2
178. Reznor, Jacob	"		Freeman Hunter	Missouri 11	2
179. Robinson, Edward	"		Freeman Hunter	Missouri 11	2
174. Guill, Cardinale	P. F. C.				
175. Jac. Harteau	P. F. C.				
176. Osterico, Jacques	NWCo	X	D.	Col. 12	0

[31] "Missouri," i.e., the Missouri River. Hobaugh, Reznor, and Robinson (nos. 177, 178, 179—the first two names are spelled variously) were experienced mountain men and trappers who came into the overland Astorians' camp on May 26, 1811. The camp was on the Mis-

1st Year	2nd Year	Equipt	Station	Where & When Free
1000	1000	0	Snakes	
P.P.	P.P.	D.	Ft. Geo.	at Montreal Feb. 1814
			Willam.	
200	"	0	Ft. Geo.	Time expires 1 May Free Montreal
			Ft. Geo.	
600	P.P.	D.	FT. Geo.	at Montreal Feb 1815
600	"	D.	FT. Geo.	F. des Prairies 1 Aug 1814
			Willam.	at Montreal Feb. 1815
			Willam.	
			Ft. Geo.	
			Ft. Geo.	
			Ft. Geo.	
450	"	M.	Ft. Geo.	at Montreal Feb. 1816
300	"	½ G.	Ft. Geo.	Time expires 1 May Free Montreal
600	P.P.	D & G.	Willam.	at Montreal Feb. 1816
600	600		Snakes	at Montreal Feb. 1815
600	"	D.	Ft. Geo.	at Montreal Feb. 1816
350	350	M.	Spok. Hs.	at Montreal Feb 1816
180		0	Spok. Hs.	Time expires 1 May Free Mont.
			Willam.	
	On Halves—	M.	Snakes	
	On Halves—	M.	Snakes	
	On Halves—	M.	Snakes	
			Ft. Geo.	
			Willam.	
P.P.	P.P.	D.	Kootonees	Columbia 10 May 1816

Courtesy of the Hudson's Bay Company Archives
HBCA/PAM F.4/61 fos 6–7d.

souri River, just below the mouth of the Niobrara, along the border of present-day Nebraska and South Dakota. They joined the party at Hunt's invitation. They were also with John Reed on his last trapping venture in 1813–14. Ronda, *Astoria*, 149–50.

BIBLIOGRAPHY

Primary Material

Manuscript Collections

DeWitt Clinton Papers, Butler Library, Columbia University, Special Collections

Albert Gallatin Papers, New-York Historical Society

Books and Government Documents

Brown, Everett S., ed. *William Plumer's Memorandum of Proceedings in the United States Senate*. New York: DaCapo, 1923. Repr. 1969.

Coues, Elliott, ed. *New Light on the Early History of the Greater Northwest: The Manuscript Journals of Alexander Henry and of David Thompson*. 3 vols. New York: Francis P. Harper, 1897.

Cox, Ross. *The Columbia River*. Ed. Edgar I. and Jane R. Stewart. Norman: University of Oklahoma Press, 1957.

Fanning, Edmund. *Voyages to the South Seas, Indian and Pacific Oceans, China Sea, Northwest Coast, Feejee Islands, South Shetlands, &c, &c*. Introduction by E. W. Giesecke. New York: William H. Vermilye, 1838. Repr. Fairfield, Washington: Ye Galleon Press, 1970.

Franchère, Gabriel. *Journal of a Voyage on the North West Coast of North America During the Years 1811, 1812, 1813, and 1814*. Ed. W. Kaye Lamb. Trans. Wessie Tipping Lamb. Toronto: The Champlain Society, 1969.

Glover, Richard, ed. *David Thompson's Narrative, 1784–1812*. Toronto: The Champlain Society, 1962.

Irving, Pierre. *The Life and Letters of Washington Irving*. 4 vols. New York: G. P. Putnam, 1864. Repr. 1967.

Irving, Washington. *Astoria, or, Anecdotes of an Enterprise Beyond the Rocky Mountains*. 2 vols. New York: G. P. Putnam's Sons, 1897. [NYPL, Rare Books: annotations by Elliott Coues, October 29, 1897].

Jones, Robert F., ed. *Astorian Adventure: The Journal of Alfred Seton, 1811–1815*. New York: Fordham University Press, 1993.

Lewis, Meriwether. *The Lewis and Clark Expedition*. Ed. Archibald Hanna. 3 vols. Philadelphia: J. B. Lippincott Co., 1961.

Message from the President of the United States, communicating the Letter of Mr.

Prevost and other documents, relating to an establishment made at the mouth of Columbia River (January 27, 1823). (U. S. 17th Congress, 2d sess. House Doc. 45) Washington: Gales & Seaton, 1823.

Payette, B. C., comp. *The Oregon Country Under the Union Jack: A Reference Book of Documents for Scholars and Historians*. Montreal: Payette Radio, 1961.

————. *The Oregon Country Under the Union Jack*. Postscript Edition. Montreal: Payette Radio, 1962.

Rollins, Philip Ashton, ed. *The Discovery of the Oregon Trail: Robert Stuart's Narrative of His Overland Trip Eastward from Astoria in 1812–13. To which is added: An Account of the Tonquin's Voyage and of Events at Fort Astoria [1811–12] and Wilson Price Hunt's Diary of His Overland Trip Westward to Astoria in 1811–12*. New York: Edward Eberstadt, 1935.

Ross, Alexander. *Adventures of the First Settlers on the Oregon or Columbia River: Being a Narrative of the Expedition Fitted Out by John Jacob Astor, to Establish the "Pacific Fur Company"; with an account of some Indian tribes on the Coast of the Pacific*. London: Smith, Eden and Co., 1849. Repr. Ann Arbor, Michigan: University Microfilms, 1966.

Wallace, W. Stewart, ed. *Documents Relating to the North West Company*. Toronto: The Champlain Society, 1934.

Periodicals

Boit, John. "A New Log of the Columbia." Eds. Worthington C. Ford and Edmond S. Meany. *Washington Historical Quarterly*, 12, No. 1 (January 1921), 3–50.

Bridgwater, Dorothy Wildes, ed. "John Jacob Aster [*sic*] Relative to His Settlement on the Columbia River." *Yale University Library Gazette*, 24, No. 2 (October 1949), 47–69.

"Captain Black's Report on the Taking of Astoria." *Oregon Historical Quarterly*, 17, No. 2 (June 1916), 147–48.

Douglas, Jesse, ed. "Matthews' Adventures on the Columbia." *Oregon Historical Quarterly*, 40, No. 2 (June 1939), 105–48.

Elliott, T. C., ed. "Last Will and Testament of John Day." *Oregon Historical Society*, 17, No. 4 (December 1916), 373–79.

————, ed. "Sale of Astoria, 1813." *Oregon Historical Quarterly*, 33, No. 1 (March 1932), 43–50.

SECONDARY MATERIAL

Books

Campbell, Marjorie Wilkins. *The North West Company*. New York: St. Martin's, 1957.

Carpenter, Kenneth J. *The History of Scurvy and Vitamin C*. Cambridge: Cambridge University Press, 1986.

Chevigny, Hector. *Russian America: The Great Alaskan Adventure, 1791–1867*. New York: Viking, 1965.

Chittenden, Hiram M. *The American Fur Trade of the Far West*. 3 vols. New York: Francis P. Harper, 1902.

Clarke, Charlotte Bringle. *Edible and Useful Plants of California*. California Natural History Guides 41. Berkeley: University of California Press, 1987.

Davidson, Gordon Charles. *The North West Company*. New York: Russell & Russell, 1918. Repr. 1967.

Dietrich, William. *Northwest Passage: The Great Columbia River*. New York: Simon & Schuster, 1995.

Driver, Clive E., comp. *A Selection from Our Shelves: Books, Manuscripts, and Drawings from the Philip H. and A. S. W. Rosenbach Museum*. Philadelphia: Rosenbach Foundation. 1973.

Dulles, Foster Rhea. *The Old China Trade*. Boston: Houghton Mifflin, 1930.

Fernald, Merritt Lyndon, and Alfred Charles Kinsey. *Edible Wild Plants of Eastern North America*. Rev. ed. New York: Harper & Row, 1958.

Gough, Barry M. *The Northwest Coast: British Navigation, Trade, and Discoveries to 1812*. Vancouver: University of British Columbia Press, 1992.

Gourlay, Robert, comp. *Statistical Account of Upper Canada Compiled With a View for a Grand System of Emigration* I. London: Simpson & Marshall, 1822.

Granville, Wilfred. *A Dictionary of Sailors' Slang*. [London]: André Deutsch, 1962.

Haeger, John Denis. *John Jacob Astor: Business and Finance in the Early Republic*. Detroit: Wayne State University Press, 1991.

Irving, Washington. *Astoria, or, Anecdotes of an Enterprise Beyond the Rocky Mountains*. Ed. Richard Dilworth Rust. Boston: Twayne, 1976.

———. *Astoria, or, Anecdotes of an Enterprise Beyond the Rocky Mountains*. Ed. Edgeley W. Todd. Norman: University of Oklahoma Press, 1964.

Johansen, Dorothy O. *Empire of the Columbia*. 2nd ed. New York: Harper & Row, 1967.

Josephy, Alvin M., Jr. *The Nez Perce Indians and the Opening of the Northwest.* New Haven, Conn.: Yale University Press, 1965.

McClane, A. J., ed. *McClane's Standard Fishing Encyclopedia.* New York: Holt, Rinehart & Winston, 1965.

McKay, Douglas. *The Honourable Company: A History of the Hudson's Bay Company.* Indianapolis: Boss-Merrill, 1936.

Merk, Frederick. Fur Trade and Empire: George Simpson's Journal. Rev. ed. Cambridge, Mass.: Harvard University Press, 1968.

———. *The Oregon Question: Essays in Anglo-American Diplomacy and Politics.* Cambridge, Mass.: Harvard University Press, 1967.

Nokes, J. Richard. *Columbia's River: The Voyages of Robert Gray, 1787–1793.* Tacoma: Washington State Historical Society, 1991.

Phillips, Paul C. *The Fur Trade.* With concluding chapters by J. W. Smurr. 2 vols. Norman: University of Oklahoma Press, 1961.

Porter, Kenneth W. *John Jacob Astor: Business Man.* 2 vols. Cambridge, Mass.: Harvard University Press, 1931.

Pusey, William Allen. *The History and Epidemiology of Syphilis.* Springfield, Illinois: Charles C. Thomas, 1933.

Ronda, James P. *Astoria and Empire.* Lincoln: University of Nebraska Press, 1990.

———. *Lewis and Clark Among the Indians.* Lincoln: University of Nebraska Press, 1984.

Ross, Eric. *Beyond the River and the Bay: Some Observations on the State of the Canadian Northwest in 1811.* Toronto: University of Toronto Press, 1970.

Ruby, Robert H., and John A. Brown. *The Chinook Indians: Traders of the Lower Columbia River.* Norman: University of Oklahoma Press, 1976.

———. *A Guide to the Indian Tribes of the Pacific Northwest.* Norman: University of Oklahoma Press, 1986.

———. *Indians of the Pacific Northwest: A History.* Norman: University of Oklahoma Press, 1981.

Russell, Carl P. *Firearms, Traps, and Tools of the Mountain Men.* New York: Alfred A. Knopf, 1967.

Smith, Philip Chadwick Foster. *The Empress of China.* Philadelphia: Philadelphia Maritime Museum, 1984.

Stark, Raymond. *Guide to Indian Herbs.* Blaine, Washington: Hancock House, 1981.

Swainton, John R. *The Indian Tribes of North America.* Washington, D.C.: Smithsonian Institution Press, 1952.

Valeri, Valerio. *Kingship and Sacrifice: Ritual and Society in Ancient Hawaii.* Trans. Paula Wissing. Chicago: The University of Chicago Press, 1985.

Van Alstyne, Richard W. *The Rising American Empire*. Chicago: Quadrangle, 1960. Repr. 1965.

Vaughn, Thomas, and Bill Holm. *Soft Gold: The Fur Trade and Ethnographic Exchange on the Northwest Coast of America*. 2nd ed. rev. Portland: Oregon Historical Society, 1990.

White, Richard. *The Organic Machine: The Remaking of the Columbia River*. New York: Hill & Wang, 1995.

Wilfred, Granville. *A Dictionary of Sailor's Slang*. [London]: André Deutsch, 1962.

Wingate, Isabel B., ed. *Fairchild's Dictionary of Textiles*. 6th ed. New York: Fairchild Publications, ca. 1979.

Articles

Barry, J. Neilson. "Archibald Pelton, the First Follower of Lewis and Clark." *Washington Historical Quarterly*, 19 (July 1928), 199–201.

———. "Astorians Who Became Permanent Settlers." *Washington Historical Quarterly*, 24, No. 3 (July 1933), 221–311; No. 4 (October 1933), 282–301.

———. "Washington Irving and Astoria." *Washington Historical Quarterly*, 18, No. 2 (April 1927), 132–39.

———. "What Became of Benjamin Clapp?" *Washington Historical Quarterly*, 21, No. 1 (January 1930), 13–17.

Brown, William C. "Old Fort Okanogan and the Okanogan Trail." *Oregon Historical Society*, 15, No. 1 (March 1914), 1–38.

Carlos, Ann. "The Causes and Origins of the North American Fur Trade Rivalry: 1804–1810." *Journal of Economic History*, 41, No. 4 (December 1981), 774–94.

Drumm, Stella M. "More About Astorians." *Oregon Historical Society*, 24, No. 4 (December 1923), 335–60.

Elliott, Thompson C. "The Fur Trade in the Columbia River Basin to 1811." *Oregon Historical Society*, 15, No. 4 (December 1914), 241–51.

———. "Wilson Price Hunt, 1783–1842." *Oregon Historical Quarterly*, 32, No. 2 (June 1931), 130–34.

Favrholdt, Ken. "'Cumcloups and the River of Time." *The Beaver*, Outfit 67, No. 4 (August–September 1987), 19–22.

Giesecke, E. W. "Search for the *Tonquin*." *Cumtux* (Clatsop County [OR] Historical Society Quarterly), 10, No. 3 (Summer 1990), 3–8; No. 4 (Fall 1990), 3–14; 11, No. 1 (Winter 1990), 23–40.

Gough, Barry M. "The 1813 [British] Expedition to Astoria." *The Beaver*, Outfit 304.2 (Autumn 1973), 44–51.

Hanson, Charles, Jr. "The Point Blanket." *The Museum of the Fur Trade Quarterly*, 12, No. 1 (Spring 1976), 5–10.

Howay, F. W. "A List of Trading Vessels in the Maritime Fur Trade, 1785–1825." Royal Society of Canada, *Transactions*, Ser. 3, Sec. 2, 24 (1930), 111–34 [1785–94]; 25 (1931), 117–49 [1795–1804]; 26 (1932), 43–86 [1805–14]; 27 (1933), 119–47 [1815–19]; 28 (1934), 11–49 [1820–25].

————. "The Loss of the 'Tonquin.' " *Washington Historical Quarterly*, 13, No. 2 (April 1932), 83–92.

————. "The Voyage of the *Hope*, 1790–92," *Washington Historical Quarterly*, 11, No. 1 (January 1920), 3–28.

Jones, Robert F. "The Identity of the *Tonquin*'s Interpreter," *Oregon Historical Quarterly*, 98, No. 3 (Fall 1997), 296–314.

Judson, Katherine B. "The British Side of the Restoration of Fort Astoria." *Oregon Historical Society*, 20, No. 3 (September 1919), 243–60; No. 4 (December 1919), 305–30.

Kytr, Hobe. "The Lady Is Changeable. Catch Her When She Is Angry." *Sea History*, No. 61 (Spring 1992), 46.

McCusker, John J. "How Much Is That in Real Money? A Historical Price Index for Use as a Deflator of Money Values in the Economy of the United States." *Proceedings of the American Antiquarian Society*, 101, Part 2 (October 1992), 297–373.

Perrine, Fred. S. "Early Days on the Willamette." *Oregon Historical Society Quarterly*, 25, No. 4 (December 1924), 310.

Porter, Kenneth W. "Roll of Overland Astorians, 1810–1812." *Oregon Historical Quarterly*, 34, No. 2 (June 1933), 103–12, 286.

Santee, J. F. "Comcomly and the Chinooks." *Oregon Historical Quarterly*, 33, No. 3 (September 1932), 271–78.

Thompson, A. W. "New Light on Donald Mackenzie's Post on the Clearwater, 1812–13." *Idaho Yesterdays*, 18, No. 3 (Fall 1974), 24–32.

Unpublished Material

Kime, Wayne Raymond. "Washington Irving's *Astoria*: A Critical Study." Ph.D. diss., University of Delaware, 1968.

Myers, Andrew Breen. "Washington Irving, Fur Trade Chronicler: An Analysis of *Astoria*, with Notes for a Corrected Edition." Ph.D. diss., Columbia University, 1964.

INDEX

Note: A number in brackets after a man's name is that given to him in the "List of People on the Columbia . . ." presented here as the Appendix; some, especially the Northwesters, appear only in the Appendix. In the log, individuals were frequently mentioned only by the task they were performing, e.g., "blacksmith," or "cooper." Where an identification seemed reasonable, a job designation was indexed under the name of the likely person, e.g., George Bell for "cooper." Such identifications should be regarded as tentative, since practically all the trades were represented by more than one man at Astoria. All references to a shallop or shallops were placed under "Dolly," the name of the one that was certainly assembled at Astoria. References to other kinds of watercraft were placed under "Canoes and boats." Many names, both of individuals and tribes, were spelled differently, depending on the person transcribing the log. I have indicated the preferred spelling as the one that seemed to be most commonly used.